Library of Congress Cataloging-in-Publication Data on File

For inquiries about volume orders, please contact:

TitleTown Publishing, LLC
PO Box 12093
Green Bay, WI 54307
920-737-8051

ISBN 9780996295109

Published in the United States by TitleTown Publishing
www.beaufortbooks.com

Distributed by Midpoint Trade Books
www.midpointtrade.com

Printed in the United States of America

Interior design by Michael Short and Mark Karis
Cover Design by Michael Short

MY JOB

REAL PEOPLE
AT WORK AROUND
THE WORLD

SUZANNE SKEES

TitleTown
PUBLISHING

DEDICATION

To every Muhammad, who toils too many hours a day just to feed his children;

Every Mayra, who tends the land to cultivate her dreams of home and freedom;

And every Matt, who invents the future of technology and paves the way for all youth to fulfill their potential.

To workers everywhere who labor through aches and exhaustion, solitude and invisibility: Thank you for your striving, your hope, your tenacity and strength, which quietly build a better world for all of us.

CONTENTS

MUSIC & ARTS

ACKNOWLEDGMENTS

This book began as a collaboration, when my friend Steve Schwartz, who cofounded Upaya Social Ventures (a job-creation funder for ultra-poor families in India), tipped his head sideways over a bowl of Thai noodles in San Jose, California and declared: "Suzanne, every story you write turns out to be about people in their jobs. You should write a book and call it, *MY JOB.*"

Then Steve accompanied me to India to meet eco-manufacturers Arindam and Debaleena (Chapter 2), whose innovations with disposable palm-leaf dinnerware in rural Assam are outdone only by their anti-fairytale love story.

Daniel Kaufman, cofounder of Third Plateau Social Impact Strategies, shared our lunch that day and agreed wholeheartedly that a follow-on to Studs Terkel's 1974 masterpiece, *Working*—updated to how the world works now—could enlighten and connect people from all occupations and cultures. Then Daniel, together with his brother Jonathan Kaufman, his adopted-brother Mike Berkowitz, and their talented San-Francisco-based team, conducted market research and hatched our social-mission strategy for a book that would create a conversation about the impact of existing jobs and raise funds for future jobs.

Traveling to Haiti with changemakers from The Haiti Development Institute, I was fortunate to form a bond of simpática values and vision with Andrea Atkinson, founder of OneSquareWorld, who became the book's project manager and tireless champion. Working with me from Boston to San Francisco over months that turned into years, Andrea created a platform for broadcasting voices of unsung heroes who toil every day to build a better world with the work of their minds and hands.

Wendy Ledger transcribed the interviews with incredible interest. Working long into nights and weekends to sift through translations and accents and attitudes, Wendy admitted to falling madly in love with each radiant one of them.

Collaboration turned into serendipity when I met publicist Jill Lublin at a conference and she referred me to agent Randy Peyser, who saw the potential of *MY JOB* and connected us to the perfect small publisher. What are the odds? Out of 63,000 publishing houses in the U.S. (and we'd talked with several), one editor—Megan Trank—insisted that Tracy Ertl of Title Town read our proposal. Tracy took a gamble on this book, devoting equal parts talent and passion to producing it. Megan cultivated the content in exquisite balance between our heft of material and what the market will bear, and she pared down the final manuscript with kindness and grace.

My globe-trotting niece, Brienne Nicole Skees, dissected the manuscript for factual accuracy and cultural fairness while maintaining a strong loyalty to each narrator's viewpoint.

And my creative-genius son, Isaac Skees Hinman, designed our logo to reflect the confluence of villages and cities, ideologies and geographies, that *MY JOB* represents.

My family, beginning with my parents, Jasmine and Hugh—who in their eighties still practice what I call "philanthropy of the hands," and my sons, Jonah, Isaac, and Benjamin, who've taught me authenticity and compassion with their never-wavering examples, have offered time, insight, and support to me throughout the years of listening and editing that preceded these printed pages. Our extended family, which encircles the globe and includes a rich diversity of individuals, joins together in our common value of equal opportunity for all. Toward this ideal, the Skees Family Foundation has adopted *MY JOB* as a social-mission project. Our dedicated board members have donated tangible ideas and intangible moral support:

Brienne Nicole Skees
Elisabeth Skees Deogracias
Jasmine Panchot Skees
Sally Skees-Helly

Shelly Shepard Skees

Along the way, both this book and I benefitted from kind advice from the following fellow authors:

Bryan Welch
Darian Rodriguez Heyman
David Bornstein
Jim Kouzes
Mike Cerre
Peg Conway
Praveen Madan
Sheri Sobrato Brisson
Steve Shukis
Susan Skog

And connections and support from these treasured colleagues and friends:
Adnan and Nadia Mahmud
Anchal Bibra
Bernadine Rosso
Cheri Lippmann
Cori Toler
Elizabeth Lee
Elizebeth Tucker
Erna Grasz
Greg Khalil
Jeffrey Chow
Karen Ansara
Kari Hammett-Caster
Karl Grobl
Kathy Lynn Jackson
Lucille Ma Switzer
Manjula Dissanayake
Marie Kagaju Laugharn
Melanie Russell Hamburger
Paru Desai Yusuf
Peter LaFond
Rachel Wisotsky
Reverend Angel Lightfeather
Risa Romie Wight
Sachi Shenoy
Shirley Chen

Susan D. Johnson
Vincent Oviedo
Wendy A. Leonard
Zeenat Ariswalla

If readers resonate with these stories, we hope to publish a series of *MY JOB* books that—as you can imagine—will help the voices of even more amazing narrators reach more hearts. Meanwhile, I am profoundly grateful to the many friends, from Cambodia to Israel, Colorado to Honduras, who gave generously of their time in long interviews, and opened up their life-stories, in chapters we hope to feature in future editions of this book.

Underpinning every word I've been privileged to hear and transmit, every hour on a bus or airplane getting to the far corners where our narrators live, every minute of intense focus in sculpting these stories into chapters, is the miracle of opportunity that I've been granted by life, God, luck—whatever you may call it. I give thanks every day for my chance to work with the stellar people listed above and in the pages that follow. Not sure why, but somehow, I get to work in the best job on Earth.

PROLOGUE: WHY JOBS?

BY SUZANNE SKEES

Fifteen chapters narrated by unique people from Hawaii to Hong Kong: *MY JOB* takes you on a journey from the dusty streets of Dhaka, Bangladesh, where Muhammad pedals hard to pull his rented rickshaw twelve hours just to feed his family two meals a day; to the rolling foothills of the Appalachian Mountains in Eastern Kentucky where horse-coach Robin leads a trail ride for at-risk teenaged girls; to a sleek stand-up desk in a cavernous Silicon Valley warehouse called Google X, where Matt sketches out his next top-secret project plan with engineers and partners.

These true stories, told in each narrator's unique voice, delve deep into how they ended up in their current job, what it's really like, and what frustrates and motivates them.

There's Darius, who grew up with his single-mom and grandma and works at a Chicago Target full-time, while producing hip-hop music on nights and weekends; Pablo, an Argentinian who works for the American behemoth Xerox but would rather launch his own venture if not for the financial risk to his family; and Purnima, a young award-winning interior designer in Sri Lanka who feels pressure to end her career, marry and stay at home, to please her family.

The *MY JOB* narrators begin with what the world calls them: "equity investment manager," "head hunter," "architect," "online entrepreneur."

Then, to my surprise and (I hope) your delight, along the way they reveal themselves as fully three-dimensional human beings with unique perspectives and insights, staunch opinions and endless strength. They reveal their childhood trauma and lifelong dreams that have shaped them into who they are. They share their ambitions to hone their particular skills, or to get just far enough ahead not to worry about monthly bills, and more than that: for someone to love, something to give, a way to imprint our world as no one else has done before.

Some narrators talk about feeling invisible as they work long hours, whether punching a time clock or not, eking out a few dollars with occasional gigs or small-scale sales. They share an unknown kinship with each other, and maybe with hard-workers the world over, in their willingness to strive further when their heads and backs ache; to push harder when a report is due or a design is nearly complete; to give far more than their community or even their closest coworkers and loved ones will ever know.

When I first decided to combine my own long string of odd jobs with my experience in writing and editing, to pursue the project that became this book, I believed that most people on this planet work because we have to: We log the hours to get the paycheck to provide a roof over our heads and food for our families.

I was so wrong. First, I learned that most workers on this planet have no career options: The International Labour Organization estimates that up to three-fourths of nonagricultural workers eke out whatever living they can in the informal sector, with no job security or benefits—like hawkers selling goods on the street of whatever country you may have toured, or musicians busking for tips in the subways of a U.S. metropolis.

Then, for those with some degree of choice, career paths are never straight trajectories. Many people wind their way from the odd jobs of youth to some desk or truck or booth that becomes a specialty, and only when crafting our resume or maybe interviewing for a job, do we attempt to impose a logical narrative onto the path.

While I have no formal training in the sociology of work (my studies were in English literature and world religions), I spent three years listening to workers in vastly different settings. So far, my interviews covered ten U.S. states and twenty-four countries.

Having written hundreds of short pieces on people in their jobs, and conducted over fifty interviews for this book, I discovered a shared sense of purpose in people from all ages, genders, cultures, and occupations. Virtually everyone said essentially the same thing: "I am who I am because of what I do."

Every person I interviewed told me, "There is no typical day;" and almost every person uttered some version of this poignant point: "Even if I had all the money in the world, I would keep doing what I am doing." Regardless of fame or fortune, everyone strove to be their best, and to create some positive impact beyond their own needs, to improve their village, city, world.

Our job, for better or worse, deeply impacts our sense of purpose, identity, and wellbeing. It propels us to prosperity or locks us in paycheck-to-paycheck survival mode. It yokes us to coworkers and clients in ways we cannot avoid. Jobs stimulate the economy and create efficiency in society, with each of us doing our small part, whether it is by building roads, teaching children, protecting people, preparing food, or weaving words.

Curating and editing these stories has taught me that we need our jobs like we need air: Without meaningful connection to society through some sort of contribution, we flounder, nosedive, and crash.

How do you define yourself? Even if you're a complicated, multidimensional being, I suspect within five minutes of meeting a new person, you've mentioned what you "are" or "do." Second only to sleep, work takes up most of our living hours. The common experience of work unites us across all our exterior differences. It may irk you when I say:

our job = our self . . .

but, it turns out to be true.

—*Suzanne Skees, San Francisco, California*

FOREWORD

Our stories unite us. In disclosing the narrative facts of our lives, we share, in a relatable way, the common humanity of our lived experience. Journalist Suzanne Skees knew this when she first came up with the concept of the *MY JOB* book. What she did not know until she dug deeper, was that the lens of "a job" provides a more intimate view of a person than looking through their bedroom window.

Suzanne grants us access: the chance to get to know people in unique professions all over the U.S. and the world. As the narrators outline information about their jobs—skills needed, salaries earned, pros and cons—they can't help but divulge their vision and values, their failures and achievements, their upbringing and their legacy —all the grit of life and all the glory of the spirit that make us human.

Through my work with Suzanne, I have had the chance to reflect on my own job in community development. At its essence my job revolves around connecting people -- to each other and to the power we hold to create our own paths and lift each other up along the way. The *MY JOB* book embodies these values, *my* core values: empathy, connection, and the belief in human potential.

MY JOB provides insight into the highly diverse but essentially unified experience of what it means to "work" today. It also reveals what sets us apart. It highlights that in addition to our personal experience and perspectives, our struggles and triumphs are very much shaped by our spot on the map. Where, to what family, and in what skin we are born plays deeply into our stories and our outcomes as each societies' constructs of our race, gender, religion, or socioeconomic level perpetuate systems that either lift us up or try to cast us down.

The choice of jobs (or lack thereof) opens up conversations about access to freedom, economic power, and justice. A job can show the values that an individual and an entire society place on money, power, family, education, and success.

Prepare for a virtual journey through a range of cities and villages, unique personalities and professions, as you read through the chapters of *MY JOB;* and get ready to reflect on the daily struggles and infinite potential of your own distinct story.

Andrea Atkinson, Executive Director, One Square World

Quantity Product Details

My Job: Real People at Work Around the World

1 Suzanne Skees

SKU: 82000
ASIN: 0996295100

02774006 RRDR

TO REORDER YOUR UPS DIRECT THERMAL LABELS:

1. Access our supply ordering web site at UPS.COM®
or contact UPS at 800-877-8652.
2. Please refer to label #02774006 when ordering.

ENTREPRENEURSHIP

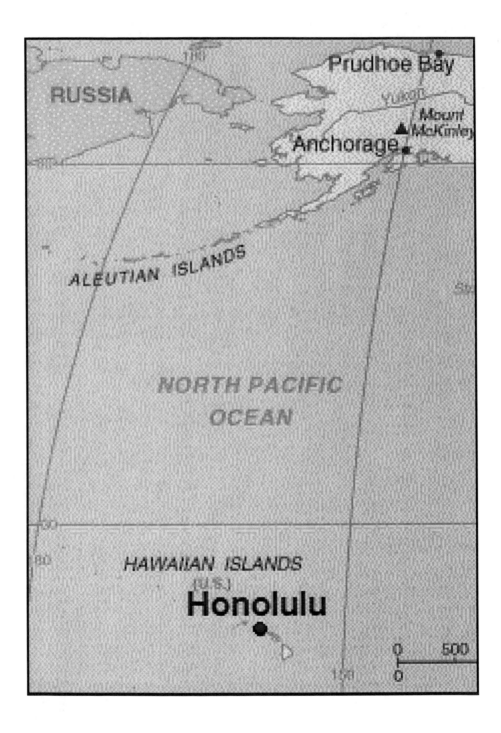

MAKANA

SLACK-KEY GUITAR MUSICIAN

HONOLULU, HAWAII, U.S.

Editor's note: Hawaii, "the Aloha State," is a paradise raised up from volcanoes that many Americans only dream of. The site of the 1941 Japanese attack on Pearl Harbor, Hawaii became the nation's fiftieth state in 1959.

More than the majestic scenes and peaceful culture we've seen through popular shows like *Hawaii Five-O, Baywatch,* and *Lost,* the 1.5 million residents of Hawaii face real-life problems, too: traffic, crime, racism, poverty, homelessness, drugs, and food and environmental issues. It's the most expensive state[1] to live in, and if you grew up here in a long line of Hawaiians, as Makana did, you might struggle to balance your indigenous heritage with an incoming tidal wave of tourists and high-rises, Starbucks and Costcos.

Thirty-six-year-old independent musician Makana (no last name; just "Makana") embodies all the modernity and tradition of the island state. He's a

---

1 Cnbc.com/2015/06/24/americas-most-expensive-states-to-live-in-2015.html?slide=11.

slack-key guitarist[2] with the same name as a mountain (also known as "Bali Hai") on Kauai, next to Oahu, where he was born to a French-Chinese-model mother and a Midwest-Minnesotan-engineer father.

"I just camped under the shadow of Makana Mountain last week," Makana tells me during our interview. It was a rare moment of downtime that he took to recharge his inner self. His spiritual mentor bestowed his name to reflect the power of the islands and the connection of his artistry with his native roots: His soul on display. The word means, in Hawaiian, "a gift given freely." And that suits him. He's given Hawaii a 21st-century interpretation of its musical legacy,[3] describing his genre as "not just mimicking my ancestors but creating in honor of them."[4] People say he sounds like four people playing all at once.[5]

Makana lives at the intersection of social justice and activism,[6] musical art and native Hawaiian culture. "It's never boring," he laughs.

During a performance at the Asia-Pacific Economic Corporation (APEC) World Leaders Dinner on the island attended by President Barack Obama in 2011—at the height of the Occupy Wall Street movement[7]—Makana commenced a quiet protest just by opening his suit jacket. He revealed a T-shirt that read, "Occupy with Aloha"[8] and began singing the protest anthem he'd just composed, "We Are the Many."[9] He stole the show and made CNN news,[10] and his song became *The Rolling Stone*'s official theme song for the movement. He was later invited to perform the song at The White House.

Years later, his 2016 video "Fire Is Ours"[11] protested governmental status quo and inspired viewers—especially young liberals—to "rise up and BERN" (i.e., vote for Bernie Sanders, junior senator of Vermont) in the presidential election. His anthem went viral. Fox News[12] reported he spent $11,000 of his own money to produce the music video. Why would he bother?

---

2. Hawaiian slack-key, or ki ho'alu in Hawaiian, is acoustic guitar music with the guitar strings loosened to give "slack" which changes the tonality, often producing a full major chord or a chord with a major 7th or 6th note. Makana evolved traditional slack-key music into a more contemporary style, dubbing his new genre slack-key rock. See makanamusic.com.

3. See Makana in his Hawaiian home, introducing his ancestry and the history and culture of slack-key guitar: makanamusic.com/video/makana-thoroughly-modern-mele.

4. As reported in an interview with Rootsworld: rootsworld.com/interview/makana10.shtml.

5. Makana describes his version of slack-key rock in a TED Talk: "I started to look at each string as an instrument," he says. He plays barefoot and blindfolded, becoming "at one with the guitar:" youtube.com/watch?v=i4hluGnH3TM.

6. Makana's nonprofit mobilizes Hawaiians to vote, donate, and volunteer for clean water, air, and food: gotkuleana. com.

7. The Occupy Wall Street protest movement was a large populous and social-media movement decrying social and economic inequality. The Rolling Stone magazine explains: rollingstone.com/politics/news/occupy-wall-street-welcome-to-the-occupation-20111110.

8. Dailymail.co.uk/news/article-2061255/Hawaiian-musician-Makana-Occupy-Aloha-T-shirt-played-protest-song Obama.html.

9. Youtube.com/watch?v=xq3BYw4xjxE&feature=channel_video_title.

10. Makanamusic.com/video/makana-cnn-occupy-ing-apec-dinner.

11. Youtube.com/watch?v=BIX5zcitEaY.

12. Video.foxnews.com/v/4757946102001/artist-writes-unofficial-anthem-for-bernie-sanders/?#sp=show-clips.

"The working class has been left behind," Makana says, and the fact that Sanders "takes on Wall Street" is why he decided to take a clear, artistic stance behind the democratic-socialist candidate.

Makana's music is very calming.[13] His voice, both singing and speaking, is soothing. His presence seems steady, but, being bipolar,[14] he experiences radical emotions that he says are "like having a mad elevator in a shaft of my soul. You know, like it drops suddenly to subterranean floors, and in a flash, it skyrockets to heights far above the safety of the structure of any mental scaffolding and gives me an impossible viewpoint. It's totally unstable..."

He chuckles. "That's art."

To meet Makana is to become mesmerized, not just by the cacophony of harmonies that he and his old beat-up acoustic guitar create, but by his relentless flows and swirls of thinking on all topics, from music to money to meaning. He's deeply intelligent and caring. He constantly ponders issues of art and justice: Not just what he thinks, but how he can help create a better Hawaii and a better world, whether through planting an organic garden, speaking to students about self-esteem, or playing free gigs to old-timers who cry for joy at the melodies of their memories.

He's not about fame. Makana is about fulfilling his dharma (life's mission) and connecting with his audience. But 43 million people "like" his seven independent albums on iTunes. ReverbNation counts 92,785 registered fans. He performs for Hawaiian cultural commercials and composes backdrops for movies.[15] This year, he opened for Bad Company and Joe Walsh's "One Hell of a Night" tour.

"My own style is high-octane, intense, passionate," Makana tells *Rootsworld* in a podcast.[16] Yeah. His music is kind of like that, too.

Out of all the people I interviewed for this book, it was Makana who addressed in the most depth the nature of work in the world today, how seeking and holding a job impacts our view of self and life, and what a job *ought* to be.

Not only does Makana model for us a person who's worked long hours and striven relentlessly toward his artistic/career dreams since childhood—and achieved them—he also expresses deep compassion for others with dreams of their own. He's a spiritual artist who believes our materialistic society blocks our experience of one another as divine and whole; he explains his version of "religion" in the chapter that follows. And on the topic of jobs, he's inspired, sickened, and torn. He's a natural to open this book.

---

13. Compare this traditional instrumental Hawaiian tune with Makana's upbeat flare in "Napo'o ka la" with the jazzy duo "Slackmenco" he performs with Jeff Peterson (makanamusic.com/makana-jeff-peterson-live-khnl-hawaii-news-now), with his blissful sunrise with the ocean in "Ka'ena Dream" (youtu.be/LV8IwBWj47I) and his plaintive love-lost ballad full of regret in "Tears" (youtu.be/7OkNKf2HiDU).

14. Bipolar disorder affects about 5.7 million (2.6%) of American adults, according to the National Institute of Mental Health. One in four Americans experiences mental illness in any given year.

15. For example, Hawaii Visitors and Convention Bureau's (HVCB) new media campaign (makanamusic.com/makana-scores-go-hawaii-tv-campaign), #LetHawaiiHappen and the musical score for documentary film Kuma Hina (makanamusic.com/makana-score-composer-documentary-kumu-hina), and George Clooney's movie Descendants (makanamusic.com/video/deep-ancient-hawaiian-forest-descendants).

16. Rootsworld.com/interview/makana10.shtml.

I WAS BORN IN HAWAII, WHERE I'VE GIVEN BIRTH TO MUSIC

I live in Honolulu, in Chinatown. Right now, we're in a very fancy audio shop that my friend owns. I live right up the street. This is where I'm born and raised, though I float around a lot.

I'm thirty-six now. I've been working as a professional musician for like twenty-two years officially, meaning getting paid for creating music.

I started my own company,[17] which is my record label and holds my copyright material, back in 2001. It's funny: When I look back to my teenage years of just breaking into the industry and gigging and doing demos and not actually being a professional recording artist yet, there was a lot of beach time. It was just pure inspiration. I could play for eighteen hours a day if I wanted. I would surf every morning. I mean, it was like a dream life.

As soon as I started to experience some career traction and success, then the name *Makana* started to get out there. My market presence grew. It was like watching an hourglass with sand dripping through from the abundance of free time, dripping down to the other side of obligation.

I would say from my mid-twenties to mid-thirties was the most difficult time. I'm just coming out of that now. Growing a small business alone—occasionally I had a partner, an agent, a manager, but essentially I was doing it all—took anywhere from ten to eighteen hour days every day, not including playing music.

It's cost me more than I could ever recover, but it's also given to me more than I could ever imagine. You know, I've watched a lot of my peers, pretty much all of them, have kids, get married, get mortgages, do all of these things. Every dollar I've made, I've put back into my business. I make really good money, I think, but sometimes at the end of the year, I'll look and I'll go, "Oh, my gosh, personally I made nothing, like less than a teacher." [Laughs.]

But everything has gone right back into my art, whether it was for production or travel, logistics or legal, or whatever. And my music is my child. It's my baby.

I've been through so many different phases, and now my "baby" is about a couple of years off from leaving the nest, and my career is like just a year or two off from really launching on a world scale.

I've really done well in Hawaii, and I have pockets [of fans] in different parts of the world. But the sacrifice that the dedication has taken, I never could have even imagined.

I was just talking to my best friend about this. He's like, "Let's go to dinner."

And my response is a constant, "Oh, hey, so-and-so, I'm so sorry. I've been so busy." It's like, "I've got fifty of my friends I haven't gone to dinner with yet."

And they say, "You're always busy, man. You've been busy like that for twenty years."

So all the people in my life have come to deal with it or just left and dropped out. The rest who stay just really honor that I'm married to my work.

---

17. Makana produces his own music as an independent artist: makanamusic.com.

WHAT A MUSICIAN REALLY DOES ALL DAY

So, my *job*. What do I do? Oh, there's a million answers to that question. My job is to inspire curiosity and movement and emotions, to move people emotionally. *Makana* is more than just music. It's my brand.

I do a lot of different things. I started out doing music, but I have so much creativity coming through me that music's not enough.

So I use language and all sorts of media to move people. On the business side of it, I own all of my IP [intellectual property].[18] Everything I create, I own. I manage myself. I represent myself. I have a very key select team of people around me. I have a wall of attorneys. I have my CPAs and my tax people, and I have an agent, and everything else I do pretty much myself.

BEHIND THE MUSIC: SIX INCOME STREAMS

Essentially, for my job, there are many, many aspects. Number One is to manage finances for the company. To make sure that we're in the black, that there's money coming in through different income streams.

Now, in music, there are at least six major income streams.[19] (There are actually like forty-two miniature ones.) They start with live shows and **performances** and **touring**. That takes a lot of energy. It's my passion. I do a lot of that. Last year, I toured all around the world. The year before, I flew over a hundred times. I'm very active with live performances.

There's **selling music**, which, as everyone knows, has severely dropped off. There's **selling merchandise**, which I do a little of, but not a lot because I don't like material things very much. There's licensing and publishing, which I'm really getting into, and it's very lucrative, like doing soundtrack work for film and TV or commercials or whatnot.

There's **crowdfunding**, which I've done successfully. Like for my previous album, I raised almost $70,000 through Kickstarter, an online platform where your fans become your benefactors. It's like the ancient model of how musicians used to survive, in a modern context with technology.

And then the sixth one is **corporate or organizational sponsorships**. I don't do many of those. I'm very particular.

So I manage all of that, and I make sure that I'm constantly reviewing and going, "Am I maximizing each of these for the vision of my brand?"

And then, with each gig, there's a world of things that happen. With each licensing deal, with everything, there's the negotiations, the contracting, the accounting side, the technical, the logistics, the production, the travel, and all that, and insurances. It's just like any other business. You have all those aspects for everything you do. And if you ignore them and go, "Oh, it's cool, I don't need that," you can skate by sometimes, but you'll get into trouble other times. So it's good to have a system.

---

18. IP: intellectual property of one's own creation or invention. See: wipo.int/about-ip/en.
19. See this list and infographic from Hypebot: hypebot.com/hypebot/2013/06/6-income-streams-to-become-a-full-time-musician-infographic.html.

And then there's managing media and fans. That's a huge, huge expense in terms of time. I'm constantly doing press.

So, I put a lot of time into marketing, and it's a very tailored marketing. Then I spend a lot of time with fans, whether it's online or after shows—some nights I've hugged four hundred people. I just offer free hugs, or I'll stand around for an hour or two and take pictures and sign CDs. I have probably one of the highest industry rates of merchandise sales and CDs. At my gigs, people just go crazy. They love it.

So there's a lot of that, and it takes a lot of time. People are moved by your art, and then they want to open up to you. I'm slowly weaning myself off of feeling obligated to respond to everything, because it's become like an avalanche. I have over 300,000 emails in my inbox. That's just from about five years, not including spam. So, it's a lot.

Emails are like that game at Fun Factory, whack-a-mole. [Laughs.] It's like, as soon as something comes in, I just try to get rid of it. It's endless.

So that's a little bit about what the business requires. I mean, that's not even the making-the-art part. That's another whole story.

WHAT MY ADOPTED DAD TAUGHT ME ABOUT MARKETING

I'm really good with PR, and when I was younger, my *hanai* (adopted dad) taught me about marketing. I never went to college or anything. But when I understood what marketing is and what it meant and how it worked, it made my career exponentially grow.

My hanai dad is Persian. The first thing he said to me was, "Marketing is what is in the mind of the masses. To know what is in the mind of the masses, the first step is to know this."

So I started to do a lot of research into psychology and understanding what motivates people to fall in love with a song and spend money. And I didn't let that change my art, but it helped to open my eyes so that it wasn't a blind process.

It's so easy to get caught up in being an artist and say, "Well, this is my art. You know, the world should just accept me."

That's called *entitlement*. That's not going to bring success! So connecting with people in marketing is really about understanding how much people are barraged by data these days.

THE BALANCE OF SCARCITY AND AVAILABILITY

The other big realization for me was, "Don't be *too* available," and how scarcity works.

One of the things I've done over the years is that, every once in a while, I'll go away for like six months or whatever. I go to L.A. or travel. I move around a lot. And then when I come back, quietly, in that period and then following, it's incredible how much people start to fear that you're not going to be around, and they can't hear your music anymore. So, they stop taking you for granted.

So, you know, it's the classic thing like, "Oh, hey, brah, how is it?"

"Yeah, I saw Makana over at the store, or at the beach."

It's like you have to create a sense of mystique and scarcity and—I don't want to call it *exclusivity* because I like to include people, but it's *value*. People assign value according to certain markers, and one of those markers is that they want to feel special, like they're having a unique and special experience. That's a social marker. So, I don't oversaturate the market. I'm very particular. It's like riding a seesaw. I think a lot of people become too available.

When you don't carefully manage your appearances, if you go to do something big, it fails. It's like spreading your seed around too much [in romantic relationships]. You know, if you want to have an important relationship, you have to save that and channel it.

FINDING MY MEDITATIVE CENTER IN A HECTIC BUSINESS

I used to surf every day, every morning. I don't surf that much anymore. I just don't have time. It's become challenging. My time is so valued. It's like every hour in the day is accounted for, every minute. Fom the moment I wake up, I'm doing so much.

I get called every day by the activists. I do so much community outreach. I've made a New Year's resolution to cut that down, because I don't want to go in circles. Essentially, I want to be in this industry and not be beholden to a corporation where they're like a bank, spending money and putting you into debt on your behalf, telling you how you should dress and how your art should be, and all that. The major-label model is dying off.

But I never wanted that. When I was fourteen, I got offered that. All through the years, I turned down everything because I really believed in myself. Essentially I've created a model of being a truly independent artist. It's rare to find someone who still owns all of their intellectual property and controls it. And it's taken every waking hour for over the past decade to get myself to this point. Now, it's about whittling down, saying no, being discerning and selective, and regaining that balance so I can take it to the next level.

BEING GOOD IN BOTH BUSINESS AND MUSIC SHOULDN'T BE SO RARE

It's very rare, first of all, and it bothers me that I'm rare, because I want to have peers. I want to have people to club up with and *huii*, we call it, to make groups and help each other. It's very difficult.

I go and lecture on the music industry all the time. It's incredible how much it's like a gamble. It's like the American Dream: nobody ever sits down and really analyzes what a load of crap it is, you know? To actually make it, there needs to be a very fine-tuned machine going. I mean, how many millions of musicians will you never hear of that are struggling? It's such a small percentage that make it anywhere.

For me to be able to make it, I try to build teams. Although right now, I'm in a lawsuit with my ex-manager; and my first manager ripped me off for tens of thousands of dollars. That was *my* college. [Laughs.] So, you know, it's difficult to trust people in this industry. I think, for me, I look at the business as an art as well.

My passion in life isn't just music. My passion is understanding God and understanding the Tao,[20] the way that energy moves, the way that molecules interact with each other and orient to each other.

And so I can learn that through anything—yoga, surfing, accounting, politics, watching money flow, watching nature. I'm into farming. So, to me, business is just another aspect of that. The only thing that I don't like about business is my body doesn't get to move as much as I would if I were exercising. That's really unhealthy, and it takes endless amounts of hours. So I try to balance that out.

But in terms of doing business, it's just like an art. One of the first things I learned was that when someone calls or emails you and they have an emergency, you don't let that become your problem. People will try to transfer all the time like a hot potato—in business, too, not just in personal relationships, "Oh, my god, Makana, this happened, and our deadline moved up."

And I'll say, "Okay. Well, I don't have to agree to that right now. Just because your situation changed doesn't mean I need to be impacted."

Let me tell you. It's taken me twenty-plus years to learn that. You get in these situations where it's so easy to feel obligated. And so business is a deeply spiritual thing for me. Just because I think I have that framework for it, it's very interesting. I love it.

My dream would be to be able to experience being a CEO for a large corporation. I would love to know what that feels like.

Why? Because I am a master of detail. Nothing ever slips through the cracks. I am a Gemini. So communication is so natural for me. Articulation is my gift. I understand management and contrary forces working together to build structure. The only difference is that I work alone. I would love to be able to interact and work with people and create something that functions highly and brings benefit to the world on a larger scale. That interests me. So the business to me is exciting as long as it doesn't steal too much from everything else.

MY GLOBAL *HANAI* FAMILY AND MY HAWAIIAN BLOOD FAMILY

My family now is my new friends, relatively new friends, Shane and Ajie. They've become like family to me. We live together. Shane and I did my last record together. He's an amazing audiophile. I have an extended *ohana* or family that goes around the globe. It's incredible—I probably have twenty or thirty sets of amazing *hanai* parents.

Do you know what "hanai" means? Hanai is like if you were raised by your grandmother instead of your mom, she *hanaied* you. It's like being adopted. It doesn't need to be a legal adoption. So I have many, many hanai family [members], on all the different islands, and we're very close. I'm like a hundred people in one, so it suits me to have a very diverse, extended, geographically spread-out family.

As for my blood family, my mom was born and raised in Hawaii. Her mother's from China. She's French-Chinese, my mom. Her name is Toni Suling Reeves. She's in her early sixties. She was Miss Waikiki and Miss Hawaii International. She was born a triplet,

---

20. Taoism (also called Daoism), which means "the way," is a Chinese religion from the 4th century BCE (Before Common Era) that emphasizes living in harmony with the life-force present in all. Find its tenets in the I Ching and Tao Te Ching by Lao Tzu.

premature, two pounds, and survived without her two sisters. She's pretty extraordinary. She's suffered from major, major, major, major mental-health and chemical-imbalance issues.

And my dad is from Minnesota. He's all sorts of European and some Native American. They're not still together—nope. My brother and sister and dad all live in Nevada, and Mom and I both live on the island.

My dad was in telecommunications. He worked for Motorola for almost twenty-five years. He was at the top of everything he did and won awards and everything, and then they laid him off in a downsizing. So he started his own telecommunications consulting firm, and he's become very successful. He's on the road at least as much as I am, and I rarely see him. He's extraordinary in his own way.

My dad is my inspiration for seeking knowledge and understanding. He has a burning desire to improve the lives of others. When we were children, he exposed us to everything from the secrets of the origins of the Federal Reserve, to Area 54 and UFOs, to the powers of hydrogen peroxide therapies and ozone and every water purification system you could find, to Ayurvedic practices and pyramids. In our home, we had pyramids. I mean, anything you could think of, we were exposed to as a child. It was incredible.

What brought my parents together? My mom was super, super hot. *[Laughs.]* My dad's *dad* was like flirting with my mom before he met her. It was so funny.

My brother is three years younger than me. He's more of a techie. And my sister is ten years younger than me, and she and I are very close. She's a very accomplished chef and has worked with some of the top names in the industry since she was a teenager. Right now she's a restaurant consultant, in-between permanent gigs.

MY MUSIC IS COMPLETELY AUTOBIOGRAPHICAL *IF* THE WORLD IS THE SELF

It depends on the context. If I look at the world as myself, which I often do, then it's completely, personally speaking, an individualistic viewpoint. My original compositions, many of them, are a large percentage autobiographical. And then in more recent years, I began utilizing my imagination and composing songs out of my personal experience realm. So that's starting to shift more.

You asked me about my bipolar brain: "Do you think one needs emotional instability to create brilliant art?" Are you looking at what's the link between creativity and being diagnosed as having a mental dysfunction?

I don't know. I guess then my question would be, "What is brilliant art? Does it just validate, or does it elicit a sense of intimacy and aversion, like at the same time?"

ART IS MY MEDITATION, MY SPIRITUAL PRACTICE, AND MY LITHIUM

Art is bipolar in a way—meaning that art, if it's effective, should at once grab you and draw you in and relate to you, but it should also repel you from some other static state, because that's movement. It's like magnetism.

Here's a crazy, crazy metaphor: It's like having a mad elevator in the shaft of my soul. It drops suddenly to subterranean floors, and then in a flash, it skyrockets to heights far above the safety of the structure of any mental scaffolding and gives me an impossible viewpoint. It's totally unstable. That's art. It's dangerous. In fact, I think art exists to destabilize. So those who are less stable mentally sometimes have access to viewpoints that are expressed as art easier than the common person who might have decided to function within a controlled confine that doesn't destabilize them mentally or emotionally. Does that make sense?

Art redefines what normal *is*, obviously. That's a huge part of it. I mean, I have the ability to fall on the ground and collapse and wail and cry where I'm hyperventilating and can't breathe, because I have such a sad thought while I'm writing something, but inside my heart of hearts be hysterical, laughing, because I've hit the jackpot of expression and articulation, and that's my reason for being alive, to be able to articulate things that no one was ever able to do in that fashion. That's my dharma.

For me, meditation is a disengaging of the part of the brain that is kind of like a public restroom [laughs], that's got just whatever can go in and out of it. And I engage something that's not so transient, something deeper. *That's* my meditation. So that could be doing nothing, or it could be doing something. It doesn't matter.

My roller coasters serve me well artistically, but they just really destroy the people around me. [Laughs.] It's a big issue in my life. I mean, you know, I've had to have a restraining order against my mom at some point. It just all depends on how you channel it. It's like, for me, everybody's got a hunk of clay. It's what you do with it.

FIREFIGHTER OR MUSIC MAKER?

I was going to be a fireman. My grandfathers on both sides were fire captains. My mom's father was captain of a fireboat in Honolulu in the 1950s, and my dad's stepdad was a fire captain in Minnesota for decades. So, it's on both sides, and I just loved the idea and the schedule and everything. But I was already doing what I was doing before I was out of the house. So, by the time it was time to make a living, I was doing music. It was never an abstraction for me.

The idea of a "job," I've never thought about in my life, ever, even once. I never worked for anyone else. I mean, call me whatever you want—lucky, blessed, spoiled, whatever—I put in so much work when I was a child, hours and hours and hours, thousands and thousands of hours. Music was so important to me. I learned from such incredible teachers, and I wanted to honor them.

So, by the time I was fifteen, I was singing for an assembly, and I remember the feeling between the audience and me, and I thought, "This is incredible. This is magic." It was like, "I want to do this more."

And then I would play in the bars. I started when I was fourteen. Well, really twelve, but I had my own gig when I was fourteen, and the old-timers would come—guys way older than my grandparents, and they would just sit there and cry. They loved it.

"Hey, boy, play old-time music for me," they would say.

I knew how to do it, and I was the only one who knew how to do it. There are very, very few in my generation even to this day who know how to do [slack-key]. And, it was just the right place, right time, my destiny, or whatever story you want to make up around it. Life molded me into this, and it was never an abstraction. It was never about, "What are you going to do? How are you going to make a living?"

HOW TO DISCERN WHAT TO DO WITH YOUR CAREER: FIND YOUR DHARMA

I've got to make a super-important point right now. The whole idea of, "Oh, what do you want to be when you grow up? What field do you want to go into?" It's abstract, right? It's not direct. So you go into that thought.

And you're influenced by fear and pressure, and your parents and your peers, and media and social media, and blah, blah, blah, and then that determines your future. I mean, let me tell you, it happens to billions of people like this.

So that, to me, is a bad idea. It's not the right way to approach it. I'll give you a metaphor: So many people say, "Oh, when do you want to have kids? When are you going to get married? When are you going to have a partner?" People ask me that every day.

I say, "Listen, I don't talk about having kids because I don't have a partner. Having kids is sacred. I don't just want to go find someone to use their womb to have a child with me. I don't objectify people."

So, to me, this whole process has to be symbiotic in order for it to be fulfilling and *pono*, as Hawaiians call it—real and healthy and enriching and nurturing. Whether it's your job or your life partner or whatever it is, it needs to happen naturally, organically. Instead, we've created this false, mechanistic, debt-driven notion. It's like a deficit if you're a woman and you're thirty-five, and you're not married. You're a failure in so many cultures. You're weird. It's disgusting. Society is based on status-quo markers that everyone enforces on each other because they automatically feel that they have to abide by them. So we all project that violence onto each other.

I never was a part of that. I've always been a rebel. I never said, "What am I going to do?" I was *doing it* already. I was helping my parents pay rent when I was still in school. Music was my passion. I never said, "What do I want to go sacrifice eight hours a day of my life doing so I can be happy?"

I never asked myself that horrible question. That's slavery. I don't believe in that. That is a failure of upbringing. That is a failure of society, of schooling, of everything.

Everything needs to happen naturally and organically. Like for me, I haven't met my life partner yet, or if I'm going to have one or whatever, but that's okay because I'm going through all of the spiritual development I need to go through. I still have things to work out. I'm still immature in many ways. I don't know if I'm mature enough even to raise a child without projecting all my crap onto them. You know, does anyone even ask themselves this question?

Instead, we only think about the end results as a society: "Hey, what's your degree in?" "How much money do you make?" "Where do you live?"

All these status-quo markers turn us into programmed beings with a relative judgment on the next person and our relative value to them. None of that is love. Your work needs to be love. That's what Khalil Gibran[21] said, "Work is love made visible."

When I was seventeen years old, my English teacher gave me that book, *The Prophet*, and it changed my life. I was like, "Work is love made visible." I printed that page up and put it on my wall in my room wherever I went.

My work has always been my first love. If your work is not your love, you're killing yourself.

Don't mind me…I get very passionate.

EVEN SUCCESSFUL MUSICIANS MAKE ALMOST NOTHING

Let's be real clear about this: There's gross and then there's net. My gross is, you know, twenty-five times what a teacher makes. And it varies so much. But my net, meaning after I pay for everything that I need to do in order to do my business, has been as low as $16,000/year.

Does that mean my quality of life was low? No, not at all. Out of that, I paid for my travel, because I live on the road a lot. I've paid for my truck. I've paid for a lot of essentials. The company pays for a lot of it.

So I'm just saying a lot of time it's a wash, like, "Oh, great. I just got a $5,000 check for a gig," but "Oh, wait. I have to pay out the techs, the sound company, the graphic artist, the musicians. I've got to pay the dancers."

Sometimes I feel like a pass-through for money, and then I just get caught holding the tax bag. I mean, it happens often. If you're not smart, you really get screwed. I've got tons of musician friends who, on the front end, life is great, and, on the back end, they're whining because they're totally in the red. So, I mean, I'm a quarter Chinese: thankfully, that means I'm good with money.

MANAGING THE MAKANA TEAM

I have no direct employees. I don't employ people. I have independent contractors. The number fluctuates. I have two or three different lawyers for different purposes, and I also have a tax lawyer. I have a CPA, and a booking agent, and a guy who handles a lot of my tech things. That's my core business team. It's about five to seven people. And then I have my personal assistant/massage therapist. That's important: I play so much, and I beat myself up playing. The way I play guitar is so intense, I constantly need to get massaged. Otherwise I can't play fast anymore.

I have my production partners, the engineers I work with. It's not like everybody shows up at an office like, "Okay, time to start working." It's nothing like that. I interact with each of these people in different timeframes, depending on the task at hand.

When I'm in Hawaii, I do bigger productions because I'm based in Hawaii. So, I'll have more musicians and dancers and whatnot and do bigger productions. To fly a whole team anywhere else is very expensive. But, when I'm on the road, generally I'll play solo. For example, I'm about to fly to Los Angeles for a music festival. So I'll do a solo set,

---

21. Khalil Gibran (1883-1931) was a Lebanese-American artist, writer, and poet, best known for his inspirational book, The Prophet. Read about him at: poetryfoundation.org/bio/kahlil-gibran.

and I'll also do a set with some of the other slack-key guitar musicians. It's kind of like a throw-together. I don't actually pay them. We're all paid independently.

Often when I tour, I tour alone. In fact, the last tour I did on the West Coast, I did like over twenty shows in a month. That was just me. I flew myself, drove myself, took care of all logistics. Before I go on the road, I plan everything, book everything, make sure every detail and address and venue and contact and tech and hotel, and restaurants in the area that have the kind of diet I want. I do all that research, assemble all of that, and then I go on the road. That is hard work.

WHAT I WOULD DO WITH INFINITE MONEY AND TIME

If I had a billion dollars right now, I would immediately build a mixed use live/work space where we could grow a massive amount of food and record all of our music and produce all our videos and hold conference meetings for activism and have a health-food storefront; and then I would put together a production team and put everyone on payroll and immediately start pumping out media—video and art and music that would influence society.

And I don't necessarily want to get into politics as a politician, but I would definitely use my influence, that greater financial influence, to start countering a lot of the corporate lobbyists. Those would be the two main things I would do.

Oh, and I would fund a food forest.[22]

MY WORST AND BEST MOMENTS ARE INTERTWINED AS ONE

My worst day and best day are all the same. That's the thing: It's like worst and best is the same for me.

One moment that comes to mind: In China, years ago, I was representing the state of Hawaii and doing a series of concerts. For one show in Tianjin, China, at an opera house, I had a very small team of performers and a translator. They flew all of us in, in the morning. We arrived at the theatre by like 9:00 a.m., and doors were opening at like 6:00 p.m., and I had to stage and produce an entire large-scale production, concert performance with all these moving parts, in eight hours.

It's comical now to look back. See, it was a worst moment because of the impact of the stress that I went through, but it's also a best moment because of the memory and the stories. I walked into that theatre that morning and thought, "Okay, I have enough experience to know that this is not enough time. So everybody listen to me very carefully and do exactly as I say," and it was awesome.

I had two Hawaiian guys who were musicians and one was a dancer. I had one hula dancer who was Miss Hawaii, one *butoh* [modern Japanese style] dancer, and one translator. Everybody did twenty things. Then we had a staff of Chinese people that didn't speak English. It was so funny. We spent an hour and a half getting the sound right, and then, all of a sudden, I realized the guy wasn't labeling anything—it wasn't a

---

22. A food forest is a sustainable agroforest plant-system that produces fruit, nuts, vegetables, and greens for human consumption. See: edibleforestgardens.com/about_gardening.

digital board. There was no recall. So everything we were doing was a waste of time: He had to reset everything every time. It was ridiculous.

So, I'm like, "Oh, my god, this is a nightmare. We just wasted an hour and a half. The guy didn't save anything."

So they like hauled him off. I don't know if they hung him or what happened, you know? I never saw him again.

Then it was like 3:00, and we were finally getting this thing together. You have a lot of lighting, design, and stage, very elaborate things. There was smoke and dragons, and blah, blah, blah.

So then one of the people who's in charge shows up and says, "Oh, Makana, we have a small favor to ask."

I say, "What?"

He says, "A local ballet school wants to dance *hula* [traditional Hawaiian style] tonight."

All of a sudden, before I can even respond, thirty-five or forty Chinese girls stumble onto the stage from out of nowhere, and we're supposed to teach them hula.

I'm like, "You've got to be kidding me, right?" But thankfully, Miss Hawaii and the other guy both knew enough to teach them, "Going to a *Hukilau*."

And then finally, the show was about to start, and then I heard all of these crashing sounds. I run out of my dressing room, and it's like New Year's Eve with dragons dancing, lions dancing, smoke cannons, and stuff.

I was like, "That wasn't part of the plan."

They're like, "Ah, well, they're Chinese. They've got to do that."

The whole thing was just insane. I was so frazzled, but it came together, and one of the cool parts was that I actually play Chinese harp, and so I had ordered a Chinese harp and hid it behind one of the curtains; and when we unveiled it midway through the show, the audience just went crazy—they gasped. I played this beautiful song that I wrote, and I said, "I'm a quarter Chinese, and I just want to honor my roots."

It was really emotional. It was really beautiful. There were two thousand people in the audience. And I became one with them.

So, my best days are my worst days; my worst days are my best days. I mean, they're all the same.

I think, if I didn't have a body to be concerned about, then I would never have a bad day. [Laughs.] But your body can only handle so much stress. I burn my adrenals really hard. I push really hard, and I give 100 percent in everything I do, whether I'm doing a concert or doing dishes. So that's just how I am, intense.

WHEN I AM CREATING, THERE IS NO "ME"

When I'm creating, there is no *me*. I mean, there's never a "you"; it's just a recognition. People say, "Oh, you should be self-aware." I don't understand what that means. Awareness is just transcendence of self. Self is a blocker of awareness.

However, when I'm performing, I become very observant of my body, because my body is like the instrument, not the guitar. When I'm playing slack key, the guitar and I are one, period. So the sensations come through my body, my nerve endings, my skin, my musculature, different trigger points that I'm managing. I'm in my breath. When I'm doing my most intense guitar work, I go into almost like a hyperventilation, but it's controlled.

So, I mean, I'm not somewhere far away at that point. There's a very calm place, like the center of the storm inside, very calm. Around me is an oscillation of many, many states fluctuating in a harmonic pattern that create like a kaleidoscopic give-off, a light and sound experience. I'm focused.

I think the main thing that happens is I'm *feeling*. Instead of a symphony of notes, it's a symphony of emotions, of feelings. The deeper I go into the feelings, it's unbelievable how it affects the musculature of the voice and the fingers. There's a language of emotion in muscles, and that comes into play when I'm creating music.

BEING FAMOUS, AND INFAMOUS

I've won a few awards. Awards *should be* for people who risk their life; I don't know why they give musicians awards. Just being a musician is a reward; getting to go onstage is a reward. People have already rewarded you with their attention. I mean, yeah, rewards, I just don't understand why we have to reward each other things. It's so weird. Anyway.

I've been harassed. I've been stalked. Of course, I must have created it, but yeah. My guitar was stolen. Houses burglarized. I've also had druggies come try and garner checks from me and steal from me and threaten me. This was in the early days. People generally don't fuck with me now. But when you're a kid, you know, it's easy to mess with you.

THE ILLUSION VERSUS THE REALITY OF BEING A SUCCESSFUL MUSICIAN

You know, you see something on the TV or on the Internet, and it's so different than being the person directly experiencing it.

It's easy to create this fantasy level. But I think when you can find an experience of the divine in the seemingly mundane, then you can see through fame. Fame is the faucet of attention, like the fire-hose of attention shooting at you. When you want to be heard, it's awesome, but you don't want to be heard all the time. I mean, when you go sit on the toilet, you don't want someone listening. When you are talking to your best friend and having a beer, just letting off steam, you don't want to be heard by anyone else. You want privacy.

Fame doesn't allow that. Fame is a magnifying glass that magnifies things that should never be magnified. Fame draws attention to things that are not worthy of attention and plasters them everywhere. It distorts things.

There's a time and place for distortion. Jimi Hendrix did great with it—he made distortion cool and did awesome things with it musically—but you can never turn it off.

I talk in metaphors…There's a time and place for distortion, you know? But to be stuck in a distorted reality with everyone around you, where everyone looks at you not as *you* but as their story of you, which happens when people meet you through media, it gets real weird. It's very dangerous.

A lot of people worship me in the sense that they treat me differently than they treat other people. Why is that? People that I'm not close with. It's strange, don't you think? Like if you walk into a restaurant, and, "Oh, look, it's somebody famous," and all of a sudden, the other people become less important.

Fame serves a purpose when you need to be heard or seen because you have something to share. It's the greatest thing in the world then; but other times, it's pretty terrible.

I've avoided fame as much as possible. That was part of my reason for choosing to do traditional music when a big music management company wanted to sign me and make me a pop star. There was no market for my music, and I loved that, actually. I'm creating a market for it.

FAME IS NOT ABOUT GETTING ATTENTION; IT'S ABOUT FINDING YOUR JOY

Bigger isn't necessarily better: After all, McDonald's is the most popular restaurant on Earth.

When I speak in our local schools and kids say to me, "Oh, you know, I just want to be famous," or, "You're so lucky. What's it like to be famous?" it's disturbing.

Media is a relatively new phenomenon. Two hundred years ago, there wasn't really a media scene. So we don't know what to make of it yet. We let it into bed with us. We let it into our lives. You can be laying in bed, or in the shower masturbating, and Facebooking with ten thousand people. It's just a little strange. You could be making love to your wife, and have the TV on, and watching terrorists in the Middle East. It's like, all of a sudden, everything is decontextualized.

So human beings haven't evolved yet. Hardly anyone's even discussed it, how much media affects us, how unnatural it is for our senses as animals. All I'm saying is, a lot of the things that seem to be cool aren't, and to pursue those things for the sake of getting attention for people is a bad idea.

I think what's important is to put your energy and passion into something that brings you immense inner joy, immense fulfillment, that makes you feel proud and share that with other people, and if it makes them feel the same way, then make a living doing that. And then the audience will come. The right people will come.

When you go about it backwards and try to get a quick access to a huge amount of attention, it creates pressure on you that you can't even fathom until it's there.

I look at Pearl Jam, one of my favorite bands when I was growing up. You know, they blew up so fast. After [their album] "10," nothing they did could follow that. It just couldn't. Nothing they did was that epic. They got too big too fast. Everybody knows it. I mean, we all still love Eddie [Vedder]. I love Eddie. I love them, but it was just like anticlimactic.

HOW BEING HAWAIIAN SHAPES MY APPROACH TO ART

Being born and raised in Hawaii and growing up in the context of a host culture that is still very much alive and prevalent, was a blessing. I had a *kumu*, a teacher, named Nova-Jean McKenzie. She just passed away last year. She was the one who gave me the name, *Makana*. She instilled in me the Hawaiian mind.

I have always been attracted to my elders. I have always valued time with them, to hear their stories, to be in their presence.

You know, when I was a boy, my dad told me about this study. It really affected me. He said that scientists took two control groups of archers. They were both beginning archers, but one group, they put through training. They had them shoot every day and practice and practice. The other group, they actually didn't have them shoot at all. All they did was have them spend a week with the greatest archers in the world, eating and drinking and talking and hanging out. And at the end of the week, they tested both control groups, and the archers who had never shot an arrow but who had actually spent the week with the masters scored higher.

I realized early on there was an immense importance and value in absorbing the wisdom and just being in the presence of my elders. So, for the past three decades, I've spent immense, countless hours with all sorts of Hawaiian elders.

The other thing my dad told me about culture was, "Take what works for you in any culture and leave the rest behind. Don't feel obligated to absorb and agree with the whole thing. Just take parts, what works for you, and build your own thing."

He gave me permission to do that at a very young age. It was amazing because there are a lot of parts of Hawaiian culture that I didn't agree with in certain timeframes. There was a time where sixteen generations of no weaponry making, no war. It was the "Aha Council,"[23] a time when there was peace and harmony, and each *ahupuaa* or land division was governed by a council of elders. That is an idyllic time that I look to, but before and after that, there were many violent eras, slaves, a caste system, and all those things that I didn't like about India.

So those parts I don't need and I don't take. The part I do take is the breath of life, *aloha*, the recognition, *namaste*, of the light in you and the light in me. "I am you." I don't just love you. I *aloha* you, which is a verb. I *am* you. I recognize that. We are intertwined. We are one. *Malama pono*, to care for the balance.

THE HAWAIIAN MIND: WE SEE SACREDNESS, NOT EVERYTHING FOR SALE

The Hawaiian mind is a frame of reference for seeing the world. We don't see everything for sale. We see there is a sacredness that needs to be honored and the importance of *ohana*, family, the importance of sustainable relationships with our resources, with managing the fisheries and oceans, taking care of the reefs, managing the aquifers and watersheds—all of these things that most people take for granted.

The *'aina* is sacred. It's the relationship with that, that becomes first and foremost, not how much money you make, where you live, what kind of car you drive, all this other stuff that is the *haole* [white person or non-Hawaiian] mentality. What's first important is your relationship with your ancestors and your family and the land, those three things.

Only a select group of people are still learning and speaking Hawaiian. This is happening everywhere—languages and cultures are being lost all over the world. It's

---

23. Cds.hawaii.edu/kahana/downloads/curriculum/SectionII/Unit1/1.B.Aha/1.B.2.AhaReading.pdf.

definitely a minority. It's on the upswing though, because there's a movement called *Pūnana Leo*, which is an all-Hawaiian language school platform where all subjects are learned in Hawaiian language.

If we can turn off the devices, tune out, do some breathing, hug someone, have a juice, an organic vegetable green juice, have some wheatgrass, you know…

Get in touch with what's real, unlike the people shaping the world and telling you this is important and you need to become a slave so you can acquire "this" thing. I don't believe in evil, but they would be the closest to that.

So it's exposure: the summation of your environment is absorbing into you, and you're absorbing it. That's why it's important to protect your senses. It's important to not constantly be exposed to materialism and fear and greed and hypersexuality and all of these [societal] distorters of beauty.

THE ANTIDOTE FOR CRAZY CONTEMPORARY SOCIETY

If you can go back to the quiet place of the resonance of the earth and your heart and tune into who you really are and remember that, that's how you determine what your *dharma*[24] is.

You don't need a "job." You need to find your dharma. When you discover your purpose for being, then the money is just lubricant so that the gears keep churning, but you don't do it for the lubricant. You do it for the circulation in your own veins, that feeling of blood pumping through your heart. It feels so good. It makes you alive. That's enough.

When you do something for the sake of doing it, you don't need a reason. It's like if you really love someone, you can't say why.

You could say why, but if you love them because of something, then you don't really love them. It's like breathing. The only way to feel a lack of love is to deny it entering you. It's always here.

It's really tragic and misleading that we look at the job market as, just give a man a job and find a job. But I think when we go back to personal responsibility—we call that "*kuleana*," when we recreate our roles, recreate ourselves as healthy, grounded, awake human beings, then all of a sudden, a lot of solutions appear on the horizon that we were blind to before.

It's a tragedy that people shut down *en masse* when they don't have a job *per se*, or they feel like they can't find a job, and they feel trapped, when there are so many things the creative mind can do to open doors to abundance. It's not that it's easy. But I think we need to reconsider our options.

WE'RE ALL JUST STORIES THAT HAVE AN INEVITABLE END

I'm not saying there's anything wrong with Muhammad's life [Chapter 6]. It may be a beautiful story, but I'm just saying it's sad. He has to pedal [a rented rickshaw taxi] twelve

---

24. Dharma is Sanskrit word from Jainism, Hinduism, and Buddhism with multiple meanings; in this context, your life purpose or sacred duty.

hours a day just to feed his kids. It's sad that someone would have to forego all of the potentials of being human and do this one thing every day of his life just to survive. It's tragic, but it's true, and it's true in many places with millions of people.

The only thing that matters is the stories. We're all expendable and disposable. We're all going to die. So it's the story that's interesting. At this end of this whole thing, you get a book out of it. All the readers are going to meet the people [us narrators]. They just get the story; they don't get to live our lives. Obviously they have their own.

It's tragedy and comedy and all the things in-between. It may be enriching and worth reading. But to have to live it, that's another story. [Laughs.]

All humans are just stories, not just the people in this book. No, no, no, I mean it—this whole trip is just a story. Whatever story it is—there is no greater feeling than the camaraderie of social interaction through storytelling. Every culture has that. And when you die, that's all you take.

I'm not demeaning the value of the story; I'm exalting it. I'm saying there is only the story. We are expendable. We're not even real. We're temporarily animated clay.

WHAT'S THE TRUE WORTH OF A JOB, AND A LIFE?

Look, as long as we all keep going along with the emperor's new clothes, like, "Oh, yeah, his clothes look great," like, "As long as you have a job, life is good," I think we're missing the whole point. Jobs don't bring fulfillment and joy. Certain jobs do, but *having a job* doesn't.—It's like the difference between living and existing.

And so, being inspired in your work changes the nature of what you produce.

Man, there are so many millions of people who hate their job, and they produce crap. That's why there's so much shit that you buy that breaks all time and doesn't work, and people's houses are filled with crud from China that's toxic. Their babies are chewing on things that are toxic with arsenic in them.

It's because we live in a surface part of the brain, that says, "As long as everything looks according to what we were taught by the TV, then we're happy and successful," and I'm saying that needs to shatter. That needs to change. If we want to see real improvement of the conditions of life for humanity in general, we need to shift our value system.

If you do the work and make the best of your life, the universe will show up and give you opportunities.

That's where I'm an idealist. But I'm not a one-way idealist, saying that everyone deserves this or that. I'm a two-way idealist. I say, as long as you show up for yourself, the world will show up for you.

WHAT I TEACH: COLLEGE ISN'T FOR EVERYONE

Is everyone going to have a perfect happy story? No, it's not that simple, but we need to shatter the belief that what success and happiness look like is a house and a car and a white picket fence, this whole culture of getting.

All of a sudden, what happens? It means that everyone who doesn't have that is impoverished. Children get pressured by their peers if they look different. They don't have the same things their other peers have, so they're mocked. Going to speak in schools for the last fifteen years, I've met hundreds of kids who have gone through this.

The violence is in our *view* of what is wealth, is success. That's violent in itself because that's what drives people to do things like have kids when they can't afford them or to send their kids to a college when the kid's miserable. I mean, let me tell you.

Every year I go to one of the most prestigious private schools in Hawaii, and I do a class called the "Search for Meaning in Life" class. And I cannot tell you how many times a student has come up to me and after they wait for everyone to leave, says, "Makana, can I talk to you?" and then just bursts into tears.

It's the pressure of trying to make their parents happy.

"My parents are working three jobs because they want to put me in an Ivy League school, but it's not what I want. I really want to do my art," or "I'm a swimmer. I love to swim," whatever it is. "But they're worried. They want me to be a lawyer or a doctor."

Oh, my god. I've heard this a million times. I've heard it from almost every kid. That is an epidemic. It's the generational transfer of the disease of conditioning. We put that on our children. That's the impoverishment we raise them in, even the wealthy families.

"JOB," TO ME, IS SUCH AN ICKY WORD

So this all routes back to *the job*. The job is how we define our pride, our place in society. It shouldn't be all about the job. It should be all about the individual being in harmony with who they were born to be and who they would like to be.

That doesn't mean, "Oh, well, I want to be just a hippie that smokes pot and do nothing and get welfare." That's not what I'm saying. What I'm saying is this: When we apply ourselves, when we give, life gives back to us.

The job implies this colloquial view of working for someone, being underneath something. Billionaires don't have jobs. Why does everyone else have jobs?

So I don't know what the *Webster's Dictionary* meaning is, but this is a colloquial implication. As long as we rate each other on jobs, then we get pressured to have a certain kind of job.

In some tribal cultures, families are very happy with very little. They're happier than I am, and I recognize that. I'm not saying everyone needs to live at a certain standard. I'm just saying as long as we look at life and each other on the level of *job*, we're not seeing each other or ourselves, and that's a tragedy.

I may be miserable or overjoyed at times doing what I do, but I keep doing it, and I never think about the money. I have played more free gigs than I have paid gigs in my life by far.

It's so funny. "Job," to me, is such an icky word. [Laughs.]

It's all about creating opportunity. Oftentimes I get written off as like, "Oh, you're lucky. You're blessed. You're special. Well, you're talented. So it's different."

To me, that's all bullshit. Yes, I am blessed. I was born in Hawaii. That's the greatest blessing you could ever have in your life. But there are a lot of people born here that didn't do anything with their life.

Society looks and says, "Well, certain people have better lives or better opportunities because there was this gift that was born into them." A lot of people who are in my position who made a living off of their own talents *per se* don't necessarily agree with that, because the amount of sacrifice and work and dedication just gets kind of overlooked.

But the biggest tragedy is, if other people think to themselves, "Well, those people are special, and I would never have that opportunity," and I just want to eradicate that kind of thinking, because everyone is special. Everyone is God. Everyone is an aspect of The One. Everyone has *immense* potentiality.

I mean, if we look at the stories, again, that exist in the human consciousness, everything from *The Little Prince* down, it's like there are so many—*The Alchemist* is a classic one. You know, we read that story from Paulo Coelho because it's a great story, but it's not about a billionaire or a very talented person. It's about a humble shepherd.

Greatness doesn't come out of some investment that came before birth. Greatness comes out of the determination and inspiration that drives a person to evolve. And it's not measured by the amount of money or the amount of recognition.

IF IT'S TRUE THAT OUR JOB = OUR SELF, I'D LIKE TO SEE THAT CHANGE

That's why this book is important, because a lot of people don't get the recognition, like the rickshaw guy. Everyone's life is equally important, and no one should ever limit their future based on their circumstance.

I've seen too many miracles, so we shouldn't say, "Well, college is the only—education is the only way." I do not believe that. I am probably the only person who doesn't believe that. I never set foot in college except to lecture. College can't teach you shit about my industry. It can set you up for a fall because it creates a false illusion of security.

So, obviously there's a place for college. I'm a huge fan of trade schools, by the way. But I'm just saying the dialectic, the language, to move beyond *college and job*, because as long as kids hear that, they dread it. There's nothing exciting about growing up and going to college and a job.

There are other ways. I'm living proof. I want people to explore that. I want kids to know that. I tell kids this in the schools. We duct tape the teachers and throw them behind the desk.

I just want to say one more thing. I'm looking at the *My Job* website [myjobstories. org], and it says, "Our job = Our self." I really want you to reflect on what I just said. I understand the starting point of saying, "In the current context of culture, our job does equal our self," and that is totally true, but I'd like to see that change.

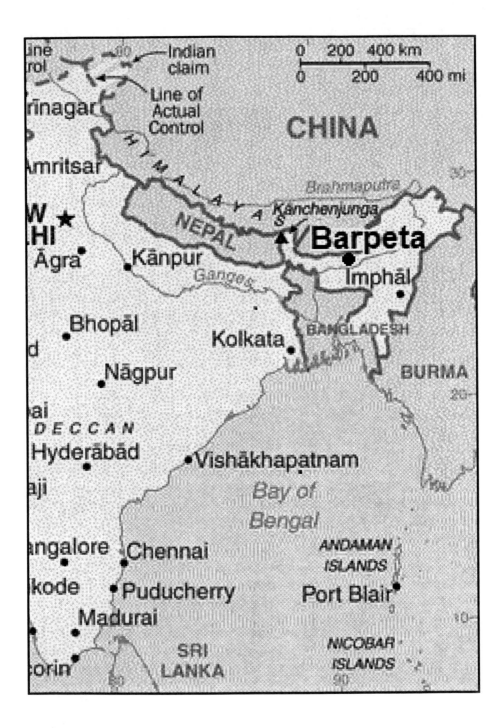

ARINDAM AND DEBALEENA

ECO-MANUFACTURERS

ASSAM, INDIA

Editor's note: She's a social worker who's into women's empowerment. He's a cigarette-smoking workaholic with persistent stubble and an edge of curmudgeon. Their love story sounds a little bit like a Hindi Bollywood film…

Yet, it's definitely no fairytale. Their first date was at the mall—for coffee on a Sunday morning—but it was set up in conservative Bengali tradition, by their mothers, as the first step toward an arranged marriage. They then returned to their respective homes and jobs—she, in the cosmopolitan center of Kolkata, and he, in the middle of nowhere in rural Assam. He waited a month, then wrote her a long email in which he detailed all of his flaws: He shaves only once a month, he smokes, and he has no money whatsoever. His only assets, he states bluntly, are his friends.

Debaleena calls this "The Arindam Dasgupta Syndrome." "What a load," she says. "Who would want to marry him?" But it turns out, *she* did.

Debaleena saw his heart and his vision. She liked his honesty and matched it with hers. They emailed further and when he invited her to come and see if she could handle life in the northeastern hinterlands, she came, saw, and fell in love.

"What he was doing was audacious," Debaleena marvels, "especially at his age." Arindam, the reluctant groom, eventually embraced the good luck that had brought his beautiful bride long before he thought he was ready for her. He not only married her: He also hired her.

Together, they run a small factory called Tamul Plates.[1] They employ 750 locals in three ways: leaf-collectors gather fallen areca nut[2] palm sheaths; home-based village units rent their machinery and make products that Tamul Plates then sells; while another team of factory workers at headquarters cleans and dries the sheaths and presses them into disposable dinnerware for parties and weddings.

Located in the Himalayan foothills, the lush green wetlands of the state of Assam is home to 220 ethnic tribal groups,[3] tea and silk plantations, and thousands[4] of native areca nut palm trees—a tall, skinny palm tree with a cluster of nuts at the top. Every spring, these trees shed the skins, or sheaths, from their palm-nuts. The fallen sheaths used to just pile up and rot, until Tamul Plates figured out how to convert this bio-waste into dishes.

Arindam and Debaleena may hold the only two graduate degrees in the village— his in rural management; hers in social work—and they're determined to make their triple-bottom-line[5] social enterprise succeed by doing the opposite of what seems profitable. Located in the remote countryside with sparse education or electricity, they design machinery that runs off-grid on biofuel. They hire ultra-poor women, youth, and men, and pay 1.5 times the going rate in India.[6] They spend their newlywed years living on their extended families' credit. They work long hours and pay everyone else ahead of themselves.

They work together 24/7, live together, eat together, watch movies, write proposals, everything, together. They've just begun to eke a profit out of their company. They've built a real-life romance and a full-spectrum friendship. The only "baby" they've birthed so far, though, they laughingly admit, is their business.

My conversation with Arindam and Debaleena flowed naturally between the two of them. You can see by the way they communicate that their relationship has a balance of power, a synergy of intelligence, and a healthy dose of humor.

OUR SOCIAL ENTERPRISE TRAINS LOCALS TO TURN BIO-WASTE INTO DINNERWARE

Arindam: My name is Arindam Dasgupta, and I am thirty-five years old.

Debaleena: I'm Debaleena Ray, and I'm thirty-one years old.

---

1. Their name, "tamul," is the English spelling of the Assamese word tambul, which means "betel nut." See: tpmc.co.in.

2. The areca nut is also known as the infamous betel nut chewed by millions (one tenth of the world's population, the BBC reports) in Asia and Africa for its caffeine-like stimulant effect.

3. Assam is on the brink of becoming a tribal-majority state, says The Times of India.

4. The Indian government estimates 100,000 hectares (247,000 acres).

5. Triple bottom line: social, environmental, and economic benefits. Also known as TBL or "three Ps": people, planet, and profits.

6. According to the World Bank, the average annual salary in India is $1,600USD. Tamul Plates pays their full-time staff $2,400 per year.

Arindam: I am the founder, promoter, director, and also the CEO of Tamul Plates (tpmc.co.in). We registered in 2009. We started off our operations in 2010. Tamul Plates is a social enterprise that promotes original areca nut-leaf plate manufacturing.[7]

These are disposable plates made out of the areca nut sheath amongst rural communities in northeast India. We promote small village units producing these plates. We support them through various services like financial, marketing, technical, and other areas of training. We help them produce the plates, and we then buy the product back and market it across India and the export market.

The focus of Tamul Plates is to create a livelihood employment amongst the rural communities in northeast India, making an ecofriendly product, which also reduces pollution because we are replacing Styrofoam and other non-biodegradable disposable plates.

Debaleena: I'm the documentation and training manager of Tamul Plates. I've been part of the organization for the last two years. Based in Barpeta and initially working only on the documentation process, I'm now also looking after the training programs as well as doing the reports and various proposals, and EOIs [Expressions of Interest] business proposals. Many times we also need to submit documents to various awards or competitions, for which we need to draft documents. So I work with Arindam closely on all of these. I also do some PR material: Facebook, marketing brochures, and all these things.

WHERE WE WORK IS REMOTE, RAINY, AND RURAL

Arindam: We are based in Assam in a small town called Barpeta. Assam is in the northeast corner of India. It's a little bit cut off from mainland India. It's just joined through a very small tract of land, which is called the Chicken's Neck. The land is very fertile. It's a biodiversity hotspot: You get various kinds of species out here.

Debaleena: One characteristic feature of Assam is the tea gardens.

Arindam: Assam and other states of northeast India have quite a different culture from the rest of India. Basically, in terms of population, this region is divided amongst various small tribes throughout the area. We have the Brahmaputra River Valley in the center, surrounded by the Himalayan foothills.

The people out here are very simple. Since we are landlocked and a little bit cut off from the mainland, many people out here don't have an exposure to India, and we are surrounded by international borders with China, Burma, and Bangladesh.

Barpeta is a very small town. If you start from one end of the town, you can reach the last end of the town within ten minutes' walking. The Brahmaputra River itself is just ten kilometers [6.2 miles] away. It's a huge river, and there are tributaries flowing throughout the region.

The agriculture out here, due to the high rainfall and the fertility of the soil, is good; but at the same time, it is affected by a lot of floods due to all the rains that fall on the Himalayan foothills. So that flooding creates a loss of livelihood in this region.

We are just around 100 kilometers [62 miles] away from the Bhutan border. Close to

---

7. See a video of Arindam talking about the company: youtu.be/C8LSvLkuTic.a

the border is the lush green where you find a lot of the tea plantations, and that region is mostly inhabited by the Bodo tribals. They're of Mongoloid origin.

Debaleena: Barpeta is a place which is diametrically opposite to any metropolitan city of our country. Lots of greenery, no high-rises, no malls, no luxuries, anything.

WAYS IN WHICH WE ADAPT OUR BUSINESS TO FIT THE CLIMATE AND CULTURE

Arindam: We get a lot of rainfall, and the moisture maintained in this region is very high. So what happens in a concrete room during the monsoons, it gets very damp, and then the moisture doesn't get out. By using local materials in construction, even if the moisture gets in the room, whenever there is sunlight, the moisture can [also] get out. So that makes it more feasible for our kind of work, because too much moisture might lead to a fungus problem in the raw material, since we're dealing with a completely natural material.

So, our factory is made out of all local materials. We only have a concrete structure in our machine room. The flooring is concrete. It's all a bamboo-based structure using a lot of local construction materials with an open kind of a feeling between.

Around a kilometer [.6 miles] from the factory, we have our office and our packaging facility. It's a big enough area, both together. Being in a small town, the rentals are not so high out here. So we can afford a bit of more space.

Debaleena: The people out here are very simple. The culture obviously is a bit different. It's a mixture of broadmindedness and tradition. There's some bits of it that you would think, oh, we are far more ahead than what people might think of here. They are very warm, welcoming.

They might not have gone to university; but these people—over the last ten years that Arindam and Tamul Plates have worked with them—have greatly enriched their own skills. They have taken us to the level where Tamul Plates is today. They work very hard, very hard; they're very honest, very simple people. Any time of the day, if you think of a job that needs to be done, you can call them up, and you can tell them, and they'll do it.

Most are from the surrounding villages. The most important characteristic they have is ownership: The community completely owns the factory and the work that we do. They say, "This is our job, this is my factory," and do the work on their own completely.

Because this is a producers' company, many staff members are literally *producers* who have a share in the company. Even those who do not have a share in the company, have a sense of ownership. So the whole team works towards the project. I don't think we get to see this kind of work culture anywhere outside, in any other metropolitan city.

When I compare it with the professionals I have met with outside or worked with outside Barpeta, the professionalism level or the skills level is not up to that mark. Probably to make the company grow further, we will in the future need other educated professionals coming into the company; but even after we do that, we really cannot undermine the efforts these people have put in to take the place where it is today. So that is a plus side of working in Tamul Plates, and staying in Barpeta.

WE BOTH GREW UP IN CITIES IN BENGAL: ARINDAM IN STEEL CITY . . .

Arindam: I was born and brought up in Jamshedpur, one of the esteemed cities of India, home of Tata Steel. I was born in a joint family where my uncle, my father, and all the extended family used to stay together. My own father was working outside.

The main people in the family were my uncles and cousins, who were living with me. So that was a great thing. There was a lot of sharing, and a lot of family values came through my childhood, through that. Among the extended family, we have seven [cousin-]brothers.[8] We are quite close. My own sibling, I have just one elder [direct-] brother.

We have cousins across the world now; some are even in the U.S. My uncle's elder son, he's a banker based in New York. There's one in the shipping industry now also. He's traveling across the globe. My elder brother is an IT guy; I am in rural management. There is one that is making films, one doing photography, and one in the shipping industry.

I have, I would say, a very unique relationship with my [actual] brother. He's four years elder to me. We hardly talk in the sense of casual talk between ourselves, but I know that he's always there for me, if there's any trouble; and he knows I'm there for him, if he needs any help. It's a very strong bond, but if you see us from the outside, people would say that we hardly ever deal with each other.

In my childhood, both my parents worked. My father worked in various places, and my mother was a teacher, a college professor in economics. I was born and brought up in a Bengali family where education is very important. You need to do well in your studies. That's a primary part of your responsibility, to excel. That always has been a good focus for me. Because of that stress, I got an opportunity to study at various prestigious institutions, like Sri Ram College of Commerce in Delhi, then the Institute of Rural Management Armand (IRMA) in Gujarat. So that's been great.

Also, I would say that my friends were as close as family to me, both from my school days and post-graduation days. With many of them I've actually worked together as part of this Dhriiti-Tamul[9] team, and many of them have also extended support externally without being a part of the team. Actually when me and Debaleena had met initially, I had told her that the only assets that I had were actually my friends and family: that's it.

. . . AND DEBALEENA THE ONLY CHILD, NEAR KOLKATA

Debaleena: I was born in West Bengal, around a hundred kilometers from Kolkata, the capital. I was raised in a nuclear family. My father worked in sales with the Steel Authority of India Limited.

---

8. In Indian culture, extended families grow up very close, sometimes (as with Arindam) in the same home. Cousins seem like siblings and in fact are referred to as "my cousin-brother" or "my cousin-sister."

9. Driiti, which means "the courage within," is Arindam's first company, a nonprofit he cofounded in Delhi and later moved to Assam to promote microenterprises in agriculture. The two companies now coexist and share staff, vision, and resources; although, as Arindam explains, he decided to structure Tamul Plates as a social-mission, for-profit company (rather than a nonprofit) with the hope that it could become self-sustaining and maybe even profitable.

I was an only daughter. I don't have siblings. For my parents, it was very important: I am the third daughter of my extended family. My other uncle has two daughters, and I'm the third girl. I come from a conservative Bengali family, where, you know, you look out for a male child. So, being the third child and female, it was not a very high point for my extended family.

But obviously my parents are very happy about it, and they chose to give me the best possible education. I went to a convent school, at a point in time when girls from my town never went to convent school. I studied there until Class 10, and then I went to another school for my Plus 2, and then to university. I did my degree in geography, and then returned back to West Bengal to study racial parity. I did my master's there in social work.

So that's it. I'm very close to my mother. My father died in 2010. And as for friends, I have very few friends, but friends who have been there for a long, long time—like ten, twelve years that we've been together. I started working soon after my completion of my master's in social work in 2006, from Shivaji University.

And then after my master's, I started working in various places. First, I was in a small town in West Bengal, and I then came to Kolkata and worked there, and I then got married to Arindam. As there are no sisters in his family, I not only became the daughter-in-law; I became the adopted sister.

And then we came to live in this small town in Assam.

WHERE WE WORKED BEFORE THIS 24/7 JOB

Arindam: For me, basically, this is what I've done all my professional life. After doing my studies at IRMA, I worked for four or five months at an institute called Entrepreneurship Development Institute of India (EDII).

In-between my graduation and post-graduation, I had worked for the Confederation of Indian Industry (CII) for a year. After that, me and some friends got together and started Dhriiti. So within six months of doing my post-graduation, I started working full-time for Dhriiti.

Debaleena: I've been working with Tamul Plates for around two years now. Before that, I worked for an organization called Child In Need Institute. It's a not-for-profit organization. Out there, I was implementing a program on HIV/AIDS prevention among the migrant population. So before joining Tamul Plates, I had work experience of around seven years, in HIV/AIDS, before that, anti-trafficking and youth development for Sanlaap India in Kolkata.

WE MET THE OLD-FASHIONED WAY: AN ARRANGED MARRIAGE BY OUR MOTHERS

Debaleena: Ours was an arranged marriage, at least initially. I come from a conservative Bengali family. Here the tradition is, when you're going in for an arranged marriage, you post in a matrimonial site of your hometown newspapers, if the girl or the guy has not been able to find a partner for himself or herself. So, because mine was that case, my mother insisted that we should put up my profile.

So then one day, I was out with my friend watching a movie, and my mother calls me and tells me that there is this lady who has called her. Her son has an NGO [non-governmental organization] in Assam. And my mother has this assumption that just because her daughter works in the development sector, she knows *all* the NGOs in India. So she calls me up and says, "Hey, do you know of this NGO?"

So I was like, "No clue." I told her, "If you like, I'll get back home and then I'll let you know."

The next day I told her, "Yes, I saw this NGO [online], but I've never heard of it."

Then my mother and Arindam's mother started talking over the phone. Around August, Arindam's parents decided to visit our house.

So that day, as any typical Bengali about-to-be bride, I had to get all decked up in saris and everything. And the conversation started with his parents. Arindam's father told me that Barpeta is a completely opposite place. You wouldn't find any mall or marketplaces. I told him, yes, it wouldn't be a difficult task for me because I'd stayed in Bankura and other remote places for work.

Our conversation went off well, and later on, me and his parents decided to meet once more in Kolkata. I remember Arindam was about to come to Kolkata for some work, and they decided that we should meet.

So that meeting also was completely coordinated by our mothers. They decided this place, this time, my son could go, and my mother consented that I would also be present. We did not meet before that. We did not talk before that.

THE RELUCTANT GROOM DOES ALL HE CAN TO UNDERCUT HIS ODDS

Debaleena: On the day of the meeting, Arindam comes in shabby clothes, all beard, no shave, nothing. I called up my mother and I told her, "Is this the person you asked me to meet? He's not even shaven, and he goes out to meet a girl?"

So we meet, and there's this funny incident. We met in this mall, South City Mall, which is quite famous in Kolkata. It was around ten on a Sunday morning. The mall wasn't open much yet. Both of us were very nervous. So we started climbing the wrong escalator, just climbing the down escalator and trying to go up, just out of nervousness. Then I was about to stumble. I balanced myself, and we got down and went over to the right one, and then we went to the coffee shop.

Basically, before that, I had met ten, fifteen people, guys. So I knew how the process goes: The guy keeps on asking questions, and I keep on answering. Sometimes if I have questions, I'll ask them.

Arindam was the complete opposite. He didn't have *any* questions. So I had all the questions in my mind. I kept on asking him. And because he didn't ask me any questions, I thought I might as well answer them for myself.

After a while, it occurred to me that he was not interested to get married. Some way, I got that, "This person is not interested, but there is parents' pressure on him that he should get married."

So I asked him that, and a very honest reply came, "No, I'm not interested to get married, but obviously there is a responsibility towards my parents that I have to do it.

So, you know, I'll do it, and I'll be very true to that person, whomever I get married to."

A very big turn-off. And then the conversation is over, and he gives me his card. I remember telling him, "I'm very amazed by the kind of work that you do, especially at your age, when you started off so young. I don't know whether this would work out or not, but let's keep in touch."

STARTING OFF A PARTNERSHIP WITH A LONG LIST OF FLAWS

Debaleena: So, me being me, I generally have a lot of questions in my mind. I wanted to talk to him more, just to explore him. I kept on emailing him, and he being Arindam, he never replied to my emails. I had to tell my mother, "Okay, look, he's not replying to my emails. What's wrong?"

My mother then inquired of his mother to find out what went wrong. What was wrong was that this person doesn't check his emails! His company is his "lady." So, our conversation started with hiccups. A month later, I got a big drafted letter from Arindam, stating all his flaws. I remember calling this "the Arindam Dasgupta syndrome." Then he writes, "I don't have any assets. My friends are my only assets." It was a big kind of big load…Who would want to get married to him?

And then because it was an arranged marriage, I was discussing everything with my mother. Why not? We discussed it, and my mother thought this would be a bizarre thing if I get married to this guy. So obviously she had problems.

But by that time, we both liked each other. The first meeting, although we didn't disclose it, we had liked each other.

Then somehow, we started talking once more. His thought was like, "Let's give it a shot. It might work into marriage. It might not work into marriage." That was a very big step for me. By that time, there were other men also wanting to get married. I didn't know what to do.

By December, we had pretty much decided that we wanted to get married. Then again, my first job—I'll just take you back a little—my first job was in very deserted and isolated town, and I had left that job overnight after joining. So Arindam knew about this. So he felt that maybe someday I could marry him, and the next day, I would run away from Barpeta.

So, because of that, he insisted that, before we get married, please come and visit Barpeta and see whether you'd be able to stay out here or not. So, without telling our parents, I flew to Barpeta, saw the place, and I think I was pretty impressed with the work and the audacity of doing something like that at his age. By that time, we convinced ourselves that we wanted to get married, and in November 2012, we got married.

ARINDAM TELLS HIS SIDE OF THE STORY

Arindam: I think she has told the story very well. My part was that, when we had met initially, I was not too keen on marriage because one of the immediate concerns was that my financial situation was not too good. That was also a transition period for me between Driiti and Tamul Plates. The new company didn't have too many resources. So I was not even taking a salary at that time.

So, that was a major concern. My problem was with my family: My brother had decided not to marry. My parents had tried to persuade him for quite some time, but then when they were unable to do so, they put their attention on me. [Laughs.] So I was also telling them, "No, no," for quite some time, but it was difficult. Basically, I thought, somebody has to give in.

When I met Debaleena, I went [appearing] a certain way because I felt that this is my true self. Not shaving is quite often. I hardly shave. My shaving part is that when I go for a haircut, I do the shave. So it happens once in a month. I thought, "This is my true self. She needs to know this." If I put up something which is not my true self, it might invite further disaster.

Then when I decided that, yes, a marriage is something I can handle, then I thought that this girl, Debaleena, seemed quite good and it might be that would solve it very well. Then I started looking into the relationship more positively.

During a visit of my parents out here in Assam, I had a big fight with them. Once I wrote that email to Debaleena about my flaws, and that email went to Debaleena's mother, and, from there, it also went to my mother. So she was quite upset. I had written about my habits of smoking and all. She was against my smoking, but she had accepted it. But she was really upset because of those other things, too.

DATING A FANTASY VERSUS PUTTING THE TRUTH OUT THERE

Debaleena: What happens in our age group, many times, I think in both arranged marriages and love marriages also, when a guy and a girl are dating, they try to put up the best of their selves to each other, trying to impress. So what we tried, we both did it the opposite way. We put our flaws out there at the first go. We said, "This is what we can do. This is what we can't do."

So I was well prepared for it, not just in terms of quality of life, but also in terms of professionalism and the people I would be with and also the quality of life. Sharing the flaws has worked for us.

If we had not shared, if Arindam had not told me that he was without a salary, and that in 2011 they all went without salaries, I would have run away. I think I would have just vanished from Barpeta and told him, "Look, this is not working. I want a divorce."

We were quite true to ourselves. We were quite true to each other also. And in that respect, our parents have also supported us in the whole process. Whatever hardships we are going through, they, our parents, our family and our friends, they have helped us to go through them. I think, without their support, we wouldn't have been able to make this journey.

BEING TOGETHER DAY AND NIGHT, AT WORK AND HOME

Debaleena: Very honestly, if I just look at the professional piece of our relationship, it is difficult.

Arindam is a difficult boss. He is a very hard taskmaster. He is never impressed with anything that you put to him. Also for me, I have not studied entrepreneurship or management. I come from a completely different world. My world was like HIV and anti-trafficking and gender issues and all of that. I started learning entrepreneurship and enterprise and promotion and all of this after getting married, not before that. So it was not in my agency at all.

But I'm open to learning. I don't have that kind of block that I have to stay stuck to the kind of job that I was already doing. When I came here, initially, I knew Barpeta didn't have many options for me. Yet, I cannot stay back at home and just be a housewife. That, I cannot be.

The first option that Arindam gave me was like, you can start volunteering for Driiti. I worked there around four months; then I started volunteering for Tamul Plates. I went in every day, working on different programs and proposals and basically learning the trade. Five months later, Arindam gave me the proper official letter stating, "You are a part of the team now."

So it's difficult, because I am learning this firsthand, and also because Arindam is a complete perfectionist by nature. You might have done a good job, you might have put extreme hard work into it, but he would find that, "Okay, this is wrong, this is wrong, this is wrong." It's difficult to convince him unless you really have a strong point, and to get that, "Yes, you've done a good job," from his mouth. So that kind of gets you down at times, but it also, at times, increases your skill and your ability to work. I think it also develops you as an individual, as a professional. That is one part.

The other part is, I think, living with an entrepreneur means it's a 24/7, 365-days job. You don't have holidays. You don't have Sundays, nothing. And you don't have any off-hours: There'll be people who will call you at around 10:30 at night and at 7:30 on Sunday morning. And Arindam is the kind of person who cannot just shut off his work, because he's an entrepreneur, and he's the promoter and the head of the organization.

So, if he needs to work, he will work until 1:30, 2:30, 3:30 a.m., and I will also have to stay up with him to go over the proposal, because it was me who wrote the first draft of it. He doesn't have that kind of compassion to say, "You are my wife. You can go to sleep, or you can go back to your room and take a rest." That isn't there. So you have to do your job.

There are no exceptions. Just because I'm his wife, I don't get extra added brownie points. On the contrary, we put in more extra effort to be on time and to be able to deliver better work. He needs to get justified that he has done a good job, and, at the same time, I also need to justify to myself and to him also that I have done a good job.

But to my advantage, I'm the kind of person who likes working. So that is a good part. And I am getting to live with an entrepreneur, learning the traits, how to run an enterprise, what are the nuances of an enterprise, just by getting married. So that is an added advantage that I've got after marriage. It's like getting an MBA without getting a degree for it.

I HAVE TO BE THE BAD GUY

Arindam: It's difficult. [Laughs.] Being the head of the organization, you need to be the bad guy. These were also the basic reasons why initially I was not too keen on her joining Tamul Plates. As she said, initially I was thinking that it would be better if she gets into the nonprofit side, and I continue with Tamul Plates. At least then there would be some little bit of segregation. I had that concern, like if we were working together in the same organization and also staying together, then it becomes twenty-four hours. There's no full-stop to my work. So then it becomes much more when both of us are working in the same organization.

So I was a little bit skeptical, and also, because Tamul Plates was going through a bad patch, then both of our incomes were affected. That was a point of concern for me.

But, on the other side, Debaleena's presence within the organization has helped us a lot. One of the reasons we were able to turn it around in the last one or two years was the fact that we started writing a lot of proposals and applying for a lot of competitions and applying for a lot of funds that way. So that really helped, due to Debaleena's presence.

As she says, I do criticize a lot. Because I am so stretched out in so many activities in this organization, many times, I don't find time to teach her. It becomes much easier for me to just work on it.

Another hard part for her is that, other than me, there are hardly any professionals here in Barpeta. So I am the only professionally educated person that can write proposals. The rest of the team is very capable, and they're picking up a lot of skills, but it's very difficult to pick up a proposal-writing thing, if you don't have the basic education in place.

Before she came in, everything had been done by me. So she's in a very difficult position because I'm always comparing her work with what I would have written.

But surely, without her presence, it would have been very difficult to get to where we are now. Many times I've told her to go ahead and put it out there. And she did it completely, without my intervention. And then we got the bid.

I am admitting very openly that she's doing a great job. But, to me, I also have to point out the mistakes. [Laughs.]

OUR RARE MOMENTS OF DOWNTIME: FOOD, TRAVEL, AND TV

Debaleena: In our free moments, when we are not working, we are either watching movies—that's one thing we both like doing—or indulging in food. I think we both are kind of great foodies.

Arindam: And we also like to travel and see new places and new things, meeting new people. One way we've been fortunate is that, due to work, we have been able to travel to some good places, both within India and outside India. But, at the same time, we have not been able to take a complete holiday.

Debaleena: So together I think we went to Mauritius for our honeymoon, and then we went to Istanbul and Nairobi for awards. We were in Istanbul for the Changing Markets Award, because Tamul Plates was one of the finalists. We went to Nairobi because we won the SEED Award.[10] And in India, we keep traveling to Mumbai, to Bangalore, to Kolkata, and many parts of Northeast India.

Arindam: With food, we try to explore a lot. We like traditional Indian cuisine: Bengali, South Indian, various kinds of cuisine. Then also we enjoy outside restaurant

---

10. See the write-up by the United Nations's SEED ("Promoting Entrepreneurship for Sustainable Development") program, on how Tamul Plates' award for their employment of local youth and reduction of plastic waste. Includes a case-study analysis of the Tamul Plates business model: seed.uno/images/documents/719/seedcasestudytamulindia.pdf.

cuisine, like Continental and Chinese. We like roadside food also.

Debaleena: Arindam doesn't cook. I do. I can cook some Bengali dishes and then chicken, and some desserts. As for movies, we like to watch thrillers, science fiction not that much, and then—

Arindam: Debaleena likes gender-issue movies a lot, women-involvement, that kind of movies, a lot. The women are the main leads, true stories of women, that kind of thing. She also likes romantic comedies. I also enjoy those movies, true stories, but there are obviously some action movies I enjoy a lot. And I like detective movies, thrillers, and all sports-based movies.

One of the things we miss in Barpeta very much are the good movie theaters out here. So whenever we are traveling, we make it a point that we go to the theatre and watch a good movie. At home, there are days when we are completely saturated from the morning to the night. We are watching movies either on the TV or on the laptop.

We do also share a lot of light moments, at the office and also at home. I think that's a way to relieve stress. Many times, we are just laughing out loud at our problems and just enjoying the situation.

Debaleena: In the morning, we do a lot of quality talking, like when we're having breakfast, around 8:30 to 9:30. We talk about our families, what's going on in the country, or in political affairs and sports. And later, after coming back from the office, while having dinner, we watch TV and we kind of make fun of the news anchor.

Arindam: During weekends, our coworkers will come, and sometimes we have a good drink and have a party. That happens at least once or twice a month. All of us get together, not discussing work, but just other things happening around us. We like it when people come here. We like it very much.

But we do have our alone time. Most of the time, after coming back home, I'll be watching TV, some news or sports show, and Debaleena would be glued to Facebook or something. She's quite active on the social media. I just cannot understand the social media thing very well.

Debaleena: I also do a little bit of reading, or chatting with my friends or my mother. So during those times, we're in different rooms because in our house, we have two floors. On a Sunday afternoon, though, many times we're watching the same movie together.

Arindam: Practically speaking, the last two years, we have spent a lot of time together, either for work or personally. But sometimes I travel alone for work, and that time, Debaleena is alone out here, and other times, Debaleena is visiting her mother. But that would be what? Ten percent of our life, probably.

WHAT I THOUGHT I WOULD BE WHEN I GREW UP: EXACTLY THIS

Arindam: Since my childhood, I was always interested in doing something which contributes actively to the betterment of our own country. I've always felt very patriotic. I was very keen on that.

When I was in school, I imagined I would join the Armed Forces and contribute in that way. That was not possible for me [physically]. I didn't get a chance. But working in the development sector, I had an opportunity to serve in a similar way.

I was never interested in a kind of a 9-to-5 job, working out of a corporate office in a glass building. I always wanted to do something in which I could travel, see various parts of the country and outside places. This particular job gives me that opportunity.

Debaleena: For me, joining the development sector was initially a career choice. I chose a career which would get me a job faster. So in my social-work program, we had job placements offered to us after two years. But at that time, the development sector was very amateurish. It didn't pay you well and was not as professional as the corporate sector would be.

The added advantage [to a social enterprise] is the difference you get to create in the people's lives.—*That* you don't get to see with an immediate effect in any other sector. So that is what pulled me in, and that is what made me continue in this sector.

When I joined Tamul Plates, when I came to Barpeta and saw the organization and was volunteering, I was kind of amazed with the dedication they have. I was amazed at the audacity Arindam had to pull off an organization, in a place which was completely new to him, and to do something so different in such a place where, you know, we would not come to by choice.

So that was one. That inspired me a lot. And also the kind of impact this organization had or is still having in each of the staff's lives. It has transformed their lives completely. For example, one staff member, Arup, was running a cycle shop out here ten years back, and today he's installing machines, designing dryers, delivering them, and representing our company in international forums.

You don't get to see this transformation every day. He's building his own house, got his sister married, got his brother married, and has become a part of our family and very close, a very dynamic person. So this kind of growth keeps on inspiring you and tells you that, if you do a little bit more hard work, there are many more people whom you can reach. It perks you up. So that is what made me join this management and makes me still stay in this organization.

Arindam: I saw more value in going for a for-profit, which had a social motive. Then you are not totally dependent on external funders.

THE COMPETITION DOESN'T ADAPT AS WE DO

Arindam: There are various other institutions working with ecological waste and turning it into product. I won't be able to give names, but there are quite a few. But with Tamul Plates, the product was new, the market was new, the technology was also new. And, the geographical issues of this region, which has also a long history of insurgency and instability, have made our journey a little more complex.

We've had to work through things like complete scarcity of electricity in this region. The supply of electricity is very poor. We just designed a dryer, which is non-electrified, fueled by biomass. We have to work on machines to provide an alternative to electricity. There are also areas, such as the borderline areas where we are working, that did not have connectivity until now.

We have to work around the basic technology to make it applicable in remote rural areas. What we are trying to do is that the value addition takes place at the village itself, adaptable for rural locations with the kind of facilities that they have.

WHAT WE (DON'T) EARN (YET)

Arindam: We are far, far away from earning a fair living wage, I think. [Laughs.] When I compare myself with my friends or people who are on salary, it's much, much, much less. I earn maybe 25 percent of what I could be getting paid if I had accepted a [corporate] job straight out of graduate school.

Last year, I got a salary of 25,000 rupees [$367] per month. This year, although my salary has been booked at 75,000 [$1,100] per month, I have not received one paycheck until now. So we're actually processing a big government order now. We are expecting the payment. So this one month's pay will probably be my whole salary for the year.

Debaleena: I get a salary of 20,000 [$294] per month. So, yeah, it's little. I think last year's whole salary, I got at the end of February. And the previous year's salary got here by December.

When we compare with the kind of salaries, the kind of financial growth our friends and classmates have been living, it would be much less. But I think we both have chosen it that way.

This financial year was tough for us because we were both not getting any salaries. Also, whenever there is a money flow in the company, Arindam prefers to pay wages first to the factory workers and then the staff. And, at the end, whatever is left, if we can manage a salary, then I will get a salary, or we'll have to go without.

So there have been months when the company couldn't afford my salary also. But when the company is in a better position, Arindam will give us a raise. If we start giving the salaries at regular intervals every month, that will be good for us and for the families.

THE BANE OF SOCIAL ENTERPRISES: GETTING FUNDING EARLY ON

Arindam: Our worst moment was in 2014. We had a financial crunch, and we had to stop production for quite some time in that financial year. Basically, the company was growing, and we needed more funds to support our growth. Although we had an understanding with both the buyer and the investor, the processing took a lot of time.

The decision regarding the investment had already begun in March, but it took a full year to process all the documents and get the funding. That's the way it works, at least out here in India. I don't know about the rest of the world.

My experience with bank loans is if you don't have much money, you don't get bank loans. So the people who have money, they're able to grow absolutely, and only then you are able to get bank loans.

Debaleena: There's no concept of an unsecured loan over a certain amount at a bank in India. The kind of money that we needed to continue working would be a secured loan, which means that there would be a collateral against it. That could be in the form of fixed deposit within the bank, or other kinds of products that you'd have to pledge, against which you'd take the loan—Collateral which the company didn't have.

Changing laws and paper delays just took so much time. The season came and he had to go and collect raw materials and ensure the production of them, but he didn't have working capital to go and purchase his raw materials. Similarly, he couldn't pay employees regularly, and, hence, a lot of them chose to leave the company. So the company went through some attrition.

Arindam: We were expecting it would take two, three months for the money to come in. So with that expectation, we were targeting a much larger scale of operation. So basically what we had saved, we spent all that on expecting a larger scale of operations. And then we were practically without anything. Our bank accounts were practically zero. We didn't have money to even support materials, or gas, or pay the workers to do the production. So basically we had to shut down our operations completely in June.

Earlier, the route that was available to us was private loans, which we took from people who know us, people who have seen our work. We have some good will amongst leaders, people in the community, my friends and all. They used to help us with private loans. But the new investor blocked that option. So now we can only take loans from financial institutions. So that made things really difficult.

OUR TOUGHEST TIMES: WE NEARLY WENT BANKRUPT

Arindam: That year was very tough, very tough. Probably sometime in July or August, I was in a mindset, for the first time in my ten years, to end all this. But there were previous liabilities that we had. Even if I wanted to, I could not close it down just like that before I cleared those liabilities, those previous loans that we had taken.

We had to continue the business to pay back those loans we had taken from friends and family. There were salaries outstanding of our staff for six months by that time. So all of that needed to clear up. And then there was a lot of support that I got from my friends and my family. I probably wouldn't have been able to pull through without Debaleena's patience.

Without her support, it would have been very difficult. And then my brother and some of my very close friends told me, "You have been doing it for ten years. This is just a matter of another probably six months to a year. You hang on, and we are there for you. You don't worry about your personal finances or anything. Don't worry. All that needs to be done will be done. Just keep on hanging on. Things will improve."

And we were able to pull through somehow. Now we are in a much better position.

THE BUSINESSES WE'D LAUNCH IF WE HAD TONS OF MONEY

Debaleena: If we became independently wealthy overnight, we'd both want to take a sabbatical for a year and work, go somewhere. If the financials were taken care of, then we'd work for some organization in India, or beyond. It would be a social enterprise or a not-for-profit organization [the developmental sector]. We surely cannot go and work for any corporate sector.

Arindam: In terms of my vision for Tamul Plates, I think now the company is in a stronghold of growing fast. We have now the resources to put in over the next two to three years, to expand fast across the region. And then someday, we would also like to develop this model into various other productions at a much faster pace, wherein the gestation would not be so long as this one.

We could produce various, like bamboo-based products. We can do something with tourism, some hand-loomed handicrafts. We would create jobs at the rural level and supply quality eco-friendly products in the urban market.

As Debaleena was sharing, some time in-between for both of us would be good, like a year's break. I have reached a point where I'm a little bit saturated. I've been under this constant pressure for the last ten years. So I have been living on the edge. A year's break would help me to refresh myself and gain some new ideas, new perspectives, and get on to it in a much bigger way after the break.

Basically there are two sets of institutions working in the development sector: the funding and the human implementation. I've been always associated at the implementation level doing the work. And from this side, the grass always looks greener from the other side. So later in my career, I would like to graduate to the funding side and become an investor, to bring out some new innovations at that level. Probably my understanding of the implementation side will help me to provide better opportunities as a funder.

I'D LIKE TO LAUNCH AN ENTERPRISE TO SUPPORT OTHER WOMEN ENTREPRENEURS

Debaleena: For me, I wanted to be a journalist when I was young: maybe because, from my childhood, I've been very passionate about women's issues. My wish was also about empowerment. So my journalist idea was the result of the admission test that goes on in the university. I applied for those, and the social work option came up for me earlier, and the journalist one came up later. So the one that came up earlier, I got admitted in that.

In my master's program, I think my first internship was at an organization which works on anti-trafficking. And from there on, I always wanted to work with women's issues.

So that's what I dreamt of. Obviously Tamul Plates to date doesn't have that many women entrepreneurs on board, but because of this NSDC, the National Skill Development Corporation award that we won this year, we are planning to host webinars to train women. I can train and support them in establishing their own production units in the villages, give them all the support that we generally provide to any entrepreneur, buy their products, and market them.

This program got conceptualized after many discussions that Arindam and I had, because I really believe that empowerment will happen once we start making the women feel *financially* empowered. This sustains the whole family, as she starts contributing more to the decision-making process.

With my experience, we thought it would be wonderful to try this program out. So this is what we've pitched and if all goes well, I think in the next year, it will be implemented.

One more thing: I really want to see Tamul Plates go online and do ecommerce, where we can supply to the major cities of India and take the marketing to a different level all together.

If it all goes well and if I think I'm equipped enough to do it, if I have enough hands-on experience of learning and working with an entrepreneur, probably to start up my own enterprise in one or two years in Barpeta—for women, working with women.

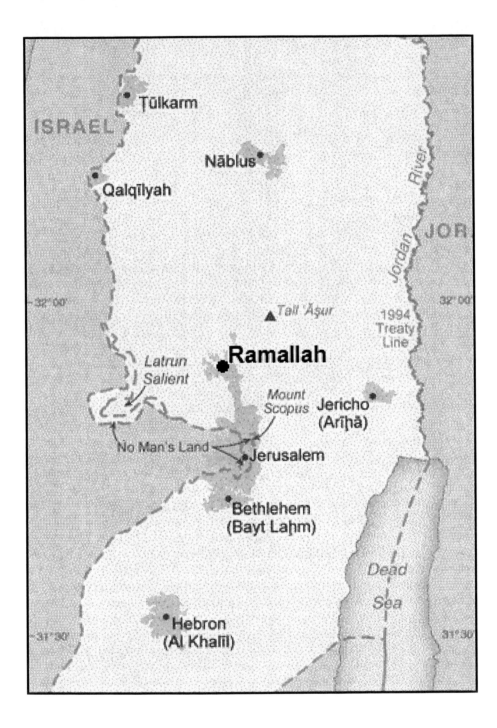

CHRISTINA

ONLINE LINGERIE

ENTREPRENEUR

RAMALLAH, PALESTINE

Editor's note: If any topic could unite MENA (Middle Eastern and North African) women with other women around the world, it could be underwear. And if any woman could bring disparate corners of the planet together through underwear, it could be Palestinian-born, American-raised, Ramallah-based, ecommerce entrepreneur Christina Ganim.

She's smart and self-deprecating, professional and utterly feminine; and she believes that a love of pretty underthings unites most women and, frankly, most men, too. Moreover, it's a product we'll need and use every day, all our lives.

She also believes that women in many areas of the world—whether due to lack of brick-and-mortar stores and Internet infrastructure, or because of restrictive cultural norms, lack basic access to lingerie products.

To Christina, the freedom to express one's womanhood, whether under a burka[1] or a pair of jeans, is a basic human right. And to her, the quickest way to liberation and prosperity for her local community is by creating jobs and revenue. She's not relying on lumbering, often-corrupt politics to effect peace

---

1. Burka, hijab, veil—what's the difference? bbc.co.uk/newsround/24118241.

in the Middle East.[2] Entrepreneurs like Christina, crunching code in a hipster coworking (shared-office) space in downtown Ramallah, are convinced that the fastest path to freedom is through innovation.

Born in Palestine, Christina fled with her family but returned, prompted by patriotism, during the First Intifada (Palestinian uprising, 1987-1993). The Ganims believed in equal rights for all human beings, including their compatriots back home. However, when violence prevailed they returned to the U.S., where Christina completed elementary and high school in North Carolina. She earned a bachelor's in international studies from DePaul University in Chicago and a master's in international law from the School of Oriental and African Studies (SOAS) at the University of London.

Christina then returned to the U.S. to work as a research project manager at Harvard Law School's Berkman Center for Internet and Society, focusing on the impact of the Internet on democratic reform in the Middle East. She also served as development officer at the Civic Forum Institute in Palestine. Then she got recruited to work for an international nonprofit managing digital-solutions projects connecting donors with social-justice causes in Africa and Asia. She also spent a few years helping to produce a documentary film on Palestinian women racecar drivers.[3]

Calling herself a born entrepreneur, Christina downplays her intelligence. She says she just "gets bored easily" and hops from thing to thing to express her creativity...She never imagined she'd end up working as an online lingerie peddler.

Her latest venture is called Kenzwoman.com. Christina explains, "Kenz means treasure in Arabic. That word reflects the beauty of a woman as well as the treasure inside the delivered package of lingerie that's really pretty and fits perfectly at the same time." According to Christina, "Eighty percent of women in the world are wearing a bra that doesn't fit them." The company's goal is to help every woman find the perfect bra.

"The lingerie you're right now wearing has an impact on how you feel all day," their bilingual Arabic-English website proclaims. "It's the first piece of clothing a woman puts on her body in the morning, and the last piece she pulls off at night."

Immersed in a region where conservative religion rules—whether Islam, Judaism, or Christianity—Christina and her American cofounder are thinking inside the box: a plain small box ordered online and delivered quickly and free, right to a woman's home, with expensive, boutique-crafted articles of intimate attire that fit flawlessly (due to an online fitting survey), feel utterly comfortable, and change her day from the inside out.

If Kenz makes it, there's a truckload of money at stake. The Palestinian tech sector accounts for at least 6.6 percent of its nearly $13 billion GDP, according to the Palestinian Central Bureau of Statistics. "Saving the world, one bra at a time," as Christina jokes, Kenz will stand firmly on the merits of its own underwire.

---

2. The Middle-East conflict has a long, painful history: globalissues.org/article/119/the-middle-east-conflict-a-brief-background; merip.org/primer-palestine-israel-arab-israeli-conflict-new.

3. See this article: theguardian.com/lifeandstyle/2015/jun/15/speed-sisters-palestine-female-racing-team or the film's website: speedsisters.tv.

I'M AN ENTREPRENEUR SELLING LINGERIE ONLINE TO WOMEN IN THE MIDDLE EAST

My name is Christina Ganim. I'm twenty-nine years old. My birthday is on Christmas Day. I live in Ramallah, Palestine. I am an entrepreneur who, along with my partner, Nicola, has started Kenz, a company that sells lingerie throughout the Middle East. Our website is Kenzwoman.com. We're self-funded; we do everything ourselves. We just launched.

MY BACK-AND-FORTH CHILDHOOD IN TWO CULTURES WHERE REALLY ONLY ONE IS HOME

My parents are Palestinian. They met in university in Cairo, actually. My mom was born and raised in Cairo. She's not Egyptian; she's originally Palestinian and Greek but was born and raised in Cairo. There were a lot of Palestinians that actually immigrated to Egypt in the 20th century.

Then they came to the United States in the 1970s and got married. I have an older brother and an older sister who were born in North Carolina in the seventies.

My family lived there for maybe twelve years. I always ask my parents why they chose North Carolina. My father is one of ten kids, and some of his brothers had gotten a scholarship to go to university there, and so they stayed. And then how it typically is with families that are immigrating, they just go where they have family, basically. So everyone just kind of followed the pack and went there.

Then my parents were really still connected to things here in Palestine and wanted to come back. So they decided to move back in the 1980s, and that's why I was born here.

I was born in 1985 in the Palestinian section of Jerusalem. Over the years, during all of the political process and everything, checkpoints have moved around, but where I was born was considered what is Jerusalem now.

We were living in Palestine during the First Intifada. The political situation was actually very, very bad, and my brother and sister weren't able to go to school. So then my parents decided to move everyone back to the States. So I grew up there, and I went to grade school in the U.S., in North Carolina.

My parents were moving back and forth a lot and were still very connected to being in the Middle East. They were very political. So we learned from an early age about injustice and inequality, not particular to the Palestine question, but in general.

My father was very political in his early twenties. He was arrested for being in the Communist Party when he was this young college student. My parents were always talking to us about these things and sharing with us, "This is now how the world should be, and hopefully we'll make a difference, and hopefully you guys will make a difference."

RETURNING TO THE HOMELAND TO PUT DOWN ROOTS AND BUILD A BUSINESS

My father had his own real estate business here. He opened an office in Ramallah, and he had a lot of opportunities here. My dad's definitely a role model for me.

So we moved back, back to Ramallah, and I went to high school here. I graduated from high school during the Second Intifada. They chose very difficult times to come back, but it worked out in the end. I've always been connected obviously to being here. I was born here. I have friends here.

In general, Palestine is, I would say, a very secular place. There're Christians and there're Muslims. My family happens to be Christian, but, you know, we all grew up together, and we all kind of had similar opportunities. Life has not been any easier or more different for me because of being Christian.

BEING IN THE TOP ECHELON—FOR HERE, ANYWAY

I went to a private high school in Palestine. The Christian population of the high school was 2 percent maybe. The majority of the people were Muslim. But we were all a part of this elite type of sector of society in Palestine, the top 10 percent, if you will, that had the opportunity to attend this school.

I will say that I come from a different sector in the society than most Palestinians. I think Westerners have this perception that it's a religious thing, but it's not a religious thing actually at all. It's more about having the means to do things. So if you come from a family that has means, the opportunities are there. Otherwise, you're struggling. You're in a much more different position if your family has the money to send you abroad.

We're definitely in the top 10 percent, economically. For Palestine. I don't know for the world, but for Palestine, yeah, definitely.

I STUDIED POLITICS AND INTERNATIONAL LAW BECAUSE OF THE SITUATION AT HOME

Going to high school and living here during the Second Intifada had a huge effect on me. It very much influenced what I did during college. So I finished high school here, and then I went back to the U.S. for university. I attended DePaul University in Chicago. I was very involved in the student groups, like the Students for Justice in Palestine and all of these kinds of international human rights groups. I'd go to protests. I really thought I'd be doing something [in my career] along those lines.

Then I did my master's in London at the University of London, SOAS, The School for Oriental and African Studies, and then after that, I was kind of figuring out what I wanted to do, where I wanted to live, what I wanted to do for work.

I studied politics and international law. The reason that I studied that is because of the political situation here. It was very important for me to try and pursue finding a job in that field. But I actually didn't have a lot of luck, and I didn't find something that was really good or suitable where I could see myself growing in my career. It's completely different than what I'm doing now. [Laughs.]

COMING BACK TO PALESTINE, BECAUSE NOT MANY OF US CAN

After I finished my studies at the university, I did think about staying in England. I did look for opportunities there, and didn't find anything, but I felt that I could always return. I also felt, if I ever wanted to go to the States, that was there too, and I could do that at any point.

For me, it's really important to be in Palestine, because many Palestinians actually can't come here. They can't come back. They have issues with their visas and their passports and face many, many difficult issues with their papers. So the fact that I have the ability to be here, too, is actually a privilege for me, and I'm very thankful that I can do something.

You would think it would be the reverse, that I have the opportunity to be in the States and it's a privilege to be *there*, but I don't see it that way.

I am very thankful for my parents for actually being the immigrants that they were and immigrating to the U.S. and trying to pursue the American Dream at one point, but also exposing us to different things in life and showing us that there's a lot more out there.

So that's why it was also very important for my family to come back and to make sure we all went to school here to learn Arabic, to make sure that our culture and our heritage is very much embedded within us, especially as we get older and start our own families. That stuck with me.

WORKING ON A DOCUMENTARY FILM ON PALESTINIAN WOMEN RACECAR DRIVERS

I came back here to Ramallah. Then I switched gears completely. I had always been really interested in film. So I had an opportunity to work as an associate producer on this documentary film. It's called *Speed Sisters*, and it's about Palestinian women racecar drivers.

They were looking for a young woman who spoke Arabic and English and could help with scouting locations and the whole crew. So that's where I came in. I worked on it for almost two years, but the film in general took almost five years to complete, due to issues with funding and editing. I was helping with the crowdfunding campaign that they put together. I was the associate producer.

After that, I worked on a couple of different film projects, smaller films. I thought about pursuing that more. But I feel I have this issue with commitment, where I can't do just one thing, and I'm constantly changing and adapting and trying to do something new. Maybe I get bored easily. I don't know what it is.

I STUDIED ICT AND DEVELOPED A FEW APPS

Then I started becoming interested in this whole online space and tech and the whole ICT [Information and Communications Technology] sector in general. That's growing in Palestine, and a lot of my friends had been working in that field and exposed it to me and told me there were good opportunities. So I actually took this online course to learn about mobile application development.

Through the course, I outsourced technical work and published three mobile apps in the app store. So I was doing that for a while. It didn't produce that much revenue for me, but I did get almost 100,000 downloads in general. My apps were games, and they were free. So I would make revenue from the ads that would pop up. If I had continued doing it, if I had stuck to it, I think I could have made revenue eventually, but I was basically just breaking even.

I COMBINED MY PASSIONS FOR SOCIAL JUSTICE AND MOBILE TECHNOLOGY

After that, I then switched gears again and I got the opportunity to work at this mobile technology company, SoukTel, based in Ramallah but also with offices in Washington, D.C., Canada, and Jordan. Our clients are the United Nations, Save the Children, and other huge NGOs [nonprofits]. They use our software to reach out to their beneficiaries, all through SMS [Short-Message Service for mobile devices] technology. It targets people that don't have access to smartphones. So I was still involved in the tech sphere and the ICT sector, but more from the NGO point of view and the whole aid sector and combining those two together.

I worked at SoukTel full-time as a project manager. That was my first real 9-to-5 job. It paid well, and it was definitely a place where you could grow. There were opportunities, and the fact that I spoke both Arabic and English and was from Palestine was appealing to the company.

I did that for a year and a half. Then I just felt it wasn't the right fit for me. I couldn't see myself doing that type of job for a very long time. So I decided to leave. I'm still helping them on a part-time basis on specific projects here and there, also to help me with making some money.

AND THEN I ENDED UP IN UNDERWEAR

And then I came up with the idea of Kenz with my friend, Nicola Isabel, who was working at SoukTel as well. We had been friends prior to that. We helped each other get our jobs at SoukTel, because we both knew the CEO, and he had reached out to us at separate times, asking if we knew of someone that would be interested in applying for the position. So we recommended each other.

We realized that we wanted to start something together, because we worked well together. And then we came up with the idea of Kenz. "Kenz" means *treasure* in Arabic. We came up with the idea of wanting to sell lingerie because we both shared a mutual interest in the product, and we realized that there could be a huge potential in selling it in the Middle East. So we were just thinking of names, and this came up. I thought it was really fitting because these pieces of clothing are actually so intimate, they should be treated as "treasures."

THE POWER OF LINGERIE TO UNITE WOMEN AND ENHANCE THEIR DAY

Kenz is made by women, for women. I feel like that bond is a treasure in and of itself. So the name relates to the women that are eventually going to be purchasing the product and to the intimate space that we're trying to create for women to be able to shop online, as well as the products that we're selling, that are so important to a woman's life.

Lingerie matters, because it's the first thing you put on in your day. In my own experience and in the experience of other women that I've talked to, if you're not comfortable in it, you're really uncomfortable for the rest of your day. If you're wearing a bra that is constantly falling off or too tight for you, it can give you back problems.

So there's an important aspect of making sure that the products we sell fit the woman properly and perfectly. We're trying to do that by creating an online quiz. That will happen later on, once the site is launched and we actually have the means to pay an engineer that can put it all together, but that's definitely in the pipeline to create that. We're coming up with an algorithm and creating the quiz that will ask women very intricate questions about their bras, what their current situation is with their underwear, and how it fits them properly.

About 80 percent of women around the world wear the wrong bra size. So we want to share that knowledge with women in the region and be this source online, as experts that can provide you with really good fit advice and really good products that can be compatible with whatever size you are.

MY WORKDAY MAY LOOK OUT OF CONTROL, BUT I FEEL COMPLETELY IN CONTROL

In January of 2015, I started working part-time at my job at SoukTel, and we really started seriously pursuing our idea of Kenz. Since then, we've been working on the new venture full-time.

We work at an office four minutes away from where I live. I drive here in our family car, a 2004 Chevrolet. It's down this big, big hill, and I don't really want to walk it.

I don't even know what full-time means anymore, because I stay here at work from when I wake up to when I go to bed. We don't start super early because we stay really late, but we start maybe around 10:00 a.m., and we leave around 10:00, 11:00 p.m.

This crazy work schedule, it's not a 9-to 5-thing: It's a 7 a.m. to midnight type of thing, and I'm so happy about that. It's really rewarding to me that it's something I can contribute to and hopefully help other people get jobs one day, if I'm able to have an actual staff and hire people.

That's the idea. But it's something that *I'm* in charge of and something that I have control over. It's a modern way of working and making money. I tried doing the 9-to-5, and I just wasn't happy. [Laughs.]

WHAT IT TAKES TO BE AN ENTREPRENEUR

Not everyone is an entrepreneur. I think it's a very specific type of person that becomes one. I can see that my past trajectory led up to where I am now. I'm understanding a lot more about myself, especially as I'm becoming older and turning thirty in a few months. I'm trying to reevaluate everything. It makes so much sense that this is what I'm doing.

What I mean is, it's my choice that I'm doing this and choosing to be here all day. The actual results that happen daily, change drastically. But if it doesn't work, you move on to something else, and you move quickly. That's appealing to me.

There's so much I've learned from this journey, from Day One, things I had no idea how to do in terms of business and finances and just like understanding how a website works. I feel like I have all this knowledge right now. And it's still so little compared to what other people have, but I've learned so, so much and become not an expert, but I'm getting there, especially in the field of lingerie, and I think that's so cool.

I wish I could do something with programming. I wish I could do some graphic design stuff. I've been trying to teach myself more about understanding financials and projections. So I've been focused on that and seeing how much money we can make with this down the line.

FIGURING OUT QUICK-FREE SHIPPING IN A GEOGRAPHY WHERE THAT DOESN'T YET EXIST

We've been trying to figure out this whole issue with shipping and logistics and talking to different shipping companies around the region, and it's such hell. We don't know how to wrap our heads around it, and there's all of these customs and tax and VAT [Value-Added Tax].

I still don't understand how it all works. That's one of the major aspects of the business that could actually either make or break us because, if we can't figure out that, then our customer service goes down the drain. Our customers won't want to keep buying from us if it takes forever to get the product to them.

The goal is to ship it to them in less than a week, and that doesn't exist in the region, like you don't get anything that you order online so quickly. People are used to having things delayed, and I want to change that. I want to say, "If you shop on Kenz, you'll get something as soon as we promise." I want to stick to our promises.

Women shop online. If they're shopping for underwear, for example, a lot of times they'll shop brands from the States like Victoria's Secret. Our other big competitors are brands in shopping malls in the region.

We don't really have shopping malls in Palestine, but going to shopping malls in other areas is very much seen as a social activity. You go there together with your friends, like anywhere in the world, I guess. People like to go to the malls. But, in general, the whole online space and ecommerce in general is growing rapidly as well, which is why we're starting this business. I mean, we wouldn't be starting it if we thought that there was no market for it.

Basically, our manufacturers will ship their products to a partner of ours in Dubai at a warehouse facility that will fulfill the orders and ship them out to the customers from there. So that's the plan.

WHERE WE GET OUR PRODUCTS: FROM ALL OVER THE WORLD

We're not manufacturing our own products. We're selling other brands. In February, we went to a lingerie trade show in New York City, and we met with brands from all over the world, and many of them expressed interest in entering the Middle Eastern market.

And so when we went there and we made these contacts, we narrowed down on the brands that we wanted to sell, that would really cater to women's styles here in the region.

We've narrowed it down so far to three brands that we're launching the site with. They're all very small, boutique brands, kind of like startups themselves, and all run by women. It's become really important to me to work with like-minded women in the industry. It's really cool to talk to these women and share whatever our frustrations are and our interests in the product.

Our brands are from the U.S., Turkey, and Australia.[4] The American brand is called Clo Intimo, and they're based in New York City, although they're actually made in Colombia. The Turkish brand is called Else, and it's beautiful, beautiful stuff. I have a feeling that women will very much like that product. The one from Australia is called Kiss Kill. Theirs are edgy, but I feel their styles will really match people's taste in the region. They have really bold colors. They have zippers on their products.

LINGERIE IS CELEBRATED IN THE MIDDLE EAST

I think often, other people have this perception of lingerie in the Middle East as this taboo type of product, but it's actually so celebrated. You see bras being sold in the center of town, hanging down, being sold by men. There's actually a huge market for it, which is why we're starting this business.

We look for brands that combine both beauty and comfort. It should be a combination, because you don't just want something that looks nice that doesn't feel good as well. When we met with these brands and we saw the products in person, we narrowed it down to the ones we thought looked very nice and very beautiful but also fit really well on women's bodies, especially women's bodies here. Women here tend to have larger breasts and bust sizes.

There are certain brands that make their products for women who have larger breasts, and others that are for more petite women. We're not looking at those brands at all because I know that's not my market, and I wouldn't want to sell something that caters to small-figured women.

If you look at our social media pages, many of the models that we post are actually fuller-sized women. I personally am totally against the idea of selling something because it's on a slender woman. That's not the market here. I feel like I would be selling a lie, basically. So our products are meant to be for larger sized women.

At this point, the pictures we post are photographs of the brands from our partners. Eventually we want to do a photo shoot here in Palestine of women that really look like women from here. I have a few friends who do modeling, and they're not your typical idea of what a model is. They're not tall and thin. One is shorter than me and has wide hips, and she's beautiful. She's gorgeous.

Of course, we couldn't do a photo shoot in the middle of Ramallah. We could do it near a window so we get the backdrop of the city. Or we could take photos far out somewhere with just the landscape. It's a very conservative community.

OUR TARGET MARKET: INDEPENDENT WOMEN OF ALL AGES

In terms of marketing, The Middle East is full of a lot of different people. [Laughs.] And in Ramallah in particular, there's a lot of different people.

Our focus is towards more independent women, working women, women between the ages of twenty-five to forty-five, who are in charge of their own selves, you know,

---

4. Check online for additional brands since the time of publication: kenzwoman.com/en.

their own being, their own self-worth. It's women that are established, making their own money. Or if they're married, they have the money to buy online and stuff. It's important for them to want to have these products in their lives.

So it may not be so much for women who aren't able to choose whom they wed, but as for women that are wearing the hijab, for sure, absolutely. And we're not trying to *not* market to anyone, either. We definitely don't want to have our products available for certain people and not for other people. I mean, if you can afford it, you know, buy it, is our thing—but our products are expensive.

Saudi Arabia is probably one of our largest markets, because women have higher incomes there, and they have credit cards. We're trying to target places where we know people actually have a high credit-card usage.

Palestine's definitely somewhere we want to target as well, but we want to focus on other parts of the region to see if it's actually an idea that could be embraced all over. Lots of women have expressed interest in buying Kenz here, but it's a product line that the entire region could partake in.

FINDING STARTUP FUNDING AND ONLINE PLATFORMS

Kenz is all self-funded at this point. We don't have a technical person because we can't pay for that. So we are using a website called Shopify, which is an ecommerce platform used by websites from all over the world. Shopify is our CTO [Chief Technology Officer]. [Laughs.] We pay a monthly fee, a subscription fee of about thirty bucks.

We're uploading everything, doing everything. My partner learned how to use Photoshop the other day. We're having help from a friend who's a graphic designer. Basically, it's a lot of friends that are helping. We have one woman that's doing translation work, helping write all the product descriptions in Arabic and English perfectly, and we have another person that's a marketing student at a local university who's just looking for an internship, and she's helping with our marketing and writing our newsletters.

So we're not paying anyone [yet]. We're not getting paid. But the goal is to approach VCs [Venture Capitalists] and try to get funding.

In Palestine, there's one VC here, and then there're other funds as well that are popping up. I'm not really sure what the main difference is between a fund and a VC, but basically this one VC has already backed like five companies. Then there are a couple of other funds that are emerging, and then there are other organizations that have accelerators [mentoring programs].

So a few people have approached us, and we've applied to a couple of funds. We got accepted, but we turned them down because we didn't agree with the terms in the terms sheet. We didn't feel that we could just sign the company away, and I felt that we would not be able to fulfill our company's vision if we signed on with them. So we decided to go the self-funding route and just do everything ourselves and really bootstrap it and kind of see where it takes us, if it takes us anywhere…That's where we're at now.

We want to launch before the *Eid al-Adha* [Islamic festival commemorating Abraham's willingness to sacrifice his son Ishmael to God]. So Muslims would have like a week off. Actually everyone in the Middle East, not just Muslims, but, you know, it's like a week-off celebration, and that's around September 23rd. So our goal is to launch before that holiday.

We'll probably be really busy around other holidays, too, like Christmas and Ramadan, times when people get gifts.

I ALSO PUBLISH ARTICLES ON THE ENTREPRENEURIAL SCENE HERE IN RAMALLAH

I also publish articles. It's one of the side things that I do to make some money.

I'm not making any money with our business now, so I have to try to be creative and find different opportunities and ways that I can make some type of livelihood. I don't make much at writing either; I wouldn't say it's that much. For example, I wrote a cultural piece on Palestine for *The Guardian* in the U.K.[5]

I'm also publishing articles on a website called *Wamda*. It's an online site that focuses on business and entrepreneurship in the Middle East, and it's in Arabic, English, and French. They reached out to me and asked if I wanted to be a contributor for things that are going on in Palestine. It's a great way to make contacts and networks and spread the news about Kenz.

BUILDING A BUSINESS AND BONDING OVER THE ANXIETY OF IT ALL

My partner and I have bonded because we share similar fears. We've changed things around. First we said we're going to carry *this* many brands; then we narrowed it down to three. It's just so much time and back and forth, and all the brands and figuring out what we think women would really like here, what would cater to their interests and taste.

And we also don't have money to place the orders from the brands, which is what you typically would do. You would place the order, and you would have it in a warehouse. We can't do that. So we're doing a presale period for three months, trying to really ramp up our social media and our marketing, and we have a landing page where we're collecting email addresses.

A lot of people have expressed interest, which is great, and I feel these will be our first customers. Hopefully they'll place the first orders, and then we'll go to the brands, similar to kind of a drop-ship service, where we would ship directly from the brand. But that's not the long-term plan at all. That's just our initial three-month plan to kind of alleviate the fact that we have no money.

Right now, collectively, on our social media, we have over a thousand followers. On our mailing list, we have over a hundred emails, but our goal is to get a couple of hundred more before we launch.

We've also been approached by the press because, to them, it's an interesting story, I guess, women selling lingerie in the Middle East. So I don't anticipate us having a difficult time in getting publicity and getting the name out there.

---

5. Theguardian.com/cities/2015/apr/20/insiders-guide-ramallah-misunderstood-cosmopolitan-bubble.

NEGATIVE INTERNAL FEEDBACK AND POSITIVE EXTERNAL REINFORCEMENT

Our best moments are when we have small successes during the day: when we secured this new brand that we were trying to carry, knowing that they really wanted to come here, and hearing a lot of positive feedback from people.

I feel like we're so self-deprecating. We're always saying, "We are just so dumb. Why are we doing this?" We're always questioning things. Well, obviously it can fail: That's a fear that we have. Every single day, my partner and I will say, "Are we going to fail? Is this going to fail? Is this a good idea? Are we stupid?" We constantly talk this way.

And then when we hear feedback from other people in the community telling us, "You know, you guys are working really hard, and you're on to something, and we think that this has potential," just those little words, honestly little positive reinforcements, little words of encouragement, are really huge. They help us to get through it all.

LOOKING FOR ROLE MODELS IN A PLACE WHERE FEW WOMEN HOLD LEADERSHIP POSITIONS

There's this entrepreneurial community that's growing in Palestine. People have been very welcoming and open and helpful. We have a lot of role models, but they're men, most of them, all the CEOs [Chief Executive Officers] with their own companies. They've all shared their own struggles and experiences with us, but there aren't really that many women-entrepreneur role models that are starting their own initiatives and ventures. And in the U.S., I haven't come across a lot of women that have been really inspiring to me, in my opinion, in the field.

But I have a friend, Humaira, who is the director of an NGO in Nablus. She's Afghan-American, and she's definitely a role model for me. She's just so strong, and she's able to manage a huge staff of people. I don't know how she does it. It's really inspiring.

If one day this business grows and we have a whole staff, I don't know how I'll be managing a lot of people. Will I be shy and timid? Will I be strong and aggressive? I have no idea what characteristics will come out; but she's definitely taught me a lot about how to deal with people, how to interact with people. She has challenges in a very different way than in Ramallah. Nablus is a much more conservative place than Ramallah. And so she deals with challenges on a daily basis. She uses humor as a way to overcome things. She's definitely someone that I always think of when we're struggling and having a hard day.

YOU HAVE TO GET USED TO QUESTIONING AND REJECTION

I would say we've definitely had a lot of worst moments, so far, being rejected from certain programs and being told that our idea can be imitated and replicated very easily. Of course, it could be imitated, but it wouldn't be imitated in the same way, because *we're* the ones that are behind it. So, being told that anyone could do this, that it's not so creative and so on, is such a big "wow" type of thing.

And we've applied to a couple of things, like different types of fellowships and programs here and abroad, and I've been a semifinalist, and then I don't get through to the next step. So it's definitely been difficult when that happens. But, you know, I'm learning to take it with a grain of salt and just be like, "Okay, well, that's your opinion, and we'll see where we are five years from now."

My partner and I are really encouraging one another and supporting one another. It's really nice to have that support. We pat each other on the back, basically. [Laughs.]

I LIVE ALONE AT HOME, BUT MY FAMILY REALLY SUPPORTS ME

I currently live at home. I haven't actually got into my own place, because I don't really see a need to. I've been able to have the support from my family and been able to pursue different opportunities until I find the one that fits. [Laughs.]

I have a very supportive family. They have been supportive since Day One with all of my crazy ideas and all the different business ideas that I come up with. I think they just want me to be happy, as cheesy as that sounds. But I'm very lucky in that way, because I haven't had such a setback from family, whereas other young women my age might have had issues with their family accepting their career choice and not being able to pursue something that they really wanted to pursue.

So it's just me living here right now. My siblings are in the States, and my parents go back and forth between Palestine and the States. They are currently visiting my brother and sister. Neither one of them lives in North Carolina anymore. My brother lives in New York City. He's a doctor, and he's not married. My sister's in Florida, in Miami. She's older than my brother by a year. She got married when she was twenty-eight, to a Palestinian-American. She's been married for fifteen years. She has a son, Roman, who's ten years old. I'm very close to him; he's my godson.

My sister is now a stay-at-home mom. She had studied history and religion and was also kind of all over the place, like me. She had worked earlier in interior design. Now she's trying to look for something that she can do. And she's actually been helping me with Kenz. Before she worked in interior design, she was a rep for a furniture company and she traveled around with a lot of different companies. So she knows how to talk to brands and sell an image. She's been giving us advice and stuff.

EVEN WHEN YOUR FAMILY NEEDS YOU, YOU HAVE TO PUSH THROUGH AND WORK AT 2 A.M.

For the first few months of the year, I was all wrapped up in my family. My aunt passed away in March, so I was in the States for a while and wasn't able to really get a lot of work done. I was also in Canada visiting where my aunt had lived. So I was having calls with our shipping company at two in the morning when I was there.

I understand that this is what you do as an entrepreneur. Regardless of what's going on in your personal life, you just have to really push through. You can't really stop, in a way, the first year.

I don't envision myself being able to stop really anytime soon. I don't want to stop. I feel like I have energy right now, and I just want to take advantage of that energy before I do reach that wall or burn out or whatever. I'm not burnt out yet.

A few weeks ago, I did go to Greece for a few days, for a weekend. It was just a really cheap ticket. So that was my main incentive to go. [Laughs.] I didn't pay for a hotel. I had a place to stay with a few friends. But that was the first vacation that I took all year.

But, at this point, I'm really self-motivated, and I think that's a characteristic I've had with a lot of these different endeavors that I've taken on. If I'm interested in something, I will pursue it, more than 100 percent. I will just try my best, even if I don't make any money from it or anything. I just want to know that I tried.

MAYBE MARRIAGE SOMEDAY . . .

As I'm getting older, I've just been starting to think about marriage. I'm really lucky—I don't know if "lucky" is the right word—I haven't had a lot of pressure from my immediate family. They definitely want me to do my thing.

My mom got married when she was young. She had taught French, but then she became a stay-at-home mom. I think she just doesn't want that for me. She wants me to do all of these things that she wasn't able to do, because she got married when she was twenty-two.

So I do want to get married one day, have maybe one kid, I don't know. [Laughs.] But, at this point, this has been my life. It's really hard to try to think of dating or having a serious relationship.

You've got no time. It's really tough.

MY PATRIOTISM STEMS PARTLY FROM THE TRAUMA OF WHAT WE'VE BEEN THROUGH

I think I am more patriotic to Palestine because of what Israel has done to us. My family hasn't been extremely affected by the occupation because of our external opportunities, because of the fact that we're also American. But at one point in time, we were actually very affected by it. Before we got our Palestinian IDs, my parents were denied entry and weren't allowed to come back here.

My whole life, I had an American passport, even though I was born in Palestine. In the 1990s when [the peace accords at] Oslo happened, all of the Palestinian leadership came back, and they issued lots of Palestinian IDs. But at the time, we weren't here. We were still in the States. We didn't feel we actually needed to have them, because some people just thought it wouldn't matter, and it didn't really mean much. So we never got our Palestinian IDs.

And then in the 2000s, when my family started coming back, my parents were going in and out a lot through Israel, through Tel Aviv, through Ben Gurion Airport, and strictly because they were Palestinian, having nothing to do with the fact that they hold American passports, Israel denied them entry. So that meant that they couldn't come back here unless they had specific papers, which would cost thousands of dollars to get from a lawyer. And we did hire a lawyer, and we got the papers, and my parents were able to come back. They were only given a one-week visa to come back.

MY BROTHER WAS IMPRISONED BECAUSE OF HIS GENDER AND AGE, EVEN THOUGH HE'S AMERICAN

The same thing happened with my brother, Nader. My brother was treated much more horribly than my parents, because he's a young guy. He was in his early thirties then. So they arrested him and put him in jail overnight, even though he only holds an American passport.

He flew into the airport. That's all he did. He hadn't been here in three years. It wasn't like he was frequently coming to cause some sort of suspicion. But he wanted to visit my parents that were here at the time (this was back in 2006), and they denied him and they kept him in jail.

He was telling them, "I'm an American. I was born in the U.S.," and they were like, "No, you're Palestinian. You're Palestinian." He said, "Thank you for acknowledging that my roots are Palestinian, but I'm actually also an American, and I have the right to be here according to America and according to Israel."

They didn't like how he responded, so they put him in jail overnight, and they deported him back to the U.S. He was traveling, and he had a layover in Italy on Alitalia. He thought that he could go into Rome and figure out what he wanted to do and then try to fly back and talk to our lawyer. Throughout this whole process, he had no access to his passport or his ticket. They gave it over to the pilot of the plane to hold, because he was considered a criminal because Israel denied him entry.

So when my brother got out of the plane in Rome, he said he felt like he was Yasser Arafat in the 1970s with two Mossad [Israeli CIA] agents waiting for him when he got off the plane. They put him in the back of a police car and took him to a holding center in Rome. He was screaming and yelling and shouting and saying, "I'm an American. How can you do this? I've done nothing wrong."

They said, "You have two options. You can go back to jail in Tel Aviv, or you can go back to the U.S."

So he came back to the States. I had called the U.S. Embassy in D.C. Basically they told me, "With Israel, there's nothing that we can do. We can't help you. If he's been gone for seventy-two hours, call us, and we can report him as missing."

My mom was freaking out. She was hysterical. She thought that he was probably being sent to Guantanamo Bay. We couldn't get ahold of him. We had no idea where he was for forty-eight hours.

But at the end, when we saw him and we found out what happened, we weren't—I don't know what word to use—we weren't scared. We understood that this is very expected treatment. It was nothing compared to if we were living in Gaza, for example, or if my family were refugees.

WE'VE BEEN MUCH BETTER OFF THAN MOST PALESTINIANS

Our background and our upbringing, we're very privileged. We've had a lot of opportunities. We're affected by the occupation in different ways, because we wanted to come back. My parents wanted to come back and create opportunities and contribute to a growing Palestinian economy: I feel that's a big threat to Israel. That's probably Israel's biggest threat: educated Palestinians coming back and wanting to make a difference for a land that they believe is their home as well.

Since then, Nader also has been able to come back. This lawyer that we found was amazing. He was able to get a court order from the Israeli Supreme Court to get him a visa to come back in for a month.

Nader came back this past spring, and again, they gave him a very, very hard time. They were just yelling in his face. They wanted him to react in a way that would be destructive or aggressive, even though they were aggressive towards him. He was very calm.

My brother's a doctor. He's really good with talking to people. So he told the guy, "Why are you so angry? What's going on?" [Laughs.] He was being a psychiatrist towards him, and the guy got even angrier at him. The officer said, "You're Palestinian. If I let you come in, then you have the right to go [only] to Tel Aviv and to Ramallah," and my brother said, "Okay."

Then the officer said, "*I* don't get to go to Ramallah. What if I want to go to Ramallah?" and my brother said, "Well, actually, the last time I checked, you guys come in whenever you want."

The officer didn't like that as well. He said, "I'm going to let you in, I'm going to be a nice person and let you in, but this is the last time that you'll come."

He said that to him. Those were his last words. My brother just took his passport and ran.

ATROCITIES THAT HAVE HAPPENED TO ME ARE TOO PREVALENT IN THIS WORLD

These are stories that we can kind of laugh about on the surface, but they're not laughable matters. They're so depressing, and they're so disgusting. It's amazing to me that in this day and age, I'm Palestinian and I see things going on all around me.

There are atrocities here, and there's things going on around the entire world. I've traveled to Brazil. I've seen the *favelas* [slums]; I've seen how people live there. I haven't been to many other places, but I read about them all the time. I try to keep up with what's going on around the world and make sense of it.

I don't think I've been through particularly very hard times, relatively speaking. I've been interrogated for ten hours when I was traveling, before I got my Palestinian ID.

Like the other day, for example, I was with a friend and we went out in Jaffa, which is near Tel Aviv. We went out to dinner there. I'm able to go there because I have a permit to cross the checkpoint.I had a permit from my previous job, and I also got a permit through the church, but I'm very lucky to have a permit. Most people don't have permits.

So I have the opportunity to go there, but I'm still only allowed to go through certain checkpoints. We were on a road that's actually not very much used by people other than [Israeli] settlers. We're still allowed to be there, but they stopped us. They heard that we were speaking English, and so they started asking for our IDs and everything.

My friend, who's American, she gives them her passport, and for me, they were saying like, "You, you, you," and I gave them my permit. As soon as they found out I was Palestinian, they made me get out of the car.

My friend was staying in the car while I had to get out of the car. I was wearing a dress. We had just been out, and we were coming back. It was so humiliating. Those are the things that I experience, but I'm so used to them that I don't consider them to be such a huge factor.

I don't think it takes such a huge toll on me until I sit down and I think about it. It's horrific. They kept telling me, "I know you speak Arabic. I know you speak Arabic." And I refused to speak to this soldier in Arabic because, Number One, he was butchering my language, and, Number Two, I don't feel comfortable speaking to him in Arabic.

So I chose to speak English to him, and he wasn't happy with that. He was looking at my permit and asking me all of these questions. And then, anyway, he let me get back in the car, but it's just things like that, like my friends can sit in the car and drive through a checkpoint (regardless of the fact that there's a checkpoint), but I have to get out of the car, and I have to cross by foot, strictly because I'm Palestinian. I can't drive my car through to Jerusalem, because I have a Palestinian ID. There are Palestinians inside Israel that are able to drive back and forth, but because I have a West Bank ID, I have to go down and walk by foot.

So those experiences are very, I guess, traumatic in a way, but they're so embedded with me, so ingrained in my life, like it's normal to me that I have to do that. It's become normalized, and that's so bad.

Another time, I was stopped at a different checkpoint. I had to get down, and the soldier, she told me to get down and cross. I had to literally walk down the side of this mountain, this valley to walk through the area where the checkpoint is where you walk by foot, while my friend drove through.

And when I was walking by foot, there was this elevated platform with all of these soldiers pointing guns at us as we walked through. It looked like Auschwitz, you know? I mean, the turnstiles to go through the checkpoints are—they are like prisons. They *are* prisons. So that's just how we live here.

My friends are either American or they're Palestinians that have IDs that allow them to go through. I don't have a lot of Israeli friends. I mean, I have Jewish-American friends that I've met in university and abroad and stuff, but I don't have many Israeli friends. I just don't.

HOW TO CHANGE THE WORLD? START A COMPANY

I feel like maybe starting a business would have actually a larger effect on the Palestinian situation than being directly in politics. The more you live here and the more you witness reality and daily life, you just want to not do it.

I wouldn't want to work for the Palestinian government, for example. I wouldn't want to work for the U.S. government, and I wouldn't want to work for the U.N. either, actually. There are a lot of things that I don't agree with that they all do and adhere to.

So I feel doing a business is another way to kind of address the situation. It's really important for Palestinians to have opportunities. If you're contributing to an economy and you're expanding and working with markets abroad, and becoming more of this really international place where people take it seriously.—That will have a more long-term effect on whatever happens here on the ground.

WHEN I CAN AFFORD IT, I WANT TO TOUR THE ISLANDS OF THE WORLD

Personally, if money were not an issue, the number one thing I would like to do is travel, to go to places that I've only seen pictures of online. I want to go to Micronesia because it just looks really beautiful. I want to go to islands around the world. I want to go to the Philippines. I want to go to Vietnam. I want to explore Asia and other parts of South America as well. I mean, I can't do that at any point right now.

I would also like to dabble in creative things. When I was a little girl, I thought I was going to be a ballet dancer and an actor.

I danced ballet my whole life actually, from when I was four years old. Right now, I'm not dancing. I mean, for fun, I sometimes will take a class here and there, but no, I'm not pursuing that at all. So, in the future, I think I would like to definitely pursue more creative things like dancing and acting.

I always thought I would be onstage. I would like to learn how to play instruments. I don't know how to play any instrument. I wish I had learned. I also would like to maybe make films. I've tried to dabble in things that have really interested me, but also I haven't been able to make any money from them.

THE OPPORTUNITIES FOR KENZ ARE ENDLESS

I do picture a lot of things happening in my business in the future. But, for now, I don't want to start huge and fail, so I think it's best to focus and narrow in on one particular type of product line and one market segment in general. If we ever get venture-capital funding, the opportunities for the brand to grow are endless.

Eventually, we want to manufacture our own line. That's the plan. There are factories here. We could probably get the material and go to a manufacturer and make them. I'm not such an expert at this point to do that. First, I'd like to understand the market, test it out, gauge it, figure out what the demand is and what the products are that people actually like more than others, and then enter that.

And then eventually I would love to create a Kenz Man and a Kenz Girl and a Kenz Boy, you know? There are so many opportunities. I want to try to make Kenz a really large company. I want to revolutionize the bra and underwear industry in the region. And that's the goal: to save the world, one bra at a time. [Laughs.]

Imagine if this is something that becomes so big, and it's like the go-to site for shopping online five years from now, for underwear and for swimwear and fun accessories. That would be so cool.

Imagine if we had different offices in different cities in the Middle East, and then we become this global brand that had its original roots in Palestine. That's something way down the line that would be so awesome. I do want it to be something that becomes really, really large.

I don't want people to think of me as just doing this little fun side project selling bras. It's a serious business to me. I'm here all day long. So I want to be taken seriously.

WE COULD BUILD AN ALL-WOMEN TEAM

Also, it would be so cool if we had an all-women team. We would love to have a CTO that's a woman, just because you don't really see too many women working in the industry, even in Silicon Valley. It's still so many men all over the place. Maybe one day we'll just have all of these awesome women that are working here and doing things like running our technology, marketing, and production.

We'll be pushing boundaries, breaking stereotypes. Granted, we're selling underwear, but at the same time, it's a real business, and we're making revenue with it. That's the goal.

I think definitely there's more freedom for young women now. I think of the diaspora, you know, Palestinians who are similar to me, that have had the opportunity to study abroad and live abroad, etc.

I would say nowadays, more and more women here are very much taking charge of their own lives. I don't know if it's a characteristic that is shared among all Palestinians, but I see it in young women that are going to university and pursuing their own interests, definitely facing challenges from family and culture and society and religion. I see things changing.

INDUSTRY AND

TRANSPORTATION

· ·

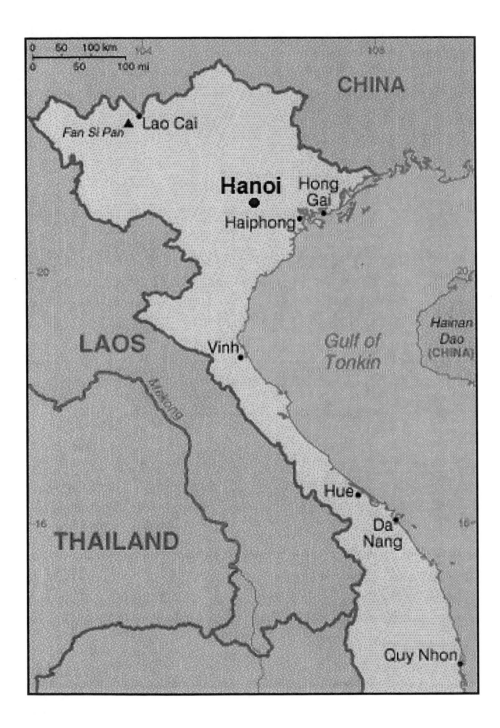

NGA

LIFE-VEST BACKPACK

MANUFACTURER,

HANOI, VIETNAM

Editor's note: One rainy evening in a small rural village in Vietnam, a mother and her teenage son watched in horror as the television evening news reported that a record-high nineteen children had drowned that day en route to school.

Rain pelted the tin roof of their little home. Heavy monsoon-season mist hung in the warm mountain air, closing in on them, ethereal and ominous. Their tropical country's annual rainy season swelled in a land where children climb from mountaintop to mountaintop over unpaved muddy roads, and board overloaded rickety wooden ferryboats[1] to cross rivers-turned-rapids, to get to school. The roads they walked and biked; the boats they boarded in their long commute; even the grass-and-twig buildings in which they studied; could be washed away in an instant, plunging them into an early death.

Every year during the monsoon, rivers became floods and the valleys in-between Vietnam's jagged mountains became rapids, and too many children perished. The mother and son looked at each other and decided to do something about it. The

---

1. Many also live on boats.

mother, Dinh Nga,[2] shared a business with her husband where she made school backpacks and he made life-vests for boats.

"Why," asked her son, "don't we make the school bag into a life-vest as well, so that if my friends go to school, that can save them from the flood if the flood comes?"

Together, the family then designed a life-vest backpack that went on to win awards and save an estimated 200,000[3] children per year from drowning in Vietnam's monsoon floods. They'd received funding from an American nonprofit that led me to their Hanoi-area factory to learn more.

My friend Erik Schultz and his wife Linn Kincannon, who run a unique nonprofit called Thriive[4] in Idaho, connected me with Nga. Erik and Linn devised a new type of nonprofit model—they call it the "pay it forward model"— in which they create jobs, prosperity, and philanthropy all in one simple step: by investing in capital equipment to build small businesses in low-income areas. The small business receives a loan that they must repay in the form of goods or services to their local community. They also get intensive capacity building and pro-bono advising. Once they "pay forward" the loan, the Thriive team hopes, the sense of empowerment and culture of giving will live on and multiply far into the future.

Nga's company, Nam Thang Long,[5] became a social enterprise (a business with a social mission) and received equipment from Thriive and other investors[6] plus advisory services from Thriive's in-country partner, the Center for Economic Development Studies at the Vietnam National University (VNU), in Hanoi. VNU professor Nguyen Huyen ("H-when"), who also serves as Vietnam country director for Thriive, has worked with Nga since her first loan ($10,000) in 2010.

"She bought about twenty-three sewing machines," Huyen recalls as she and I ride in the backseat of a car hired to take us to the Nam Thang Long factory. "With that, she started to produce the life-vest backpack. She made 60,000 items per year." Nga created forty-two new jobs and grew 92 percent during her two-year Thriive loan period.

Five years later, Nga wanted to upgrade with a higher-quality machine, "a kind of technical sewing machine," explains Huyen, "that allows her, instead of one [stitched] line to make three lines very straight and beautiful, making it a safer and longer lasting product."

Nga had realized that the problem her country faced—children perishing in

---

2. According to Vietnamese tradition, the surname goes first; her given name is "Nga" or "Ny-ah." Also, in the more formal culture of Vietnam, and out of respect, we refer to her as "Mrs. Nga." Here in her chapter, however, I've adopted the U.S. practice and put us on a first-name basis with Nga.

3. According to the World Health Organization, 372,000 people per year die from drowning. The International Life-saving Federation cites 1.2 million deaths by drowning each year.

4. See: thriive.org. To learn more about their pay-it-forward model, see thriive.org/how-thriive-works/pay-it-forward

5. Csip.vn/en/csip-social-enterprises/nam-thang-long-co-ltd.

6. Read more about Nam Thang Long in these blogs by Nevada-based Third Creek Foundation: 3rdcreek. com/3rd-creek-foundation/2015/10/20/vietnamparti, and 3rdcreek.com/3rd-creek-foundation/2015/02/27/supporting-small-business-to-save-lives-in-vietnam.

floods on mud roads and in decrepit boats and buildings—plagued a host of other countries as well, from Asia to Africa to the Americas.[7] She wanted to manufacture a sturdier product and sell it on Amazon and Alibaba.[8]

Although Nga's company had surpassed the growth and impact of Thriive's typical startup companies, Thriive decided to make an exception and approved a second loan to Nam Thang Long for $9,800.

"We almost said 'no' to her," explains Huyen, "because of how far she'd come already. But, because of the impact she was already having in her area, and what we believed she could do next for the [global] community," they approved her second loan.

Nga has donated over 1,500 backpacks to schoolchildren in impoverished areas and flood zones, and she's become one of Thriive's most active members of her local "Thriive Soup Club," where small-business-beneficiaries join forces to make soup for hungry neighbors by bringing and combining whatever ingredients they can gather up.

"Nga is one of the people that keeps inspiring more people to give. I think her successes have come from her attitude and heart. She really has the soul of Thriive," Huyen says as, two hours' drive from the city, we pull up outside of the factory.

The first thing Nga does when she meets me—is hug me. She bubbles over with excitement, enthusiasm, and warmth that are utterly contagious. Even when disclosing the headaches of endless work and the loneliness of a hollow marriage, Nga reveals not one shred of self-pity; on the contrary, she considers herself to be one of the luckiest people alive.

"My role models are Steve Jobs and Hillary Clinton," she tells me: Jobs for his inventiveness and Clinton for her endurance despite having an unfaithful husband. Nga learned to manage her company, she says, through her experience of being a mother.

I GREW UP THE ELDEST CHILD IN A VERY POOR FAMILY

My name is Dinh Thi Song Nga.[9] I'm fifty-one years old.

I was born in a village, eight kilometers [5 miles] away from here. I grew up in a very poor family. I am the oldest child. I have five younger siblings, four girls and one boy. As the oldest child, I helped my mother take care of my younger brother and sisters. I helped take care of them and feed them.

I am the most successful person in my family. My mom was a teacher, and my

---

7. See this report by the World Health Organization and UNICEF: who.int/violence_injury_prevention/child/injury/world_report/Drowning_english.pdf.

8. View Nga's backpack products here: made-in-vietnam.com/business/71428f38/cong-ty-tnhh-nam-thang-long/home. And yes, she made it onto the Alibaba platform: You can purchase her backpacks here: alibaba.com/countrysearch/VN/lifesaving-bag.html. It costs about $10 to save a child's life.

9. Her lyrical name has meaning: "Nga" is short for "beautiful girl" in Vietnamese, "Song" stands for "chrysanthemum," and "Thi" is "poem."

dad was a freelancer. He was a mechanic, and he worked wherever he could, fixing motorbikes, bicycles, and sewing machines. Any kind of machine, he could fix it. He did many different types of jobs for income for the family. Two of my younger sisters are merchants of clothes, and the youngest boy is working for a a big Korean-international group. He's in charge of security equipment.

When I was seven years old, I started to work with my father. We fixed bicycles for the neighborhood. They donated [paid] the money to my father, and then he gave the money to me. So I saved by putting the money into a bamboo box and buried it in a hole, but my younger brother stole it. And after I realized that my money was lost, I just cried.

I earned money for my education. After high school, I had only two months to learn from a relative, my cousin, about how to sew and master the sewing machine skills.

I started with only one scissors and one ruler. While I was studying at a professional Vietnamese secondary school, I made clothes and shirts for my friends to earn income. I brought things to a shop to finish them, and in that way, I earned some money for my education.

I trained for two years to become a teacher. I learned very well. At the professional secondary school, I graduated second in a class of two thousand students. Here, how it goes is high school, then professional secondary, then maybe college and university after that.

WORKING AS A TEACHER FOR TWENTY-TWO YEARS, I ALSO TRAINED TO BE A TRADITIONAL DOCTOR

I worked as a teacher for twenty-two years. After ten years, I started to learn traditional doctor skills. The teacher from the Institute of Traditional Medicines came from Hanoi to here, to teach in this region. I studied traditional medicine for four years.

I wanted to study traditional medicine because, when I was twenty-five and my daughter was about one year old, I was very often sick. I had very low blood pressure. I was tired all the time.

In Eastern terms, we would say the negative and positive sides of my body were unbalanced. At first, I had money to buy the medication, but later on, I didn't have enough money to buy the medication for my health. And I didn't understand why I got sick all the time. I wanted to learn about the body and health and medicine so that I could know why I get sick so often like that. That was the motivation for me.

Now my health is more stabilized. When I feel tired in my body, I know what to do. Every time, I treat myself through medication and acupressure, and I feel better.

The term for modern medicine is "Western medicine," and what we practice here is "Eastern medicine." Western medicine divides people into different parts, like lung or leg or heart, and every time you have pain in the heart, you treat it in the heart; so, separately in different parts of the body. But Eastern medicine considers the body as a system of all the parts with different functions. Every time a disease comes, they consider the entire function of the body. So this will be related to different parts of the body, but this will be one function. We consider the body as a system, as a whole.

I treat in two different ways. One, I have a pill made from a leaf or tree: all natural ingredients. The second way is not using any kind of medicine at all. For example, when a representative came here from Thriive, she got sick on the way. Her head was very hot, and her feet were very cold. I just used pressure to help her to reorganize the energy of the body. The next day, she was healthy again.

TWO MARRIAGES, TWO CHILDREN, THREE CAREERS

I was twenty-three years old when I married for the first time. I met my husband through his parents. They were neighbors, and they liked my appearance and saw that I was hard working and took care of my family. The parents of my husband told him about me. He worked ninety kilometers [56 miles] away from the home, but the parents asked him to come home and see me. So, we got married.

It was an arranged marriage, but I was happy to get married to him. We were married for sixteen years. During our marriage, I realized there were many differences between us that were hard to get resolved between the two persons. We later got divorced.

But, we had two children together, a daughter and a son. Our daughter is now twenty-seven years old. She is already a university graduate and has worked for four years. She just got married three months ago. She lives in Hanoi. Our son is twenty-one years old, and he studies at the Technology University in Hanoi.

After that, I married a second time to my current husband. I was still a teacher when I got married to my husband now. We didn't organize a ceremony, like a wedding ceremony, but we legally registered.

He's sixty years old now. He was my patient. Somebody introduced him to me [as a patient] and I checked his health. Through the process of helping him restore his health, we got to know each other and we felt it was a good combination. I also knew his family. We've been married since 2007.

MY SECOND HUSBAND MADE BOATS, SO I MADE LIFE VESTS

In 2005, I started my current business, and then I built this factory in 2008. During the first three years, it was just a very temporary factory, but after 2008, we had this factory that you see here. Although I now have my own business, I still check the health of my family members and all my employees. So I'm a businesswoman and a traditional doctor at the same time.

My husband is a businessman. He's the director of his own company. He makes boats and ferries from composite material.

On the boats, they needed life-vests, and I had the sewing skills to produce those. So, in the past, I made the life-vests so that he could sell them through his boating business. But during that time, we had different ways of doing business. I'm very safe [fiscally conservative]. I do it carefully, but my husband wants to be quick, to be on time. So we are different in that point of view of doing business.

BRANCHING OFF TO ESTABLISH MY OWN FACTORY BUSINESS

Eventually, I separated and started my own private business, in 2005. We started on the same land we own now, right here; but it was a makeshift building, made out of a fabric cover over some bamboo frame, like that. We started with five employees. They worked for both my husband and me.

When I hire employees, the first thing I look at is their *attitude*: If they have an open mind to learn, are a little bit intelligent, clever. Everything else, I can train them.

In 2007, when he was fifteen years old, my son created the idea of the life-vest backpack. So there are about 200,000 children in Vietnam who go to school every day by ferries or boats, who are at risk of the floods. Before my product was invented, there were so many newscasts on TV about five children dying at once, or seven…the top number we heard was "nineteen children die at once." But after I invented this product, I didn't see any news or hear any stories about children die of flood anymore.

In 2008, my son brought the idea of the life-vest to a design competition in Taiwan, and it was the winner for most innovative product. He was fifteen at the time. The idea came from my son, but the whole family, me and my husband and the son, tried to develop it into a good product.

So more customers began to come, and there was more demand for the product. That required me to stop teaching after twenty-two years and work full-time for the business. I think that if I continued to teach and manage the business, it's not good. So I decided to fully devote myself to the business.

Now my husband has thirty employees, and I have sixty.[10] So, altogether we have ninety employees.

I have different departments—sales, marketing, and floor production. All of the employees are important. There's one head of each department in the production. Even though we are in charge of different departments, we all share the work when we are busy, or we can design a product together working across marketing, sales, and production. We work together and design the products.

We produce about 6,000 items per month. So it's about 70,000 per year for all types of products. It could be a life-vest or life-vest backpack or plain backpack.

MY REVENUE: AM I WEALTHY YET?

The revenue last year was 12 million Vietnamese dong [$538]; that's about 6 to 7 percent profit. I don't know how much I pay myself. [Laughs.] We don't have shareholders. So I don't have to share the profit with others. I keep that for my business, so for myself, but I use that to reinvest in and expand the business.

You could say that I'm not rich yet, but what is rich is understood differently for different people. For me, some people are rich in money. Some people are rich in relationships and friendships; others are rich in social values. For me, creating more social impact and more social values is to be a rich person.

---

10. Nga doesn't mention it here, but "approximately half of the employees have disabilities, and the other half are from dire financial situations where they are the sole breadwinners for their households," reports Third Creek Foundation. Hiring employees who most need the job is part of Nga's social mission.

I'M RICH IN SOCIAL VALUES, LIKE BILL GATES

I care a lot about social values. Education is very important for a person's life. Personal development is the way to complete everyone, to keep learning things like that. The top social value is for me to create a good working environment for my employees to develop all of themselves.

It's like Bill Gates, where he earned a lot of money, but he didn't give that money to his children; rather, he's giving back to the community and helping people. The same with me. Getting rich and earning money is not the biggest goal of my life, but I can realize that around me so many people have a lack of opportunity and are in more difficult backgrounds.

So I think I can do something for them. I can help the disadvantaged people. Here in Vietnam, we have a lot of disadvantaged people, and like women in violence. I want to see an end to violence.

A DAY IN THE LIFE OF A FACTORY OWNER: IT DOESN'T END

I usually start very early, like 4:00 or 5:00 a.m. in the morning. I read either a printed book or something online. At 6:30, I do some morning exercise and I have breakfast. After that, I go and check the work in the morning for different departments, to see how it's going.

At about 8:00, I go to the open-air [food] market, and then I bring the food and ingredients in here and give it all to the kitchen. The kitchen will cook for my family and some of the staff.

Most of the employees will go home and eat lunch at home, but some of them stay here. So after we are sure that the menu is set for the meal, I go and check the work again, to see if anybody needs help. After that, I can go online and search the Internet to see if there is a good business model I can learn from, anything I can learn from the Internet, and then I share that information with my employees.

At 11:30, we have lunch, and after that, I have about fifteen to twenty minutes, and I take a nap around noon. I have a sleeping room over there. So the employees will work steady from 7:00 to 11:00 and break, and then they start again from 1:00 p.m. to 5:00 p.m.

I usually finish the whole day at 10:00 p.m. My home is about 600 meters [2,000'] away from here, but I don't live there often. Only me and my husband are at home...

So lonely! So I usually stay here. My husband also stays here. I continue working in the evening, like looking online for a job, more collaboration opportunities, and things like that. I also enjoy reading books.

MY BEST DAY? WHEN I SIGN A BIG CONTRACT, OF COURSE

I have a lot of energy. I'm a happy person. I have a job I like. So I spend full-time on it. I'm very happy about that. I also have an ecosystem of organizations and individuals around me. The organization is a nonprofit organization, which serves my customer, Thriive, and individuals like Linn and Huyen, and like you, individuals that share the same point of view that I have about the world. I have a lot of support like that. That keeps me energized and gives me all the energy for my work.

The best moment in my work is when I sign a big contract. For example, I recently signed another contract with UNDP [United Nations Development Program]. It's about 1.5 billion to 2 billion Vietnamese dong [$60,000-90,000]. It's a big contract. When I sign that contract, I feel like, "Wow!"

THERE AREN'T WORST MOMENTS—ONLY HEADACHES AND LESSONS

I don't have a worst moment. I do have challenges in my business, but I don't have the feeling that I don't like it. I have a headache and feel tired, but then I find the solution for it. I don't feel like that's the worst moment of my life or my business. I actually like it because it teaches me and it helps me to grow.

Every time I have troubles or challenges, I go slowly one by one and gradually I overcome the challenges and problems. And after that, I feel like I grow up. So I feel happy to have the challenges. That makes me grow and helps me be better.

CHALLENGES OF A SOCIAL ENTERPRISE: LACK OF CAPITAL AND MARKETING

The lack of capital at the beginning was really hard for the business, but I went online and checked available sources, and I found Thriive. We applied for that, and, luckily, we got the loan. And after that, we had the machines and the technical expertise to help us to improve our products. So we overcame that.

The second challenge is the marketing. For this small business, we don't have good money for marketing and advertising and things like that. But I discovered a very good tool, the Internet. So we do marketing online, and the customers know us from the Internet, and some of them come for three times, five times, and ten times. The old customers keep coming again and again, and we have new customers who learn about us. So we just go slowly and keep plugging away. Also, we use online marketing to sell our product.

WE'VE WON AWARDS FOR OUR LIFE-SAVING PRODUCTS

I have received awards. Our first award was a gold medal in Taiwan for the life-vests for boats or ferries. We also received a gold medal from the International Intellectual Organization and a gold medal from the Ministry of Industry and Trade and the gold medal of the Marine Ministry, all for our boating products.

It's also a very good feeling when I receive feedback from my customers that it's a good product and the children love it. The parents still report to me that their children have been saved, and the children feel very safe and don't worry about floods when going to school.

OUR BUSINESS IS GOING GLOBAL, BECAUSE OF THE NEED

My vision is to see my business achieve globalization, to sell the products globally. This year, we plan to have a page on Alibaba to sell my products. In the future, I want us to be global, but to still keep the main value of the business on life-saving products for both children and adults.

In the world, I believe there are many more people at risk of drowning by floods.[11] I don't know exactly how much is the demand.

We work in the garment sector. The garment sector here in Vietnam doesn't contain much value compared to, for example, Korea. They have a lot of value and income because they design their products. They have a whole long history of processing garments. So they have a better value, better price, and a better income.

But, in Vietnam, we just do like subcontractor work or we do very basic skills. So our garment sector is not adding a big value. However, in my business, the value for me is when we save the children. So the product is for the children, to save the children's lives. So, even though, compared to other industries or other countries, in Vietnam, the garment business is not so valuable, that's what I can do, and I love it.

MY RELIGION IS HUMAN RIGHTS

If I had all the money I could dream of, I would be a doctor, and I would be working at a hospital for orphans and for the elderly.

And I'd build schools for children. This would be the best model of education, in that school, where people are respected, are developed for all potentials, and generally human rights is respected.

I don't have any religion. I learned all the best wisdom from all the different people, religions, or books. I respect and I apply different aspects of all that for my own life. But I thank the Buddhist religion because it teaches me one thing about life: When somebody does something to hurt me, or somebody does something that is not good for me, I don't get angry or upset. I don't want to get revenge on them. I feel sorry for them that they are hurting themselves. They are thinking and doing something not good, but it's not good for their life. So I feel sympathy or I feel sorry for them, but I don't want to get revenge on them, and that is the Buddha religion that taught me about that.

HILLARY CLINTON IS MY ROLE MODEL—AND WE HAVE A FEW THINGS IN COMMON

I rarely watch TV, but I enjoy reading books. I do not like novels or fiction; I prefer the truth. My favorite topic in books is true stories about human development or stories or about the soul. I have so many books over there on my shelf about stories and about soul and about humans.

For example, I like reading about Steve Jobs and Hillary Clinton. I like Steve Jobs because I spend all my energy for work. Hillary, she's very strong, like me.

It's like her [Clinton's] husband and my husband, maybe they have the wrong relationship, or as women we endure things like that, but I learn from her that I need

---

11. According to the World Health Organization, 372,000 people per year die from drowning. The International Lifesaving Federation cites 1.2 million deaths by drowning each year.

to be strong. I cannot push things away, but I try to keep the business because I have workers. I have people who rely on me. I need to be strong.

My husband is not faithful, but he is helping my business. He has business connections. He's advised me. He's helping the business. So sometimes I think that I have to push my personal life down rather than the business. There is pain here when I know my husband is not faithful to me, but in my mind I say that we should keep it away, don't think about it too much, because I'm thinking about something bigger.

GENDER ROLES IN VIETNAM

I'm different from the women around here. No woman in this province can be so open to learn like me and love the Internet like me. [Laughs.] I haven't traveled outside of Vietnam yet. [Laughs.] Only virtually, online.

So, women around here, they don't read books a lot. They don't like looking for information on the Internet. They are not creative. They follow the life in a traditional way. So, as a woman, I have to take care of the business and also take care of the family.

Even now that my children are grown up and they are in the university or have graduated, I still have to direct them in the way they look at the world.

MY MANAGEMENT STYLE EMANATES FROM MY MOTHERHOOD

I read a book from Harvard to learn the skill of the Americans and other countries, the skill of being a good mother. So I read that book and took from the book how to be a successful mother, and I learned how to direct my children. I don't ask them to do things, but I share with them and support them.

I also use that skill to direct my employees. I don't work on them or show them every detail of the work, but I show them where to look for it: what book they should look up, or what they should do to learn themselves. So, in that way, I can save my time, and I can do a lot of things at the same time, but I don't have to waste too much money on the details.

The men here are almost all the same. It's the weakness of Vietnamese. It's the same as the problems of Vietnam in general. The political mechanism is making people lazy, so that not all the potential of the person gets developed.

The political situation in Vietnam does not facilitate the personal development. The educational system does not encourage people to be creative. When I was a teacher, I was the only teacher to teach the children the methods of learning, how to describe a literary piece they've read, rather than just memorizing it.

Other people gave a sample literature for them to learn by heart and just have them memorize all the samples, poems and things like that, and when they see a question, they just memorize the answer and write it down. But I didn't do that. I taught the children how to be creative and use their own language, to develop their own observations.

THREE WISHES BEFORE I DIE

I am going to try to live until I reach seventy-five years old. The three things I wish for the most before I reach that age:

1. The first is to bring my business to success, where people love to work and live here as a family, and it's a successful business.
2. The second wish is to give orientation for the younger generation, including my children and my grandchildren, where they have a good view. They know how to see life, and they overcome challenges, and they have a good overview and a good attitude for life.
3. And the third thing I want is to help disadvantaged people, like women in violent situations.

For myself, I just want to be healthy. Only that: just my health. I live for others. I listen, and I share with others. That's the base for all my success.

It's like this Vietnamese poem that I love. It goes like this: "So please live the new day when it comes, even if you are very tired of life. My life, our life, may we just be happy with it, although we lack the shoulder of someone to lean on." So that means the man or somebody you rely on.

So, even if you don't have the shoulder of a person you can rely on, we are in this life together. We can enjoy it, and we can always find other joy or happiness in our life.

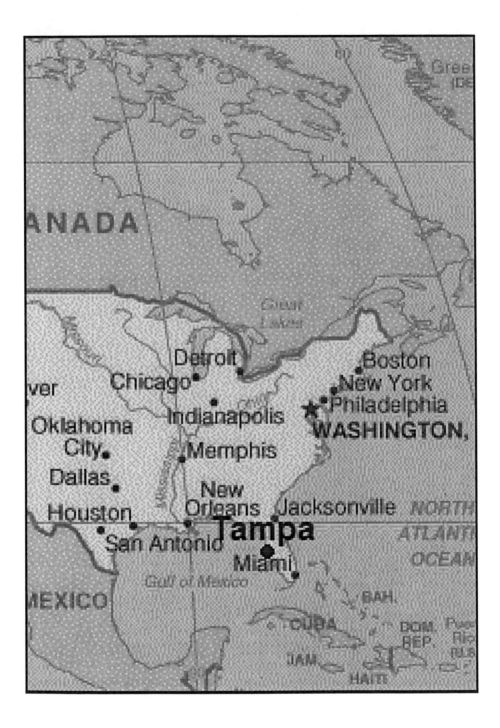

·····················

HANNAH

RECRUITER-HEADHUNTER,

TAMPA, FLORIDA, U.S.

Editor's note: Hannah happens to be one of my dearest personal friends. She and I like to say that families don't turn out the way we'd envisioned when we were naïve young women getting married and having babies...Sometimes, they turn out better.

We'll call each other from Florida to California and say, "I'm having a Norman Rockwell moment!" which means, *my family and I are all in harmony.* It means we're managing to nurture and celebrate the real, raw, flawed, brilliant mothers we are and the families we've created...

More than managing, we're thriving. With the divorce rate still hovering around 50 percent in the U.S., we're not exactly atypical in being single parents. Yet Hannah has experienced more challenges, raising her children truly alone, than anyone I've ever met—all while building her career as a recruiter, keeping a roof over their heads, and retaining a stubbornly optimistic view of the world and people.

We met during one of our darkest moments, when two of our family members descended into drugs, violence, mental illness, and trauma that would ripple through both families and rip us apart for years to come; but Hannah and I clung together in the way that compatriots of crisis do. As I came to know her gentle soul, I was stunned by her unconditional love for her four children—who, between them, have endured challenges from rape to jail, ADD to PTSD, suicidal hospitalization to transgender transformation.

Hannah somehow managed to cry and love her way through not just years, but decades of days on which anything could happen, and often did. I observed from across the continent as she tackled one emergency after another with the same steady patience as she had once changed her babies' diapers. She never complained, not once.

Hannah also never let her children go hungry. She worked long hours to keep the mortgage paid and leveraged that mortgage a few times to put braces on their teeth and keep them all in counseling.

Her children have always known one stable home. They've all had the chance to study at private schools and take lessons in speech therapy, drama, singing, and music. They've had Passover Seders and Hanukkah parties, road trips to visit relatives in Maryland, and vacations with their great-aunt at the beach. Behind the scenes, Hannah was resourceful and resilient in ways they cannot even imagine, always the rock they needed to come back to for a hug, a ride, a bailout, or a loan.

What struck me about Hannah was that she hadn't a shred of superiority or self-pity. Like so many parents of both genders, and often grandparents and adopted caregivers, she's been the quiet hero of her children's lives, loving them rather imperfectly and yet with all the strength and grace they've needed to build a solid foundation for their own happy adult lives.

As our hair goes gray and our children finally leave our nests, I see Hannah begin to blossom into a joyful woman whose heart has always been open, and whose life is now free. She has a seven-syllable laugh that interrupts nearly every sentence. She cries over sappy commercials; she has an insatiable sweet tooth; and she adores her Yorkie-poodle, Banjo. Hannah still wants to travel to new places, still hopes to find her soulmate, and still believes in happy endings.

The trauma of her two broken marriages, the chronic anxiety over children on the edge, and the 24/7 struggle to keep the bills paid, has begun to crest into a wave of relief: Her kids have reached young adulthood, all intact, all well. As for Hannah, she's earned the right to be really proud of the way her Norman Rockwell life has taken shape, as she's painted the portrait with her own two hands.

I'M A RECRUITER, AKA HEADHUNTER

My name is Hannah Kalderon. I'm fifty-five years old. I work for Maxim Staffing Solutions. My title is Senior National Recruitment Manager. I get people jobs, and I help people to understand how to get jobs. I not only recruit and hire, I also manage a team of traveling therapists through their career with us as external caregivers. We serve locations in all fifty U.S. states, in all clinical settings including schools, hospitals, outpatient clinics, skilled nursing facilities, home-health agencies, and government agencies.

There's a difference between human resources and recruiting, what I do. Human resources is like an internal department for a company. Recruiting may be a part of human resources or a standalone company all by itself. What I do is more sales- and commission-based, whereas human resources is almost always salaried only. So I find people and I find their jobs, and, depending on how good I am at it, I make commissions.

I am a *headhunter*. That's the term that people use in every industry. We sell *people* in a couple of different ways: by hiring them directly, and by placing them with our clients. When we hire someone, we hire them contingent on having a place for them to work. We make a percentage of what they make. We pay them; the client pays us; we make money off of the middle.

I've been in recruiting for twenty-three years. I spent more than ten years recruiting information technology [IT] people. Then I recruited accounting people. After that, I recruited engineers, and then in the healthcare industry.

We also sell people into permanent positions. So, let's say a client wants to hire somebody. They don't want to do their own advertising or screening. So they put the job order out to a company like ours, and we find somebody. They pay us only if we're successful. They can put that job order out to a dozen different companies that may spend tons of money to find the person, but they can pick and choose and pay for only what they want.

I worked for a small company launched by four people. The focus was strictly therapies: physical therapists, occupational therapists, and speech/language pathologists. It's a very small niche within the healthcare industry. About seven or eight years ago, we were bought by Maxim Healthcare, which is a huge healthcare provider, with a wide range of services. So now we're the division of Maxim Healthcare that works specifically with therapy.

Maxim was on an upswing back then. Since then, things in the therapy world have gone downhill. The government has put caps on [insurance] reimbursement. Somebody might need ongoing therapy until they get better, but they're not going to get more than three physical therapy visits. The government stepping in has made it very difficult. Over the last few years, my income has gone down each year.

Currently, the company as a whole places between eighty and one-hundred and fifty people a year. It's a pretty wide range; we're on the low end right now. My travel team fluctuates between twelve to twenty. If I can get to twenty, then I will not only have a better commission, but I'll be able to get stock payout and stock ownership in the company and a bonus trip. So twenty is kind of my goal. It's been my goal every year.

MY TYPICAL DAY: COMMUNICATING BY EVERY MEANS POSSIBLE

On a typical day, my alarm goes off between 6:30 and 7:00. I don't really think about work too much in the morning. It's the last thing I think about at night, though. Before I turn out the light, I always check my email. Maybe it's the Jewish thing: The day starts the night before when the sun goes down. [Laughs.] When I go to bed, the last thing I do is to check my work email.

First thing in the morning, I'm usually not in work mode. I don't know. My mind doesn't wake up well. I'm probably thinking, "Get my nose pill." I have allergies, so the first thing on my mind is, go get my nose pill. [Laughs.]

I'll shower, dress, get into the office around 8-8:30, depending on whether or not a kid has missed the bus. If a kid misses the bus, which still happens now that there's only one kid left in high school, I'll make a detour. Nate's[1] school starts at 7:30. So then I'm at work before eight.

I turn on the computer, get a cup of coffee. I try and control my day by looking at emails and prioritizing, but there's always fires to put out. So I jump into it and start putting out fires, making phone calls.

For example, somebody wasn't able to get through the computer application the night before. So I tell her, "I'm sorry. This is what you need to do," because the faster I can get that moving, the better. Or, somebody had an interview the night before, and the client said, "We want to extend an offer." The candidate doesn't know it yet, and I want to get to that person early in the day before they go to work.

Recruiting is a rollercoaster of ups and downs and things going on. Somebody's paperwork hasn't gone through…you think the deal's on, and then it's off. You think the deal's off, and then it's on. It's always just jumping from one extreme to the other. It goes ups and downs and crazies all day long.

I'm in an office, in a cubicle. Over the years, I've had offices; I've been in cubes; I've been in bull pits. During the workday, I'm at my desk on the computer or on the phone. I can sit down at 7:30 in the morning and have a hard time taking a pee break [laughs] because there's just one more thing to do, one more thing to do. I have to force myself to stop.

I rarely take lunch, because that's the easiest time to get in touch with people. I never want to miss a call because I'm making calls all day long. If somebody calls back when I step away to go to the bathroom or get a cup of coffee, Murphy's Law [i.e., if anything can go wrong, it will] is the way it happens. So I'm always tied to my desk, hoping that I'm not missing anything.

It's a very busy day. It takes me completely away from being a mom. I get totally focused on what I'm doing. However, one of the things I really like about recruiting is that, if something else does come up Mom-related, at the drop of a hat, they understand.

When my son Aiden had to be bailed out of jail—my boss didn't think twice about it. Then, again, before that, I wanted to get a dog. She didn't think twice about that either, when I was thumbing through, looking for dogs. When I found one in a pound, she said, "Go out and look at it now." [Laughs.] They're wonderful people to work with.

My days are never predictable. My official hours are 8:30 to 5:30, but when the calls come in, you take them. It's quite possible that I can make 100-200 phone calls in a day, and all I'm doing is leaving messages. So, if a human being wants to call me back, I'll drop everything and talk to them about whatever it is they want to talk about, for as long as they want to talk about it.

---

1. Hannah explains: Nate, 19 and a senior in high school, was born as my youngest daughter, *Naomi*. He/she decided in his late teens that he was a boy born into the wrong body. I'm completely supportive of him being transgender. Nathan, or Nate as he prefers, also has high-functioning Asperger's and developmental delays. Being a boy hasn't seemed to make him happier or more comfortable, socially. But my other kids and I still respect his choice. When he turns 21, he knows he can go into therapy and start the process of gender-reassignment.

I really make an effort not to work nights and evenings. When I was first recruiting and Rachel (she's my second oldest, after Aiden) got sick with cancer, I learned to constrict my availability times: I was 100 percent Mom when I was out of the office; I was 100 percent recruiter when I was in. I just didn't have the bandwidth to let them overlap.

Now there is some overlap, but I try and still turn off work on the weekends. I try not to take calls, although I'll answer emails all weekend long. On Saturdays, I'll wake up late, take the dog for a walk, maybe hang out in the backyard if it's sunny, and maybe go kayaking. On Sundays, I'll hang out at Starbucks and read a book. So, my weekends are pretty laid back.

MY BEST MOMENT IS WHEN SOMEONE GETS HIRED!

In terms of best moments, bright spots at work happen whenever anybody gets a job. It is so rewarding. For example, California takes forever to issue a [therapy] license. So a young couple I've been working with, had to stay longer in Texas, waiting for California to come through. They finally got jobs up near San Francisco with the same company. Coordinating two people is an extra tough thing, but I did it. They got jobs with a client that we know is nice.

And so I got to tell this guy that I've been working with for over a year, "You and your fiancée are finally going to California!"

I have so much fun finding the right people and jobs for each other, and I find it so rewarding on both sides when I get to tell someone that the other person accepted their offer.

DO WOMEN MAKE BETTER RECRUITERS?

As for harassment or abuse at work, that happened a little bit back in my IT recruiting days. It was a small, family-owned place. Since I did not have a direct counterpart in the firm, it was not apparent that I was unequally paid. When I left, however, I have no doubt that the man who replaced me earned much more.

The guy that owned it hired his sons. He was Italian. It was a very macho cultural thing. He felt that women were strategically used best in a certain way. One of the guys was setting up after-hours events that I thought were work-related, that were actually opportunities for him to hit on girls. I was outraged later to learn I was a draw to the males in IT. It was not honestly spoken of as a business decision, because I was an asset as a pretty woman, not as a recruiter.

But now, for the most part, you're over the phone, so there's no physical opportunity for taking advantage or abuse. They don't even know what I look like.

Some people feel like women are better recruiters. In my experience, women *are* better recruiters. I don't know why. Maybe it's because it does take quite a bit of nurturing to draw out of people what they do best and to hear and focus on them to find them the job that's right for them.

The men that I've seen try and make those kind of matches have been more focused on the money and trying to force things. They'll say things like, "Oh, you say you want a permanent job, but I've got a great contract job for you over here. You'll really like this."

I think I get along well with my coworkers. We actually do a lot of feedback in my current job, and I know I'm well respected for my knowledge and my abilities. Nobody doubts my word. If I say I can do something, I can do it. In relation to some of my other coworkers, I'm not the superstar that I was when I was in the IT world. There are two women who are substantially better than me. They make substantially higher revenue and are earning stock every year. I'm usually in third place behind them, and that's OK with me now. When I was in the IT world, I was always in first place by far, but I think now I prefer a little bit more life-balance. Also, neither one of them has outside families or kids.

THE INTERNET AND SOCIAL MEDIA HAVE TURNED RECRUITING INSIDE-OUT

I'm open to embracing new technology. I'm on Facebook. I'm on LinkedIn. I'm not stuck in old ways. I'm always embracing whatever's new. Keeping up with fast-paced changes in industry has been the biggest challenge, but also is one of the things I like best about my job. It seems there's always a newer, better tool to use. I find the technology exciting and feel like a detective as I sleuth out new and creative ways to find people.

When I started recruiting, employers would either place an ad in the newspaper or perhaps hire a recruiting firm. Recruiters would have paper files with resumes and their brains were the computers that would try and match up the people with the jobs. As computers and the Internet became available to more of the population, the job notices and resumes were exchanged, stored and remembered differently. I've seen newsgroups and job boards, Monster, Dice, CareerBuilder, Facebook Careers, LinkedIn/Jobs, online licensing boards…so many resources that it's hard to keep up.

The world as we know it has become very specialized. People no longer start a job and retire from that same job. Transitions from the academic world to the professional one now require help and often a lot of luck. Recruiters help keep people working and provide employers with the workforce they need. We are the talent scouts of the sports industry, and the matchmakers of the dating world. A recruiter has seen thousands of resumes that allow them to know how yours stacks up against the competition. No individual could have that perspective.

Sometimes I forget that I change people's lives. When I hear someone years later say, "That job you got me was the best move I ever made," that's one of the benefits of Facebook that I love. I can become "friends" with someone, hire them, send them to a job in a place that they didn't know existed, where they may meet their soulmate; I can stay in touch and help with future job placements, see them marry, have kids, and post pictures of it all, as their lives develop.

In my short lifetime in recruiting, the industry has gone global, with no barriers to entry. Anybody can recruit with a phone and the Internet, but there are very few that can last 20+ years at it and do it well.

I think recruiting tends to burn people out. So there aren't as many recruiters that have lasted as long as I have. It's not a job you go to college to get. It's a different skill set. It's not a job that a lot of people know exists.

I know now that I'm good at recruiting. I can hear what people say they want. I can fix their resumes to say what they do, and I can be quick enough to get the right people in front of the right opportunities. People do come to me often, too—asking me to consider changing jobs, and try and recruit me away from what I'm doing. So, although I'm not the top superstar anymore, I could be if I wanted to. I just prefer a little bit more life-balance.

MY JEWISH MOTHER WANTED TO NAME ME "JESUS CHRIST"

No joke: My Jewish mother, who was only seventeen when I was born, is a little wacky. She wanted to name me *Jesus Christ Kalderon*...None of the relatives was going to accept that! At my twenty-first birthday, she gave me the name of "Joy" instead of the first name "Jesus."

I'm divorced, with four children: one son, Aiden, age twenty-three; two daughters, Rachel and Gabrielle, ages twenty-one and twenty; and a transgender girl-to-boy, Naomi/Nate, age nineteen. I've learned to not wait for somebody else to help.

I grew up in Maryland. As a curious kid, I looked around in my grandparents' bedroom when I was little and came across a letter about my birth and my mother running away and eloping. She was writing to her dad saying, "I'm sorry, Dad, but I got pregnant, and so we're eloping and getting married."

My parents were divorced when I was still an infant, and I went to live with my mother and her parents, Madeline and Marion. The families loved each other, but my mother was only seventeen and not really interested in being a mother at that time. She wanted to be a career woman. So her parents pretty much raised me while she went on, finished college, and got a degree as a lawyer. She worked as an economist. She was always much more into being a professional woman, whereas I always emulated and wanted to be like my grandmother and be a stay-at-home mom.

My dad and his family also wanted to be involved. They had custody every second weekend of every month, every other holiday, and for a month every summer, and they only lived between Baltimore and Washington. So, most of the time, it was just a car ride and an inconvenience.

I was the only kid with a split family in those days. I had two grandmothers that doted on me, loved me to death, and a mother that was a bit of a whack-ball. This may need to be edited out.[2] [Laughs.]

I also had a wonderful aunt, Ruth, who was my mother's sister. She saved my sanity many times. It was a great, loving, although different family.

I GREW UP IN A STRANGE FAMILY OF REBELS

There were all sorts of weird, wacky stories in the family...My great-grandmother and my great-grandfather were niece and uncle. They had a little incest back there.

My great-grandfather, my mother's father, came over from Europe, somewhere along the Polish/Russian border. He was one of those immigrants that came over to work, worked hard, sent back money, and brought over one family member, then another one,

---

2. Hannah chose a pseudonym to protect her family but decided to allow this and other honest comments.

then another one. He had a disagreement with his father about religion and Judaism. His father was a very Orthodox rabbi, and he didn't want to be that extreme. So he left. I think he was maybe around thirteen when he came over to this country and just started bringing relatives over.

When I grew up, there was a huge extended family that all started with [Great-Grand] Papa Davey. One of the people he brought over was that niece that he married, Mama Rachel, whom my daughter's named after.

HOW I BROUGHT FAITH BACK INTO THE FAMILY

Everybody in my family is Jewish, but I couldn't go to Sunday school consistently every Sunday in either place; so I didn't go to Sunday school in either one. Neither family, when I was growing up, belonged to a temple. I guess it was my great-grandfather's rebellion against his father: We were Jewish, but more culturally Jewish. Nobody belonged to a temple or a synagogue.

When I was raising my kids, that was one thing that I wanted them to know and to have that foundation. So, because I didn't have it, they did, and I learned as they learned about it. In Judaism, Conservative, Reform, and Orthodox are the three biggies. Orthodox came first and is the most restrictive. Reform came next, and that's what we are, and that's what I call "Jewish Lite." And then because some Jews felt that Lite was too far from Orthodox, Conservative was developed in-between, and that's too strong for me. [Laughs.] So we're Reform.

To be honest, I don't know if my religion has impacted my thinking or my career choices in life.

I WANTED TO BE A HOMEMAKER, NOT THE CAREER WOMAN I AM NOW

As far as education, I attended public school (elementary, junior high, and high school) in Maryland. Math was probably my best subject. I was a straight C student until I got to high school; grades were not that important. It seems everybody in my family rebels against everything else. When my grandfather was raising my mother and my aunt, he demanded straight As. At least, that's the story I heard. But I was the doted-on grandchild. Everything I did, I walked on water.

So, if I brought home a C, "Oh, that's great." If I had brought home an A or a D, that would have been equally great to them, I think. So I didn't have a whole lot of drive through school. There was never anything I really wanted to do, and my mother, being the Women's Libber[3] that she was, wanted me to have a career. She was very aggressive. She was going to law school at the time, and all I ever wanted to do was be a housewife with a station wagon. It drove her up the wall.

I did well with statistics and math, but I think that's because I had teachers that enjoyed it and friends that couldn't do it. And if I explained it to them, it helped explain

---

3. The Women's Liberation or feminist movement peaked in the 1960s-1980s striving for equal rights, pay, and opportunities for women. See: novaonline.nvcc.edu/eli/evans/his135/events/womensliberation/womensliberation.htm.

it to me. I did worse in English and in writing. So I muddled on through and did fine, graduating not at the top or at the bottom of my class.

I didn't have anybody to marry and become a housewife for [laughs], and no valid excuse or job, not to go on to college. And, my parents were fighting over who was paying for it! So, I went on to college. I didn't particularly have any drive to go to college, but I didn't have anything better to do. I was like, "I don't know what I'm going to do." I couldn't get my MRS ["Mrs."] degree, so…

"Well, if you don't have anything better to do, go to college," my aunt Ruth said. "You can always stop [later]."

I went to the University of Maryland. I got kicked out after the first year, for poor grades, not really from too much partying, just a lack of caring. But I later went back to the University of Maryland because, once again, I didn't really have anything better to do. And, one year at a time, Ruth just kept kicking my butt through.

I was taking psychology, computer science…Nothing really stuck for me. In psychology, it just seemed very inefficient to take five hours of your life and only get three credits. In computer science, those stupid machines were smarter than I was. [Laughs.]

So, eventually I tried an economics course, which was my mother's degree, only because my boyfriend at the time thought that that was an impressive thing that I should do, and I got an easy A in it. It just didn't seem to take much effort, three credits for three hours. So I stuck with that and got my degree in economics.

WORKING THREE JOBS WHILE MARRIED AND IN COLLEGE FULL-TIME

I met my first husband, Alan, when I was twenty-one. We married when I was twenty-three. Since I got kicked out of college after my first year, the whole four-year plan took six with me. And during that last year, I was already married to Alan.

He was feeling like we were stuck in a rut and never going to succeed financially. "How are we going to get out of this apartment?" he would say. "How are we going to get ahead in life? We're just spinning our wheels."

I was like, "We are going to finish our degrees, and then we're going to have better opportunities."

I ended up finishing before he did, even though he was a year older than I was. He failed classes. The less he worked outside of school, it was like the harder it was for him to actually pass the classes. For me, it was the opposite—when I took on more work and I took more classes, I did better at both.

For a while, when I was an undergrad, attending school full-time, I had three jobs. I was waitressing at two different places part-time and working in retail at Garfinckel's, so I could develop a professional wardrobe.

When I finished school, I didn't just sit back and say, "Okay, you're right. We're stuck in this hole." I got a job at Merrill Lynch. Actually, it was funny because I didn't know that the world of headhunting existed. Nobody ever told me how to get a job. No one in my family helped me write a resume.

I GOT MY FIRST PROFESSIONAL JOB THROUGH A SLEAZY HEADHUNTER

So eventually I fell into a headhunter's lap, and he got me an interview at Merrill Lynch. He was the kind of a headhunter was supposed to be paid by the candidate. So I was supposed to pay this guy that got me the job. I said, "Fine, I'm desperate enough to need a job. You know I'm desperate enough, but I don't have any money to pay you."

So he got me the job and then he said, "Okay, there'll be payments. You'll pay me so much a month for the next year."

I said, "Okay, fine. Send me the bills, and if I'm making enough money because of the job you got me, I'll be happy to pay you."

He ended up never sending me the monthly tickets [bills]. Well, now, years and years later, I know how the industry works. There are people that will charge you to redo your resume and to get you a job, and those are the wrong recruiters. Those are the ones that are unethical, and they don't usually disappear as nicely as this guy did for me.

But after I got the job at Merrill Lynch, I was there for two years and doing very well. Alan eventually got his degree. I was a bookkeeper. I was doing accounting. My degree was in economics. The work at Merrill Lynch was nothing like anything that I'd learned, but I got a month of training internally, and then I was very good at it.

I liked Merrill Lynch a lot. It was very much about what you did and not whether you were male or female, which was nice.

But then, someone authorized payment of a bad check at Merrill Lynch, and as a result a bunch of people were fired. That opened a rare opportunity for promotion. It was time for me to grab my chance and fight for the promotion, but I could not get my head in the game...

I was totally distracted because I felt so awful about our two cats. Alan and I had a pair of kittens. One had just died from feline leukemia. (It was too late by the time the vet told me there was a vaccine to prevent the disease, but nothing to cure it.) Within a couple days the other one got lost when Alan came home drunk one night and took it outside for a walk. Both cats had been kept only indoors and declawed. The promotion at work and the loss of our cats was right at the same time.

It just wiped me out. That could have been my time to be cutthroat, put my name in front of people and say, "Okay, now's my chance. Somebody's out, and I can get their promotion," because that was the only way anybody ever moved up was if somebody moved out. But I missed my chance.

Months passed. I thought, "Who knows when the next catastrophe will happen or person will die? I'm going to be stuck at this level forever and ever. It's time to start looking for something else. How are we ever going to get ahead? We've got our degrees but we're still barely making ends meet."

WORKING MY WAY INTO MANAGEMENT AND THE D.C. PARTY SCENE

So I got a job at The Wyatt Company in Washington, D.C. They were an actuarial consulting company, and I was again in the internal accounting department. I was probably twenty-six or twenty-seven. I was still married, still struggling with Alan, kind of beginning to realize that he was not the right guy. He'd planned to go into the Foreign Service, but he failed the exam, and it was very demoralizing. He was just depressed and couldn't shake it. He couldn't get a regular job. I also saw us stuck financially. I thought, if I'm going to do anything about it, I'm going to have to achieve.

So I got a new job with more money. I kept achieving and going up and up. I didn't realize it at the time, but it was making things harder on our private life because I was succeeding and he wasn't. He thought that he was going to end up taking care of me, and I was going to be the housewife. That's what we both kind of signed on for.

But The Wyatt Company days were fun. They also became very alcoholic days. A big group of us would go out after work Monday through Thursday and drink and drug and have fun. It was mainly cocaine.

Alan would occasionally come along. But Alan would be also hitting on other women, and that was offensive [laughs], not just to me, but also to my friends because it was my friends he was coming with, and then he'd be up at the bar ordering a drink and hitting on somebody else.

Jack, who was my best buddy at work [and later became husband #2], would see how Alan was treating me, and he was horribly offended. So Jack and I got to be good friends, but just good friends; because I still thought Alan and I would somehow live happily ever after, which, of course, didn't happen.

Then my boss left The Wyatt Company. She and I were very close. Once she left, the company changed. It wasn't the fun bunch of us anymore. I started looking for another job.

I stayed in the accounting field, because that's what I knew. I got a job as an assistant controller for a nonprofit run by a Catholic priest. I thought, how wonderful this must be. It was a not-for-profit. It was a noble cause, providing low-cost loans for higher education because, at that time, you could get loans for your undergraduate degree but not your graduate degree.

Boy, was I naive. He was very crafty, very financially successful, and slightly unethical. He was putting together deals that were so complex that a lot of the money fell out of them and into his pockets. He had properties and accounts and crazy things happening all over the place, and the actual human beings that were trying to get these low-cost loans and trying to pay them off were really struggling. It was a real eye-opener for me. He was, I guess you could say, a Catholic-priest loan shark. I wasn't there very long. I think I was there for less than two years.

THE LEGACY AND LOVE OF MY GRANDPARENTS

During this time, my grandmother and grandfather on my mother's side, Madeline and Marion, the two that raised me, both died. My grandfather was the rock in the family when I was growing up. Physically, he was tall. He was big. He was quiet. He was the provider. He was just the central core when everybody else was going crazy around him.

They were childhood sweethearts. Their parents actually wrote a book together: His father and her father wrote a poetry book together, and because of the friendship of the two men, when the wives had their babies, Madeline and Marion were strolled around together.

They were six months apart. She was older than he was. But she was also very different from him. He was the quiet, stable rock, and she was the social butterfly. They didn't date right from the start, but eventually in high school, they got together, and it stuck. They were married fifty years. They still died too young. [Cries.]

And she did say that at one point, she tried to leave him, but in those days, you didn't leave your husband. She walked home—they lived in a small area in Baltimore. Nobody went very far away. She walked home to her mother. She had had it with Marion. Her mother said, "Go back to him. You don't do that. You go back to your husband."

She was more quiet and behind the scenes. She wasn't the one that got things done. My grandfather used to take her to three grocery stores because she figured out who had the best sales going on.

He had a stroke first. After my grandfather died, it was up to me. I taught my grandmother how to write a check. I taught her how to pay the bills. When she died, only six months later—I was just numb, and I couldn't cry. I remember my relatives all coming to me and saying, "Why aren't you crying? Why aren't you crying?"

They knew it was big, but I just didn't feel like I could do anything else. So now I've still got all of these pent-up tears I'm working off the rest of my life, I guess. [Laughing and crying at the same time.]

At the time, I was coming to realize that my marriage was screwed from the start. I mean, like I said, Alan was drinking. I should have known better. Before that, when he failed the Foreign Service exam and didn't know what to do with his life, I should have known better. I liked his family a lot, but he was just clearly not the right guy.

Alan had become a minority of my time. I had gotten strong enough to know that if I wanted to do anything, if I needed to do anything, I just didn't figure him in on it. I sat at home and did nothing, or I went out with my friends from work.

MY CAREER TAKES OFF AT ARTHUR ANDERSEN

Then I got the job at Arthur Andersen. I loved it. I was assistant controller for the internal offices, eleven offices in Washington, D.C.

That just sounded so impressive to me. At one point, I had twenty employees under me; our accounting department took care of several offices. I had somebody that took care of the reports. We had a whole room full of paper reports that were replenished every day. It's amazing to think of how many trees we killed back then. [Laughs.]

It was huge. And I was pretty darn proud of myself, considering I never took a single accounting course in college. So, basically, I was off and running, figuring it out as I went along.

The people there were beautiful and smart, and I really liked that job. Eventually it got kind of absurd, though, because in management there were a lot of meetings. I would have a meeting in my boss's office about things that he wanted me to do. I would walk back to my office, and my phone was ringing when I got back to my office, and he wanted to know how many of these things I had accomplished.

And then we realized, of course, we're having too many meetings. So, as a group, we had a meeting on meetings to determine how many meetings we should have. Meanwhile we're meeting instead of getting any of the work done. [Laughs.]

My first marriage lasted about eight years. We sold the house after much time and difficulty. Everything was settled and in place and dispersed, and by around November, I was ready to decide what I wanted to do. I knew I didn't want to be in D.C. anymore. I hated being in the cold weather all of the time.

My aunt Ruth was up in Wisconsin. I always vacationed up there with her—nice people, good food, roaring fires. I thought about going there. It would be a much simpler life than D.C. And then my best buddy from Wyatt, Jack, had moved down to Tampa, Florida. I thought, that might be fun, too.

FALLING CRAZY IN LOVE

But he and I had never even kissed yet. We'd been best friends for eight years and had never kissed! And to pick up and leave and go a thousand miles for somebody that you have never dated, not even once, seemed a little bit crazy. Then he came up to D.C. for a mutual friend's wedding, and I went with him, and we kissed for the first time, and I decided to be crazy for the first time in my life.

So I quit my job, and I gave them a month's notice. My boss said I was crazy. He said, "We'll give you time to think about it." [Laughs.]

For the first couple of weeks, my boss didn't believe I would go through with it. I had never done anything like that. Eventually he hired someone whom I could start to train to take over what I had been doing. And I came to Florida, to see whether or not Jim and I could date and hit it off. And we did.

And then I sold my house up there and bought a house in Florida. I was twenty-nine and didn't even know if I could have kids but knew that I wanted them, and Jack was like, "Fine, that's secondary. I've got you. We'll figure out the kid thing." We had started talking about, "Well, if we can't have kids, we'll adopt."

I got a job when I first got to Florida…I didn't know I was already pregnant. I knew I was moving down to be with Jack. I worked in the accounting department for a very small legal firm. I found out I was pregnant a few months later. So then we got married in the backyard with a justice of the peace that we didn't even know. Each of us imported our best friend, and just the four of us stood in the backyard.

STRIVING TOWARD THE AMERICAN DREAM

Our thought process was that, if we could do this all on one income, with two incomes, we could get a fifteen-year mortgage on the house. We could pay it off fast. We could have the financial flexibility to send our kids to private school, if we wanted to. We could certainly have enough money by the time that they were going to college that we wouldn't have a mortgage, and everything would be good. But [laughs] what happened was, *I* got the job. *I* got the mortgage. *I* got the house I've been in for twenty-four years now.

I was thirty. I know with Aiden, it wasn't a high-risk pregnancy, but by the time I got to Rachel, the next one, two years later, they did an amnio, and with the other two kids, they considered me an old mom. [Laughs.]

Then I stayed at home. Jack was going to be the one that was working and supporting us, and I was going to be the housewife. But Jack didn't have the career stability or growth to support what we had in mind. Then we had another kid, and there was certainly more financial need. So we started to figure out what I could do, short of going back to work and without having to pay for daycare.

So I started picking up accounting clients privately. Meanwhile, Jack was doing computer programming, and recruiters were calling him, and I was answering the phone, so I started making arrangements for new gigs for Jack, acting as his agent. This was before cellphones.

A world we didn't know existed fell into our laps, with me taking messages and making deals behind the scenes. A programmer friend of Jack's was saying, "Damn, my wife won't even pass on a message. [Laughs.] Can we get your wife to take care of this for me?"

So I did. I got his friend placed in a job, and I got a fee for it. I started a recruiting business as a stay-at-home mom. It was called Employment Services. Jack came up with the name. I did the accounting for it, and we set up articles of incorporation. We had the two of us as our only employees, and we stated that our employees had 100 percent paid childcare. So all of our childcare was being written off through the corporation. We paid ourselves as little as possible, and we did creative things to make it work.

We did this for a couple of years. When I was pregnant with third one, we realized I wasn't really making enough money on straight commission, and I wanted the stability of a salary. So I started looking for another job.

CMC, the Computer Management Consultant Company, had paid me my first fee for that first friend of Jack's. I'd developed friendships with recruiters that were now calling on a regular basis. They were saying, "You'd be great at this." By the time our fourth child was born, they needed somebody, so they hired me.

I worked at CMC for over ten years. CMC was family-owned and relatively small. They got some pretty big deals though; for example, with Price, Waterhouse, and Coopers. So, for a while, it was fantastic. But even though I loved them all, some of them were not competent. I had to do everything if I wanted anything done right. I learned a lot. It was great. I worked there through lots of good times and bad times.

MY JOB SAVED MY LIFE WHILE MY DAUGHTER BATTLED CANCER

When our daughter, Rachel, was four, she was diagnosed with leukemia. It was very treatable, but still, our lives were taken over by getting her to the hospital on time when she needed it, and she had to be there at minimum weekly. At maximum, she was there for a couple of months at a time. We had no relatives. It was just Jack and me, juggling jobs and kids and keeping us all together.

My CMC coworkers brought meals to us. I got a laptop so I could work from the hospital and still take care of Rachel. So we managed to have dinners at the hospital every night. Rachel got all of the chemo that she needed. We met a wonderful bunch of people through all of that.

I really appreciated that job. I could do it anywhere with an Internet connection and a phone. And there weren't the kind of deadlines that there were in accounting. In accounting, you had the end of the month, and you had payroll, and you had deadlines. In recruiting, if you didn't make your deadlines, there were no federal penalties. There were just bigger consequences.

Rachel was in treatment for two-and-a-half years. Jack was somewhat helpful through that. I was working, and he was not. He was in-between gigs. During our marriage, Jack worked about 40 to 60 percent of the time. And he tried to be Hospital Dad, but he didn't really have the temperament for that.

THE LOVE OF MY LIFE TURNED TO ALCOHOL, DRUGS, PROSTITUTES—AND VIOLENCE

While I was working in recruiting, Jack was working as a programmer. All was going well, but he just couldn't let the happiness be, or grow, for whatever reason. I think alcohol was the crux of his problem, but he let it lead to much worse drugs. He let it destroy his life.

Because our lives were attached to his, we all went down until I got the strength to separate our lives from his. He imploded and started doing stupider and stupider things to where he ended up going crazy and in jail and homeless.

It was just before Aiden's bar mitzvah that things really came to a head. I didn't see it coming. We knew Jack was an alcoholic, but he'd stopped drinking. He was doing community service, going into jails, helping other people. He was in therapy because he knew he needed that as well; he was actually seeing two different therapists. We were behaving as a family, going places as a family. We were working. I thought everything was great.

At that time, my oldest was twelve. We had been through cancer by then. Rachel was ten, Gabrielle was nine, and Nate was eight. And Jack bought some crack cocaine. I didn't realize how bad he was getting. He also was working out and decided to get some steroids. He started going crazy and getting more and more erratic, and it got scary.

I wanted to believe in him. It was like almost overnight, things were fine, he'd been my best friend for all these years, and then, all of a sudden, I didn't recognize him and didn't understand what was going on. This had to be a temporary blip. Once we figured it out, we'd be fine. But one night just before Hanukkah and Christmas, he got scary to the point where I called the police.

He did not hit me, but he got up in my face, nose to nose with scary angry eyes. At that point, he had been working out. So he was completely muscle-bound. I never, ever, before that felt threatened by him. He could be angry at everybody else. Everybody else in the world was stupid, but I was always his one person that he could talk to. That was a heavy weight on me. It wasn't always a good thing; but I had never seen him turn angry at me like that. It was scary.

I HAD TO CALL THE COPS ON MY HUSBAND

He had just been mean to the kids at dinner, just totally out of character. He loved his kids. He wasn't always great, but—I said, "Don't you think you should—is there someone I can call? Can I call a sponsor for you?" and he was like, "No, if you feel scared, you call 911!" and I did.

And the cops came out. I think that was Halloween. And Aiden was dressed up like his dad, like a programmer, for Halloween. Jack ran away before the cops got there, and then he came back.

The cops talked to us and asked whether or not I wanted to press charges, and I said, "No. I don't know what's going on, but this has got to be a temporary blip. This isn't the guy that I've known for twenty years. Please, no;" because if we got something permanently on-record right there, I feared for HRS [Health and Rehabilitative Services] taking the kids. I feared for Jack's record.

So the cops left. They wished us luck, and, unfortunately, something else happened again. It was an argument over laundry. Jack pushed me.

He pushed me out of the way, trying to put his laundry into the washing machine. I guess I fell down and got scraped a little bit. It's not like he hit me. He didn't break anything. He was never primarily a physically abusive guy, but it was just—I knew that his attitude had changed, and then it was the first touch that landed me with a scrape on my arm. And I said, "OK, I'm going to use this as an excuse to get you out of here," and I called them again.

I took a picture of it, because I knew it would fade fast. I didn't even bruise, but I had to do something. I couldn't ignore it that time. I realized by then, the kids were being affected by these events. Aiden started showing bad behavior and got kicked out of school. I got him into a new school and got all of the kids into therapy.

The therapist said, "Hey, I can keep seeing your kids every day of the week, if you want to keep bringing them out here; but until the home life changes, nothing's going to change."

There was a more extreme event one night, where Jack grabbed me by the back of the hair and held up a baseball bat and tried to bash my head in. [Cries.] When I went to sleep, I had my phone in my hand under the pillow so he couldn't see it. He was pacing around the room, talking about how he could kill me, and how he could hide the body.

Then I finally went and got a restraining order against him. So he was in jail when Aiden got bar-mitzvahed at age thirteen. We didn't have to worry about him showing up and making a scene. But Aiden also didn't have his father at his bar mitzvah. By then, none of us had his father. I didn't know what happened to him. This was all within a couple of months, you know? I lost my best friend and I got this crazy person. I didn't know what was going on.

One night during this time, he came in and threw over a chair, and I scooped the kids out of bed and went to a friend's house for the night. He was suicidal. He was a danger to himself and others. His therapist talked him into going into the emergency room to pick up a prescription.

Jack is a very smart guy. So I got to think a part of him knew what he was doing, but he walked into the emergency room to get a prescription for an antidepressant, and because it was Christmas Eve, he couldn't get it from the pharmacist or whatever in the regular way.

And they said, "OK, Mr. Kalderon, walk through the door over here, and we'll get this for you," but, each time, he was walking behind a locked door. By the time he realized, they had to restrain him. They had big guys holding him down. On Christmas Day, we came to see him in the psychiatric ward, and he was just an angry caged animal and just spewing such vile things. I regret taking the kids there to see him.

I first found out what was going on when they let him out four days later. It wasn't just the steroids. It was that he was doing crack cocaine. [Pauses. Takes a breath.]

That's the first time that I knew that he was doing crack cocaine. And apparently that's the hardest thing to quit, the most personality-changing. I had no idea that was something he—I should have known, in hindsight. If you're an addict, you're going to be an addict looking for something stronger and stronger, but I had no idea that he would go that far, and he did, and he was.

JACK FELL APART, AND I HAD TO KEEP THE REST OF US TOGETHER

He lost his job at that point, too, because he was saying all of these crazy things about wanting to kill people at work, too. He had started obsessing on a girl at work. There had never been any other woman, ever. And now he was obsessing on this girl at work, and another girl at AA, but he wasn't doing anything about it.

So, in the months following his release, when we found out about the crack, things just kept going downhill: There was a woman that gave him crack. Then there was the therapy appointment after that, when he told me about the prostitutes that he was seeing. It was all so confused in my head.

In the middle of all this, I was still just in awe that it was even all happening. I got him out of the house. I got the restraining order. I got to buy us some time. He was in jail. We could get some breathing room and some space. He went in and out of jail a couple of times, but the restraining order kept him away, and it was months that he was away, but I was still miserable, not knowing where he was.

At that point, he was living on the streets. He had a car—a car that he loved, a Trans Am that he'd special ordered. He managed to keep the car longer than he kept the family, it seemed. But eventually he ended up losing that as well. He sold it for drug money or something.

He was always trying to get a clean start. So I tried to do that, too. I don't know. There were lots of ups and downs, but still it was just so hard to believe.

A year went by. At one point, I took him back in again and really quickly realized that was wrong. I tried to get another restraining order, and the judge said no. The judge said, "You let him back in again. You're clearly not afraid of him."

Then I was really stuck because, when I called the cops to say, "What can I do now?" they said, "You can't do anything. The house may be in your name, but you're married. If he's there, we can't remove him."

So then I had to get a divorce to be able to keep him away from us. We had been married for fifteen years. I had to trick him into the divorce because he did not want it. He wanted to see the kids. But by then I realized that any interaction with the kids with him was bad for them.

THEN MY KIDS BEGAN TO NOSEDIVE, TOO

The kids were being affected. They were all in therapy. Aiden started to be a tyrant and really enjoyed it. He was terrorizing his [siblings]. He was the oldest. He had his father's name. And so he somehow identified with the idea that "all Aiden Jack Kalderons are crazy."

And he was doing things to [his siblings] that I wasn't believing: Rachel said that he tried to burn down her bedroom. He didn't burn down the house; there was no burn mark, but she was convinced. And I couldn't tell the difference between siblings blaming siblings for things and reality. You know, I'd walk into the room, and they're nowhere near each other, and Rachel's crying, "Ow, don't hurt me! Ow, don't hurt me!" like kids do.

I didn't believe it for a long while, unfortunately, when he really was probably tormenting them. But Aiden also was with multiple therapists, and eventually I had the same sort of dilemma with him that I did with his dad: What am I going to do with this kid that is a train wreck? There was some physical harm, but he never left a bruise, never broke an arm. If he did any of the things physically to them that I didn't see, that they claimed, he did it really artfully; but I think it was more mental torment.

In terms of diagnoses, Jack was very clearly depressed. Aiden had many diagnoses. I think ODD, oppositional defiant disorder,[4] was the most appropriate diagnosis for Aiden. OCD[5] was also applied to Aiden, but I don't think as accurately.

I think all of the kids had anxiety and PTSD [post-traumatic stress disorder].[6] At that time, I knew Aiden was also doing a lot of marijuana, but I knew a lot of fifteen-year-olds were doing that. I didn't worry so much whether or not he was going to be an alcoholic at that point. I thought the stronger problem was his identity with his dad and that craziness that he saw so strongly in his dad and thought he was going to go down that same path.

I had no family in Tampa. The summer after his bar mitzvah, Aiden went up north to be with my relatives for a month because I thought, "What on earth am I going to do all summer long? He's now thirteen. He's too old for camps in the summer, too young to get a job, and he's going to do nothing but cause trouble all summer long."

So that summer, he did half-camp and half-relatives. By the next year, I didn't know what to do with him. I had him talk to the rabbi. The rabbi said, "Hey, what if we had an angel that could pay to have him go someplace that could help him?"

I had cut off my thumb by then, trying to take care of household chores. Aiden scared me—he threatened to smash it while it was still healing, so when the rabbi offered to rescue us by giving us the money to get us some breathing space and get him some help, finally I said, "Okay, let's do this."

---

4. ODD is a condition in which a child displays an ongoing pattern of uncooperative, defiant, hostile, and annoying behavior toward people in authority, disrupting family and school activities. Many children with ODD also have other behavioral problems, such as attention-deficit/hyperactivity disorder, learning disabilities, mood disorders (e.g. depression), anxiety disorders, or conduct disorder.

5. Obsessive-compulsive disorder (OCD) is a potentially disabling illness that traps people in endless cycles of recurring and distressing thoughts, fears, or images (obsessions) they cannot control. The anxiety leads to an urgent need to perform certain rituals or routines (compulsions). People with OCD may be aware that their obsessions and compulsions are senseless or unrealistic, but they cannot stop them.

6. Post-traumatic stress disorder (PTSD), once called shell shock or battle fatigue syndrome, is a serious condition that can develop after a person has experienced or witnessed a traumatic or terrifying event, such as a sexual or physical assault, the unexpected death of a loved one, an accident, war, or natural disaster. Families of victims can also develop PTSD, as can emergency personnel and rescue workers. Most people will have reactions that may include shock, anger, nervousness, fear, and even guilt. These reactions are common. For a person with PTSD, however, these feelings continue and even increase, becoming so strong that they keep the person from living a normal life.

Aiden was fifteen when I let him go get the help he needed at a residential treatment center for at-risk teens in Utah. My dad came down to help. We had the police standing by in case he didn't go willingly, but Aiden knew that what he was doing had to come to an end at some point. So by the time I pulled him aside one morning and said, "Hey, instead of driving you to school today, I'm going to drive the two of us to the airport, and we're going to go to Utah," he went willingly. He said OK.

HOW MY JOB HAS KEPT ME SANE, AND KEPT MY FAMILY FED

In the years since I've been divorced, I've thanked God that I fell into the recruiting field. This career has put me in touch with such wonderful, supportive people. In the accounting field, there's no commission. I was always nervous in sales and commission, but since I've been in the recruiting field, it's a base plus commission. So I've got the stability and I've also got the ability to make enough money to support us.

My kids think I'm a workaholic! In the good years, I made six figures in IT. In the current years in the healthcare industry, I was grateful to get less than half when I took this job, just to have a base again. I make a $40K base plus commission. So the commission wavers, too. I've earned over $60K. But now I'm going down these last three years, because the industry has gone down. But we've always had food.

My grandmother grew up with the Depression mentality of, "We store. We buy on sale. We buy in bulk. We buy smartly."

I learned from her. I've redone the mortgage a couple of times. I bought smartly, but that initial plan to pay it off in fifteen years is long gone. I think I've got more than fifteen years left now. So, I've gotten money out of the house. And, for a while, I had excellent credit, which I totally destroyed through Aiden's Utah time, but, you know, I did what I needed to do, and, one thing after another, it's been able to work.

WHAT I STRUGGLE WITH: WANTING TO TAKE CARE OF EVERYONE

I also know my weakness clearly. It's come up often: I'm a softie. I'm like this in my professional as well as my personal life. So I can be inefficient with my time. I can spend a lot of time quickly with the assistants in my field. There's currently a glut in the market of PTAs [physical therapy assistants] and CODAs [Commission on Dental Accreditation assistants]. And I'm a softie for those people. They get on the phone, and they can't get work. I spend way too much time with a bleeding heart [laughs], trying to place people.

The same thing happened in IT after the dot.com bubble burst. These guys were all working as bag boys, and they would call me up looking for jobs. I would listen to them, and I was compassionate, and I would do what I could for them.

I'm like my grandmother Madeline in that way. I'd like to carry on her legacy. I think I just want to take care of people. Just hearing her name makes me cry. I miss her so much. I'd like to be like her. My grandparents had what I've spent a lifetime wanting. I don't know if I have time now for a 50-year marriage, but...

THE AMERICAN NIGHTMARE

If I had all the money in the world, I would be volunteering for lots of different things. During my unemployment years, when IT imploded, and Jack was gone, and Aiden was in Utah, I lost my last IT job. So I was actually totally unemployed, getting unemployment, getting food stamps.

This was just before Maxim, about seven years ago. I knew I had to do something to not go crazy with nothing to do every day. I had to fill my days with some structure. So I looked for places that I could do things to make the world a better place. I started volunteering.

I volunteered with cancer support groups, a lot with them. During the cancer years with Rachel, one of the groups would take the kids away for the weekend. That was the only break that I got. It saved my life. So we helped with their fundraiser, a fashion show. I organized the silent auction.

I also fostered dogs. That forced me to get up in the morning and get out and get walking because someone's got to do it, and it was my project, not the kids'. We fostered about a half-dozen dogs and got them into happy homes. I volunteered in the office at the Tampa Theater, which is a historical landmark in Tampa that I love. I volunteered on the library board for the county. I also volunteered with Big Cat Rescue. And I was on our temple's religious committee.

Despite everything, I would still say that I am an optimist. I found that every time things were really bad, it was just that I didn't know that what was coming around the corner would be really good. [Cries.]

So when cancer came and that was really bad, it turned out to be a wonderful blessing. I met great people. Rachel's alive. We're all much better off for it. We had opportunities we would never have had.

When Jack was going through his meltdown and I was losing him, it was awful. But I've built a great life since then, and done such wonderful traveling. I've done things I would never have done if I were still married to him. So I just don't know what's coming around the corner next. When life seems bad, I can't get stuck in pessimism.

I get to actually take responsibility and direction for where I'm going and choose the jobs, not to accommodate my spouse, but for what I want. I don't have to be dependent on anyone else. I can choose to do volunteering or whatever I want with my time, and to go out with people that I want to. I'm not accommodating to anybody else, and I think that's good. Now I have the opportunity to figure out what *I* like.

MAYBE NOW, IT'S MY TURN

Turns out, I've always loved the water. So I have my kayak, and I can take it wherever I want and put it in the water. I like boating. I like to travel. Lately I've been traveling more. Now that my kids are old enough, they no longer need a babysitter for me to leave them alone. My passport still has blank pages on it, and I'd love to fill it up.

I want to clean up the house and maybe even eventually have the opportunity to pay it off or sell it and live someplace different.

I used to like crocheting and sewing and stuff like that, but now I have old-people eyes, and that's no longer as enjoyable because I just can't see it as well. I did that kind of stuff for years and years and loved it. I made the kids' outfits; I've got pictures of them all dressed up in clothes I made. My great-grandmother and my great-grandfather were tailor and seamstress. I have Rachel's old sewing machine in my attic and her dressmaker's model in my bedroom. Gabrielle used it to make an outfit just last month.

I'm trying to meet more adults for "un-kid-related events" in Tampa. So I go out to dinner with Meetup groups. It would be nice to "meet up" with a guy that could be a date and a relationship, but I haven't found that yet. [Laughs.] I haven't given up yet, either. I would like a marriage like the one my grandparents had.

I've given my kids the stability that I've wanted to give them, and now I'm not trying to walk on eggshells or accommodate anybody else's thoughts about where things are going.

They've had one home. All of them have been born since I've been in that home. They've had one mom who's consistently been able to put food on the table. They've never known really any sort of financial deprivation, although they, of course, are kids, and feel that they didn't get everything they wanted. They've been well cared for and stable and they've always had that. So I'm sure they'll look back one day and realize that . . .

The American Dream? I don't know. I mean, the American dream of escalating your career and having a house and a stable family? It hasn't exactly come true for me.

Maybe I'll have another chance to find someone that's more in alignment with what I want. And when I'm a very old lady and passed from this earth, I want to leave behind happy, healthy, responsible, respectful kids who will hopefully do the same.

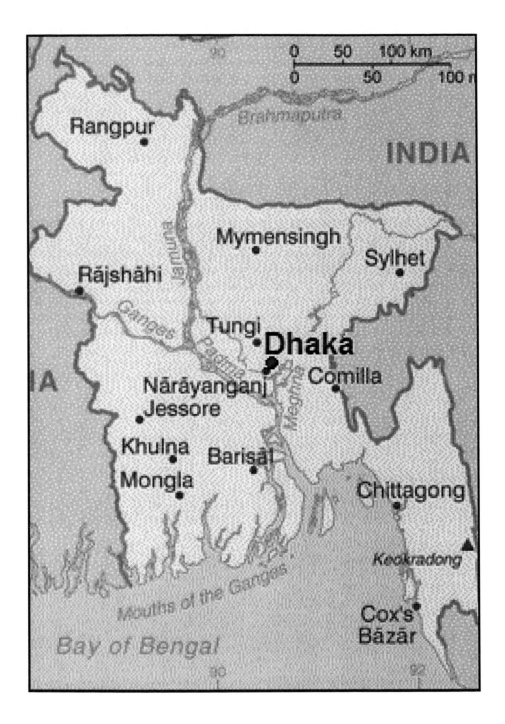

MUHAMMAD

RICKSHAW PULLER

DHAKA, BANGLADESH

Editor's note: The soil on which fifty-three-year-old Muhammad stands was once a part of India. It became partitioned off as part of Pakistan in 1947, and won independence as Bangladesh ("The nation of Bengal") in 1971. Muhammad remembers well the Bangladesh Liberation War, because he was ten and already working to support his mother and siblings. His father had divorced his first wife to marry his mother in the hope of bearing a son; but then he died young, leaving Muhammad as the man of the family.

"I had to carry the whole family on my shoulders," Muhammad recalls. He worked all day as a sharecropper on someone else's farm, and got paid one meager meal—rice and vegetables—each night. He would then take that meal home to share with his mother, brothers, and sisters.

One of the world's most densely populated countries, with 162 million people living in an area the size of New York state, the brand-new democracy then underwent decades of searing poverty and famine, political turmoil, and military coups.

Muhammad realized the only way to find work was to move from his small rural village in the lush countryside, to the dusty capital city of Dhaka, population fifteen million. Here, he could rent a rickshaw on the cheap, especially if he got a fake license—which the vast majority of the city's rickshaw pullers do—at $7/year[1] rather than $500. To buy a new rickshaw would cost up to $1,000.

"The job pays well," he says at first. Then, he soon corrects himself: What he means by "well" is that his family of nine can afford their one-room rent in a Dhaka slum and can eat two meals a day.

An estimated 500,000 people—some say they are all men—pedal their bicycle-rickshaw taxi-carts around Dhaka. Originating as a human-pulled cart in Japan around 1869, the cycle-rickshaw evolved in the 1930s in Singapore and India. The rickshaw emigrated to the United States at the Seattle World's Fair in 1962.

Petrol-powered auto rickshaws, prevalent next-door in India, were banned by the Bangladeshi government in 2002, due to pollution. About a decade later, a company that had been marketing batteries for cycle-rickshaws brought them into Bangladesh.

Muhammad saved for and purchased one. He was thrilled to have a bit easier time maneuvering his cart and passengers; but the combined drain on the city's electric grid compelled the government to ban these rickshaw batteries just a few months later. Drivers were back to thigh-power only.

I met Muhammad not atop his rickshaw, but in the office of a school where his two youngest children are enrolled. Launched by a 21-year-old just out of law school, Korvi Rakshand, in 2007, JAAGO Foundation (jaago.com.bd, a partner of SFF, skees.org) has expanded to 350 employees assisted by 20,000 volunteers, providing free education for 2,200 children in thirteen schools.

Ironically, in a job where muscle- and lung-power wield great influence, a great portion of rickshaw pullers smoke cigarettes. Not Muhammad. He exudes honor, pedaling his way through long days in a city where the air stands still and the sun beats down at up to 118 degrees in summer months, and the rains flood the streets until only the top rims of his bicycle wheels appear above muddy waters during the annual monsoons.

He's plagued by headaches and feels far older than his 53 years. He can't see any way out of this life for himself, but he feels certain that, by becoming educated, his kids will be able to create a life of prosperity and choice.

HOW I LANDED IN THIS JOB

My name is Muhammad. I am 53 years old. I live with my wife and other people in my home. I have been driving a rickshaw for twenty years in my life.

Before I drove a rickshaw, I used to work in a factory for six years that was a [textile] washing plant, producing dyes and garments. I used to work in there, but the salary wasn't sufficient enough to run my family. And now I am riding the rickshaw, and I am getting the proper amount that I need to run my family.

---

1. The Bangladeshi taka (100 taka = $1.29) has been converted to USD throughout this chapter.

I never had schooling in my life, because my father was not there. My father had to marry twice: My mother was the second wife. The first wife had four daughters, and then they got divorced. My father died when I was four years old.

If I started to tell the story of my life, I would start crying…[His voice trembles.]

At age five, child labor began for me. My mother, my wife, and myself have all been through struggles.

I started working before the Liberation War. I used to work on farms for other people. The deal was this: no salary, and food only once a day, at night—rice and vegetables. I used to go back to my home and share that meal with my whole family.

After the war, it was tough to find a job anywhere. We used to have only one meal a day. I came to Dhaka, started pulling rickshaws, and got married. Life was still very hard.

MY TYPICAL WORKDAY

The whole day I spend pulling the rickshaw. In the morning, I start from 7a.m, until 7p.m, for twelve hours. Often I ride until 10p.m and the next morning, I get up and do it again. It's a very long day, but it's necessary to work all day to make enough money for my family to eat. I earn on a daily basis. It depends on who is riding on the rickshaw. My expenses are high. My profit is 300 to 400 taka ($4-5) each day. I also hire [rent] my rickshaw from the rickshaw owner for $1 a day.

When I drive, I just go around in my neighborhood, to easy places. Most of the time, I become sick, riding this rickshaw. It's like, yesterday, I was very sick.

My guess is that most of the rickshaw pullers, like me, have come from the outlying villages. I'd guess there are 500,000 pullers. The legal limit is far less: 100,000 to 200,000.

There is a rule in the number of rickshaws. Supposing my [license] number is five: There is another number five in the next town over. If I had to get a legal license, I would have to chase after the police and then pay $200-250. For a duplicate or counterfeit, it only costs around $7.

How do I compare with all these other rickshaw pullers? I usually ride very safely. If a part on my rickshaw is damaged, I have to pay for that. The difference is, I drive very slowly and carefully, and I avoid traffic jams. The rickshaw is not mine, so I have to be careful.

MY JOB IS MAKING ME SICK

The hard part is, I just have my breakfast in the morning, and then I have my dinner, and in-between that I don't have anything at all, which makes me really weak and sick. The whole day—the hot weather, the hard work—that's what's making me sick. Lack of food. Sometimes I become cold. I am 53 years old, so I have a lot of headaches.

Sometimes, my head aches, and I have memory loss, and so I forget where I am going, and I can't find my way home. I reach home very late, sometimes.

Some years ago, I became sick. I hurt my right knee. I had some savings, but I had to take loans from some other people. Now, I am almost clear: Twenty years later, I owe one lakh [$1,286]. I save about $6 a month, and I pay $6-12 per month on my loans. I really have no idea how much interest I've been charged.

I have no savings, because I took a lot of loans from banks and people, so I am in big debt. My head still goes spinning all around. I have headaches. My legs hurt a lot; my cartilage is decaying every day.

I ride the rickshaw just for the expenses of my family. If I miss one day, we don't eat that day.

WHERE I LIVE

I have lived for many years with my wife and seven children in one rented room that is very small. Now the older ones are married and just two children remain.

We have no balcony. It is smaller than this room [the JAAGO school office, about 8'x10']. My building has eleven rooms, with one family in each room. We have a shared kitchen and two common latrines for the apartment where we all bathe and use the toilet. We have electricity at home, and we have mobile phones, too.

[He puts one hand on top of the other wrist, on his lap. Muhammad has a kind face. He is perfectly groomed, with well-trimmed hair and just a few gray hairs sprinkled through his goatee.]

Today, I am looking very fresh. But every day, I would have a torn *lungi* [the traditional male skirt] and torn shirts. I would be full of dust from head to toe.

MY FAMILY

I have a lot of family members: my wife and seven children. My elder son, Sohel, is age eighteen. He studied until the eighth grade, and for the poverty of the family he started working at a pipe factory. The eldest daughter is twenty-eight.

One son and one daughter still live with me. My two youngest children study at the free school for street children here in the slum where we live. The school is called JAAGO and it's just next to my house. See the rooftops out that classroom window? That's my building. My younger son, Sujon, is fourteen years old. He studies at JAAGO. He intends to study hard and go to college, and then become a doctor: a dentist. My daughter Mukta is twelve. She wants to go to college, too.

My wife, Julikha, is a housewife. She's pretty, like her name. I've been married for over thirty years. It's a long time. My mother brought the proposal to me, and I liked her, and she liked me. So, we got married.

My father died when I was very young, and my mother had to struggle very hard to take care of us. I was the only son. I had an arranged marriage. My mother is no longer alive, but she arranged the marriage for me. I married at age twenty-one. It was probably not a love marriage: I just saw her and married her; but now we have a good marriage, and there is love.

My wife is a very nice lady. She supports me 100 percent, in every way. She teaches the Quran [Islamic bible] to children in the slum, ages six to seven. She earns very little, just $2-5 each month.

As my wife earns a little bit, so I give her all my money, and she manages it. It's easy to manage our finances because of her. She studied until twelfth grade, and she studied Arabic.

I never got a chance to study at all, in my life. I wish I could read and write. Then I could do many things. When I was a kid, I used to want to study accounting and work in a bank. I had a dream of studying and working in banks and offices. Everything related to money, I would like to do.

Now we are off from a lot of troubles, so now my family has two meals a day; sometimes three and sometimes only one, but usually two.

MY JOB WAS EASIER, BRIEFLY

For a short period, I had a battery in my rickshaw. When I had a motor in my rickshaw, I earned a little more, about $8 per day. I brought home $3 after expenses.

I had my battery for about five months, but I had to remove it, because the government said to get rid of it. All the rickshaw pullers with batteries were using up too much electricity in Dhaka each night when we were recharging them. So, they made the batteries illegal.

I WOULDN'T WISH THIS JOB ON ANYONE

It's very tough work. Nobody would want to do this. I hope you will promote the work of a rickshaw puller [in this book]. It's the toughest job you would ever do, but it's an easy way to earn money. Not everyone can do this.

I'd prefer any job that would give the same amount of money as this—in a factory, in the garment industry, anything. I really want a motor for my rickshaw, because that would be easier.

It's all mental strength. If I don't work, my family won't have any food. Physically I am very weak, but all I want is for my children to get educated. I might look physically strong, but inside, I am weak. If I get any time to rest I will fall asleep, even if just for one to two minutes.

I would prefer any job that's not so physically hard. My body is in pain when I get home.

MY DREAMS FOR THE FUTURE

I have dreams, but it all depends on the Almighty, if he wants to make my life good and better. I would like my sons to be educated, to be in a good position. I want them not to be like me—not to have to work so hard. Until my sons get educated, I have to do the same work every day. Everything is aching. Everything in me hurts.

Rather than pulling the rickshaw, I'd rather do anything else. It's a tough operation. I would prefer a job that would be easier, at my age. All I want is to have my children get an education. I want them not to have to work so hard, like me. I want them to be a good person. We all wish that we can fulfill all the dreams of our children, but we are very poor, so we cannot do much.

As a father, we try. We brought them here and JAAGO School is helping them a lot. My daughter wants to be a doctor. We need help from a lot of people, for that [to happen]. I believe my children will become a very big success in their lives.

I thank you, and I hope you will share my story. I've never been outside of Bangladesh, but most of us rickshaw pullers come from hometown villages, and so we've seen more of the country than just Dhaka. We hope our sons and daughters can travel to the United States and visit you, and travel to many other countries as well.

I've said everything I need to say. I hope our life gets better, and better for our children, too.

What would I say about my life? The whole thing is a struggle. The only thing I wish is for my children's education. My life is at an end.

FARMING, FOOD & ANIMALS

• •

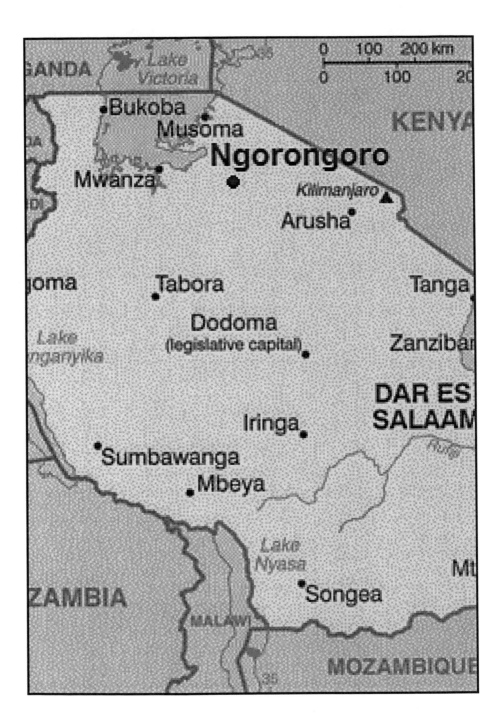

WANTAY

AFRICAN WARRIOR

NGORONGORO, TANZANIA

Editor's note: Wantay Mosses Irmakesen grew up in a round mud hut in a *boma* (family complex) with one father, four mothers, and twenty-nine shared children. Living on wildlife preservation land in Ngorongoro Conservation Area (NCA)[1] in Tanzania,[2] East Africa, he compares the fate of his Maasai[3] tribe to that of Native Americans relegated to reservations. Until adulthood, he lived his entire life just temporarily camping on his ancestral land.

At age 15, Wantay became a Maasai African warrior. He's also one of the few

---

1. Ngorongoro Crater, a 2.5-million-year-old volcanic crater, was named one of the Eight Natural Wonders of the World in 2013. It has Earth's largest unbroken caldera (volcanic crater), with 30,000 animals including the "Big Five" safari favorites: the lion, leopard, rhino, elephant, and Cape buffalo. Read about the history of the crater: pbs.org/edens/ngorongoro/fiery.html, and see the wildlife of Wantay's homeland: youtu.be/wBwP62cXW2E.

2. People call Tanzania "the soul of Africa" and Ngorongoro "Africa's Garden of Eden." This is where the earliest archeological evidence of hominids was discovered: 3.6 million-year-old footprints that represent, to many, the cradle of human evolution.

3. The East-African Maasai tribe of about 1 million people live a semi-nomadic, subsistence economy in Tanzania and Kenya. Read about their lifestyle and customs: maasai-association.org/maasai.html.

people on Earth today who has killed a lion, legally, with nothing but a spear, a shield, and a few other skinny teenage boys to help him get the job done. Training for ten years prior, he'd learned to build fences around the *boma* or circle of mud huts occupied by all of his father's wives and children. He herded the clan's sheep, goats, and cows, dodging hyenas and lions—and his father's hand, if he lost any of their precious herd. Puberty brought three tests of his manhood: decorative cutting of both earlobes, burning of his right thigh, and circumcision—all performed without anesthetic and without the slightest twitch.

"You had to look straight ahead and not cry; not make a sound; not react in the slightest," Wantay recalls. He passed the tough-guy tests, and then matriculated to the lion project, a shared hunt with his age-group cohort of about five males. He was a full-fledged warrior by age fifteen.

The prize for succeeding? Not only did he get a lion's paw to decorate his spear, Wantay also could now grow a long strand of hair, wear a ceremonial headdress made of many species of birds he hunted himself, and enjoy the company of girlfriends, who were forbidden up until then.

"The lion is as smart as men, and can maneuver through the bushes faster than a human being," says the Maasai Association. The lion Wantay killed[4] weighed over 400 pounds—more than four times as much as he did.

"Well, I didn't throw the first spear," Wantay protests, as though he wants to convince me that he's not all that fierce. "I was like the fourth," he laughs. "We celebrated for two months in my village. People still talk about it, so many years later. They point at me and say, 'That's the man who killed a lion.'"

Wantay's American-born wife, Tina, who lives with him and their five-year-old daughter in Karatu, Tanzania, chimes in, "It's kind of like getting your Ph.D. in *Warrior*."

I met Wantay by accident, when I wandered through Karatu, a small tourist town in the shadow of ancient volcanic mountain Oldenai and just about an hour's drive from two world-renowned safari parks, Ngorongoro and Serengeti.

My American eyes lit up at the words "Internet Café" and when I ducked inside, I discovered a treasure trove of good coffee and food, the only decent Internet service in the area, and a family of new friends: Wantay and Tina owned the place. Their Karatu café (now closed—they've moved to the countryside and started a new business[5]) became our refuge after long days of walking to visit local schools on the dusty roads.

We kept in touch, and their nonprofit organization AID Tanzania (aidtanzania. org) also became a partner of SFF (skees.org).

Wantay's American wife Tina grew up Libya and Iran, studied business at

---

4. These days, warriors don't kill lions; instead, they compete in athletic events such as sprinting, jumping, and club throwing. A video embedded in an article from the London's Daily Mail shows a few examples from Wantay's homeland in Tanzania: dailymail.co.uk/news/article-2895269/Maasai-warriors-armed-bows-arrows-slaughter-six-lions-repeated-attacks-livestock-Tanzania.html.

5. The Irmakesens run a four-wheeling adventure company that helps support their education nonprofit: facebook.com/4WheelingTanzania.

Columbia University, and then settled in Colorado—until she traveled to Africa and fell in love with a warrior. She accompanied Wantay to the interview and offered some insights that appear woven throughout his chapter.

Tina says that Wantay's education "has afforded him the opportunity to be straddling two cultures—his traditional lifestyle and then also a more modern lifestyle. He's been the liaison for his family to the outside world for a long time, as kind of a conduit." To stay connected to their relatives on Tina's side of the family, they spend time in the U.S. every year (mostly in Colorado and Oklahoma). Wantay gives talks in American schools about the Maasai life.

We conducted this interview in English. Wantay, who grew up speaking Maasai, later taught himself Swahili and English in order to advance his career in tourism and business. He speaks in a quavering, slightly raspy voice. He's left-handed, gentle, creative—not at all what you expect in a warrior—and the biggest surprise, to me, was that he's maybe Maasai's fiercest feminist.

"I love living in a community of all women," he says. "I love just to see the Maasai girls become educated." To this self-taught-warrior-turned-educator, the ideal world would have space for a mud hut and a cow, an iPhone and a university—all the richness of tradition blended with all the opportunity of now.

WHO I AM AND HOW I GOT MY NAME

My name is Wantay Irmakesen. I'm 39 years old. My birthday is April 6. I have been a Maasai tribal warrior, and I am now an elder. I am also cofounder of two nonprofits, AID Tanzania and Kiretono Resource Centre, and I am the managing director of an ATV [all-terrain vehicle] tour company, 4 Wheeling Tanzania. I have a wife, Tina, and we have a five-and-a-half-year-old daughter, Mara. We live on two acres in Karatu, near Arusha, Tanzania.

My middle name is Mosses. That's from the Old Testament. That's the one I use in all documents, like my passport and everything. Wantay is the name my mother gave me. Most people in the village and even in the town of Karatu, they call me Wantay.

I GREW UP IN A FAMOUS AFRICAN TRIBE WHOSE HOMELAND IS NO LONGER HOME

Wantay: I am one of twenty-nine children. I grew up in Tanzania. It's an East African country. There are five[6] East African countries: Tanzania, Kenya, Uganda, and Rwanda, and Burundi. In Tanzania, there is a place called Ngorongoro. That's where I grew up. That's the place where one of the very famous tribes called the Maasai live. That is my tribe. I am a Maasai.

I lived my whole life in what became a national park, before I was born. The Maasai used to live in the Serengeti. When the Serengeti became a national park, the government

---

6. Five countries comprise East Africa. There are 54 countries, 9 territories, and 2 unrecognized states, on the continent of Africa, which is the second-largest continent after Asia and has the second-largest global population, 1.2 billion, after India with 1.3 billion.

moved the Maasai[7] from Serengeti to Ngorongoro. That was in 1959. They gave the name that's called "conservation area." The Maasai, they're living on the land along with [wildlife] animals. That's my home place.

Tina: It's multi-use land with a three-pronged strategy of indigenous people, wildlife, and tourism.

Wantay: It's a very peaceful place with animals and people living in harmony. At least, it was like that when I was a little boy. The Ngorongoro Crater was caused by the volcano. It collapsed and created that big bowl. The Maasai used to live inside the crater with all the rhinos, like two hundred rhinos, were inside the crater with the Maasai people.

At that time, they didn't have any problems. The elders tell me there was a lot of grass, a lot of animals. There was no drought. They didn't have to sell their cows to get food from the farmers. They were able to depend entirely on the cows and get everything they needed to survive from them, like milk and meat. It's not like that now. Now, there's a lot of drought. And the Maasai, they don't have anything now.

THE COW IS YOUR FOOD, YOUR BANK ACCOUNT, YOUR EVERYTHING

For the Maasai, the cow is food. The Maasai depend everything on the cows. It's like their assets, their bank, you know?

But they don't have a sacred relationship with the cow, like what they do in India. They can slaughter or sacrifice the cows. For example, when the elder or the head of the family, the father dies, they slaughter really black cows—the really darkest black one. The Maasai think that this is very important. They use the oil from the meat of the cow, anoint the body, cover the body with the cowhide, and then they lay the body on top of the cow. And then when we come back the next morning, we don't see anything. The whole body got taken by the animals. We don't bury in our culture. We let the dead body be food for the animals.

As an elder now, this is what will happen to me when I die. My kid, my family, they're going to do the same thing. They're going to slaughter the cows, and then they're going to bury me like that.

FROM FERTILE GRASSLANDS TO DROUGHT AND MALARIA

Now, life is so different. The Maasai don't live in the crater. They got moved by the government to the top rim of the crater. So they live like maybe a mile, mile-and-a-half, away from the crater. There are no vehicles. You just have to walk everywhere: up to the road and down to the crater.

There is not enough rain. There is not enough grass for the cows. There are a lot of diseases for the cows. There are restricted areas and then the drought. Before, we may have had a little tiny place, but we had a lot of rain, so we had enough grass and enough

---

7. The relocation of the Maasai tribe has been compared to Native Americans being relegated to reservations. Read more about their forced move in National Geographic: ngm.nationalgeographic.com/ngm/0602/feature1/index.html.

water. But now there is a lot of drought. So even in the little place we have, there's not enough food for the cows.

There are a lot of diseases for the cows. For example, we had rinderpest.[8] Then there was a kind of disease that comes from the tick. And Rift Valley Fever happened about eight years ago. That made it so that the people couldn't even drink the milk from the cow. Any meat would also have infected and sickened the people.

So now, the Maasai have only a few cows to feed them. Let's say you have a family of ten wives, and maybe forty kids in the family, and you have like ten cows. That means you don't have enough food to feed the entire family, only for the milk and meat. You need to slaughter the cows in order to survive. Then there's not enough cows anymore.

It's getting very difficult. The population has grown; but meanwhile, with the small conservation area, it minimizes the people. You have to go to a certain place and there are certain places you're not supposed to go. More people, less land.

It used to be, if there weren't enough rain, you could move to where there was grass. But now there is more drought and you have to stay right there, so there's no grass.

Climate change is also an issue now. The weather has gotten so humid. My family lives at about 8,000 feet altitude, and they used to never get malaria, and now they're starting to get malaria. As it warms up, the higher altitudes are kind enough to the mosquitos, so they can get up there.

JUST ONE OF TWENTY-NINE CHILDREN

When I grew up in Ngorongoro, my father had four wives. I was one of twenty-nine children. We were all very close growing up, except for one of my younger brothers. We fought, you know? But recently we have become really good friends.

I think there are like four different names [i.e. different fathers or lineages] in our village. A clan size just depends. Some clans, they have few people, and some, like my clan, they have so many. It's almost an entire village, my clan.

My Maasai name is Wantay Oloi Terratoi Irmakesen. "Oloi" means "son of Terratoi." So Terratoi is my father's name, and Irmakesen is the clan name.

Growing up, we were hungry, a lot, but we were never poor.

We lived in Ngorongoro in a little mud hut, in the bush. It looked like an oval building. They build the building with sticks, and then they plaster it with the cow dung on the top, during the rain. When they see rain coming, they collect the cow dung, and they climb on the hut and plaster it with the cow dung while it's wet from the rain.

Inside the hut, it's tiny. It's like a one-bedroom. Everyone is together: people, babies, cows, everything. And inside that there were two beds: one for the elders and the warriors, and another bed for the women and kids.

---

8. Rinderpest, now eradicated, plagued Africa, Asia, and Europe until the beginning of the 21st century. It was a viral disease that impacted cloven-hoofed animals and led to widespread death of cattle: merckvetmanual.com/mvm/ generalized_conditions/rinderpest/overview_of_rinderpest.html. The tick disease he mentions is "bovine babesiosis" or "tick fever:" thecattlesite.com/diseaseinfo/196/bovine-babesiosis-redwater-tick-fever. Rift Valley Fever (RVF) virus, transmitted by mosquitos, hit East Africa hard in the early 2000s and, as Wantay points out, could make humans sick as well: cdc.gov/ncidod/dvrd/spb/mnpages/dispages/Fact_Sheets/Rift%20Valley%20Fever%20Fact%20Sheet.pdf.

They cooked inside the little hut. There was a little hole to let the smoke out. It was really smoky inside. There's also a little place for the baby cows and straw for the baby and the mother cow. So that's where we lived.

Tina: The central open area is smaller than this room. It's probably about 150-200 square feet.

Wantay: The hut was for the immediate family. So we also have what is called the *boma* (enclosure or village). For example, say the father has ten wives. The whole group of ten wives might have the huts around their boma. And then the ten wives each has seven to nine kids. So he might have like maybe forty or fifty kids, and he is responsible for everything.

Polygamy comes from the culture. The Maasai believe that if you have like a hundred wives and a lot of kids, then you are a rich man. If you are really poor, you might not have cows. You don't have anything to feed them, but you have the wives and kids. So they believe that you are a rich man. So that's why the Maasai, they have more than one wife.

Having more wives is actually a sign of status in the community. But, you can't marry more wives than you can take care of! [Laughs.]

Things are changing, but the Maasai are late [slow]. Some Maasai still do not believe in education. They're behind in life. That's why polygamy is still happening. While some say now, "We need [just] one wife," others still don't believe that if they had one wife, that would be good for them. So they still have more than one: ten, fifty, sixty. [Laughs.]

My brother-in-law has sixty-one wives. He married my sister. There's another one in my village that has thirty-two wives, and he home-schooled his children for their primary school education.

The really wealthy guys have the most.

So with polygamy, there is a surplus of men. That's why the Maasai, they have what they call "arranged marriage." For example, I can go to a wedding and arrange to marry the couple's future daughter, a girl that doesn't even exist yet. Maybe this guy has a wedding today, and he brought the wife, and I can bring the ring to the lady that says that, just in case you have a baby girl, that will be my wife. Marriage is a transaction, really.

So it might happen that they have all boys, and they don't have a girl, and I'll still be waiting for a wife. Maybe there are elders without a wife because there are no women available. Many men end up not getting married at all [due to the shortage of women], while other wealthy men have all the wives.

The men are an entire generation older—at least twelve years older than the wives. They don't know anything about the girl. There's no dowry; there's no gold ring. It's like anything will do: any ring, or a cowhide, or goat hide. Sometimes they may not even bring the ring. And there's no divorce in the Maasai tribe.

ONE WIFE IS ENOUGH FOR ME!

Now me, I have only one wife. [Laughs.] That's more common among men of my generation. Things are changing.

Of my three brothers, only one, the one who's working at the lodge, has two wives, and one of them has already died at age twenty. He was married to his first wife for a couple of years, and she didn't have any children. So he took a second wife, and she died at age twenty, a few months after giving birth. She had a congenital heart issue.

This is another reason why the Maasai have more than one wife: in case one of the wives dies, who's going to take care of my cows? That is a reason why to have more than one.

MY JOB: BEING A WARRIOR

Being a warrior is not a given. It's a job you have to earn.

When I was growing up, my childhood dream was that I would be a good warrior, that I would be able to kill lions and protect my community.

That was my dream, to become a good warrior. I didn't have any other option. There was not anything else. If you didn't go to school, you didn't see the rest of the world, so you had only that one option.

So I'm going to explain the warrior training, what we needed to do to become warriors. There's what's called an age group [cohort], you know, who become warriors together. The little boys, maybe around age five to eight or so, they take care of the baby sheep and goats. And then from the age of like eight or nine to age twelve, they will be herding the cows with the warriors.

So that is what is called the *layok* in the Maasai. An uncircumcised boy is a layok. Then they have a period, an interval, when they become the warriors. It's like a seven-year interval. And then after seven years, they retire as elders and allow another generation to become warriors.

MY WORST DAY: I LOST A HERD OF SHEEP AND GOT BEATEN AS PUNISHMENT

My worst day was when I was around thirteen and not yet a warrior. I used to herd my father's sheep and goats. There were maybe 200 or 300 animals. It's a challenge because you take them into the bush, you know, the really thick bush.

There are buffalos and all kinds of other animals there. You could be just one boy with 200 sheep, you know? And then you'll be worried that any time, the buffalo or the lion or the elephant could come and kill your sheep. So that was a big challenge, when I was little. And it might be you have a spear or it might be you don't have a spear, because you're not a warrior yet.

My first day was really bad. I took the sheep and goats to the bush, and there was a really big rain. The sheep and goats came in [and huddled] under one big tree. I tried to hide from the rain, and I waited until it finished. When the rain was almost going to stop, I looked around and saw that some of the sheep, they weren't around. So I stood up and looked around, and what I saw, I saw the hyenas. There were more than three hyenas. They were just laughing, like, "What's happening?" You know?

It was starting to get dark. I walked around a little bit, and I saw that two sheep had already been killed. They were only recently born. I had just seen them being born in the hut. Then I realized that six more had also been trapped [by the hyenas].

So I took the herd home, and as I walked a little bit, I saw then that ten more of them were already killed. I saw some of them crying. The hyenas were just, you know, celebrating. I took the sheep, and I was walking down, and then I saw another five of them dead, another ten. All the other sheep, they ran home, and I didn't know that they were home. I was thinking that they were all together here with me.

So I climbed down, and then my father and mother's people, they came and said to me, "What happened? How come the goats and sheep came home here [without you]?"

I think it was almost fifty sheep and goats that had been killed.

I was punished for that. They beat me with a stick. They wouldn't let me stay in the boma that day. I had to go stay in other people's bomas because my father and my brother, they were angry. They just wanted to kill me.

Anyway, that was my worst day. It took like, I think almost a year that I was still thinking about it, because of how many sheep and goats had been killed by those hyenas. The hyena is not even considered like a kill threat! The lion can fight with you; but the hyena cannot even fight with you. They [usually] just run away.

PRE-PUBERTY IS THE TIME TO PROVE THAT YOU DON T FLINCH FROM PAIN

When you're a *layok*, they start to train you to be a warrior. They do three things that are like a test of bravery. First, they're going to pierce the ear[lobe]. They take like a piece of the cowhide, they put it here with the knife, and they just remove the middle thing with the knife. You don't make the noise; you don't cry.

It hurts a very lot. [Laughs.] There's no anything—they don't use any painkiller. But you don't make any noise. That is a sign that means that you're ready. I was six or seven when that happened.

Then they take a roll of fabric, they just roll it like a cigarette and then light it on the top, and they put on it on your thigh, and then the smoke goes back on your skin, burning, burning, burning. Other boys are watching you. You don't cry then, as well. That's a sign that you are becoming a warrior. It's like if you took a cigarette and burned the leg, only it's much bigger. I have a big scar on my leg from that.

Then after that, your father would say, "Okay, I'm going to circumcise him now, because he's ready to become a warrior."

The reason why they do that [the two tests prior to circumcision], is that when they circumcise you, if you cry, that is really shameful to the family. It's just, you know, it's the way. So, you have to practice a little bit before you do the operation. You just think to yourself, which way should I do it so I won't blink my eyes, and I won't look all around. I won't move or make a sound.

You don't even blink your eyeballs or cry or move your toes or your finger. You just look in the same direction until they finish the operation. If you cry, you go to the side.

All of the entire village comes. It's like maybe sixty, seventy people coming, even people you don't know. They just want to see, are you brave in this operation? So they come.

Women are there too, but they'll be in the back. They don't want to see the operation. But everyone, the entire village, they're just watching your eyes, your toes, to see if you flinch. Are you brave? Are you going to survive this operation? It's the way; it's like being so disciplined.

If you cry, then your entire age group runs away. All the people who were supposed to come for your celebration, they don't come. They don't eat the food. You might slaughter like ten cows, but no one would eat them.

No one eats. No one celebrates. So it would be shame. And then people see you around, "Hey, he's someone who cried. He's someone who cried." You cannot walk in the entire village because of shame. Those boys don't even come out of their houses because of their shame and everyone is talking about that.

THE HAPPIEST DAY OF MY LIFE: I BECAME A WARRIOR

The Maasai, they have a big ceremony when they do the circumcision. The ones who have been circumcised already, they have the ostrich feather. They have the bird headdress, and then actually they can raise [you] up to be like this [overhead]. And they sing for you. And when you become the warrior, then you'll have all the freedom. You can do anything.

So I was really happy that I was able to be brave, to pass through the operation without crying. I was really happy to become a warrior. That was my happiest day, my happiest memory.

Tina: It's kind of like when people say here that college is the best time of your life.

Wantay: Before that, when you're a boy, before you're circumcised, you don't get to have the long hair, like the string, the long hair they have. You're not allowed to touch any girl, to go across [and talk to] any girl. You don't dance with a girl. The warriors, they can beat you, and you don't say anything. You aren't allowed to kill the lion.

THREE MONTHS OF HEALING AND TRAINING TO KILL THE LION

Then, they give you the training. The newly circumcised boys, maybe ten of them, they could be brothers and cousins, the same age group from the village; they train together. You have maybe three to four months while you're healing.

In that time, you'll practice things like chasing the birds. You chase a bird until you catch it. You chase the birds all day long until you can catch them in your hand. Then you have to kill the birds, collect the birds to make your own headdress.

The more birds and the more variety of birds, the better it is. So we learn the behavior of birds. We watch them. The birds nest underground at night, and then we can close off the entrance to the nest, and then we come back in the morning and lift the rock, and catch the birds as they're coming out. We learn all the behavior of the birds, because we have to catch them. And then we stuff them and put them on the headdress. The headdress has like taxidermy birds on it.

The elder warriors, they do the training for you. You go chase the birds, and you also work with spears. You do target practice with arrows and throw stones. Throw the stone and, you know, which one of you can throw the stone higher? You practice hitting the tree. As well, they teach you how to kill the lion, how to trick the animal, how to avoid them.

I HAVE KILLED A LION, BUT JUST ONE

I have killed a lion, but just one. I was fourteen or fifteen, something like that. I was not the first one to throw the spear. I participated. The thing is, it's really very important that we kill the lion. So we decide who are our most expert warriors-in-training, maybe five or ten of us who will go. We say, "Let's go kill the lion."

So five of us go to the bush, and we find the lion, and everyone tries to be the first one to spear the lion, so he can get the tail. The second one will get the paw. This is very important. Everyone tries to be the first one. But it can be like, you're not the first one, but you're among them who killed the lion. I was one of those who killed the lion. I was like the fourth person who speared him.

But you need to be prepared. Before you go, you participate in what is called the meat harvest. You attack like a bull, two bulls, really far from home, and you go kill them and stay in the bush for maybe ten days, just eating the meat. Then we're really fit and we're very strong because we'll be doing exercises and eating the meat. We grill the meat. We cook on big pots, and we can eat the soup from the meat.

We know the places, in the really thick bush, where you can find the lions. So I went into the bush and found the lion, and there was more than one. There were three of them, two females and one male. We know the bush. We know the places where they hide. We let the females go, but they're very dangerous. They can kill you in a second. We had no guns, only spears.

And then, what we do, we chase them, and they get really upset. They don't run anymore. They just wait. They look in people's eyes, you know? They just look in your eyes. They become really upset. And then if you throw the spear, they come straight to you.

So when you're ready, you throw the spear, and you run away. If you cannot run, you have the shield. You have a big Maasai shield made from cowhide or buffalo hide. It's really strong. You can't run fast with it; it's too heavy. It could break a lion's paw when they jump on you. You've got to be really ready to throw the spear. Either you can block under your shield, or if you are really strong, you have to be really strong to be able to hold the lion. The shield is *heavy*.

The lion may be on top of the shield, you know? Otherwise, if you feel like you are not very strong, you can run to the back of your friends. Then another one can throw the spear, and then the other one can do the same. It takes teamwork.

So the lion could get confused, you know? But usually the lion is not confused. He would just come straight to you, and he'd catch you.

WE DID IT, AND THEN WE CELEBRATED WITH CEREMONIES AND SONGS

Nobody died in my group. If the lion even scratches you, then there is no celebration. You don't celebrate because the lion got you. So you didn't kill the lion. The lion cut you. So if we killed the lion, but we got attacked by the lion, we make sure that the village, they don't see any blood. Otherwise there's no celebration.

The four men who were with me when we killed the lion are still in the village. Some of them, they're working, some of them not, but they're still in the village. It does form a bond between you. When you kill a lion, it's like a "wow." Everyone talks about you for the rest of your life. When they sing songs, they mention you. "Wantay, he killed the lion!" Not only your village, the whole entire Maasai land will hear about you.

When you kill the lion, you take the paw and tail. You put it on your really big white spear: the long, white [ceremonial] one, not the black one. You put the tail on that, the top of that spear. And the paw, you put that on the black spear because you're not the first one. So you put it on the spear, and then you hold it up.

Then everyone, like all the warriors will follow you [in a parade]. If you are the first one, the second one, and the third one, you will get the lion mane. They just follow you. And then the women, they come to dance with you, the girls. The people support you and cheer for you like you're playing football. They can celebrate for maybe two months. You have to go through each village, running and singing, showing everyone what you did.

I became a warrior at the age of fifteen. After seven years, when I was twenty-two, I automatically became an elder in the Maasai tribe. I was nervous inside to become an elder [laughs], because I was still young. They call you an elder even though you are young still.

THE LION-KILLING TRADITION IS NO MORE

In my lifetime, from my village, I can remember ten times when warriors killed a lion. Now it's increasingly rare for lions to be killed. For a while, if the lion killed a certain number of cows, say, 5,000 of them, the government would allow the warriors to kill that lion. But now, you can't kill lions anymore.

So now they have to pay people for livestock. Up to a certain amount [of loss by lion killings], the government will pay you for the loss.

THE MAASAI BELIEVE THEY OWN ALL THE COWS ON EARTH

You know, the Maasai believe that all cows on the Earth belong to them. The tribes around the Maasai, the neighbors, who own cows, they're still fighting with us because the Maasai, they try to go and collect the cows from the other tribe. So they go on a cow raid, kill the people, and bring back the cows. So, all the other tribes around, they don't get along with the Maasai.

The Maasai, they used to come down to Karatu and get the cows from them. I don't know if you've seen the traditional house of the Iraqw tribe, the underground house. They dig the ground, and they build a house, and they cover on the top with the dirt, and then the grass can go on the top of the house. The Maasai, when they come during the night, if there's just a house in a hill, so they don't see that there's a house there.

So the Iraqw can hear you because they're underground when you come. You make a big noise, you know, stomping around above their homes. That's how they build houses to protect from the Maasai. They don't do that anymore now [laughs], but before.

It's not quite like that today. Recently we've come together. With the Maasai, they can go work with them. They can come to the Maasai village now, and we can go to Karatu, and all of that.

THE WORK OF A MAASAI WARRIOR

The warriors have one main job: to take care of the cows. We have to take the cows far away to get the good grass to make milk. Let's say maybe we had rain here in one place, and where we are is dry. So we can move the cows to where you have the rain. Only the warriors do that. They move the cows from one place to another for grass.

They have to build temporary huts and temporary bomas and *kraals* for protecting the cows from the [wild] animals and the other tribes. The women build the houses, the huts. The warriors build the "kraal." It's like our word for "corral." They build the enclosure for the cows. And the baby ones are too small, so they can get through the fence. That's why they go inside the huts at night. When the warriors are grazing the cattle, they're gone for months. It's not like you go out for the day, and then come back. So that's why they have to stop and build a little temporary encampment.

The elders, they give the warriors the orders that, "You guys need to take the cows to this place because there is rain." Then a group of warriors have to come together to work. It could be like my father's cows: It's not like I have to do the kraal myself, you know? We can build the boma all together. We can decide to work together, put together all the cows, and do one big boma. I can just ask my fellow friends, "Can we work together?"

The cattle are divided, like each wife will have her own cattle, and then boys of a certain age will have their own cattle. So then when there's two or three boys, whether they're full brothers or from different wives, they can be circumcised in the same age group. So then they would all work together as a group.

In your warrior group, you then elect leaders. I have not been elected leader. They pick just one for the entire age group. They try to think like, this family has really good leaders, this family has a good reputation, and they take from the same family.

The warriors also have to take care of the community. When something goes wrong, we guard them from anything, from animals, from the other tribes.

MY FAMILY STAYED IN THE VILLAGE, BUT I WENT TO SCHOOL

In my family, all my sisters got married. They're in a different village, still in Ngorongoro. One of my sisters, my eldest sister, died in the childbirth, but the rest of them, they're still alive.

I'm the only one who went to secondary school. When I finished school, I came back and I found a job. I was able to work and support them, buy the food for them and try to encourage them to go for more education, and try. I was able to send one of my brothers to go to school, for vocational school. He wanted to be a tour guide. I became the provider for my family.

WHAT'S UNIQUE IN MAASAI CULTURE: RESPECT FOR ELDERS

The Maasai are always unique because of the warriors. Also, in the Maasai culture, when you are little, you listen to your older brothers or elder people. So it's not like another tribe where you can play with all the people. Like the younger people in the Maasai generation, people, you really respect your elders, your older brothers or older sisters.

You respect them. They can send you to go get something, and then it's fine; you do it. With another tribe, if you send someone younger than you, they don't agree. But in the Maasai, if it's someone younger than you, they respect that this is my older brother or my older sister. They'll do it.

The Maasai elder's job is, he's the one that has to make the decisions. If there are fights or conflicts within the family, they call the leaders, the elders, to come in and sort the problem. They see it and they talk with you, and then they finish. And then the elders, while they're there, they make a decision for the meeting. They're kind of like the Supreme Court.

So the elders figure out how to solve conflicts, and they're the ones that feed the family. They say, "We need to slaughter this goat for the family. Or, we need to sell that for the family." They're the ones that are making the top decisions for the family.

WARRIOR GROUP NAME AND TERM LIMITS

You cannot apply for a second term as a warrior, because there are new, younger warriors coming up. They want to take your place. But you can go higher, if you want to.

While you are a warrior, you also share a name with the other boys in your age group. Your age group name has a meaning. With some, they give you a bad name, like my age group has a name that means the stomach thing, like distended intestines. *It's a bad name.* [Laughs.] But no trades! No trading your name, because the older age group gave you that name, and you have to take it, you know?

Later, after seven years, when your group becomes the elders, then you can change it. Then you give yourself a really nice name, and they bless that name for you, and then you take that name. Also when you become an elder, then you have the right to marry. That is age twenty-two. The elders will bless you. You can marry, you know, and you're free to do many things.

I CHOSE MY OWN WIFE

When it's time to marry, usually it's an arranged marriage. But not for me. I picked my wife.

I had a wife arranged, but for me, it was different, because I went to secondary school. So the girl grew up and I didn't want to marry her because I was still in school, and then someone else took her, because I was too late. So when I came back, this is a true story, it was too late. She'd already been taken.

I said, "It's fine." So I finished the secondary school and went looking for a job. I found a job, and I was working in the lodge now. I was waiting to earn some money so I could marry. Then I could find a wife

…and that's what happened. I met Tina.

Tina grew up in Libya and Iran. She's completely different from my sisters. She's not only educated; she has a graduate degree. She's lived all over the world. She's run several businesses.

Tina: When I met his grandmother for the first time, Wantay put me in traditional clothes. She had lived in the Serengeti. She was alive when they first moved them from Serengeti to Ngorongoro. It was a German colony first, and then it was a British protectorate. So his grandmother was always afraid of Germans, after that.

Wantay: That's right. When the Maasai people see people in western clothes, they go inside and hide. They don't want to see them because they're worried that they're policemen or something, you know. It's not about the color of the skin; it's about the clothing. They're afraid of anyone wearing trousers.

I SAW MY FIRST TELEVISION AT AGE 18 AND GOT MY FIRST CELLPHONE AT AGE 21

I saw my first television in 1996, when I was in secondary school. My first computer, not until I got my job in the lodge. Now, I have the latest Apple iPhone. I have a thing about Apple. But it was funny when I saw my first cellphone. One of my friends had one, and I was curious to see how it worked.

I asked his permission, "Can we go see the cellphone, how it's working?" But there was no signal. We used to walk to the highest hill to try to get the signal. We all went together, and that phone, it was really exciting.

I was like, "What's inside this phone? What's inside? Is this a demon inside, or a little person talking?"

I said, "Take it away from me. I don't want to see that."

My grandmother was scared of the cellphone. She thought there was a demon or something inside it. Now, even in the village, everyone has a cellphone.

WOMEN IN MY VILLAGE COMPARED TO THE OUTSIDE WORLD

I think the women in the village are missing out on a lot. Even themselves, they realize now that they're missing out on a lot of things because of a lack of education and travel, and food.

Education is really important. So the ladies now in the village, they can feel like, "Oh, I can see that I'm missing something. I didn't get an education. I'm just sitting in the village being nothing, just feeding the family, and I don't have choices."— They're doing their own work every day to try to support the family. But they can see that they're missing something. And they try to look at the world.

WHAT I DO NOW: TWO NONPROFITS AND ONE RECREATION BUSINESS

We run two nonprofits, AID Tanzania and the Kiretono Resource Center (KRC). AID Tanzania is based in the U.S., and KRC is based in Tanzania. Through AID Tanzania, we raise funds to support KRC. The mission of KRC is to support and educate girls.

The Maasai girls, they're from the rural area, and they speak only Maasai when they're in the village. So we tutor them in the language and get them ready for the local school. They need to learn Swahili, the traditional language.

In Ngorongoro, they have a permanent structure for the primary school, but they don't have enough teachers in the area. The school could have like 400 kids and might have six or seven teachers. At the primary school in Ngorongoro, they speak only Maasai.

So when they go to secondary school, if they come into Karatu from the Maasai village, it takes them like a year to catch up with the other students because of the [lack of] quality of education and the English and Swahili as well.

But then we decided that we're going to have a dormitory in Karatu, and we're going to tutor them English and get them ready for secondary school. The first year we had eight students, and the second year, it was eleven. I think it was eleven. We currently have twenty-nine students, all girls, Standard Year 5 to 7 [middle school].

Right now, we only work with girls. We didn't have enough dormitories to accommodate both boys and girls. So we're starting with the girls now, and then later on, we could raise more money, and we'd be able to build our own dormitory. Right now, we're renting the place for them. We'd like to build a house to accommodate both boys and girls. That's the plan.

THE PAPA IN AN ALL-WOMEN COMMUNITY

For me, I love living in a community of all women. I love just to see the Maasai girls become educated. They're living in a little town, where they are exposed to other students, speaking different languages, like Swahili and English. They speak only English in their dormitory, and Swahili too. We tutor them sixteen hours a week in English.

I really love the girls. It's good to have them. They call me Papa, and I'm so happy. I'm happy for them because, you know, if you try to do something and help people and they're happy with what they're doing, then you're happy, too. So it's really nice, yeah.

It's good because some of them, they don't have fathers. Some of them have no mothers. We have two orphans. They don't want to go back home. They have only one parent.

WE WORRY WHEN OUR GIRLS GO HOME DURING THE BREAKS

When we have school breaks, some of them will say, "We don't want to go home," and I say, "Why?" It's because, when they go home, they don't have food, they don't have cows. So they want to stay in the dormitory instead of going back home.

But we're still worried that the girls could be married off young. We worry about a lot of things: early forced marriage, domestic abuse, rape, and female circumcision.

And that's why even though the school's out for maybe a month, we won't let the girls go for the entire month. We just let them go for one or two weeks because we worry about them getting married. Some of the parents, they told us that they need for their daughter to get married, because they will get cows and money for them. The father will force them to be married.

The Tanzanian law does forbid child marriage; but somehow the Maasai get around that. The government supports education for all kids, but only through primary school. There is no secondary school in our village. So, if you finish the primary school, you're a little afraid that your father can decide what to do with you [e.g., early/arranged marriage]. It's kind of like the government doesn't control them after that. The father can decide it, you know?

HOW THIS GENERATION IS DIFFERENT FROM MINE

These girls are different from their mothers because the mothers, they're not thinking about the future, you know? They are just for today. Their mothers, they know very little. So that's the big difference.

These girls are thinking about their future. They're not thinking about getting married now. They know more things. They think more, they see more. They read. They're educated.

In my generation, the girls didn't have to worry about going to school. They were just thinking about getting married, staying with the husband, and have the kids, and stay happy, you know? But now the girls, they realize that education is really important. So they don't think about getting married now. They think about going to school so they can support themselves and their family.

EDUCATION: MY PHILOSOPHY AND MY PHILANTHROPY

Education is my number one philanthropy. I have been an education funder for over twenty years. When I finished secondary school, and I found a job, that's when I started to support my relatives.

We can see the difference. We've seen the girls of Maasai, the ones who went to school, they come back home and they find a job. They buy more cattle. They're supporting their families.

This can really change the culture; because if you have more people educated, then I mean, there's more of them that can work, and they can support a lot of families.

SUPPORTING OURSELVES WITH OUR 4-WHEELING BUSINESS

Then, 4 Wheeling Tanzania is another business to support us because we're working in a nonprofit, and we're not making any money from that. So that's kind of what we do so we can support ourselves while we're doing the nonprofit thing.

Tina: And the hope is eventually, when the business is going well, then we can take part of the proceeds from the business and put it into the nonprofit. One of the reasons that we've set it up nearby the dorm and the school and everything is because we want to take people past our project so they can see it and expose them to the charitable work that we're doing and have one feed into the other; so that when the clients of the ATV business are exposed, they may decide that they want to help support us, sponsor a student or help us build. And then also the plan has always been to have the beaded merchandise out—to sell handicrafts that their moms make back in the village.

Wantay: We just started 4 Wheeling in November. We're not covering our costs right now. We're not covering the loan for the bikes yet. But we've just started. We have seven vehicles. So we can take six people at a time. We have anywhere from a one-hour ride to an all-day ride.

I take everybody out on the bikes and show them the local culture. It's just a recreational center, not a tour operator, because a tour operator has all kinds of registration and government fees and all that stuff that they have to do.

Right now, we probably currently have four to six groups a month, and that's been entirely residents in Arusha and locals, like expats and their friends coming to visit from out of the country. We're just starting to see some interest from the tour companies. There's a high season starting in like late October through the middle of January.

HOW WE SURVIVE

Tina: We have monthly income from a house I own in Colorado that's rented out, and then we're living off of savings and investments and stuff like that.

If we hadn't had Mara, we'd be all in, in Tanzania. The issue is that we don't want to handicap our daughter and her education opportunities. There's a hesitation to jump in again with a lot of capital investment into a new business, and then feel like, you know, by the time she was ready for school, to feel like we had these golden handcuffs on to where the business was starting to make money, and so we couldn't leave because we were just going to start recouping.

And we've come to the realization that there are good international school options in Arusha. It means some sacrifice from us and more expense, but if the business is successful, then it will fund that.

So that's what we're hoping for. Because right now there's not another company doing this— we're the only ones. It's like, people go out for the weekend to Serengeti, and go out and see the wildlife, and then you've also got all of these foreign visitors coming through. So we're sitting in a really good spot.

The terrain is perfect for the ATVs, absolutely perfect. There's so much to see and do, and nobody's doing it. Wantay wanted to do a tour company, and I basically kept trying to talk him, over the years, like nine years now, "No, no, no, I don't want to compete with everyone else." So this is something different, and we're hoping to work *with* the tour companies.

WHAT I WISH FOR THE FUTURE, FOR MY ALL THESE GIRLS

Wantay: In the future, what I wish for Mara is not that far from us, from what we have now. I wish her to be able to speak both languages, the Maasai language and the Swahili language, but as well, I would like her to get a good education.

So I need her to be able to know both cultures, the Maasai culture, the Tanzania culture, and then the other [global] culture as well. If we live in Tanzania, I think she'll be able to go to an international school, to have a good education. They still speak Swahili. They can speak Maasai. That will be a good option. Otherwise, if we would go for education in the U.S., maybe I can speak Maasai with her. Otherwise she will forget Maasai.

My dream is, after maybe twenty years, I want to see that the girls we're trying to support for their education, that they would be able to go for further education. They would be educated and not get married while they're still in school, and then they can come back, and they can look for a job. They can work and support their community and their families, and they can support their own children to go to school. That's what I need to see.

WHAT WILL HAPPEN TO MY MAASAI VILLAGE IN YEARS TO COME

I think, in twenty years, it might end up that no one lives in the village, because you cannot do anything in the village. Otherwise, you could work far away from home, like Arusha or other places. You can come back home and buy the cattle—you might be working somewhere else, but the family's still there because home is always home, you know? So I think that people, they might still be there.

Now I'm really sad, because I can see that in the future, a lot of Maasai, they won't be able to speak Maasai. They don't want to be able to follow their culture. They'll never sleep inside of a mud hut. So I can see that we're losing our culture.

I wish the Maasai could keep their culture the way it is. Even if they advocated for and wanted a high education, but still I wish they can retain their culture, like they can have a place. There are so many ways that they keep their culture unique. They're proud of their culture. I wish they could have permanent houses. I would like to keep our Maasai dress, jewelry, and the language.

If I could give away parts of the culture, I'd give away the warriors' ability to sleep with girls whenever they want to. When you become the warrior, they give you freedom. Right now, the warriors can dance with the girls and celebrate with them. And they can stay in one house with a girl. You can be close like that. There's always the risk to get the girl pregnant when they're still young, before they go to school. So, you know, that's the thing I don't like, the warriors to be really very close to the girls all the time. In the Maasai culture, they don't like the girl to be pregnant before they get married, but it happens sometimes.

I would also do away with the arranged marriages. I would like the girls to be free to decide themselves what they want to do.

WHAT I WOULD GIVE MY PEOPLE, IF I COULD

If I had all the resources in the world, I would want the Maasai people to be able to farm. I would want all of them to go to school so they could know what their future is. They could think that, "Okay, I need to do this to support other people." I would want all of them to be able to have houses, not the temporary houses, but permanent houses.

If you think about that, that's the only thing they need. But the government, they will never allow them to farm or to build the permanent place there. If the government could give the Maasai the really good land, give them a pasture and everything, they can herd their cows. They could have farms for the cows, the grass and hay, you know? They can create so many things, like they can make cheeses for sale. Some of them can do the farming and some of them can build houses.

The only thing is, and you can put it in the book, if you want to, for me, to come through all this is really something.

I grew up really poor in a Maasai village. Then I went to the U.S., and saw the American culture. I saw how people become educated.

What I see now is that, for example, if you help just one person from a poor family or a tribe—not only the Maasai but from the other people in the world—if you help one person, that means you help a hundred people in the world. They will become educated and go back, and then they can help others to be educated. They can create a nonprofit like what we're doing. You can help many people that way. It's possible.

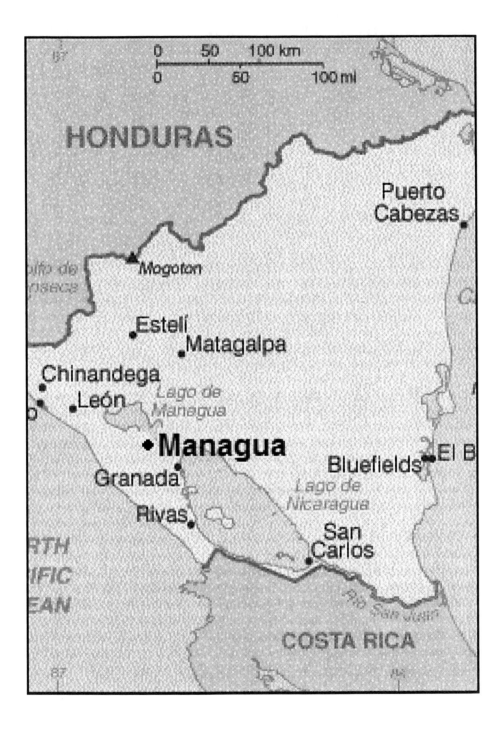

· ·

MAYRA

COFFEE FARMER

SAN RAMÓN, NICARAGUA

Editor's note: Forty-seven-year-old Mayra Gámez sits across from me in a white plastic chair, in a cement-and-brick building she built with a handful of other women on a patch of land she bought herself, from the proceeds of corn and coffee beans.

The building, called "The Center," is the direct result of Mayra's dream to create a space where their women's coffee cooperative could build related enterprises (such as coffee grinding and packaging) and grow stronger together. Having survived violence and heartbreak, poverty and chauvinism, Mayra took the best lessons of the Nicaraguan Revolution (the 1962-1990 Sandinista populist uprising against a decades-long family dictatorship and subsequent Contra War) and applied them to her neighboring farmers in the central mountains of her farming village, San Ramón,[1] population 2,744.

---

1. The small farm-town of San Ramón sits atop the central Nicaraguan mountains at 2,297 feet above sea level. It's known for coffee and tourism. A Cornell University student writes a detailed description of life in San Ramón and Mayra's coffee-farmer cooperative: blogs.cornell.edu/ccenica2012/about-san-ramon.

"Living together in a community," Mayra muses, "the problems are the same for all of us, economically and in production aspects. So I think it's really necessary to work together and help each other mutually."

She is tiny, petite, somehow softly feminine even with her hair pulled back and not an ounce of fat on her wiry frame. She's all business, Mayra. She talks very fast, in the English she taught herself as an adult. (To get further ahead in business, she needed it to communicate with NGO people and coffee marketers.) Mayra has given many talks like this before, about her life as a Central American coffee farmer and a hardworking woman...

Yet here and there, she veers off-script. Her eyes well up as she talks about the man she married at sixteen who fathered five children with her and then fell in love with someone else—right here in San Ramón—leaving her to raise them alone. She's learned not to need a man, any man. The wound still festers, decades later.

And then her eyes brighten, and she smiles, recalling the years she picked coffee beans as a migrant worker with her mother, dreaming little-girl dreams of someday owning a tiny plot of land and a pretty little *casita* (cottage).

"I feel very grateful to God," she says, "because I was able to achieve that. I not only have my house, but I also have land that I can work." She owns a farm that grows inch-by-inch whenever she has a good year with a few *cordobas*[2] leftover after expenses. She's also president of two coffee-farmer cooperatives: one for women only and another regional collective of co-ops. Her children and neighbors look up to her. She's made more than a few of her dreams come true.

Self-taught since she dropped out of school in fourth grade to work to help feed her younger siblings, Mayra has proved she can do anything. But she's not looking to rest on any laurels; she's saving for a corn mill to expand into the service of grinding local corn. What's next after that? A tortilla business, of course...and on from there.

How does she stay strong, and so determined? Mayra, whose ancestry dates back to Native American Mayans, might say that her strength, just like her dreams and her wellbeing, comes right up to her through the rich mountaintop soil of the land itself.[3]

WHY WE CREATED A WOMEN'S COFFEE COOPERATIVE

My name is Mayra Gámez. I'm 47 years old. I work as a farmer on my eighteen *manzanas* (31.5 acres) of land in San Ramón, in the north of Nicaragua.

My main crop is coffee, but we also cultivate green beans, corn, *malanga* (a root vegetable; a type of taro also known as "Japanese potato"), bananas, and other fruits as well.

I work on the land with my children. During the coffee harvest, I employ more workers, but during the rest of the year, it's just us at work, myself with my children.

---

2. One cordoba in Nicaraguan currency, equals about 4 cents USD.

3. See Mayra speaking about her work and the collective power of farming cooperatives in this 3-minute video (in Spanish with English subtitles): youtu.be/DLKC28_CIm0.

I'm the president of a women's cooperative.[4] There's a men's cooperative here in this community that's been in existence for around twenty-five years. A group of women also wanted to organize, and we went to the men to see if they would give us the opportunity of working together with them. They said yes, but they never listened to us. They never gave us opportunities to participate in anything. So we were just sitting there doing nothing. We would just listen to what they decided, and what they were doing.

We decided to figure out a way to organize ourselves, by ourselves, because we felt like we were just wasting our time with the men. So that's how the idea first became promoted. We started a program called GEMA, groups of women-solidarity savings groups. That's how we began to organize ourselves.

We remained in that group for a couple of years. At that time, we didn't have any place to meet. We'd always be looking for a house or a little space we could borrow for our meetings. It was very important, the support that we received from CECOCAFEN and also from the San Ramón Union of Agricultural Cooperatives or the UCA, the second-tier cooperative. They provided training.

WE RAISED OUR OWN FUNDS TO BUILD OUR CO-OP CENTER

San Ramón UCA provided training in cooperative principles, in self-esteem, and in sexual and reproductive health. That support was really important to us. Once we were trained, we decided that it would be important to become a constituted cooperative ourselves. We then went through all the paperwork and procedures, and our cooperative was officially established in 2001.

We have eighteen members in our co-op. When we first started, we didn't have a place to meet. So I said to the women, "Let's find a piece of land that we can build a building on, so we can have our meetings. And they said, "Well, how would we ever buy something like that if we don't have any money?"

So I said, "We're producing coffee. We're producing beans. We'll each kick in a certain contribution and with that, we'll be able to save and buy it."

So that's what happened. They offered this piece of land to us, and we did the accounting. We needed 330 cordobas—that's $12—each at that point in time. And that's what we each contributed to buy the land for the Center.

We also made other contributions. We needed another installment in order to build the house itself. First, we made a house that was made of wooden walls with a tin roof. That was the original building for the cooperative. It was about 22,000 cordobas [$778]. We didn't have any seats to sit on, any chairs. So we each put in twenty pounds of beans during the harvest time. We sold those beans, and we bought our chairs.

We now have this building. This was pretty expensive. It cost about $6,000. Two Danish organizations, MS [Mellemfolkeligt Samvirke] and ActionAid, provided support to us. They helped us to work on the business-initiative plan, to write out the project proposal in training, and also to purchase some of our equipment and the building itself.

---

4. Coffee cooperatives, says "Resilience" blog (resilience.org/stories/2016-02-04/how-impact-investing-is-saving-nic-aragua-s-coffee-industry), really move the needle on the entire coffee industry in Nicaragua, the poorest country in Latin America. Coffee comprises 6 percent of Nicaragua's exports, according to MIT's Atlas Media ranking: atlas.media.mit.edu/en/profile/country/nic.

I'M THE VOLUNTEER PRESIDENT OF TWO COOPERATIVES

When we first started the cooperative, I was elected president. Having a responsibility in the cooperative, it's not a permanent position; it's for a certain term. You serve as president for a minimum of one year and a maximum of three years. I've been the president three times. I was the first president, and then I served a second term after that. Then other people came in, and now I'm president again.

I'm also the president of the San Ramón Union of Cooperatives, the Union of Agricultural Cooperatives [UCA]. It's a second-tier cooperative, a group of eighteen cooperatives with a membership of a little more than 1,000 farmers, like 1,070 or something like that.

I don't receive a salary for being president of either of the co-ops. I work as a volunteer. But I've learned that if we don't work hard as a grassroots cooperative, we don't get recognized. It's difficult to apply for project funds. It's hard to obtain financing. The same thing goes for the UCA. The only difference there is, we're not talking about just one grassroots cooperative but a number of them.

There's a lot of work to do in the grassroots cooperative. We have to look after the organizational part. We've improved our coffee plantations.

As president of UCA, I look after the organizational part, mainly. I help to seek resources for the membership for the different cooperatives. And I provide oversight for all of the different functions of the UCA. We don't have any computers or anything in the coop centers. The recordkeeping is all on paper, ledger books and so forth. It's similar to the work that I do here.

BEYOND THE BEAN: LAUNCHING A BUSINESS TO ROAST AND GRIND COFFEE

I'm also an entrepreneur. I helped launch a little business initiative that we started with the [coffee-bean] roaster and grinder. This is another thing I never would have imagined that we would have the opportunity to do, but we did.

We've achieved some important goals: We wanted to buy a mill and a grinder so that we could grind corn for the community. We had the opportunity, and this dream has become a reality. We also have this roasting initiative, this new business that we started.

Did you see the little building that we're building down here? [Points out the window, and then to the new coffee grinder shown in her chapter-opener picture.] And this is the grinder here. We're going to sell the grinding service to the community to grind corn for tortillas; because there isn't a mill here in the community. We think that we'll be able to make good income from that.

We sell our corns and our beans on the local market. We can learn about the price for coffee through the media. It's on the radio. It's on television. Every day, the price of coffee is in the newspaper. It's on the radio, too. When it goes up, when it goes down, we hear about it.

MY INCOME FLUCTUATES WIDELY, DEPENDING ON FERTILIZER AND FUNGUS

Two years ago, we had problems with the coffee-leaf rust fungus.[5] That disease really damaged most of our coffee. Before that, I had a pretty good income compared to others. I could get $5,000 or $6,000 earnings in a year in order to work the next year. So that would be net, after my debt and all of my costs. But since the coffee rust affected us, it's much less. This year, it was about $2,000. That's very little income to be able to work my farm, because it is a lot of work.

I don't have any money in savings right now. Because of the coffee leaf rust and the drop in coffee prices, I haven't been able to save. I've had to invest it. I haven't taken out any loans right now, but there are times when we do need loans in order to get the fertilizer to put on the coffee.

I GREW UP IN THE MIDDLE OF THE SANDINISTA REVOLUTION

My father abandoned us when we were all very small. I was seven years old. One of my siblings was ten years old, and another was eleven years old, and then there were a bunch that were younger than me.

My father left my mother with eight children. My mother was a good mother. She worked hard, and she fought for us. She taught us to work. She taught us to be responsible people.

When the Revolution[6] occurred, we worked picking coffee. And then the Revolution had a program to give land to the peasants. They gave a piece of land to me, and also one to my mother. And we began to work it.

We lived in a city called Estelí. My mother worked as a maid. There was no Contra attack or anything here; but Estelí was very much part of the insurrection, the revolutionary movement. They called it "the three insurrections" in Estelí before the triumph of the Revolution.

In the fight against Somoza, there were three battles that occurred right in Estelí against Somoza's National Guard and between the Sandinistas and Somoza. It was pretty stressful there. We lived through some strong moments of the war at that point.

I HAD TO DROP OUT OF SCHOOL AFTER 4TH GRADE

When I was in Estelí, I studied for four years, up to fourth grade. But then I didn't go to school because we moved here to work.

5.Coffee leaf fungus is a disease that appears reddish-orange, like rust, and can devastate entire crops: apsnet.org/edcenter/intropp/lessons/fungi/basidiomycetes/pages/coffeerust.aspx.

6. The Nicaraguan Revolution began in the early 1960s and 1970s with opposition to the 43-year Somoza Family dictatorship, led by the Sandinista National Liberation Front (FSLN). People from all sectors—workers, businessmen, peasants, students, and guerrillas—joined forces and finally defeated the Somoza dynasty and the National Guard on July 19, 1979. The FSLN then governed Nicaragua from 1979 until 1990. During this period (1981-1990) the Contra War was waged between the FSLN and the U.S.-backed Contras. Read more about the Nicaraguan Revolution: vianica.com/go/specials/15-sandinista-revolution-in-nicaragua.html.

We were eight children, and I had to work, because my mother earned very little as a maid. It would have been beautiful if I could have continued school. If I had had the opportunity and the resources to be able to do that, that would have been really great. I think I would have studied something that's related to the work in the fields, agronomy or something like that. Instead, I've been in the school of real life.

In 1982, we moved here to San Ramón. There was no contra attack here or anything here. We were kind of like migrant workers, picking coffee. Then the Revolution had a program to give land to the peasants. They gave my mother and me eight manzanas (14 acres) of land, and we began to work it.

And then I remained here to live, and now I'm still here in this place. I don't rent my land. I own it. It's what they gave me in the Revolution.

And I settled in and started also to have children. I have five children. My mother died seven years ago, but I still live in San Ramón.

I BECAME A SINGLE MOTHER, LIKE MY MOTHER

I am now single. My husband went off with another woman. I have five children—four sons and one daughter. I also have one brother and one sister that live here in the community. In my free time, I go to church. I go to an evangelical Protestant church.

My oldest child is married, thirty-one, and lives in Matagalpa. The second-oldest is twenty-eight, lives and works in Managua. I have a twenty-five-year-old son who lives here and works with me in the fields; one who's twenty-three, and then a little girl who's nineteen.

I just have one daughter, but I have a granddaughter because my daughter has a one-and-a-half-year-old baby girl. Her name is Mayra—Mayra Junior! She always wants to be on my lap.

I ALWAYS DREAMED OF OWNING A PATCH OF LAND AND BUILDING MY DREAM HOUSE—AND I DID IT

I've told my children that when I was a young girl and worked picking coffee, I was always very friendly, but I was very shy, too. I feel like the organization has helped me to overcome my shyness quite a bit. I was not like with some people who're friendly with everybody. If it was somebody that I didn't know very well, I was shy.

Something I've talked to my children about is whenever I was working picking coffee, I always dreamed about buying a small piece of land and building a house and living there peacefully with my children.

I didn't know if it was achievable. And I feel very grateful to God because I was able to achieve something that I always wanted. I not only have my house, but I also have land that I can work.

In comparison to others, I would call myself a small producer, a smallholder, because I'm a small farmer. But I don't really compare myself. It's rare that I would compare myself to others.

My work is on the farm and my land. It's within my family, in the cooperative. When there are social projects in the community like on water and other things, I participate in those, too. Not everybody has the desire to sacrifice like that. So there are some things that you can't compare with other people because they're not willing to make those kinds of sacrifices.

MY HUSBAND FELL IN LOVE WITH ANOTHER WOMAN, RIGHT HERE IN MY VILLAGE

The most horrible moment in my life was when I was twenty-four: My children's father fell in love with another woman right here in this community and married her. We had been married for eight years. That was the most terrible moment in my life, but now they've moved somewhere else.

And my happiest moment was when I was able to overcome that…when I realized I didn't need men to live and to work. That, for me, was the best, the best moment.

I was able to organize. I haven't really thought about marrying again. I really feel like my life is okay this way. There are times when it would be nice to have a partner to talk privately about things with, but I don't think it's so necessary. I can work. I don't really need a husband or anybody to take care of me or help me with my children.

WE NEED TO THINK ABOUT THE MAJORITY IN ORDER TO HELP EACH OTHER MUTUALLY

It's also difficult in my community, because we don't all think the same way. There are some people that just think about their own welfare, and they don't think about the welfare of everybody else or of the majority. That's a little difficult.

As human beings, sometimes that's the way we are. Sometimes people think, "Well, I'm not going to spend my time doing stuff for other people." There are people that think that way, and I don't think that's right.

But the truth is, when we live in a community where there is a cooperative, the problems are almost the same for all of us, economically, in production aspects. So I think it's really necessary that at least some of us think alike, because that's the only way we can help each other mutually.

HOW I'VE CHANGED FROM BEING IN THE COOPERATIVE

Personally, I've changed a lot. I could say I've changed a lot in my person. Before I was part of the organization, I was embarrassed to talk to my children. I didn't feel competent enough even to ask my sons if they had a girlfriend. And through trainings that I received, I learned that it was important for me to sit down and talk to my children, that I give them counsel and advice so that they don't commit the same mistake that my father committed and their own father who left us.

So I say to them now, "Use a condom. If you have a girlfriend, you need to protect yourself, and you need to protect her." And also with my daughter, there's a lot of trust between us. I talk to her. I think that's part of what's changed.

For me, the cooperative has been like a little school for me because I've learned so many things. I've learned to value myself as a person. I've learned to figure out what I want to do, what kinds of work I want to do, and what kind of person I want to be.

I've learned how to know what I want, what I want to do, and what I like. I've learned about organization and organizing, to think about the future, not simply about the day that we're in. I've learned that I must sit down and talk to my children, to my family. I'm able to talk with my children about what we might invest financing in, if we have a loan.

I believe that everything that you set out to do for yourself, you can do if you work hard. And I've learned that, in this life, you have to struggle. You have to be strong because, if we become weak, then any wind will just blow us right over, and we won't be able to achieve our goals.

FROM BEING A MIGRANT WORKER TO OWNING MY OWN FARM

Also in the organization, a beautiful thing has been that I have taken ownership of my own work on my farm. In our training sessions, we've learned about crops and also about working on a farm.

We need to take care of what we have. I've tried to teach my children that we need to work without damaging our surroundings, what we have around us. So we need to produce, but without damaging the trees. That's something I've learned in the organization, that we have to respect life, even animal life. We need to respect trees. I've learned a lot in my life.

Another thing that's really beautiful in the cooperative is that we as women can promote working together and mutually helping each other. It's changed quite a bit over time.

WORKING WITH WOMEN: HOW FAR WE'VE COME IN THIS COMMUNITY

When we first stopped going to the men's meetings and the men heard the news that we were going to form our own cooperative, they said, "Oh, they're not going to do anything. They're just a bunch of old women."

For those members that had husbands, the men said, "The husbands are going to tell them that they need to be home, doing their work at home, their housework. They won't be able to just go this way and that, outside in the community."

But when the cooperative did form and the men saw that we really are taking important steps forward, they said, "These women have really grown some balls!" in the vocabulary that the men use. [Laughs] "Yeah, man, these are real women," because they really kind of stayed stagnant, where they were at. They haven't done anything really further.

So now there is some part of the land that is jointly held, but there are others of us that own our land outright. It's just the women.

Before, when we weren't organized, it was whatever the man decided, whatever was done on the farm, whatever was done at home. The man made the decisions—but not now. Now the women say, "My husband doesn't say to me anymore, 'You can't spend money on that.' We sit down, and we negotiate about it. We negotiate about that."

The women say, "Now things have changed. When we go to bring in our coffee to get paid for it, we both go. If we want to invest in something, now we decide, both of us."

MONEY, SAVINGS, AND PRIORITIES

In their families at this point, the women don't really have savings accounts because of what I talked about with the coffee rust [attacking our crops].

There's not a culture of savings. That's what we were trying to do with the GEMA groups, to create a culture of savings here. We've basically used all of our savings and don't have savings accounts right now because of the coffee rust. But in general, when it comes to spending, the women's priorities are for the children to go to school, take care of the family's health, and pay for expenses of farm production.

HOW I WOULD LIVE IF I HAD TONS OF MONEY

If I had tons of money, the first thing that I would do is tell my children, "I have enough for you to study a professional career in a university, a very prestigious university." I would do the best that I could do on my land, in my home, and for my health. That's what I would do.

It would be beautiful to travel, but you have to make priorities, too. So, if I were to spend money on traveling, then I might not have enough to do the other necessary things.

As for my own aspirations, I don't feel like I can go back to school. I feel like I'm kind of too old to go back to school. I have vision problems. It's not the same as when I was twenty.

But, in my dreams for the future, I'll have my land in good condition, because that's what provides me the income to live with my family. I also want to help my children, who are still in school, to continue and finish their studies. I wouldn't even take a trip to the beach, because that takes money.

NOT EVERYTHING'S ROSE-COLORED, BUT YOU CAN LIVE A GOOD LIFE WITH CLARITY

I'm very happy to be able to share part of my life with people who want to learn about our lives. I think the difficulties that I've been through or the achievements that I've been able to obtain might be important to other people in their own lives.

Not everything's rose-colored along the path of life. Not everything is beautiful. There are always difficulties along the way. There are ugly things that we have to face.

Sometimes the achievements and the difficulties that other people go through can help all of us in our own lives. For example, a young woman shouldn't have to live through what I've survived. To be clear, you don't ever have to give your whole hand, to completely give yourself over blindly to your husband or to your boyfriend; because sometimes a boyfriend or a husband doesn't really value the woman he's with.

And I think young people have to prepare themselves and become educated. If they have the opportunity to go to school, then they should go to school and take advantage of that. If they have the opportunity to work, then they should work.

Why? Because that way you don't have to be dependent on other people—because that only leads to failure. When the other person decides to take off and you're used to simply depending on that person, then you end up badly in every sense of the word. So you have to educate yourself, be prepared, and work. If you have opportunities to go to school, then go to school. If you have opportunities to work, you have to work. That's the way it is.

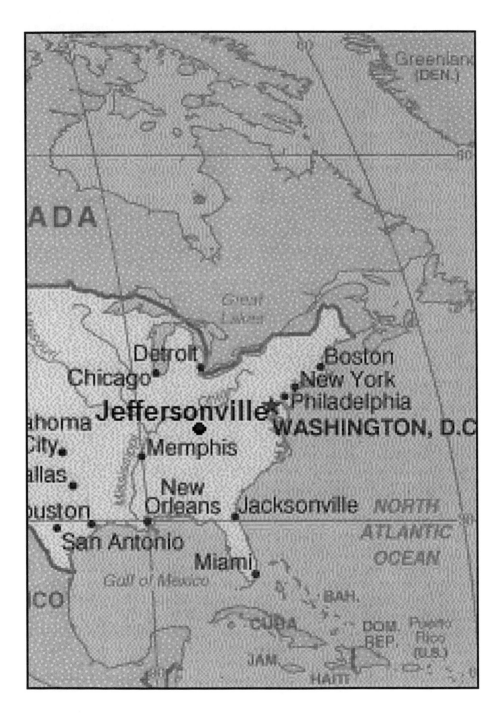

ROBIN

HORSE COACH

JEFFERSONVILLE, KENTUCKY, U.S.

Editor's note: Like many people, Robin Little-Basil works more than one job. An environmental scientist/health inspector turned horse coach, she grew up on the back of Mountain Pleasure horses, the oldest gaited breed native to North America. She and her husband also breed horses and sell them to offset the cost of her volunteer work as a horse coach for teenage girls and their parents.

"Yeah, well, I'm your fourth job—keeping me under control," jokes Robin's husband, Aaron, who works in the upstairs den as a computer programmer. It's a second marriage for both.

We're in the Bluegrass State, nicknamed for its fertile soil, lush grasses, and music. Robin has just shown me her barn and horses, and now we're sitting in the kitchen of her farmhouse, east of Lexington in Jeffersonville, Kentucky, population 1,697.

The state of Kentucky has only 4.4 million residents (that's about half as many as New York City), with one hundred people per square mile. This is The South, The Bible Belt, land of agriculture and auto manufacturing, whiskey and horses, and Kentucky Fried Chicken. Its Iroquois name, *Ken-tah-ten*, means "land of tomorrow." To the east lay the Appalachian Mountains; to the south is Tennessee; and just north of here, you cross the Mason-Dixon Line into Ohio and Yankee land.

Besides bourbon, maybe nothing says "Kentucky" like horses. And this horse owner-breeder-coach happens to be in the family: My brother Ron and his wife Shelly live on a fifty-seven acre farm down the road a piece. They've raised four spirited daughters here. Their youngest, Tessa[1]—like all of Robin's protégés—was a little girl who fell in love with horses, and survived adolescence by devoting herself to riding instead of succumbing to sex, drugs, and anguish.

I sit shotgun next to Ron as he pulls two of his horses in the trailer behind his 2004 Dodge Ram truck.

Old sedans and jacked-up pickups whiz by fast on curvy rural roads: Their drivers know every inch of these roads on which they've spent their entire lifetimes. Cows nibble tender sprouts of new spring grass on gently sloping hills, and on the right, a creek ("crick") hugs the road. Beyond that perches here an old farmhouse, there a trailer home. The landscape intersperses quaint cottages and white-steeple churches with rusted-out abandoned cars and overgrown weeds. Care and squalor compete for the same turf.

And dropped into random spots in-between are bouquets of bright yellow jonquils, riotously celebrating the triumph of another spring.

There's something about Robin that surprises me, when I first meet her in the middle of her barn. She's sipping on her insulated travel-mug of coffee in the cool, early-spring air, up to her cowboy boots in straw and horse manure. And she's *in* it, but not really *of* it. She's very pretty, almost glamorous.

We move into her house to talk. Late-morning sun slants through the windows of a house where, just like its owner's life, everything (from wallpaper to doorknobs) has to do with horses.

Robin sits back in the kitchen chair and spins the yarn of her five decades, easily moving from mental illness and alcoholism to teenage pregnancy and trailer living. The common thread throughout is her unwavering self-determination and confidence, with which she completed college as a single mom, bought acreage and horses and built not one but two homes—next-door to each other—for her and her ex.

"My life has been quite a 'ride,'" Robin jokes. "I'm happy to tell you all about it—but I have a tendency to loop stories," she warns. "I'll start somewhere, and I'll end up somewhere else entirely."

She's got a sharp tongue, a quick wit, and a fiery temper that's been known to "scatter" her girls "to the winds" to escape her wrath. What she seems not to want me to know, is that she's actually got a heart of gold.

Robin lives one county over from where she was born and puts a lot of stock into her family's local roots. She believes that as people age, they value their legacy more deeply. And in her case, that legacy has four legs.

---

1. Read about how Tessa became a horse-girl, and about Ron's and my ancestral roots in Kentucky: myjobstories.org/the-narrators/finding-my-ancestral-home-and-horse-heaven-in-kentucky.

"Horses just bring me so much joy—and I like sharing that with other people," she muses. "Being around horses all my life has definitely made me a better human being."

I HAVE THREE NAMES AND THREE JOBS

My legal name is Robin Lee Little. I didn't change it when I got married the last time, but I go by Robin Little-Basil, which is my husband's name.

I just didn't want to change my name, at this age, no children. You know what a hassle it is, as a woman, to change your name. So with this last one, I didn't. [Laughs.]

I'm forty-nine years old. I'll be fifty in August. I'm a Leo. We're sitting at the kitchen table at my home in Jeffersonville, Kentucky. My husband works upstairs. He's a software developer, and he works out of the house.

My day job is, I'm the environmental health supervisor for the Gateway District Health Department. That's a fancy title for *health inspector*. I also am a horse breeder and a drill-team coach.

I'M JUST FROM KENTUCKY

I'm just from Kentucky. I've never lived outside of it. I've traveled very little, honestly. I grew up in Menifee County, which is the next county over. That's the county I work out of as a health inspector.

I've lived in a lot of different areas in Kentucky but ended up getting a job back in Menifee County. It's relatively close to Jeffersonville. We're only about fifteen minutes from there now.

WE HAD MONEY, MENTAL ILLNESS, AND ALCOHOLISM

My mother and father were together until we were in our early teens. They weren't a very good match. They didn't openly fight, but they definitely weren't in love. My father was actually an alcoholic. My mother was bipolar. We didn't really know what that was, for years, and that was a bit of a shock. We figured that out later on.

I [have] an older sister and a little brother. I [am] the middle, but I was always much more like the older sister than she was. We were upper-middle-class, for our area. We had more money and a big house. We had things that a lot of kids didn't have. We had really nice clothes.

We were very popular in school, especially me. I was blonde. I was cute. I was really friendly. I was a very good little girl. I was always the teacher's pet, the teachers all loved me, I was the homecoming queen, blah, blah, blah.

All of that. I played basketball. I was MVP [most valued player]. I was very determined to be perfect or near close to perfect, which a lot of that was OCD, though nobody really knew that at that time. But you're very driven if you're obsessive-compulsive. So, always straight As. Everything was pretty hardcore. My sister didn't care, still doesn't. My brother is pretty laid back. [Laughs.]

Daddy's fought with alcoholism off and on his whole life. We have an okay relationship.

I had a lot of issues in my early twenties with my dad, but we're pretty good now.

My mom died at fifty-three. She had a lot of health issues on top of the bipolar. She went plumb off. I mean, there was no saving her. She was completely gone. When she went through menopause, she actually completely lost her mind.

I mean, she did the full-on Aluminum Foil Cap Club. Have you heard of that? A lot of people, when they're bipolar, at some point decide that aliens are after them. She thought electrical impulses were being shot at her. So they jokingly call it the Aluminum Cap Club, where people would put aluminum foil on their heads to keep the signals from getting in.

I've had this conversation with my doctor. Her dad was also bipolar. We say, "Neither one of us are bipolar, but we were raised by bipolar parents. So we mimic bipolar behavior occasionally."

I don't have the highs and the lows, but I get very manic at times, like getting things done, very, very fast, very quick. A lot of that came from being raised where, that's what you did. That was my mother's manic behavior, but we didn't recognize it. We thought everyone got on their hands and knees and scrubbed the carpets and the floor! That was just normal for us. So I do exhibit some manic behavior. It's actually been pretty productive for me over the years. [Laughs.] I can do more in a day than most people do in a week, especially if I get myself all cranked up, fired into it, drinking too much coffee.

Then my parents divorced, and we went from being wealthy to being extremely poor. My mom didn't get anything in the divorce. So then we lived in a little shack, but we didn't really recognize that we were really poor. When you're a kid, you don't really notice that much.

Mom was a wonderful mother. She really was. She was a good, loving, caring person. We didn't know what was wrong with her. But when I was seventeen, she basically said, "You've got to leave." I had no idea why, but it didn't really matter because I just left. I was like, "Okay."

My sister had already moved out. My brother went to live with my dad. I wasn't quite through high school yet. I went to live with the man who was [my daughter] Jenna's biological dad. I'd only gone out with him a couple of times, but I didn't have anywhere else to go. So I went and moved in with him.

I THOUGHT I WOULD BE A VETERINARIAN, NOT THE COUNTY HEALTH INSPECTOR

When I was growing up, I didn't even know there was such a thing as a health inspector. I wanted to be a veterinarian because, like all little girls that grow up in the country and love animals, you want to be a vet so you can have animals and get to play with them all day.

After I moved out of Mom's, I was a pre-vet at Morehead State University. My parents did not support me in college, but I managed, just the way people manage everything. If you want to, you can . . .

I was nineteen when I got pregnant. Back in the day, they didn't really tell you that, if you were on antibiotics, that affected your birth control pills. So I got pregnant on birth control pills. That was devastating, of course, back then, but it was the best thing that ever happened to me.

People always think that when you have kids. They're like, "Oh, my god, it's the end of the world," and it's not. It's fine. You just learn to go on.

Jenna's my only child. I was very driven and determined, so I don't know that I would have ever just taken the time out and said, "Now's the time for me to have a kid." So if it hadn't been for that, I would maybe never even have had children. Now Jenna's turning thirty this year.

So I got through college fine, kind of on my own. I don't consider myself to have had a bad childhood by any stretch of the imagination. I mean, I was very lucky. I was never raped. It could have been so much worse.

I did a lot of things that I wouldn't have smiled on had Jenna done them, but I didn't really think anything about them. I lived in a home for a while, when Jenna was born, where we kind of bootlegged whiskey. That was how we made our money, you know? That was fun. We did that for a while. But I never got into drugs. I didn't care for alcohol. My dad's an alcoholic. My sister's a bit of an alcoholic. I didn't get the taste for it, thank God. So it never was really an issue for me.

When Jenna was a baby, I had her dad sign his rights away. He was a very nice guy, but it was not working. Then I lived on my own, in an old mobile home, for years. That was kind of gross, but we were fine.

I always took her to daycare. I worked part-time jobs to get through college. It was okay. I mean, it was a little hard. When I was twenty, I decided I couldn't do seven years of the pre-vet program with a child. So I switched my major to a biology degree with a chemistry minor and ended up with an environmental science degree. Morehead is just a local regional college, but it has a really top-notch environmental science department.

GETTING MARRIED AND, LATER, WANTING TO KILL THE GUY

When Jenna was seven, I married [my ex] Drexel. We were married for pretty close to fifteen years, I guess. When Jenna went to college, I kicked into early menopause.

I wanted to kill everybody. I hated everybody. I didn't know that was normal. I just felt mean and angry all the time. Drexel was and is still a wonderful man and one of my very best friends, but I wasn't in love with him.

I finally told him, I said, "Look, we need to get divorced because I don't know really what's going on, but at the end of it, you're going to hate me. Like we really, really love each other as what we are, but you're going to hate me because I'm going to make your life a living nightmare, and I can't help it. It just is what it is."

He didn't like that at first, but it was rough living with me because I'm very demanding at my best. At my worst, I'm mean. I'm a mean son of a gun. I'm pretty scary. When I'm angry, I'm *really* angry. I've just kind of accepted it. I'm not a bad person; I'm a really good person in a lot of ways, but I know me. I'm OCD. Certain things set me off every time. If you don't want to set me off, simply don't do that. It's just that easy.

I divorced him for his own sake, to spare him from my temper. I really did. But then he ended up living next door.

Drexel and I are still best friends. When we were married, Drexel adopted Jenna, and he and I actually bought this whole farm. There was sixty-eight acres when we bought it, and then we added a little bit more to it. When we divorced, we just kind of split it down the middle. So I took the right-hand side. He took the left-hand side. I may have a little bit more—thirty-five or forty acres. We're still best friends. He lives right down over the hill.

We're both remarried. We have barbecues together. We hang out together all the time.

But I will say this: Don't make me out to be a really good person. Now he realizes our divorce was the greatest thing that probably ever happened to him, but, at the time, he was devastated. [Laughs.] But the fact is, I couldn't stand him. I really wanted him out. I loved him, but I really wanted him out. I just couldn't stand him anymore.

I did, though, fix him up with his [second] wife, Sandy. Her daughter rode on our drill team for years, and I actually went to high school with her, and I love her. She is probably one of the finest people I've ever known, much more akin to his temperament, much more quiet. Drexel is very quiet, hardworking, very stoical. Like I'm kind of loud and bubbly, and he's very quiet and mellow. So the two of them together do much better.

MY SECOND HUSBAND IS THE PERFECT MAN FOR ME

My husband, Aaron, showed up a few years ago, just a freak thing, and for some reason, he just is absolutely enamored with me. He thinks I'm the greatest thing that ever lived. Even when I'm mean, he's just like, "Oh, my god, that just makes me love you more." [Laughs.]

We actually met on Match.com. We are such a cliché. Our whole relationship is a cliché.

This is so funny. We met online, which Aaron will tell you right now, is ridiculous because it was just a freak coincidence.—I was only on there for three days. I *hate* computers; I just had nothing else to do.

It was right around Christmas. They had a free weekend thing, and I typed on there. You should have seen my profile. I mean, I was brutal. I was like, "I am mean, hateful, high-strung," which I am, all this stuff, and Aaron responded. He was one of the first ones to respond. He's very romantic. He claims he had been looking for me his whole life, desperately looking for me. He's so cute. He said, "I went on a thousand first dates looking for you."

I mean, this is his story. He's very adorable.

He'd been married before. He has three children. He'd been divorced about three years. He was the only one on Match that I talked to, the only one that I said okay to—only because he was like, "I'll come today. Can we meet today? I'll drive to you," because he was in Lexington at the time. I was like, "I'm not driving to Lexington to meet you." [Laughs.]

I think it was Christmas Eve. I said, "Well, honestly, I'm going to my dad's." My dad is a rough cat to meet right off the bat, you know? I'm like, "If you want to go tackle my dad on your first date," and he was like, "I'll be there," and he's never left. He's been here ever since. It's just funny.

We've been together now going on four years. I'm myself more with him than I've ever been with anybody else, because what I consider to be my negative qualities, he doesn't consider to be negative. So it works for us. He softens me a lot.

I had gotten very, not hard, but definitely more manly. I'm a little bit more on the testosterone-y side than the feminine side with the way I think and my behavior, and so that's difficult for a lot of men. It takes a strong man, but they can't be *too* strong, or else it's going to cause a fight.

So, you know, he's much more dominant than one would think when they first meet him, or else I'd mash him. He can hold his own, and yet he's very good with me. He's very, very good with me.

WE'RE AN ALL-FEMALE TEAM IN A BIBLE-BELT, CAUCASIAN COUNTY

I've been with the health department for twenty-one years, and I've been the supervisor for probably fifteen of those. Our team all graduated from Morehead with degrees in environmental science. So we're all really good friends, all women. That's rare throughout the state.

We actually work for the county, but we're state employees. It's an odd thing. Every district or county in Kentucky has to have a health inspector. Our district is four counties: Menifee, Morgan, Bath, and Rowan. They're rural counties, small populations. A health inspector in Lexington, Fayette, or Louisville area would have a much less area to cover than we do, for example, because they have a lot of inspectors. We have just one per county.

This is considered part of The Bible Belt. It's mostly Democratic in this area, mostly white, very, as a matter of fact; there are probably very few African Americans in Menifee County. There's a small population of African Americans in Bath County, and there's some in Rowan County, but that's because it's a college town. I would say, in the four counties, very few, very few Hispanics, almost none. Everybody else is primarily Caucasian. That's about all you see.

A lot of the counties are still very cliquish. If your family is not from there, they basically never really accept you.

TWO TYPES OF KENTUCKIANS: HARD-WORKERS AND WELFARE FAMILIES

In these four counties, you have two very distinct groups of people. You have really hard-working, agricultural-based people. Most of them came from generation after generation of farm families. Years ago, when the farming started to die off in the area, a lot of the younger generation moved to Ohio. A lot of people worked at the plants up there, where there was more factory-type work.

Then you also have a lot of people that are what we call long-term welfare.[2] A lot of them at this point are fourth or fifth generation that have never worked. They've never done anything but draw from the welfare system. That's really common in this area. They'll move into our area from outside, because we have such a high unemployment rate and high poverty level that they get more money.

A lot of them come from the coal counties, Pike County, Hazard, that area—Eastern Kentucky. Also from like Ohio and different states, because they tell me the welfare rate

---

2. According to local news station WKYT, 21% of Kentucky residents receive government assistance; more are on temporary assistance: wkyt.com/home/headlines/WKYT-Investigates-208393651.html.

is much higher in this area. So they move down here to draw a higher check. If you move to a poorer county, it increases your welfare check.

WE BARGE INTO BUSINESSES AND DEMAND CHANGES THAT WILL COST YOU MONEY

We go into businesses. Pretty much any public building that has a public in-and-out gets inspected by us. They have to follow certain Kentucky state regulations*, and we have to go and enforce those.

We do kitchen inspections, school inspections, mobile homes, hotels, motels—from food to poop, and everything in-between! We inspect tanning beds, meth labs, you know, pretty much anything. If the state police bust one, they contact us to go out, and we actually do the physical posting on the house or the car or whatever it is, at that point. We post it as a meth lab and say that you're not allowed on the property, blah, blah, blah. It's kind of like a quarantine notice more than anything else.

We're basically the throw-all. Any program that comes out that they don't know what else to do with, they just kind of pitch at us. And sometimes we have them for a while, and then they take them away. Like, we did body piercing for a while, for the whole state of Kentucky. Then they came back and said, "That's really medical. So we'll give that to medical." So they took that away from us. We still do the tattoo parlors, and we do limited ear piercing.

We do regular food inspections. In addition to that, because we're in a rural area, we also do all the septic systems. So we go out, dig the holes, look at the dirt, tell you what to put in, how many feet, that kind of thing, and then we go out and inspect them. There's also a rabies program where we quarantine and release animals. There's a lot of variety associated with the environmental field, and I really like it. [Laughs.] That's my day job.

And then I actually have a schedule book. I may do four inspections in Rowan County today. I may go to Morgan and do a site evaluation, which is where we look at the dirt. You know, I may go do a final for a septic system. I may go to Bath County to quarantine a dog. It's not unusual for me to go a hundred miles a day, every day. So I'm mostly on the road.

But when I do my inspections is not really important. And where I do my paperwork is not important. So often I bring things home. This has been a really quality job for me because I require a lot of flexibility with my schedule, because of the horses.

IT MATTERS A LOT THAT I'M FROM AROUND HERE

With my job, it's really important that people here know who you are, because of the lack of transplants in the area. It's made my job a lot easier because my family is really well known and well liked in the county.

My grandfather ran a country store for seventy years. He was a postmaster. My dad was a postmaster. A lot of the "Littles" were storekeepers. Even my brother has had stores. So people know the "Little" name, and that's made it a lot easier for me.

For example, with an elderly gentleman, especially a farmer-type, let's say I go onto their property because there was a complaint of sewage. Their first instinct is to be, "Get

---

* chfs.ky.gov/dph

off my land. You're not going to tell me what to do. I don't know who you are," you know? And I've been really blessed because I can usually just say, "Hey, how are you doing? Who are you? I'm Robin *Little*."

"Little? Who's your family?"

That's what happens. A lot of people thought it would be more difficult for me to work in the county that I grew up in, but it's actually been considerably easier because, if they know you or think they know you, then you're accepted, versus being an outsider.

I'm also friendly by nature. So it's pretty easy for me to slide into the Southern, "How y'all doin'? How's everything going? Boy, it sure is a pretty day. The weather's been nice."

I was raised in that type of situation. So I can easily fall into that, and that's usually what I do. I put on my hometown persona or whatever you want to call it. It's not fake; it's part of me. Once you've made that connection, all of a sudden, everybody's family, and that's good. People are just comfortable with what they know. It's like, the devil you know.

I try to make people comfortable because normally when I go in, I'm going to give you bad news. I'm going to give you a bad score. I'm going to make you throw your food away. I'm going to cost you money. So I try to cut the edge off of it a little bit.

Sometimes if they're really upset, I'm like, "Look, you know, it's either going to be me or it's going to be somebody else. I mean, you simply can't do what you're doing. You know, this isn't 1940 anymore. You can't run that pipe over the hill, honey. It's just not going to be okay." [Laughs.] I try to soften it with words, "honey" and "sugar."

NO TECHNOLOGY HERE: WE STILL FILL OUT PAPERWORK IN TRIPLICATE

Our normal hours, we work 37.5 hours a week, usually from 8:00 to 4:30. In our district, they've been really lenient with our time schedules, because basically people don't come into the health department to see me. So it's not like I have to be there. The office is fifteen minutes away from my home. I'm there every morning from 8:00 to 9:00, because that makes people happy. They can call or whatever. During that time, I also do a lot of paperwork and emails. We have quite a bit of paperwork associated with our jobs.

Our inspections are still triplicate, hand-filled-out inspections with carbon paper. They've tried really hard over the years to do away with those, and it's just never worked because the problem is, you go in, you do the inspection, and you need to give them a copy of it because we post it now. In order to do that, you have to have a printer. So they gave us portable printers. Well, they were always messed up. There simply wasn't a better way to do it than just to handwrite it, tear it off, and hand it to them, and go on.

And, honestly, my husband says I'm a bit of a Luddite . . .[3]

I don't resent technology, but I don't really enjoy it. I think it's very busy, intrusive. I enjoy looking at Facebook just like everybody else does. And, sure, I'm glad to text you or whatever, but the fact that people sit and stare at their phones for hours and hours and hours bugs me. I'm very active. If people sit around too long and look at things, the way I was raised, you're just ornery, meaning, *lazy*. (In this area, ornery can mean both.)

---

3. Luddite: a person opposed to increased industrialization or new technology.

When my daughter was growing up, there were no videogames ever in my house. I can't stand for a kid to sit in front of a video. It just drives me nuts. I'm like, "You need to get up. You need to move, play, occupy yourself."

I'M A FOURTH-GENERATION HORSE BREEDER OF MOUNTAIN PLEASURE HORSES

I'm a fourth-generation horse breeder. My great-grandfather had them, yes, and my grandfather, who was a wonderful horseman. So I'm the fourth generation of this same bloodline of horse. Every horse out here is related.

Right now, I have twenty-one horses. We have thirty-five acres here. We have some other acreage in other places, but this is primarily where we keep them. We have what's called "Mountain Pleasure Horses."[4] They are the oldest gaited [smooth-riding] breed of horse in North America. They did a bunch of DNA testing on them back in the 1980s, and they're proven to be the father breed of all other gaited breeds in North America.

It wasn't like I searched the breed out or did whatever. They're the only horse I ever knew. I grew up with them, and we loved them, but we didn't realize how special they were. But, as I got older, as most people do, you learn to appreciate the heritage and the history behind some things. I had always loved horses, and I had always loved *our* horses, but I didn't know what they meant to the people of Eastern Kentucky. They were the entire livelihood for these people. These people would have died if it hadn't been for these horses.

These horses did everything for them. They pulled the buggies. They pulled the plows. They took the kids to school. They were everything for these people, and the people bred them accordingly. Only the very best of the best were bred, because they couldn't afford more than one horse.

Now, they're a rare and endangered breed. There are probably only 2,500 of them left in the world, and we have twenty of those. It's a big deal. There are no larger breeders of these horses. A lot of the other breeds become more popular, as trends waft one way or the other, but I'm so proud of ours.

I had an epiphany: My true passion is these horses. This is really what drives me. I'm the president of the Mountain Pleasure Horse Association this year. We're really trying to save them. Every colt that we bring about helps keep it from extinction.

My daughter's now almost thirty. She's like, "I just don't know if I can continue this heritage when you're gone, because I just don't get into it like you do." And I'm like, "You're not there yet. This might end up being a huge deal later in your life."

We don't necessarily want to see it explode into popularity, because that always causes problems with breeding; you know what I mean? When "Rin Tin Tin" was out, all of a sudden, everybody bred German shepherds, and you got crazy German shepherds. So we don't want that to happen here, but we also don't want to see them disappear. They're just such a wonderful heritage horse.

---

4. Watch a 3-minute video on the Mountain Pleasure breed here: youtu.be/gz2acSDPeo4, and read about them here: mountainpleasurehorseassociation.com.

They're so gentle, so calm, so easy. You can take a very novice rider and put her on a two-year-old horse, and they'll grow up together. That's fairly unheard of, in the horse world outside of our breed. I mean, it's not just done. You would have somebody killed. And, yet, for us, that's just normal everyday fare.

Mountain Pleasure horses make good drill-team horses, because they're bred to do anything you ask them to. They can climb mountains and rocky trails like goats. And they're unbelievably tolerant.

HORSE CARE: YOU CAN SPEND ALL DAY OR TWENTY MINUTES A DAY

It's not as time-consuming as you would think. We don't do that much horse care. Our horses are outside all the time. I feed them in the winter. I throw them corn, ear corn out of a bucket, and let them go get it. I don't brush my horses. I don't fool with them. I mean, we take good care of them, but I don't baby them. I simply have too many. I would never get anything done.

When the farrier [who trims and shoes horses' hoofs] comes, it's an all-day event, but that's only once every eight weeks or so. So it's not terrible. It's not bad. You can pretty much spend all day every day caring for your horses, or twenty minutes a day. It's really entirely up to you.

I don't keep horses in the barn. The only reason I'm keeping the stalls clean right now is I have pregnant mares in there. If the one foals, I don't want it to be in a bunch of poop. For now, I'll clean up the stalls, but that's not very often, because I don't keep them in there very much.

Sometimes you have to put in the time. The day before yesterday, I pulled a foal. It doesn't take very long. A cow can take half-a-day to have a calf. A horse, from the time its water breaks to the time the colt is out, you've got about a forty-five-minute window. If you go past that, you could lose one or both.

We have video cameras in the barn. Aaron designed an app where there's an orange ribbon running around the inside of Keeper's [the expectant mare's] stall. There's some sort of recognition software that he hooked up, that basically the code will tell you if Keeper is below that line, and an alarm goes off. The mare lays down to have her foal. They lay down to have them. So basically an alarm comes on that says, "Keeper's down." It's the sound of a horse neighing. [Laughs.]

My husband is a genius. He's probably the smartest person I've ever met. I'm grateful every day I'm not as smart as him, because his mind is constantly running. I can't even explain to you how he wrote this out, because I don't understand the math behind it. It's crazy weird.

Before we had that app, we had to check every two hours just to make sure they're up, or that they're not showing signs of labor. And not all horses have as difficult a time as Keeper, but her colts are always exceptionally large, and she's twenty-one. She's not a young mare. You don't have to pull every colt, but her colts, you do. And this week, she had a very easy delivery. She pretty much has a colt every year.

I didn't raise Keeper. I bought her specifically to be the brood mare. I've got two brood mares, actually. There's one stallion here. We're very specific. He's over there in a field all by himself. He can't breed anybody out there, because they're all related to him, except those two mares.

INTERBREEDING HORSES IN KENTUCKY: THOROUGHBREDS AND RACEHORSES

Interbreeding is an issue in Kentucky. I don't mean to pick on a certain breed of horse. The Mountain horses are the father breed of all these; but for example, about fifty years ago, there was a stallion that had a chocolate color. He was brown with a white mane and tail, very pretty. Some people just think they're the most beautiful things ever. In order to get that color, he was the only one that threw it [passed it on through his DNA].

So they basically bred him and bred him and bred him: to his daughters and to his granddaughters, and bred him; because he was the only one that produced that chocolate color. So that's where you get the inbreeding, the really severe inbreeding.

That's the Rocky Mountain horse. Not to denigrate them, they love their horses—they're a little uppity. Wealthy people have Rocky Mountain horses, and you get the little snooty thing going on, but they're very proud of the fact that they're 70 percent taupe or whatever. I'm a Mountain Pleasure person. This is the only breed I've ever had or known.

Kentucky is considered the horse capital of the world, but that's based on the thoroughbreds. I have no interest in the Kentucky Derby at all. Racing horses means nothing to me.

Racehorse people are not anything like us. They don't think like us; they don't treat their horses like us. Thoroughbreds, Arabians, mean nothing to me. This is literally all I've ever known. These are my horses. I take great pride in them.

In general, this is a very horse-happy state, but there are lots of breeds. For my breed, Kentucky is definitely the pinnacle.

WE SELL ABOUT TWO HORSES PER YEAR TO PAY OUR EXPENSES

Our horses are self-sustaining. I usually have to sell at least a couple a year. Don't get me wrong: We're very specific about which ones we sell and how we sell and stuff, but, as a general rule, at least two horses a year have to be sold to pay for the rest of them. As long as it's self-sustaining, we do okay with it, because we enjoy it.

And a good horse still brings in a good price. We sell mostly to out-of-state people. Here, for the drill team kids, if I can find them a good horse or if I raise one and I don't have a lot of money in it, I will let them have it for practically nothing, which is $2,000, which wouldn't cover the feed bill. I mean, Keeper's out there going through a lot of grain. You've got an enormous amount of money in them.

But most of our horses end up going to out-of-state people. They'll bring in $4,000 or $5,000. A good horse is going to bring a good price. It really will. Not around here, just because most of the people around here can't afford it. But I sell horses primarily to older women, middle-aged women.

We don't put our horses up for sale. We have horses for sale all the time, but they're never "up for sale." People come; I don't know why. They just do. I do not advertise at all.

NOT THE HORSE WHISPERER, BUT A HORSE-HUMAN MATCHMAKER

I don't believe that I communicate with horses. I'm really good at matchmaking horses to riders, though. I'm not being braggy, but I'm probably one of the best people around, and it's not that I know so much. I base it on the fact that I grew up with them and watched them a lot and adored them when I was little. I read human body language pretty well, but I read equine body language *really* well.

A friend of mine wrote a book several years ago, and she put me in the book. Before we were friends, she came looking for a horse. She thought she knew what she wanted, and she came here.

I told her, "Don't think you know what you want, because you don't know what you want until you've found it."

I mean, you just don't. You think you want a fourteen-two-hand palomino [about 58 inches tall from the foot to the top of the back] that's this and that, but you've got to be attached to that horse. You've got to have an attachment. It's almost like love at first sight.

Like if you came to me, and you were looking to buy a horse, I would say, "How do you like to ride?" because horses are like people. They have very distinct personalities. You've got brave people; you've got brave horses. You've got timid people; you've got timid horses.

Do you like to ride in the front, or the back? Horses are the same way. You've got some that want to lead, and they're happy, and you've got others that are happier in the back [of the pack]. Some like to be by themselves; some like being with a group. It's the same thing.

You have to figure out which horse likes to ride the same way you like to ride, because that's where you're going to be happy. You need an animal that enjoys the same thing you do. If you don't, you're always going to have a conflict.

But the weird thing that happens is, horses will tell you whom they like and whom they don't, and they're very, very obvious about it most of the time. It's their body language. My friend was like, "How do you know?" and I'm like, "I don't know. I just know."

But there's got to be something that's cueing me off. I can tell by looking.

So basically what we do is say, "Okay. Why don't you walk around out in the field? Just walk around and look around," and the horse will actually tell me whom they like, which is really funny.

A lot of times, they'll come walking up to people. People think all my horses are friendly, but some are very standoffish, and they're the most obvious. If they come to people, that's easy. I'm like, "He never willingly comes to anybody," and, all of a sudden, he's in your pocket and behind you and wallering all over you, you know? And I'm like, "Okay, you might consider this horse." [Laughs.] I'm just saying.

COACHING TEENAGE GIRLS: OUR DRILL TEAM CHANGES LIVES

Our drill team[5] started about fifteen, sixteen years ago. It actually started when Jenna was in high school.

If you think about horse drill teams, it's a marching band on horseback, or cheerleaders on horseback. You have a very distinct choreography going on. My girls *hate* that description. Most horse girls are not the cheerleader type. A lot of these kids in the youth squad were misfits.

But Jenna was never a troubled teen. She was very much like me: an overachiever. She was valedictorian of her class. She was prom queen, captain of the cheerleading squad. Jenna was never bad. Horses were just always part of her life. She enjoys dressing up and showing off.

We wanted to do something fun with the horses, so one year we went to State 4-H competition, and they had a drill team there, and we were like, "Oh, my god, that's so fun. Let's do that." So that's how the Licking River Riders, our 4-H drill team for nine-to-eighteen-year-olds, began. It's not restricted to girls, but over the years, it's been primarily all girls.

It's a totally different mentality between boys and girls. Most boys don't really take an interest in horses until they get older. They look at horses like bicycles. When girls look at horses, it's love. Little girls *love* their horses, I mean, beyond any reasonable amount. Boys just look at them as something fun to play with, and to get from here to there.

MY YEAR IS SEASONAL—THAT IS, ALL SEASONS

I work year-round on my job. We don't take a break. And then for the drill team, we have our last event about mid-December, which is the Christmas party, and we do the Christmas parades, and then we start back up in February. So we don't really break.

We do a lot of things together. We do a lot of camp-outs. I have found with these kids, you're better off to keep them together and keep them going. They get along really well.

HOW TO HELP A KID: HAVE THEM HELP SOMEONE ELSE

I also have the kids do at least two or three community-based projects a year, because we're still [members of] 4-H, and the kids need to give back.

We do an annual deaf-blind camp where they bring in a busload of people. We really enjoy that. They bring them to the ring over there [points out her kitchen window]. We've done that for several years. They come in mostly from the Louisville area.

I've worked with handicapped adults. A lot of these people are old, wheelchair-bound. Some are visually impaired. Some can't hear. They bring them in: elderly, wheelchairs, up around eighty years old or so. They bring them in, and we take them for rides. Last year, we had over fifty people come. The kids and their parents do it. They love it. It's probably their favorite event that they do.

---

5. See Robin's drill teams here: facebook.com/Licking-River-Riders-Gaited-Drill-Team-103042226399904, and here: facebook.com/Rockin-R-Rhythm-Riders-Gaited-Drill-Team-103962979635582.

If you really want to see joy, that's where you will see joy. You want to see people crying, come to that. I have parents that sob like babies, just saying, "This is the most wonderful thing I've ever done in my life." I mean, that's pretty awesome. To be able to give back like that for a lot of people is really therapeutic, too.

We've also gone to Hope Hill Children's Home. It used to be an orphanage years ago, and now it's a home for troubled teens. A few years ago, they started an equine program there to try to help these kids. A lot of these girls had emotional scarring, baggage, whatever you want to call it; and they wanted to bring in some horses to help them out. So we took our drill team up there and did a demo for them, and showed them what a drill team is, because they thought they might start one up there.

This is all on the Rockin R Rhythm Riders' Facebook page. I think it's either on that or the Licking River Riders. I've got a couple of parents who're really good about taking pictures for us.

We also do a lot of big venues. We do BreyerFest at the Horse Park. We're there three or four times a year. We travel a lot with these horses. We do some competitions, but we also do a lot of demonstrations. We're getting ready to go to the Equine Affaire in Columbus, Ohio. We've been there every year for about eight years.

HOW WE FUND OUR TEAM

We don't get funded: It's just an organized group. We have to follow lot of parameters. There are a lot of rules associated with 4-H. We've done everything from yard sales to bake sales to anything. Right now we're selling RADA knives. They basically order crap out of the catalog, and you get 39 percent of it. A lot of the kids have sponsors.

It doesn't take as much money as you'd think, though. Most of the parents just foot the bill. Some of the traveling costs, we do have to do some fundraisers for.

COACHING ALONGSIDE MY DAUGHTER, JENNA

I coached the Licking River Riders when Jenna was in there; and then she aged out, because in 4-H, you age out when you're eighteen. So she started helping me coach when she was nineteen, and then she has been with me all these years. We do it together. Actually, Jenna designs the choreography. She is fantastic at the choreography, *fantastic*. I mean, she just pulls it out of her ass.

Jenna is also better with the kids. She loves children. Actually, she is the visually-impaired teacher for the Bath County school systems. She started out as an elementary school teacher and then went and got her master's degree in visually impaired. So Jenna works with children all day. All of her life, she's done riding lessons, swimming lessons; any kind of lessons pretty much that a kid can be taught, Jenna's done it. So she was a born teacher. She enjoys the kids.

Jenna loves the little kids. I actually love the teenagers. I do. I find teenagers to be just all kind of entertainment. But I probably get more enjoyment out of the parents. I really like the adults.

HOW I ENDED UP COACHING TWO SQUADS

We started out with the kids, and Jenna would do the riding lessons, and then the parents would be like, "I'd really like to ride," and I'm like, "Well, we can get you on. Let's help you." It's really been fun because it gives the kids something to do with their parents that bonds them together, and a lot of them still ride together.

Once the girls age out of 4-H, they go to the Rockin R Rhythm Riders, which is the adult squad. What happened was, a lot of my kids aged out of 4-H, and they still wanted to ride. So I'm like, "Well, heck, you all want to ride, we'll ride."

The number of people on the drill teams varies. Right now, I think there're fourteen on the youth squad. The adult squad can go up to up into the twenties. If the kids want to ride on the adult squad, they can, too. So it usually ranges somewhere from around twelve to fourteen.

The adult squad, we'll do all kinds of goofy stuff with them. They don't learn faster, but they kind of get the idea of spacing and timing; like, you've got to be the same distance away than that one. Adults have that mentally already set in their head. Children don't. They have no real concept of spacing and timing. They have to just repetitively do it.

Normally, when we go in for a competition, with our kids, and you've got to be horribly repetitive, like it takes them a million times, if they're doing a routine to really get the routine. So we teach them one routine a year usually, and that's their base.

Most of the kids come back. They go to college or simply get too busy to do whatever. But I seriously expect at some point to get thirty and thirty-five year olds back, because they love it. It's a lot of fun. It's a really good group, and we laugh a lot.

I'm not paid for this work. I really don't know why I'm committed to it, other than I truly enjoy it. I love my kids. I love the parents. I've got to get something out of it or I wouldn't do it. I don't know what the something is, but there's something. That, or I'm just too stubborn and strong-willed to let it go. I love it. I still love it.

THE THERAPEUTIC VALUE OF HORSES

For a lot of people, horses are so therapeutic. It's very emotional as well as physical. A lot of kids bond with horses, animals in general, but with horses, especially girls. I don't know why.

I'm blessed to be able to say that. I believe that. I've seen it happen time and time again, kids just completely and utterly changed because of these animals. And it's wonderful. If you can give somebody that, gosh. What an advantage to give somebody the chance to remake themselves.

We've had a lot of antisocial kids who bond really strongly with horses. I've got two girls on there right now, that there's probably not a handful of people in the world that would give a shit if they live or die. I mean, that's just the way it is. We've had some pretty rough kids over the years. We've had some Goth kids, and some cutters. They have a tendency to bond with horses very well. They usually end up staying on the team. They usually end up healing.

We had a girl that was taken in by her grandmother that was probably about thirteen at the time. She had a little sister, too, no father. Her mother was taken in for drug abuse, so she had lost her rights. So the grandparents took her in.

The grandmother called me and she said, "I'm going to lose her. Social Services is going to come take her. We can't do anything with her. She is cutting herself all the time. She's just very nasty. She won't mind. She won't do anything."

I said, "Bring her over. We'll see what we can do."

So she brought her to riding lessons. She rolled out of the car, and she was a Goth. She had all this black on and the piercings and the weird pantyhose with rips in them and stuff. She was overweight. She was heavy. She had a lot of issues, and she was very sullen and moody: "I don't want to do it. I'm not going to do it. You can't make me do it. I'm not going to do this."

I finally told the grandmother, "Look, why don't you all go into town and shop or whatever it is you need to do? She doesn't have to ride. If she just wants to hang out in the barn, that's fine. Just let her hang out in the barn. We have other kids that ride, if she wants to do whatever."

So I said, "If you want to go, go pet it. Go brush it, whatever. Just sit here if you want to." That was pre-cellphone days. So she was just having to sit there. [Laughs.]

I'm fairly strict on the girls, and so I told her, "Look, you can't dress this way. Number One, you look ridiculous. You can't dress this way. It's unacceptable. You've got to wear real boots." She had those big clobby black ones with the pointy things on them. I was like, "No, you can't wear those."

So eventually she started riding, and her grandmother said it was her favorite activity. We eased her on and got her on the drill team. I'm still friends with her on Facebook. She's probably in her early twenties now, and she ended up getting through high school, going to college. She has a degree, and her grandmother said, "Never would I have dreamed in a million years we would have got her through there."

She's told multiple people, it just changed her life. This was life-changing for her; but that's true for a lot of kids.

HORSES HAVE SAVED A FEW OF OUR PARENTS' LIVES, TOO

Sandy, the one that married [my ex] Drexel, was in an abusive marriage. She had been married for twenty-some years, and she just took it because she thought that was her life. Her daughter Emily is severely ADHD, and we took her in, and Sandy gravitated towards us because I don't think a lot of people had been that kind to Emily.

Sandy started riding, too. She had never ridden. She started riding, and I truly believe it gave her the strength to eventually leave her abusive, alcoholic husband. It totally changed her life.

Another example would be a drill team kid's mother, Cora. She came here when her daughter Megan started doing riding lessons. Cora was dangerously obese. She's not very tall. She's maybe 5'2", and she weighed almost 400 pounds at one time. She almost died. She's a schoolteacher.

Cora had the [stomach] surgery done. I can't remember which one: gastric bypass or one of them. She started losing weight and started coming here to ride. She was bringing Megan to riding lessons. And she said, "You know, I rode when I was a little girl." She said, "I sure loved it."

I said, "Cora, do you want to ride?"

Cora said, "I couldn't ride."

"Sure. Why can't you ride?"

And she started riding, and now she owns a horse and rides in the adult squad. Cora's told people, "I never dreamed that I would ever be able to live the life that I'm living. I just love it so much."

It totally changed her life. She went from being 400 pounds and going to die, to riding on a drill team all dressed up in a costume in front of people, riding in parades and waving at all her kids. We go trail riding and camping. I mean, Cora's right there every time. It's awesome.

I think it gives people a different view of what *could* be. If you're around this group of people, you see, "*This* could be my life. I could do that. I really could."

OUR CHRISTIAN BACKGROUND AND HOW WE DON'T REALLY TRUST CHURCHES

I grew up just Christian nondenominational. My mother wasn't so much religious as she was very—I mean, she believed. She was a very firm believer, but she didn't like church, which kind of threw me off of it a little bit. Looking back now, part of that was probably the bipolar thing, because she simply thought things were happening that weren't happening.

She had a lot of paranoia issues, I'm sure derived from the bipolar. So we were raised not to trust churches. The churches are unfortunately often misguided. They take people's money. They do bad things. Preachers do things they shouldn't do. [Laughs.] They sleep with prostitutes. Mom was a little bit like, you know, "I'll just read my Bible at home."

She loved [the Reverend] Billy Graham. She was all about Billy Graham. Other than him, I don't think she ever truly trusted another preacher. He walked his talk.

MY WORLDVIEW IS OPTIMISM

I am definitely an optimist, probably a Christian. I believe. I've prayed many, many times. I tell you what: I'm not really a club person [to belong to a church], which is odd, considering I run the drill team. I really enjoy sharing horses. They have been such a source of joy to me. I love when other people can experience that. And you don't have to own your horse in order to have that therapeutic effect. Most people start out borrowing mine, because horses are very expensive.

A really quality horse is going to cost you around $5,000. It's like a car. And then that's not the most expensive part. The upkeep over the years, taking care, is going to be thousands of dollars. The saddles, the tack, the grooming stuff. It's fairly costly. It's a hobby like any other hobby, but it's one that you just get a lot back from. It's not a bass boat.—You're going to get a lot of stuff back from this hobby.

MY HAPPIEST MOMENT IS WHEN I SEE A KID OVERCOMING HER FEARS

I've had a lot of good moments as a drill team coach. Probably the best moments were when I've seen kids overcome their fears. One of my proudest moments was with Megan, who came to us when she was about ten. It's her mother that I told you that was so heavy. So Megan came to us, and she had been to another riding lesson teacher, and they had scared her. She was young, and scared. Some kids are either very scared or very brave to start with. That's just a personality thing. And Megan was very timid.

She was very heavy, and she was quiet, very bashful. She wanted to ride, but she was so scared that she threw up every single time before she got on…But she got on. And so she learned. She is now in her twenties, and is one of the finest riders I've ever had. She's probably one of my proudest moments. She's one of the really good ones.

MY WORST MOMENT IS WHEN I LOSE MY TEMPER WITH THEM

If I'm mad, I'm *really* mad. Most of the kids have seen me mad at some point, especially when I was going through menopause. I was really angry then. I'm not so angry now.

Destructive behavior really sets me off, just things that I consider to be foolish. Probably one of the maddest times I got was when we were at a show over in Cookeville [Tennessee]. I had all of their drill team stuff in one room. When we're traveling, all their pads, all their bridles, everything's laid out. Again, OCD. Everything's exactly where it's supposed to be, and if you don't do that, everything gets lost, of course.

Tessa and her best friend Sophie were just playing. They'd been washing the horses, and one of them had thrown water on the other. I was trying to pack stuff up, and we were getting ready to leave, and one of the kids ran into the tack room, and Sophie threw a bucket of water inside the tack room.

I lost my ever-loving mind. I mean, I lost my ever-loving *mind*. She soaked everything that was in there, all the pads that I had laid out to dry for hours and whatever, and I'm not, I'm not joking: People scattered to the winds. If you didn't get out of the way, I would physically assault you. I mean, there's no doubt. I would hurt you and I wouldn't care. They're like, "Oh, my god, she's mad."

But the good news is, when I'm over it, I'm over it. Everything's fine. Get in there, clean all that up. I mean, it's over.

BAD-PARENT SYNDROME: GET YOUR KID TO MIND OR GET HER OUT OF HERE

Some of the parents are the worst. I'm sure that's true for every coach. All in all, my parents are wonderful, but some are difficult. I've had to really put my foot down hard on some of them. But most of the kids will either come around to what you tell them to do, or the parents will pull them [out].

For instance, several kids didn't get along. They had personality conflicts. Jenna and I have had to have a "come to Jesus" meeting with some of the parents. Basically I go, "Look, you have two girls that are fighting. I'm going to tell you right now, either you control your kid, or I'm going to. They're not going to run their mouth. They can sass you until hell freezes over, but they're not going to sass me."

I say, "I'm going to smack you off that horse. It's just that simple. You don't want me to smack your kid? You'd better load your kid up in the car and take her home, because I'm going to mash her mouth."

Normally, the parents are either okay with it and the kid hushes, or they take them home. I don't care what kind of bickering they do or how they talk to their parents, but they're simply not going to talk to *me* that way. And the kids are normally really good. Behind my back, they may say horrible things. I don't care.

WON THE AWARDS, DIDN'T KEEP THE TROPHIES

I've won many awards. Again, I'm an overachiever. You have to keep that in mind. We've been national champions five times and state champions multiple times—I don't count.

It's not about the trophy. Sophie's mother, Bert, she loves the trophies. So I just give her all the trophies and tell her to keep them, or drag them out if she wants to, don't if she don't. The accolades don't mean so much to me. I'm an achiever who doesn't have a shrine of trophies. I meet my goal, and I'm done—moving on. [Laughs.]

I want my kids to do well because *they* want to do well. I really don't care if they win or lose. I want them to be happy, though. They love being the champion, you know. But I'm very strict with them, like there's a no-crybaby policy. If you ride on my team, you get the talk before you go in: I don't care if you get first or you get tenth. You come out of the ring with a big smile plastered on your face.

MOST IMPORTANT LESSON: HOW TO LOSE WITH GRACE

If you cry, I will jerk you off [your horse] and whip you, so help me, when you come out of the ring. I won't have it. I will not have a sore loser. I will not have a crybaby. Do you know what I mean? It's just not cool at all.

Anybody can win. You've got to learn to lose. So I'm really strict with them over that. But they usually win. So it's not really like my big badass speech does me any good, because they usually win. [Laughs.]

It's not "win or lose," because somebody has to win and somebody has to lose. I think it's important that the kids learn that's not the end because, honestly, the trophy and the ribbons, we have buckets of them. They mean nothing in the end.

What they'll remember is, "Oh, what a classy team. They came out and they were all smiling. Look how happy they were. They got third."—You know, fake it until you make it, girls. Put that smile on and just keep going. Because a year from now, it's not going to matter. What is going to matter is that you competed with class and grace, and that's how they'll remember you.

So it's more important to me that they be good losers. Pretty much everybody's a good winner. It's easy to be a good winner. [Laughs.]

WE MAKE OUR OWN FATE

I detest whiners. I never want to be one. I really don't like people who use excuses of, "Poor, poor, pitiful me" for why I couldn't do this or why this happened. I think you're just taking the coward's way out.

I mean, we make our own world that we live in. We really do. You don't want drama: Don't have drama! It's just that simple. People are like, "Oh, I can't do this" or "I can't do that." I'm like, "Shit, why?"

I don't know where I get my confidence. [Laughs.] Nothing scares me. Yeah. That's the way I feel.

I'm not scared of anything. Nothing that I know of: death, terrorism . . .

Nothing gets me down. I don't really have bad days. I'm tired sometimes; I have some arthritis. Not bad at this point, but it's definitely starting to irk me a little. But, all in all, I'm really healthy.

MY NEXT JOB WILL BE EVEN BETTER THAN THIS

When I retire, I'm going to *retire*. I'll be done. I really like my job as a health inspector. I think I'm good at my job. I won't miss it when I'm gone because, honestly, after twenty-some years, you probably need to pull on something else for a while. I feel like everything needs young blood, and I also don't like the idea of people who stay in a job for years past when they can retire. I feel like that's really unfair to the youth who are coming up that desperately need those jobs to support their young families.

And so when my time is up, I'm gone. I'll leave that day. I'll be fifty-five, certainly still young enough to be able to do something else. So I'm like, "What do I want to be when I grow up?"

I really enjoy the adults and the horses and the therapeutic version of it. There's a thing called PATH, which is a therapeutic horse association. You've got to take classes and be certified to work with the handicapped.

So I will probably do that. I'll get certified as a horse therapy instructor and work with disabled vets, because they say that's really good for them. A lot of people with severe—what do they call it? PTSD? Really good, apparently, for them.

I don't know. I love everything about combining horses with therapy. I'll probably ease towards that, I suspect. But you can never tell with me, really. I may float off on a completely different tangent. [Laughs.]

I'VE BEEN KICKED AROUND BY MY HORSES, SEVERAL TIMES

A lot of people are fearful of horses—understandably so. You know, they're thousand-pound creatures. Yes, they have teeth. Yes, they have hooves. Yes, they can kick you and bite you and whatever; but that's not their primary goal. I've been jerked around. I've had some really severe rope burns, down to the bone. It was my own fault. I shouldn't have had it wrapped around my hand. You thought you could hang on: really? You thought you could hold a thousand-pound horse while it ran backwards? You can't.

You've got to think like a horse. You're going to get kicked if the horse gets scared, or if it thinks it's a territory dispute between two horses. You've got to be respectful. It's a thousand-pound animal that can easily hurt you with no intention of doing so.

I've been hurt several times. If you fool with horses, you're going to get hurt. I mean, they're large animals, and they are not predators in the wild.. So they react like prey, which is, "Oh, my god, it's going to bite me. Oh, my god, it's going to kill me. Oh, my god, it's going to hurt me."

So you will get hurt from a scared horse a million times faster than you'll get hurt from horses being aggressive to people. They love people. They're very attentive. You normally get hurt when they're scared. I've been hurt many times, because I've raised young horses. Young horses are very scared, just like young people.

And when you're a kid, you fall off, you get stepped on. You're doing something stupid, playing cowboys and Indians and whooping around, and you whoop in the horse's ear, and it decides to run left and you go right. And we had some mean ponies growing up. They did throw us and try to beat us down, but, all in all, I'm in pretty good shape.

BEING AROUND HORSES HAS MADE ME A BETTER HUMAN

I've never *not* had horses. I suspect much of my life has been formed by them, in ways I will never recognize or never realize. It's just like if you've never had something, you don't miss it.

So I know that horses were a huge part of my childhood and most of my adulthood. They've made an enormous contribution to whatever I've become, good or bad. I'm probably much more tolerant because of them.

When I was younger, I had a much more aggressive personality, but you can't be that aggressive with horses. You have to be quiet, calm, and assertive. Horses have herd leaders. Without them, they panic, and they're just lost. So in order to be a horse's leader, you've got be quiet, calm, and assertive.

So having horses around me has, I'm sure, made me a much better human, and also helped considerably to quell some of my not-so-attractive innate qualities. I like to think that they've been a primary factor in my life.

FINANCE & TECHNOLOGY

....

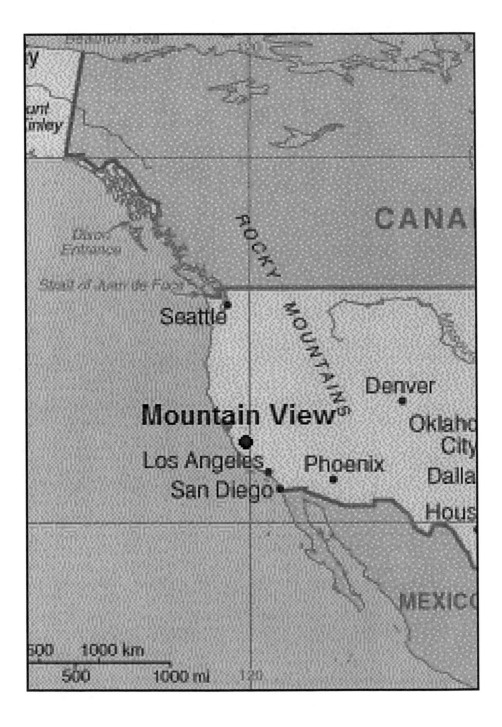

MATT

GOOGLE TECHNOLOGIST

MOUNTAIN VIEW, CALIFORNIA, U.S.

Editor's note: Matt Severson now works in business development for Google X, but when I met him, he was just a skinny college kid at Brown University.

Matt had traveled to Africa for the first time the summer after he graduated from Palo Alto High School (Paly) in Silicon Valley, California. He and his parents volunteered at an orphanage in Kenya, then spent a few days on safari in Tanzania,[1] where Matt met John Medo, the young student who would become the first scholarship recipient of The School Fund and Matt's best friend.[2]

What struck me about Matt was that he acted upon an impulse many of us *have* but do little *with:* He wanted to extend opportunity to kids whose families could not afford their school fees.

---

1. They didn't know each other yet, but Matt's graduation safari trip took him to the home of Wantay the African warrior (Chapter 11) in Ngorongoro Crater Park.

2. I wrote about Matt and John and how their friendship sparked a global initiative to graduate all the world's high-school students: huffingtonpost.com/suzanne-skees/school-fund-tanzania-_b_972986. Halfway through college, in 2016, John died in a senseless accident in a speeding public bus in Iringa, Tanzania. He was on his way to meet students as a volunteer for The School Fund: skees.org/story/3065.

Matt came home to the U.S. and started college that fall. Meanwhile, he teamed up with his high-school and college friends to create a unique web platform that crowdfunds scholarships for needy students, one dollar at a time. He tapped his computer-engineer father to build the site, his engineer mother to run operations, and everyone else he encountered, to add their skills and resources to build one of the most collaborative organizations I'd ever seen. Matt took his deep, innate compassion and channeled it into the technology of connection to allow students and funders to chat with one another in a sort of Facebook-style journaling platform. He put 100 percent of donations toward school fees, scanning and posting receipts for every single dollar spent on students.

By the time our first meeting ended, Matt and I had a handshake deal for a startup grant, plus a plan for a series of stories on their students that would take me to Tanzania just a few months later with The School Fund team.

Meanwhile, volunteering part-time as founder and president of The School Fund,[3] Matt went on to complete college, then landed a paid gig at perhaps the most famous company on the planet: Google, a subsidiary of Alphabet.

Our two nonprofits continue to work together to raise awareness about the 63 million (according to UNICEF) young women and men locked out of secondary school due to lack of funds—and the ease with which we global neighbors can pitch in a few bucks to keep them in the classroom till graduation.

The School Fund supports 1,100 students in fifteen countries in Asia, Africa, Latin America, and the Pacific Islands. Holding down one paid full-time job and one volunteer part-time gig, Matt finds free time to play tennis and ski, travel the world, and fall in love with everyone he encounters—but especially, with one special person who's become his partner at work and home.

Promoted to the Google X "Moonshots" team in late 2015, Matt's having the time of his life, working on top-secret projects that he can't talk about. He says he learns a lot both at the "grassroots," with his education nonprofit that struggles for every dollar and student; and the "grasstops," where he plays with multimillion-dollar budgets and insanely innovative ideas.

I WORK FOR ALPHABET, AKA GOOGLE

My name is Matthew William Severson. My birthday was in January. I'm 26. I have worked for Google for four years, which is crazy. My job title is new business development [NBD] associate at Google. Right now, we're sitting here in Google's Mountain View headquarters in a conference room.

My team works on partnerships, and in particular, we focus on all of Google's early-stage products and initiatives, such as the self-driving car and Project Loon, which is a project that is using a fleet of high-altitude balloons to provide Internet coverage in places of the world that previously didn't have it.

I've also worked a little bit on Google Helpouts, which was a platform to provide

---

3. See Matt explain in less than 1.5 minutes, how and why he launched The School Fund: youtu.be/S6zVR1M3CXs.

real-time help over video-chat on a range of topics from language tutoring to cooking to home and garden advice, and that product actually was later shut down.

I'm working now on an early-stage clean energy project, which is still confidential. A lot of Google's early-stage products, they win because we have first-mover advantage. Sometimes the technologies are really, really advanced, but sometimes they're a little bit more obvious. Moving first and moving quickly is important, so that other people don't copy us too closely on our tail.

I really can't tell you anything at all about this current clean-energy project—not yet! [Laughs.] I can't say where, or when, or anything.

We have a number of confidential products throughout the company, and this energy one is just one of them. Google has been focused on clean energy for a long time, because we actually use a ton of energy in our data centers, which power all of the services like search and Gmail and YouTube that people all around the world enjoy…But we also recognize that climate change[4] is a big issue, and we want to have a hand in helping to address that.

On my NBD/partnerships team, there are about twenty-five of us on the project, but the way that we work is we're actually kind of farmed out, if you will, in either ones, twos, or threes, to the product teams that we do partnerships for. For example, I'm working right now as the only partnership person for the clean-energy project. That team is very small, six people. Well, we do have a lot of other helpers, I suppose. But full-time people dedicated 100 percent to the project—that's only a handful.

Google, I think, tends to like to understaff us, to keep that thirsty entrepreneurial climate in place. It forces you to be thoughtful about how you spend your time, which directions you go down. You can't do six things at once. You have to pick a couple of things and try those. It forces you to focus a bit.

One interesting thing that I *can* share is this kind of framework that we apply to our business development. I think it was Larry [Page] who said to spend 70 percent of our resources on core, 20 percent on adjacencies, and 10 percent on moonshots.

So, 70 percent core is, "Let's put 70 percent of our people, our resources, our energy into our core activities," which are search, ads, YouTube, Chrome, the things that most people are probably familiar with. Then, let's put another 20 percent of the people and resources into adjacencies. An example of that might be Helpouts; that was certainly an adjacency. It was built on Google Hangouts, which is our video-chat product, but it was a new area.

And then you do these 10 percent moonshots, which are meant to address a huge global challenge. Moonshots are oftentimes quite technically complex and have nothing to do with your core business but are worthy of trying to tackle. "Moonshots" was coined by Google X, which is the kind of advanced-hardware-development branch of Google, like the self-driving car, Project Loon, and so on. They may build a little bit on a Google strength, but they're also totally out there.

My job is pretty diverse, and what's exciting about these early-stage projects is [the contrast with] with some of the more mature products like Google Play, where you're

4. Take a Google-Earth tour of climate change narrated by Al Gore and Ted Danson: youtu.be/ToHtpaEuZHw.

doing the same type of deal over and over, for example, getting movies into the play store. For our early-stage products, you may be doing content deals or deals to develop new parts. For example, with the self-driving car, we did a lot of deals that created the infrared and radar-sensor systems. We were building that car from the ground up, using all this new technology. So our partners were making stuff for the car that had never been made before.

Sometimes we'll do deals with entire cities. For example, with Google Fiber, we did deals with the governments of Kansas City and Austin to go in and dig up the streets to lay the fiber-optic cable down. I didn't work on Google Fiber, but this is an example of the different types of deals our team does. And, for these early-stage products, they've looked to us not just to do deals but also to help formulate the business strategy.

So, it's a pretty fun role. We get to go in at the very ground level and work closely with the product leads in engineering and marketing, to figure out the overall strategy for the product, and also how partnerships can help the product along its way.

HOW MUCH DOES GOOGLE REALLY KNOW ABOUT US?

As an outsider, people are oftentimes worried about data and so on, "Oh, is there like someone at Google who's looking up what I've searched for and can find my credit card numbers and is watching me on the video camera?" and whatever.—That doesn't happen. There's no one here looking for "Bill" in Kentucky and snooping on what Bill is doing.

IS GOOGLE A SPY, OR YOUR PERSONAL ASSISTANT?

All that stuff around tracking what you've searched for, tracking where you are physically on your phone—I shouldn't even say "you;" I should say "the user"—all that stuff is really just to provide the person with a better Web experience, right? And, yeah, the fact that your phone knows where it is; that's great! Because when you search for a Mexican restaurant, it knows, "Okay, here are the five near you," and stuff.

Hearing Larry speak, when we have a companywide meeting every week, it's not about being a creep and figuring out what people are doing in their day-to-day. It's all about providing a better Web experience for the user, one where Google kind of can anticipate, "Oh, on Saturdays, you love going on hikes. So can we suggest for you the five best hikes in the area?" or, "Oh, we saw that you bought a plane ticket for London. Here are the ten best restaurants in London."

It's more like a *concierge*. I think Larry's used that word a lot. And this product, Google Now, which has been quite popular on Android phones, does a lot of that suggesting. So, if it sees you bought an airline ticket, it will automatically put the boarding pass on your phone. It knows where your house is, because it knows where your phone is at night. So, if you're out in San Francisco, it will automatically tell you how to get home, for example, using Google Maps. We're all about building a better assistant and a better concierge.

MY OTHER JOB: BUILDING EDUCATION FOR ALL

I am also the founder of The School Fund, a nonprofit organization that raises money for low-income but high-potential high school students in the developing world. We built a website where donors can log on and see students' profiles, where you can see a breakdown of their school fees, get to know them a little bit in terms of what they want to be when they grow up, what they like to do as hobbies, favorite classes and so on, and then directly fund their education through the website.

The School Fund has grown a lot, which has been really exciting to see. We've funded over 1,100 students so far in Asia, Africa, and Latin America. We work with local field partners who have the boots on the ground, actually selecting the students and monitoring them, making sure they're in school. Once we vet these field partners, they're able to put their students up on our website. Our students are low-income, high-potential, future leaders.

SOCIAL CHANGE FROM THE GRASSTOPS TO GRASSROOTS

I get to learn all sorts of things, both from Google that I apply to The School Fund, and also from The School Fund that I apply back to Google. For example, I've learned to communicate and speak publicly. I've given a few talks for The School Fund that have helped me communicate more effectively here at Google.

And then from Google, I've learned a lot about how to professionally manage partners and how to understand what makes a good partner and not a good partner, which has impacted my ability to go out and find good partners for The School Fund. Just lots of learnings and lessons back and forth, which have been useful.

It's funny. The way my team works at Google, we help spend lots of money. [Laughs] We're placed within these product teams, and then the product teams each have budgets.

I know more or less what my product team's budget is, but I honestly have no idea what the budgets are for the product teams where my teammates are working. I would guess in the tens if not hundreds of millions of dollars though, which obviously is a stark contrast to The School Fund's budget, which is about five hundred thousand bucks.

WHEN EVERY DOLLAR COUNTS

But it makes us be very efficient. [Laughs] I see sums of money move around Google with little thought: those figures make my eyes bulge. People are like, "Oh, yeah, fifty thousand dollars, no problem." But at The School Fund, we try to make sure that we're spending every dollar in an impactful way.

For our operating expenses, we've raised money from a handful of individuals and family foundations. The Skees Foundation has been with us for a long time. The Heising-Simons Foundation has also been with us for a very long time. This year we were delighted to become grantees of the Brin Wojcicki Foundation. Sergey Brin is one of the cofounders of Google, and Anne Wojcicki is the founder of 23andMe and also The Schmidt Family Foundation. Eric Schmidt is the chairman of Google.

I realize I mention Google in both those foundations, but both of those connections actually didn't come through my Google relationships. They came through a friend of a friend in the case of the Schmidt Foundation, and in the case of the Brin Wojcicki Foundation, my high school teacher, Esther Wojcicki. She is Anne's mom and Susan Wojcicki's mom as well, and she's been kind of an advisor and mentor of The School Fund for a long time.

Most of this money goes to scholarships. We just launched two full-time roles in 2015. That's about $150,000 of that. But then the rest is going directly to the student scholarships.

REAL-TIME CONNECTIONS THROUGH ONLINE DONATION PLATFORM

And then, on the other side, on the program side, the money we raise for students comes primarily through our website, where thousands of donors all over the world have logged on and contributed typically between $50-75 at a time to support these school fees, and 100 percent of those online donations goes toward supporting students.

I think we've made some pretty innovative and important steps when it comes to transparency. The reason I created The School Fund was because I wanted to help students go to school, but I was not happy with the way that most student-scholarship nonprofits work. You know, you go to their website, and it says, "Hey, donate five hundred bucks to support this girl," but you never know who that money is actually going to. You never know if that money actually made it there. There's no direct connection to the student that you're supposedly helping.

So we wanted to create a much more transparent system, where a donor could go on and support, you know, Susie in Kenya. I know that my $25 is going to this student. I can see the progress bar fill up, and I can actually have a direct connection with that student, which we do through an online journal.

So I think that financial transparency, and then also the fact that donors and students can actually communicate with one another, is pretty novel. For a long time, you could write letters to children you sponsored, but with the Internet now, and with computers and mobile phones and all this actually allowing someone on their couch in California to fund a student in rural Tanzania and then to have a dialogue, is pretty exciting. We all have a lot to learn from one another. These journals are just one way that students in the developing world and donors all over the world can communicate and learn from each other. We've had over five thousand posts written on the website so far.

I was reading some of the posts just earlier today. And sure, you know, there's a couple of posts that are kind of that flavor, like, "Hi, Donor, I'm in school. Thanks for funding me," or whatever; but the vast majority of the posts are really cool.

It's like, this one girl showed a picture of her school and talked about how her walk to school was and so on. Another student in the U.S. said, "Here's my school. This is what my day looks like."

It's in many cases a pretty even dialogue. Some other posts are about, "Oh, I love playing volleyball. This was the score of the game, and we played for this long," dah, dah, dah.

Then the donor writes back, "Oh, some of my hobbies include x, y, z. I like skiing," or whatever.

So, yeah, I think it's cool to give students in the developing world really for the first time a chance to share their stories with a broader audience and to connect with people outside of their home village.

I GET INSPIRED BY THE GREAT ATTITUDES OUR STUDENTS HAVE ABOUT LEARNING

For The School Fund, I think one goal for me will be to try and visit a new place. I keep going back to the same place, Karatu, Tanzania, because I like it so much. It's where I met my friend John Medo, and
where his family still lives.

Another really outstanding student is Apollo, who lives in Nairobi, Kenya. He comes from our partner, Kenya Education Fund, which runs an excellent scholarship program in Nairobi, and he was Number One in every subject in his entire high school, which, you know, clearly means he's been studying hard, working hard. Apollo grew up in the Kibera slum, with no parents. I think he was living with his brother at the time. He is living by himself now in a little hut there at university. So he's actually no longer getting funding from The School Fund: He's now on a government scholarship to nursing college.

Just meeting him, you can see that he really cares about the education he's receiving, and he does not take anything for granted. I mean, he understands that his going to school is an opportunity that he wouldn't have had otherwise, and so he really takes it seriously. I think he and so many other students in Africa are such amazing role models for kids in the U.S. that I know who are like, "Why the hell am I stuck going to school?"

And it's not really just about being stuck going to school.—It's more about the general opportunities that people have here. I mean, I think we do end up taking so much for granted. Knowing students like Apollo who really value and take so seriously something that kids here in the U.S. take for granted, is really interesting to see.

WHY EDUCATION IS MY CAUSE

I don't know if I was inherently drawn to education as a vertical, versus like agriculture or health or something like that. But I've always enjoyed helping people. One piece of it is absolutely this selfish good feeling that I get when I help someone. I mean, I feel happy.

Another part of it is the realization that I've had a lot of privilege growing up, especially in the more recent years of my life, and that one hour of effort on my part can translate to a pretty radical change in the life of another person living abroad. Ten dollars is a very short amount of my workday. [Laughs] I can earn ten dollars, right? That translates into something really meaningful and powerful. It might mean meals for a week for a family in the developing world.

So I think that realization that I happened to be born over here in the U.S., where, for whatever the hell reason, my one hour of effort can translate into the equivalent of a hundred hours of effort for some farmer, we've *got* to do something about that. We've got to give back.

So I've chosen to spend a lot of my time and energy on The School Fund. Education is a really powerful way to not just give someone a handout, but to give them skills to lead their own lives of meaning and to lift themselves out of whatever situations they're in.

THE FAMILY I'M CREATING WITH MY BOYFRIEND

I live at home in Palo Alto with my boyfriend, James. We met in a very serendipitous way. I was studying abroad in London. He was working at McKinsey in Chicago. I'd flown back to the U.S. for a conference, the Clinton Global Initiative University (CGIU). That just happened to be the week that the Icelandic volcano erupted, which meant no air traffic in or out of Europe.

I was stuck in Chicago, and I ended up staying with this random guy whom I had just met, who happened to be the boyfriend of my School Fund cofounder, Roxy. And this guy was living with a bunch of McKinsey colleagues of his, one of whom was James. So that's how we met.

We were all at the conference together, Roxy and her boyfriend and myself. It was the CGIU conference in Miami. We met, and then we went our separate ways, and then a year later re-met at Google. [He works here, too.] I started working in July, and he started working in August, and I think we just remembered that we'd met a year ago and so we reconnected and had lunch.

I'm very happy with James. He's a really nice guy. He's twenty-nine. He grew up in Chicago. He's a Midwestern guy, like my dad. He's very hardworking and really a caring, sweet person as well. He has a great family and a really nice group of friends who are a lot of fun and also very smart and accomplished. His job here is on our business operations team, which is essentially a group of former management consultants from McKinsey, Bain, BCG [Boston Consulting Group], and a few other companies, and they do similar type projects for our CEO and his leadership team. So it will be something like, "Help us design a strategy for how to enter Brazil" with whatever, YouTube or something like that, and they'll help strategize.

TRAVEL WISHES AND OUR MAP OF THE WORLD

As for hobbies, it's hard to say whether I think The School Fund is a hobby or like my second job. [Laughs.] I guess just thinking about it in terms of how I spend my nonpaid work time, a big chunk of that is The School Fund, for sure, and I do think of it as my second job.

I also like playing tennis. I like downhill skiing. I like photography and traveling.

As a couple, we like traveling and eating. We go all over. We have a nice big map that's about 6' x 4' hanging on our wall in our house, and we've done little dots all over. So the green dots are where just I've been; the blue dots are where just James has been. The red dots are where we've been together, and the yellow dots are where we want to go. It's on our landing.

So every time we walk down the stairs, we get to see the map, and it's kind of fun to see all the places we've been and the places that we want to go. Both of us really like London. What's on our list? We're going to Japan in a couple of months, just for fun.

Bhutan is also on the wish list. I have things that are on just my wish list. I don't know—[laughs] I haven't run them by him. But I really want to go to like Buenos Aires and Morocco. Those are two places that are on my personal wish list. And James has not been to Africa with me. I think he'd be open to going.

COMING OUT WASN'T EASY

I think, as many gay couples find, parents accepting their dating can be tough, but we're making progress. I think meeting James and just seeing that he's a nice, caring, supportive guy is really helpful.

My dad flew down and met James's parents in Santa Barbara over the holidays, and it went really well. My dad has been amazing, and my mom is making some progress…I think I'll leave it at that.

Understandably, my mom grew up in a very different culture in Taiwan. I'm also her only child, and she's put a huge amount of energy into raising me and has been thinking of this vision of me in a good job with a wife and kids and so on, for the last twenty-seven years of her life. She's been aiming toward that. So any deviation from that I think can be tough to wrap her head around.

I had a relationship in high school, but then I dated a girl in college. So I think she thought, "Oh, great, [laughs] he's dating a girl." But, yeah, this path is the one that I'm happier on.

It's maybe a little bit of her personality and a little bit of a Taiwanese thing.

Initially, both parents were not super accepting. I think my dad was worried about the life that I would have and the difficulties that someone in a gay relationship has, but he's seeing a lot of public opinion and the tides sort of shift there. So he's really warmed up to the idea.

GROWING UP AS THE ONLY CHILD OF AN IMMIGRANT WHO'S ALSO A REBEL

My mom's name is Judy Severson. She grew up in Taipei, Taiwan. My mom is one of four children. She has an older sister and two younger brothers. She was very, very poor and was incredibly hard working. She was sort of the second mother to the two little brothers.

My mom often went hungry for lunch. She didn't have lunch money. She walked to school, forty-five minutes to an hour each way. She had one doll; that was her only toy. But, despite all of this, she wanted a better life for herself and her kids. She was the first member of her family to go to college and then obviously to go on to a graduate school. She went to college in Taiwan and taught for a year there, then saved a couple of hundred dollars to come to the United States.

I think she was very adventurous and brave to come all the way out to this foreign land, speaking no English, with barely any money. She worked in a kitchen to pay for her college and her graduate school.

Then she went to North Texas State University for computer science. I don't know quite how she found this school. Can you imagine?—back in whenever that was, probably the late '70s. I'm going to get in trouble if I tell you how old she is. [Laughs.]

So, she did that. We talk now about how there's not enough women in computer science. I can only imagine *then*. She was probably like the only woman and the only Chinese woman. She taught herself English. I ran across her Chinese-to-English dictionary a while ago, where she had painstakingly gone and circled and underlined in red pen all these translations and stuff.

I think I get my desire to be social from my mom, actually. She struggles oftentimes with English. But I've seen her in settings with her Chinese friends, and she's cracking jokes and being goofy and all that stuff. And I'm horrible at Chinese! [Laughs.] I took a year in college, and I can say like super basic things. But, no, I wouldn't even say I could get by. I can get by in Spanish. I wouldn't say I was fluent, but, yeah, I could get around in a Spanish-speaking country just fine.

One more thing I'll say about my mom is, she's kind of like the rule-breaker in her family. And by that, I mean, she came out to the U.S. She went to grad school, first off; then she married a white guy. I think relative to the cultural norm that she had grown up in, where the wife is supposed to support the husband and be there to take care of the home and so on, my mom was very independent. She had ambitions to have her own career. So, anyway, I think it's interesting, and I appreciate her slightly rebellious nature.

MY DAD IS A CLASSIC ENGINEER

My dad's name is Denis. He's one of five children. He has four sisters; he's the only boy. He grew up in Moorhead, Minnesota. He did his undergrad and master's at North Dakota State University and then came out here to California to do a PhD in computer science at U.C. Santa Cruz, but didn't finish because he started working at a company one summer and then just stayed working.

He was working at a variety of tech companies, Zilog and Wyse Technology, one in which he met my mom at, I can't remember which. He then went to Xerox Park and was most recently at Google as one of the early software engineers. He retired my senior year of high school. So, that was long before I ever applied or came here.

My dad is a pretty classic engineer. He's very short. He was like 5'4" all through high school. Only in college did he kind of get to his towering current height of 5'7-½". [Laughs.]

I remember one time I used to not like my food being hot, and so he made this thing using a model airplane engine, and he attached a propeller to it and then put it on little stilts. We called it "the food fan." You could put the food fan over your hot soup or whatever, and it would blow air on it and cool it. Just cute things like that. We were always tinkering with stuff. I'm not an expert tinkerer by any means, but I do like making stuff, and I like the idea of having an idea in your brain and translating that into something that other people can touch and use.

MY DUAL-ENGINEER PARENTS FLIRTED OVER PROGRAMMING

He and my mom met at a company where they both worked. The cute story there is, my mom would always come to my dad for help because my dad's a very good programmer, and he was like, "Who's this annoying woman who keeps coming over here asking me for help?" But, after a few times, I think he found it endearing. So they went on their first date to Kentucky Fried Chicken. [Laughs.]

Then they got married. And I'm the only kid. My mom had me late in life. My mom's a couple of years older than my dad. I was born in Mountain View technically, and we lived in Milpitas for four years, and then for elementary school and onwards, I lived in Palo Alto.

I'm very proud of my mom and how hard she's worked to get to where she is now. When I was in elementary school, she was working at Sun Microsystems as a software engineer, and [laughs] she would bring me into her office when I was sick. She would make me do math homework. Her office mate would bring her son, and he got to play computer games the whole time. I remember being very jealous of that. I had to *work*. But, anyways, I'm very proud of what my mom has accomplished. She'd worked for twenty-five plus years. She retired when I was in maybe freshman or sophomore year of high school.

THE ASIAN FACTOR: EXTREME ACCOMPLISHMENT, EVERY DAY

It was tough growing up bicultural. I was friends with kids whose parents were mostly European-American. I didn't hang out with as many kids who had Chinese parents and Asian parents and so on. I remember my friends were like, "What the hell are you doing? You have piano and violin and basketball and soccer and saxophone and swimming and tennis."

It was like fifty million things. I did swimming and tennis, both quite seriously, but I also played basketball, soccer, and baseball growing up. I played piano and violin quite seriously, also saxophone and trumpet and drums. In the summers, I went to public-speaking camp and computer science camp and outdoor camp and all sorts of things. [Laughs.] I think of myself as a generalist or a Renaissance type person or whatever.

Oftentimes, my friends would give me a hard time for having so many activities that I was doing. But, you know, from my mom's perspective, I get it. She had dreamt of doing all these things as a little girl and never had the money to try them. So I think she really wanted me to experience everything that she had missed out on. My mom definitely took academics very seriously. So, I had lots of tutors for this and that. She put a lot of energy toward making sure that I experienced lots of different things, and she would always have me try something, even if I really didn't want to, at least have that experience.

I'm very fortunate and probably not grateful enough of all the experiences that I've had, from all the millions of extracurriculars I did to, you know, the food, the shelter, and the clothing, the college that was paid for.

But there was also a bit of a tension in parenting styles. I mean, my mom is a pretty classic Asian mom in that she was very focused on me getting into a good college and all the preparations that were needed for that, whereas my dad had a much more hands-off parenting style. So there were certainly moments of tension there. But, yeah, overall, it turned out fine. [Laughs.]

GROWING UP THE SON OF SILICON VALLEY—AND TAIWAN

I grew up all my life in California. I guess that's defined who I am. Growing up in Silicon Valley in particular got me interested in technology and entrepreneurship and all that. But I love the fact that I also have this other culture that is a part of me, and I think being

Chinese is pretty cool. I have been to Taiwan. I've seen my roots. I have a Chinese family. So we'll have dinner with my mom's sister, my aunt, and go eat Chinese food where everyone in the restaurant is Chinese. There are no European-Americans there. [Laughs.]

I think I understand the challenges that first-generation Chinese parents have had to come here, and I get why they're so intent and focused on their kids being successful. I mean, I get that because I experience it, and I can relate to how my mom journeyed here and worked hard and so on.

So, whereas I think a lot of kids with two European-American parents are just like, "Oh, those crazy Asian parents," I'm a little more empathetic. And, yeah, I mean, I look different [laughs]; although, going to China and Taiwan, I think people can often tell I'm American but not Chinese.

WHAT IT'S LIKE TO GROW UP IN TECH MECCA

When I was young (in elementary school), both my parents were software engineers, but I was friends with these other people. You know, of my best friends in elementary school, one dad was a hotshot lawyer. Another's dad was like the VP of marketing at this big tech company, and they were actually quite a bit better off than we were. Not to say we were poor in any way, but we were, I would say, "middleclass."

So I actually didn't aspire to follow in my parents' footsteps. Other things mattered to me. It's like, "Oh, they have more toys." It's like the silly things that matter a lot to a young kid.

I think a lot of kids these days, if both their parents are software engineers, software engineers are being paid a lot. There's all kinds of interest and hype, and technology is really booming now. So kids like that would probably go down the tech path, whereas I intentionally did not want to go down that path. This was before my dad worked at Google, and we got very lucky in that sense because he went to Google very early, and then it went public. I wouldn't say we're in the middleclass anymore. We are in the One Percent. We now have plenty of money to live comfortably.

GROWING UP AT GOOGLE, WHEN IT WAS IN JUST ONE BUILDING

My dad joined Google back when I was in fifth grade. He was a software engineer. I don't really know what he did. He did two projects that I'm aware of: One was in the logs group, which would look at global search trends worldwide and then distill it down into insights.

So, for example, "Okay, in Japan, they're all searching for TVs."

"That's interesting. Should we be serving more ads for TVs in Japan?" or something like that.

So the logs team looked at global search traffic and analyzed all of that. That was a lot of data. And then another one he did was a web accelerator that essentially you could install on your computer, and it sped up your web browsing—back when web browsing was slower. So this was like a nice way to make it faster.

My dad joined the company when it was about a hundred people. He would bring me here, and I kind of grew up coming here. We played roller hockey in the parking lot back when they were just in one building.

Coming here, I felt very comfortable. I had a good understanding of the culture and how people got things done. It enabled me to just quickly jump in and potentially not be as afraid about misstepping or breaking a rule as others might have been, which I think for my role now is actually a really good thing. We often need to bend the rules a bit—obviously not just any rules, but sometimes to get things done quickly or to question a leader's assumption, being comfortable with that is valuable and important.

They were all just in one building. I don't remember this, but apparently it happened: I was riding a little electric scooter around because they had those to get around, and I crashed into a cubicle. My dad was very anxious, but Larry Page was there, and he said, "Oh, that's okay. Don't worry about it." I was like eleven or something.

My dad worked here for a long time, and I would come every once in a while to eat lunch or play roller hockey or whatever. So that was before I even went to college.

My dad retired when I was seventeen. So they're both retired.

My dad is now very involved with The School Fund. He's programmed a big chunk of the website, and he's also the treasurer of our board. He helps keep our financial documents all straightened out.

In her retirement, my mom has taken over management of our program in Tanzania that we started The School Fund with. We think of them as our first field partner. So she's managing that program. She's also involved in a number of other activities in the Bay Area—the Garden Club and Avenidas. And recently, which I think is nice, she's been helping some Chinese families who've moved here, to get the lay of the land and figure out what's going on. Many of them come here speaking no English. She advises them on the good tutors in the area, what schools should you be going to, and that kind of thing—helping families get acclimated.

HOW I STARTED A NONPROFIT ORGANIZATION AT AGE 18

I graduated from Palo Alto High School in 2007. That summer, I took a trip to Kenya to work at an orphanage for a week, and then did a three-day safari in Tanzania.

And outside our hotel this little boy, John Medo, was cutting the grass for his cow. I just went over and started talking to him. He barely spoke any English, but he told me that he wanted to grow up and become president of Tanzania. I learned that he was graduating from primary school and was supposed to go on to secondary school; but in Tanzania, you have to start paying anywhere from a $100-300 a year for secondary school. John was fourteen at the time.

My life was on a pretty clear path of, "on to college, then on to a well-paying job," and here was John with this big fork in the road of either going to school and being able to move up a rung of the poverty ladder, or staying right on the same course of his parents. John's one of five kids. His dad's a furniture maker, and his mom mostly stays home and grows some vegetables, which she sells in the market.

John's $150-a-year school fees were preventing him from going on to high school. So I started helping him and then from there, as I learned more about the issue, I was inspired to help more kids like John. There are 110 million students[5] worldwide who don't have access to education.

I started funding John in 2007 and then launched The School Fund officially in the fall of 2009. I was inspired by Kiva and Donors Choose. I saw how Kiva had done a really great job of connecting individual lenders with individual borrowers in the developing world, and I thought the person-to-person connection from donor to student could work just as well, if not better.—Because for a student, they're going to school year after year, and so building that relationship between donor and student means the donor may support that student multiple years in a row.

MY PASSION PROJECT: ENSURING ALL YOUNG PEOPLE GET TO FINISH HIGH SCHOOL

The School Fund has been a complete passion project for me. My mom was concerned that I was distracting myself from a good traditional job by spending time on The School Fund, but I think The School Fund has ended up teaching *me*. It's been such a critical part of my education, just in the same way that we're helping educate these kids abroad.

I am still best friends with John. We still stay in touch. He Facebook messages me on New Year's and Christmas and often in-between. So, he is definitely a tech-literate young man. He's a great guy, a special kid and really enjoys making friends with people and getting to know people.

I remember back in college, some of my college friends were like, "Who's this John kid? He messaged me on Facebook," and I'd have to explain, "Oh, yeah, remember The School Fund? Well, John's our first student. He loves reaching out to people."

John's great. He's in university now in Dar es Salaam [the capital city of Tanzania]. I have big hopes for him. He's now twenty-three. (It's crazy how fast time goes.) He's put on pause his aspiration of becoming president! He's now focused on becoming a doctor. Later, once that career has progressed a little bit, he says he wants to go into politics. That was always his plan, as far as I can recall: He would be a doctor first, and then end up being president of Tanzania when he was like thirty or forty.

MY FIRST REAL JOB WAS HERE AT GOOGLE

I had very little work experience before coming to Google. I held some internships while I was at college, at a couple of architectural firms. One was paid, and another one was unpaid. My mom decided—for better or worse—that my time would be better spent doing math problems versus delivering pizza. There's obviously a lot of great experience to be had in having and holding a job when you're younger, but, no, I was doing other academic activities. [Laughs.]

I never had to work to sustain myself or anything like that. I had an internship at an architecture firm, where I was paid a little bit, but, you know, it wasn't like I was needing

---

5. The number of children not in school worldwide varies; e.g., UNICEF reports 63 million (unicef.org/publications/files/Investment_Case_for_Education_Summary.pdf) and UNESCO reports 124 million (uis.unesco.org/Education/Documents/fs-31-out-of-school-children-en.pdf). Regardless, to Matt, that's about 64 to 124 million too many.

to save for college or anything like that.

How I got to Google wasn't anything fancy. I was in college at Brown. Google goes around to several good schools throughout the U.S. and the world and recruits on-campus. I just applied and threw my resume into the pile and interviewed; and then they extended me an offer to join their people-operations team in a three-part, nine-month rotation program.

I don't think my dad working here had a role in my being hired. I don't think anyone would have made that connection. I applied totally separately and never really mentioned throughout the interview process that my dad had worked here. It's not like he was the VP of engineering or anything like that. While he contributed in big ways, he wasn't running the show by any means. He had retired in 2007, and I applied in 2011.

The one award I've received here was during my very first rotation, in "learning design," from the Brandon Hall Group Excellence Awards. It was for a training that we put together that went around to all of Google. We did some interesting things with it. We basically gamified it. As you went through the video lessons, you earned points. And then as you answered the quiz questions, you earned more points. The style of the video that we did those trainings in, was innovative.

WHAT A TYPICAL WORKDAY LOOKS LIKE HERE

I work very reasonable hours, usually between forty and fifty hours a week. The culture of my team is one where it's very flexible. We do a lot of vetting of our teammates up front. It's like, if you earned your spot on the team, we trust you not to screw up and not to take advantage of that flexibility. So it's a very flexible team. If you do your work, you can set your own hours, for the most part.

I lived in San Francisco and did the Google-bus thing for a year but quickly tired of the three hours per day commute from San Francisco to Mountain View. If there's no traffic, it's like forty minutes each way, but typically you hit something unless you're getting on the 6:00 a.m. shuttle or whatever.

So, after a year of that, I moved down to Palo Alto, where I'm from. I now live like an eight-minute drive from work. I usually wake up at seven, get here by eight, have my coffee and eggs over at the next building [laughs], and do some emails while I'm eating, then start meeting with people or doing more emails or traveling around to visit our partners.

As in many early-stageish jobs, the weeks tend to vary. In a somewhat average week, I like to go and sit with the engineers and the product team on whose project I'm working. I feel like you get to know the team better and establish a better working relationship with them. You can quickly ask questions just in person, rather than having to wait for emails and so on.

Google has got a lot of great perks. We have over twenty cafeterias here on campus, which are all free, and a couple of them do breakfast and dinner as well. You can do your laundry. There's a bowling alley, tennis courts, and a soccer field. There are gyms that you can use. There are subsidized massages, which is my favorite perk. In fact, for your birthday, you get a free massage credit. So I'm going to get a massage later today. And micro-kitchens in most of the buildings with snacks and drinks and so on.

The latest perk: They put this new building over here [points out his window] with no offices. It's the Wellness Center, and there's like a gym, a yoga studio, massage rooms, and a juice bar. They're making these nice little made-to-order juices.

All in all, I think Google's done a really good job and paved the way for this culture of wanting to keep your employees on-campus, and not running off for an hour and a half at lunch to go eat at the Chili's down the street, or whatever. A lot of companies like Facebook and Twitter and all the startups have emulated that culture.

HOW DO WE DO RESEARCH AROUND HERE? WE GOOGLE THINGS

In a typical week, there are a lot of meetings to help us understand from the product teams where the product is headed. Then we look at the world, saying, "Okay, whom might we collaborate with or partner with to get us there?" And so it's a lot of [browsing around the Internet, or] *Googling* to find who are the players in this space.

Then it's meeting with them, flying out to see them in-person, and bringing them to Google a lot of the time. Lots of meetings and lots of emails.

I've been cautioned by my colleagues, who have all said, "Don't get too used to this. People tend to want to work with Google," whereas, in other companies, it's a bit more of a hard sell. And I've certainly experienced that.

For example, I'm working to find some social-impact partners for Project Loon, nonprofits that could use Loon Internet in Africa, South America, Asia, and so on. And we have Google.org right here, which is the big grantmaking arm, who has got their fingers in all of these different areas of the nonprofit world. So it's pretty easy to say "Hey" to my friend over there, "Can you refer me to this nonprofit?" and they almost always will jump at the opportunity to chat with someone at Google. So, yeah, it's been very easy to have those initial conversations with all sorts of exciting potential nonprofit partners. I suppose that schmoozing is a part of it. [Laughs.] And some thinking.

When I need to think, I really like whiteboarding. I'm a visual person. I'll sometimes just go into a conference room with a whiteboard and draw. There's also a nice little walking loop out here that I'll sometimes go on.

As far as travel for work, I've been to New York and Boston and Las Vegas and Chicago and Des Moines, Iowa. I'm going to Chile soon. I think that's basically it. I'm not on the road a ton. Maybe once a month, I'll go somewhere for work.

For The School Fund, I spend anywhere from five to fifteen hours a week on it. It's like a breath of fresh air. It's nice to have that contrast where I'm calling the shots. I'm getting to make decisions with The School Fund, whereas at Google, being part of a team in a large company, I don't have as much autonomy. So that's kind of a nice contrast.

WHAT SUCKS ABOUT MY DREAM JOB

I was super-happy when I got this particular role on the product partnerships team at Google. My first job at Google, though, while interesting and educational for me, wasn't necessarily the best fit for my passions. I was doing HR [human resources] which, to be totally honest, is not a great fit for me. I think it's an important function, and there are people who are good at it and people who enjoy it, but I do not like it.

There's a lot of playing by the rules and reacting to issues, versus being proactive and planning ahead. That sounded mean. [Laughs.] At Google, I imagine as at most companies, maybe not quite to this degree, you can really chart your own course. If you find an area that you're interested in, everyone's certainly very accessible here. You can slap a coffee meeting on anybody's calendar.

So I was desperately looking for a role that was a better fit for me. I found this team and thought that the people-related aspects of doing partnerships and deals and pitching to potential partners, was really interesting. Also, working on these exciting early-stage products that have to do with access to Internet in the developing world and climate change (which are two big passion-buckets for me), the actual job material would be really interesting.

I started to get to know various people on the team and had a helping hand from Megan Smith, who used to run the team and was sort of a mentor to me. I was pretty sure I wasn't going to get this job. I'm the youngest person on this team by at least three or four years; there are lots of people who have like twenty or thirty years' experience on this team. I think a lot of the work actually that I'd done with The School Fund, and the partnerships that I had forged there, proved that (even though I lacked Google business-development experience) I could get the work done. So Megan took a bet on me and said, "Yeah, I'll make a spot for you on my team," which was exciting.

That was a good moment.

I FOUND MY NICHE IN BUSINESS DEVELOPMENT

One cool thing that happened just a couple of months ago was a little esoteric perhaps: We were talking with this partner for this energy project, and there was some complexity around who would own the IP [intellectual property] rights to this new thing that we were developing; and, to be honest, this was my first time of really delving into complex IP scenarios. So I had to go talk to a bunch of my teammates to figure out what they had done in past deals, where they were paying someone to develop a new thing for Google.

And then, using my architect mind, I made a little diagram that showed, "Okay, money comes in here. Work is here, and then out comes this thing, and who owns which piece of this thing?"

I presented it in the meeting to the VPs and the partner organization, and they were like, "Oh, I've been doing this for twenty years, and I've never seen a chart like this. It's really helpful."

So that was a fun moment where I was brand new to negotiating IP rights, and I made this nice architecture-looking chart, and it really helped to clarify the conversation issue at hand. That was a good moment. [Laughs.]

There are times during the day when I become so focused on my work, I forget everything else. Generally when I'm working, I'm pretty focused. I'm not really paying attention to what else is going on. I'm very impatient [laughs], as my dad will tell you. So I like getting things done really fast. And I know that this is an area for me to work on.

Sometimes my impatience will lead to like 1 percent sloppiness, which sometimes is fine. Sometimes you actually don't need that 1 percent. You need to be fast. But at the times where I need to be 100 percent perfect, and where pace is not necessary, I need to learn to switch that.

I'm talking specifically about the paperwork of a deal. It's actually really important, exactly what those words say because if anyone goes to court over that, that's the document they're going to refer to. So, yeah, those are times when I should slow down and make sure that everything is just so.

IN TECH, YOU NEED TO BE GOOD AT RELATIONSHIPS

Looking at my job in one way, it's professional friend-making. It helps that I enjoy talking to people and getting to know people. I genuinely like to form friendships and relationships with the people I'm working with, not just like, "Hey, can you do this for me?"

No. I want to get to know them and actually understand how working together can benefit them. I think that's really useful for my job.

WASTED TIME, NEGATIVE FEEDBACK, AND JEALOUSY

My my horrible moment here at Google…Gosh, how can I answer this question without hurting someone's feelings?

I guess my job here has been pretty comfortable; but I will say that like in my last rotation, I was quite frustrated with the work I was doing for a number of reasons. I don't like following rules that I don't think are necessary. [Laughs.] I don't like doing things that only impact one or two or three people. I like doing things that will potentially impact thousands or millions of people.

Some of the HR work I was doing was just like fixing one problem for this one guy, and that felt like not a good use of time. It was too microscopic. I much prefer to do a piece of work that then impacts thousands or millions of people. I definitely had lots of moments of frustration in that role.

I've never been harassed here, but I've gotten some negative feedback, sure! Like, "Why did you do this?" or "Why didn't you consult me before doing x, y, z?"

That was in previous roles. In this role, overall my manager Diana, she's awesome. [Laughs.] She's very clear about what her expectations are of me, and that communication and that clarity just really helps so that I don't make mistakes.

I don't think I've gotten any negative feedback from the outside the company. People have told me, "You must have a great job," but not like, "Why the hell did you get that job? You must have paid your way in or something."

HOW MUCH I EARN HERE

I make a little over $100,000 with my salary and bonus, and I have some more stock options and stuff.

This is pretty comparable to my friends who graduated around the same time as I did. The computer science ones and engineers are making more than me. But I recognize that we're compensated quite well here, not to mention all the free food and stuff.

I mean, I guess it's cool to work here. [Laughs.] This may be the world's most famous company, but it feels normal to me. It feels like we're all here working to make great products. I guess I have to recognize that there's probably a unique concentration of really smart, driven people here; but I don't think it's way more special or anything like that.

I live in a bubble in many ways. Socioeconomically, you know, everyone has got all of these gizmos and gadgets and so on. I know that that doesn't really exist in such a concentration in other parts of the world. But I don't think we're doing anything particularly magical here versus somewhere else in the world. Great ideas come from lots of places around the world, like Nairobi, Kenya, or London, or all of these other spots.

HOW I ENVISION MY FUTURE: GRAD SCHOOL, MARRIAGE, AND KIDS

I might want to go to grad school. I'd love to have kids at some point. I would like to be married and have children. I like kids a lot; I'd like to have two or three. I'd like to adopt, and I'd like one to be biologically my own. Then my mom will have some grandkids. [Laughs.] It's going to be complicated. I haven't really looked into that much, to be honest. It remains to be seen.

I would love to be leading a team here at Google perhaps someday. I feel so lucky because I'm getting to work on the two issues that I care most about through some of these projects here, which is why I've stuck around. If I were working on projects that weren't in line with my values, I would leave.

But I would love to scale my impact here—whether that's working on bigger projects or working with more people reporting to me in ten years. I think continuing to work in these two areas of addressing climate change and addressing property alleviation would be awesome.

And with The School Fund, I'd love to continue on as board chair. I do a lot of our fundraising and strategic partnership work with groups like Chegg and Kathy Ireland Worldwide and JacksGap.

I'm lucky to have a job that—I don't want to say, "that pays the bills" because that's not it. It's like having the job that makes money but is still also really in line with my values and my interests, and that's flexible enough to also allow me to spend a good chunk of my time doing a second job that doesn't necessarily pay. I've managed to find that nice setup for myself, and I would encourage other people to do what they can to find that nice balance for themselves, too.

So, in the future, I would love for The School Fund to continue to scale and be doing millions of dollars a year in donations and to be supporting tens of thousands of students around the developing world.

TOP DOWN + BOTTOM UP: HOW I WORK TO EFFECT SOCIAL CHANGE

There are moments in my life where I feel very deliberate, and then other moments where I'm just sort of wandering along, and then it's like, "Oh, I guess it actually makes sense," in hindsight. But looking back, there are a couple of issues that I know that I want to spend my time and energy working on: climate change and poverty alleviation. Climate change/clean energy is a big piece of that, and with poverty alleviation, I think

‚ ‚cation is the most effective tool. And maybe second to that, access to information to those in the developing world is another huge tool.

My "grasstops" work at Google doing partnerships for clean energy and Project Loon and some of these other products, is very much in line with those two issues that I'm excited about tackling. And then my "grassroots" work with The School Fund is obviously an education project, which I think is a big part of the solution to poverty alleviation.

There's a lot of blending and learning from one chunk of work to the other. At Google, I've learned how to project manage and communicate with different types of people, whether it's engineers or marketing, or your manager or legal, or whatever. It's certainly helped my communication, both verbal and written, and so I'm applying all those learnings all the time to the nonprofit.

Google—especially on a lot of these crazy projects—teaches you to really think big, not in terms of incremental change. Thinking big is a useful lens for a small nonprofit project.

In terms of how The School Fund has informed my Google work, I've had to go and pitch The School Fund, to be an aggressive networker and build relationships with people, and that's helped me drive a lot of my partnership conversations at Google.

My dad always says I don't like to take no for an answer. I always just keep pushing, and I'll try and address why a person doesn't want to work with us or whatever, and get to a point where they do. So a lot of work I've done with The School Fund has helped my partnerships work at Google.

I WANT TO LEAVE A POSITIVE IMPACT ON THE WORLD

I want to do work that matters, that leaves a positive impact on the world, and has touched people in a profound way. I really get excited about the potential for scale.

I really like the notion of having an idea in your head, getting that out in the world, and then having that being able to kind of touch the lives of many, many people. I just think that's really cool; and with the Internet and all of these devices that everybody has, there are such great ways to do that.

I would love for my work to be addressing and tackling some of the big challenges that will really, if not addressed, negatively impact all of life for future generations. So for me, that's global warming and poverty and all of the horrible things associated with that from malnutrition to gender inequality to poor health, and so on.

I think The School Fund is part of the solution of addressing poverty. I'm just getting going. I'm a young person, and I hope I have many years of productive work ahead. I would love to continue growing my efforts in both of those areas. I guess one thing that's interesting about my work is that I've found a way to balance a couple of interests and a couple of jobs.

I realize I'm very lucky in that obviously I have lots of opportunities. I've gone to a good school and all of this.—But I really think that people should find a way to have jobs that both make money, but also give back. If you have a job that may not necessarily be aligned with your core values, add another job that may be 100 percent aligned with your core values.

As humanity progresses, hopefully some of those more tedious jobs that people had to do historically just to survive, will start to either fall away or, with the assistance of machines, become more efficient. So rather than spending a hundred hours a week washing your clothes, you can spend two hours a week washing your clothes and then have that other ninety-eight hours free to do other stuff.

People can make space in their lives to give back, to do something that's really rewarding and in line with their values. And so my arrangement happens to be a great setup for me, but I think other people should find arrangements that work really well for them.

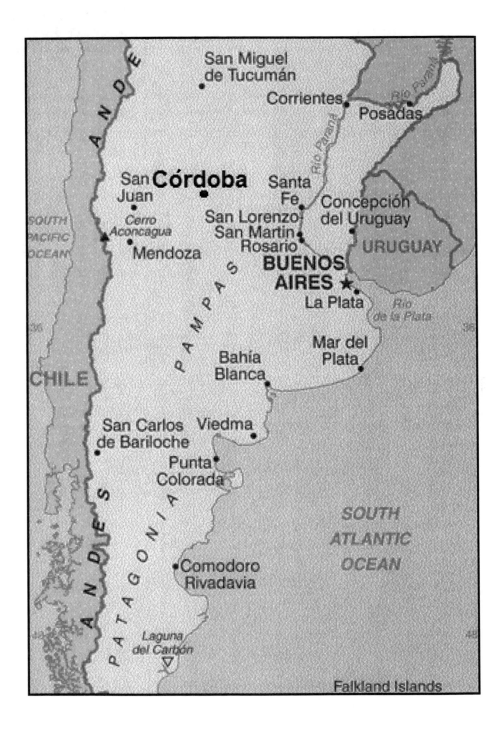

PABLO

XEROX LATAM

FINANCE MANAGER

CÓRDOBA, ARGENTINA

Editor's note: Pablo Mira and my brother Ron live about 5,000 miles apart. They both have wives and children—in fact they are straight—but they have something of a bromance going on. They work in the same enormous division for a monolithic corporation. On conference calls, they hear the sound of each other's voices more often than their next-door neighbors. These two men have been through a lot more than skewed spreadsheets and busted budgets together. If not for the camaraderie of these two coworkers, I never would have met Pablo.

Compatriots in a conglomerate-merger mess of a company, both Pablo and Ron got acquired by Xerox when it bought out their company, business-process outsourcing firm Affiliated Computer Services (ACS), for a cool $6.4 billion in 2009.[1] Initially excited to work for a company of its wealth and history, they've witnessed it spiral downward ever since. Earnings have declined 25 percent, and Xerox was ranked by Glassdoor as the fifth worst company to work for. Their sharp losses in sales prompted Xerox, in 2016, to split the company back into

---

1. Xerox.com/news/news-archive/2009/swe-acquire-affiliated-computer-services/svse.html.

pieces again: in essence, rejecting the ACS acquisition.[2]

So the two long-distance work buddies suddenly lost their grasp on the biggest perk of the job: a steady paycheck. They don't know where they will be, come 2017.

But for now, they bond on Skype over faith, family, and the dream of freedom in their professional future, if ever they manage to get past the bills of today. They giggle and shout during our interview, when it's revealed that not only do they both drive motorcycles: They even ride the same exact bike in the hills of Argentina and Kentucky: a Honda Shadow from the 1990s.

Pablo[3] recently has expanded his borders to cover the entire region of Mexico and Central and South America (Latin America or "LatAm") He leads the finance division for half the Americas in one of the world's twenty-five largest Fortune-500 information technology (IT) companies: Xerox, with 140,800 employees. He works all over the world, but he still lives in the exact same city where he was born.

He's a former college professor who never gets enough time to study and is even now taking courses in entrepreneurship on the side of a full-time career, marriage, and fatherhood. Pablo is passionate about children, education, and civil rights. He believes that mothers should put children as their top priority and fathers should sacrifice their own work and studies to help out at home.

He's a contradictory combination of conservative (Sicilian Catholic) family values and progressive (telecommuting) global networking. He's a numbers guy who sees the world in terms of dollars versus pesos and feels that there's never enough of either currency or time.

I PROVIDE FINANCIAL SUPPORT FOR XEROX LATIN AMERICA (LATAM)

My name is Pablo Mira. I'm thirty-nine. I'm a senior finance manager for Xerox Services, in charge of Latin America: that includes Argentina, Chile, Colombia, Peru, Brazil, and some others.

I provide finance support to operations leads in those countries during business decision-making processes. I've been in this job almost nine years.

Argentina is the largest country that Xerox runs down here. We have two main types of clients. The largest one is international telecommunications companies. Here in Córdoba, we have about 2,500 employees working for those clients at our [customer-support] call center.

Why Córdoba? Córdoba has one of the largest private universities in the country. Sixty percent of our employees in the call center are university students. So they're very well educated, and they're capable to take calls from first-class clients.

---

2. Phys.org/news/2016-01-xerox-sales-decline-company.html.s

3. *Pablo* is a baby nickname for Paul that means "small;" it's an endearing term. *Mira* means "look" in Spanish, peace in Slavic, light in Hebrew, and ocean in Sanskrit. It's become a slang term for "yo"—me. These are loaded words for a man who's spent nearly four decades looking for the meaning of life, religion, work, and money.

HIRING ON THE CHEAP IN COLOMBIA AND PERU

Then there's Colombia. Colombia is growing fast. It's a low-cost country. We've got about 1,500 agents or employees working there. Basically, we are in Bogotá City. Actually there are two big clients there that are communications companies, but there are also small clients coming to us such as Colgate and Direct TV, plus some Asian companies. We have started new business with insurance companies as well. So Colombia is growing fast, and the company is making a lot of effort on investing there.

Then we've got Peru, which is growing basically on servicing Argentinian clients because, you know, Peru is also a low-cost country. They have like 800 employees thus far in call centers in Lima, the capital city. That business is growing very fast. Revenue there is pretty hot compared to call-center businesses.

What *low cost* means: Just to give you an idea, an employee, a call center agent in Colombia and Peru earns 50 percent of what an Argentinian call center employee earns. We also have other types of operations in Peru. We provide public transportation services to the government of Lima.

CLOSING DOWN OPERATIONS IN CHILE

Last year was a tough year for Chile. We have shut down our operation there. We got really bad contracts with the telecommunications company—Telefónica, to be precise. We were losing money with them. We tried to renew those contracts under better terms. We couldn't. So the company decided to close that entity. We had to turn out about 700 employees there.

HOW I GOT ACQUIRED TWICE AND ENDED UP AT XEROX

Now that's my own current work for Xerox: I've been running those four countries.

Nine years ago, I was part of Multivoice, which was acquired by ACS Corp in December 2008. Eighteen months later, ACS was acquired by Xerox.

With the new structure to all the organization, I'm also overseeing other countries where we have operations; for example, in Brazil. We are running a call-center operation in Brazil for Apple. That's a large contract. There are some other smaller businesses, not call-center businesses, but businesses related to finance and accounting support to General Motors, General Electric, and Goodyear, etc.

Overall, I think they're trying to make a long-term [profit] goal in a short-time period.

MY TERRITORY KEEPS EXPANDING

I'm also getting involved in some Mexican and some Guatemalan operations, because my new role is to oversee 100 percent of the operations out of Latin America.

That now includes a pretty tiny operation in Suriname,[4] on the north coast of South America. It's a very small country. I learned about Suriname, I'm embarrassed to say, only

---

4. This tiny island is infamous for drug-smuggling and government-corruption, says Slate: slate.com/articles/news_and_politics/roads/2014/01/why_travel_to_suriname_the_former_dutch_colony_now_run_by_a_drug_running.html.

when we started working there. We acquired Unamic in 2005. Suriname is a former Dutch colony, so they speak Dutch there; so it's a low-cost country for the Dutch call center.

And so, overall, in LatAm, Xerox Services has, I may say, 6,000 to 7,000 employees roughly. I have eighteen direct reports.

Our revenue for all of Latin America, including all the countries, it's about $200 million a year. Off the top of my head, I can tell you that we have between thirty and forty different clients in the region.

I'M THE ELDEST SON OF A STRONG SICILIAN FATHER

I am the eldest son of the family. I have two younger brothers and a sister. One of my brothers (30 years old) lives in a different province with his wife and daughter. My sister (38) lives in Córdoba with her own family. The youngest one (27) is still single and still lives with my parents. My parents are still alive and together! They also live here in the city of Córdoba. My parents are not retired yet.

When I was younger, my dream was to work in finance for a multinational company. My father is an accountant as well. I think that I received a lot of influence from him. He had his office at home. I could see him working every day with all the papers, all the calculators, and the typing machines.

My father had a strong presence at home, not only for his job, but also for religion and education. I learned from my father to be the support of the family. According to him, you have to work as many hours as possible to give your family a decent life. We come from the south of Italy, in Sicily. The presence of the father is pretty strong in those types of families. So, a kid like me wants to be like his father.

My mother, although she worked during most of my childhood, was the one who took care of us kids. The main role for a mother is to raise kids and take care of the house. If the mother has time to work after that, that's fine. Both of them are Catholics and have educated us in love and respect to God. They, as a couple, and all together as a family, have dedicated time to church and charity for several years.

CATHOLIC EDUCATION FOR ME, FROM UNIVERSITY TO MY MBA

In Argentina, after kinder[garten], you know, we have primary school. Then we have secondary school. I went to a Catholic institution, a private institution, during that period. I liked foreign languages. So I started to learn English, and I spent five years studying English. Then that helped me a lot when I joined my first work with an American company [Dana] because that was a requirement.

Then I entered a public university in Córdoba. The companies look for talent from public university rather than private, because private universities are not so "prestigious." Is that the word?

The National University of Córdoba was founded by the [Catholic] Jesuits in the sixteenth century. The advantage in Argentina is that public universities are free, and there is no test to get into there. There is no limitation to study. Furthermore, there are people from other countries coming to Argentina so that they can get graduated from the university, because they cannot do that in their own countries.

So, I did my university. While there, I joined a group of teachers, to teach about cost control. That was a career I was interested in. I was studying for my CPA [Certified Public Accountant], and I worked for the university. It was like seven years working there. I learned about cost accounting, cost control, and planning, a lot more than what I had learned during the university courses. So that helped me a lot as well because that is something very specific. It took me five years, but I received my CPA degree in 1999. I am a public accountant.

During the last two years of my studies, I also worked as internal auditor for a local bank in the city of Córdoba.

My degree taught me enough to get me into Dana Holding Corporation, one of the largest auto-parts manufacturers in the world. It is based in Ohio with subsidiaries in several countries. I started there as a cost analyst after graduation and ended up working there for six years. However, I grew tired of working for a company in a permanent crisis. So I decided to start looking for a change in my professional life.

In 2006, a recruiting firm offered me a finance and planning position for a local company in Córdoba dedicated to call-center services. Its name was Multivoice, and it was owned by two persons from the same city.

I took the offer because I was interested in working in a service company, a totally different industry from auto-parts manufacturer. This company was later acquired by ACS, then Xerox.

While working at Dana, I had started a master's degree in business administration, an MBA [Masters of Business Administration] in a public university, the Catholic University of Córdoba. Regarding postgraduate degrees, that university is better than the public university, and it costs you the same. So I picked that.

I MET MY WIFE WHEN SHE WAS MY STUDENT

I met my wife, Carina, when I was teaching at the university. She was my student. She's thirty-four now, five years younger than me. She is a CPA and works in the National Bank of Argentina.

My wife comes from the countryside; so, she couldn't live in an apartment. She lived in an apartment while I was studying at the university, but it wasn't good enough for her. We now live in a small town near Córdoba city, in a house in a gated suburb with a dog in the yard. It was a must to get a house with a yard. We have two children, Marisol, who is seven years old, and Santiago, who is four years old.

BEING A FATHER, I HAVE TO STUDY LESS AND HELP OUT MORE

When I got married, my status changed. [Laughs.] When my daughter came, you know, I stopped with university and teaching. I spent more time at home and helping with homework. I like studying a lot. I'm very curious, and I'm always reading. But when my family started to grow, the time you have to dedicate to yourself is less than before. So I had to start reassigning some matters.

Actually one advantage that we have is that my wife gets home at 4:00 p.m., right when my daughter is coming home from school. She spends more time than me with the kids, helping with homework, spending time in the park, riding bicycles, etc.

What I do the most is, I take them to their friends' houses. There are birthday parties every week. And I take care of dinner. I cook basic meals—just a big salad, some smashed potatoes for the kids. And when I don't have time, I buy something. Later on at night, I take the children to the bathroom, and I help them with the bath. And then when my wife takes them to bed, I wash the dishes, and that's my chance to watch some TV as well. As far as my wife's concerned, I'm a manager just at work—not around here. [Laughs.]

For hobbies, I've got a motorcycle, a Honda Shadow XLS 600, a 1993. I like riding this motorcycle. My chance is only for the weekends when I have time and it's sunny. I am not an expert riding motorcycles, so I have to be careful.

And I play tennis at work once a week. Now I've started to run, and I'm getting myself prepared for a marathon, but I got injured. So I'm in rehab now. [Laughs.] I'm not running a lot, but I do my best. That's the kind of things that, you know, don't let me think of work. My mind flows away. I enjoy that.

MY WORKDAY: TRYING TO COMMUNICATE GLOBALLY WITH WORDS AND NUMBERS

I work from my home office two days a week. I spend three days at the Xerox office downtown. Apart from my responsibility as senior finance manager, I'm also the vice president of the legal entity in Argentina. So I'm a legal representative of the company. I have to sign contracts and checks, and approve wires [transfers]. So that is corporate. [Laughs.]

When I am at the office, my first task in the morning is to read emails—You know, the ones that I couldn't read while driving…[Laughs.] Because you are connected all the time, you know. That's the reality. I try to respond to as many emails as possible in the morning, because I'm usually up earlier than other countries because of the time zone. I'm one or two hours ahead of the rest of America. So I take advantage of that.

Based on the wide geography my position covers, I interact with several individuals every day. Since my company was acquired by ACS six years ago, I had seven managers I reported to and only met three of them face-to-face. Interactions with my direct managers are kind of impersonal, where just in a few occasions we would chat about something different than work. As we are figures people, that's OK and it doesn't mean an issue.

Communication with other people located in a different country is by email, phone, or instant messaging. That's pretty impersonal, too.

RESOLVING CONFLICTS ACROSS DISTANCES OF CULTURE AND PLACE

I can tell you that I spend the most time working with operations and sales counterparts from LatAm. Those people are located in same region, so we not only share time zone but also culture. Interaction with them is almost all online. We have daily contact and, sometimes, different objectives may generate some conflicts with these groups. As they report to a different line in the company, we have to solve those conflicts or, at least, minimize them as much as possible to be able to work together.

With regard my direct reports, I try to provide support to them not only in the formal way of a manager but also taking care of small details of their personal life— which doesn't mean that I have success with that. I just treat them same way I'd like to be treated.

My reality is that I try to work with everybody without conflict, making our hours at work happy or, at least, easy. With coworkers spread around the globe, I haven't found it easy to make close friends at work. I think that the situation for other people working in this industry is pretty similar. Every time I have the chance to talk to someone working in a service company, we have much in common.

LOTS OF MEETINGS, AND THEY'RE ALL REMOTE

In the mornings, I have my one-on-one meetings with my direct reports. So I've got my managerial reports—that's six, and the rest of the team reports to them. So I have six one-on-one meetings. I've got one meeting a week with my boss, who's in London.

My calendar is full of plenty of meetings. Most of the day, I spend time on the phone on conference calls, providing support either to operations or explaining something to the auditors, or reviewing new business opportunities.

We also have conferences where we review new business opportunities. And we present [Adobe] Flash to the management. Flash is a weekly forecast we run to cover the quarter we're working through, and we convert that against our budget or our latest forecast. We explain variances to the top management, and we get punished as well. [Laughs]. So every time I have to present reports I say, "Don't shoot the messenger!"

My calendar seems to flow between those types of meetings. Sometimes, people believe that finance professionals are the "owners" of company results just because we report them. We're just the messenger!

THE DIFFERENCE BETWEEN ACCOUNTING AND FINANCE

However, I do think that we have some empowerment, because according to our operations lead in the region, finance is the second-in-command. Nobody does anything without finance approval. That's reality.

It used to be that finance acted kind of like business police. We'd advise on what's allowed and what's not, or what's a good idea and what's not. And now that accounting and finance are split, accounting currently has that role, the role of police.

In our industry, we call that a "poke-a-yolk;" it's a test of anything, for quality or internal control. And I think that finance has become more the basis for any decision to be made, because operations tends to be more creative, and they just think aloud.

We have to put these ideas in the real life, and decide or show them whether or not those ideas are good, either for the clients, or for the company. We pay more attention to the company. So finance is a little bit more strategic and forward thinking, whereas accounting is just measuring end results.

The last recognition I received was an award from the CFO [chief financial officer]

Xerox services for work performed in LatAm during 2014. Fortunately, most of the people I report to or work with recognize my work and always let me that know. I realize that that's not something very common in the business world.

DIFFERENT CULTURES = DIFFERENT WAYS TO GET THE JOB DONE

Working across a region as vast as Latin America for a global company, you definitely find some legal and cultural differences that affect how we work together.

Geography affects several aspects on the job. For instance, for someone located in LatAm, it's not the same working for a U.S. company than working for a company with HQ [headquarters] in Asia. Time zones affect significantly the rest of the day of a professional regarding their personal life.

Argentineans are arrogant because of the way we speak, you know? In the north of Latin America, they are too polite, I would say. [Laughs.] They are always saying, "Sorry. Sorry for bothering," a lot of respect in conversation and even when you are chatting with them on IM [instant messaging], they are polite as well.

How much a professional earns also depends on the country where that person lives. Nowadays, corporations are moving shared-service centers to low-cost countries, because professionals with similar skills make less money in those countries.

I think the most challenging aspect of my work is to make people in the U.S. understand the way of doing business in LatAm. Most of the policies ruling the way of doing business in U.S. corporations are based on what clients, employees, and laws/ regulations require in the U.S. I've faced that issue in the two U.S. companies I worked for.

VACATIONS, FURLOUGHS, AND REGIONAL IDEAS ABOUT TIME

When I work with people from the States, my experience is that most people just see the world with their own eyes. They have some mental structure based on American principles. For instance, in Latin America, there might be about fifteen holidays a year in each country, and everybody takes them because that's a law-regulation in each country. In some countries, you've got a month of holidays when you join a company, and during summer, people usually take at least two consecutive weeks out.

You know more than me, that for an American, that's crazy. [Laughs.] If you're out of your office for two weeks, it means that you no longer work for the company.

I've got a short story regarding furlough, which is pretty common in this country. People can take this anytime, without compensation. That's forbidden in other countries. We cannot push people to take days out with no compensation. That's a law violation. And it took me like three months to make my first boss at Xerox understand that the regulations are different.

BEFORE I ATTEMPT TO WORK WITH SOMEONE, I GET TO KNOW THEM

So, in my own experience, when I start working with someone from a different country, my first thought is I have to learn about that person's reality before interacting with him or her. For example, for a Colombian person interacting with an Argentinean will encounter differences. Their way of asking for things is different.

So I start getting to know people by chitchatting. It's a good starting point, talking about life, you know, the weather, sports. And then we can go straight to work, but with a different atmosphere, and an understanding of how that person thinks.

I used to work with Brazilians. They're joking all the time. They're just saying nonsense. I laugh. That's very funny, but sometimes you have to be serious. But I understand it. It's part of their culture, and they're very good at work. So no complaints, you know? But that is something that people working at an international level should take care about. It's something that's really important to make people productive. That's the best approach.

USING THE REALLY WRONG WORD—IN SPANISH—IT MEANT "DICK"

I have made mistakes—[laughs.] silly things. For instance, everybody speaks Spanish or Portuguese down here, and some words, they don't mean the same, you know, in different countries. So I said something in Spanish that is a bad word in Chile, and I didn't know about that. In English, it would be like when you say, a number thirty-something, you know, and that "something" in Spanish is *pico* [spells]. You'd say, "thirty-y-pico." And "pico" in Spanish is "dick" in Chile.

So I said that in front of one of my reports, who was a lady, and she told me, "You shouldn't say that. You're in Chile, you know?" I grew very embarrassed. [Laughs.]

It's a cultural thing. In Chile, they are very conservative. So you would never hear them cursing or saying something impolite. So that is something to consider when you talk to someone from Chile. You have to be very careful with the words you use.

CHANGES THROUGH TIME AND TECHNOLOGY

When we look for someone for the company, we really look for experience and knowledge. There is no difference regarding gender and ages.

I've worked with ladies and gentlemen, old people, and young people, and the only difference is experience. Young people come up with all the technology insight. Old people have the experience because they already experienced different things that young people didn't. That's the only difference I see.

In my first years, we used Excel spreadsheets a lot. All the work that later went to computers was too heavily manual. We had to create reports, spend time creating reports. Now the softwares [programs] that we use are more record-protecting of work. Except for Essbase, the business-intelligence system we use for reports. We pull reports for that. It's changed now. But I hear that one's not going to be around too long, either. Everything changes quickly.

WORKING WITH, OR AROUND, CORRUPTION IN LOCAL GOVERNMENTS

Regarding corruption, South America or Latin America, in general, has governments that are social[ist] governments, right? They're in favor of doing more things for people and less for companies. In that kind of work, you have to set pretty good controls to avoid corruption, which is something not very feasible in our country. That would require a lot of money to spend on [creating controls].

On the average, we have very corrupted countries, such as Bolivia, Colombia, Mexico, and Brazil, sort of, Argentina, sort of. There are other countries, such as Chile, that are doing a very good job preventing corruption. They are well regarded by European countries and the U.S., because the corruption can be measured now.

I'm not an expert on the subject, but there are surveys[5] being made by international companies. There are other statistics regarding politicians' track records, cases being opened against former politicians or governments. There are companies tracking that information. And there are opinions as well, which are not really objective, because this topic can be so subjective.

But people living in the region can read the papers and the news and see discussions about politicians and government. When companies like Xerox try to get contracts with the government or the cities or the states, you can also notice the level of corruption in each state, each city in the region.

Everybody in Argentina is pretty sure that the government manipulates the statistics of the country. So I'm sorry to say that we have lost like ten years of good statistics in our country because they manipulate the inflation index,[6] and that causes the poverty rate to appear lower. And the unemployment index is also manipulated because they pay an unemployment compensation to the unemployed, and they count them as if they were employees.

We trust more the statistics prepared for by the private companies than the government itself. Actually last year, the inflation, the cost of living for, I mean, the consumer price index for Argentina was around 20 percent, and 100 percent of the unions are asking for a 30, 35 percent wage increase for their people. So that means that even the unions don't trust official statistics.

The corruption affects us a lot because we compete against local companies that aren't ruled by Sarbanes-Oxley [investment protection], for instance. They don't care about paying a fee to the politicians to get a contract. So we need to find a way to compete against those kinds of companies following our own rules and being unethical in the way of doing business. So it's not easy. I can say that. It's not easy.

As I said before, most of the contracts are gotten based on personal relationships with *people* within the market. That kind of personal relationship is sometimes is based on favors. So when you hire a sales executive from the market, you have to be very, very careful about whom you are hiring. Salespeople sometimes don't care how we get business. We have had that kind of experience prior in ACS.

---

5. See transparency.org/news/feature/finding_the_right_measurement_for_corruption.
6. Economist.com/blogs/americasview/2014/04/statistics-argentina.

I'm very careful with businesses coming from Latin America. When they say, "Hey, you could get a new business opportunity with Paraguay," I have to pay close attention at this point, you know, because I know how businesses are done in Paraguay.

Paraguay is one of the most corrupted countries in the region. Just to give you an idea, there are stolen cars driven in the country with legal licenses. [Laugh.] People from Paraguay steal cars from other countries; they get those cars into Paraguay and turn them legal for Paraguay. Nobody believes that, but it's a reality. You can Google that.[7] That's Paraguay. That's my world.

UNTAMED CURRENCIES: DEALING WITH FLUCTUATION AND INFLATION

In terms of currency, there are two macroeconomic factors in Latin America that are not so common in the U.S. One of them is currency (currency fluctuation), and the other one is inflation. We have to deal with both of them.

There are some people I work with in the U.S. who believe that they are tied together or are the same thing. That means that they are not familiar with those issues in this country. There are cycles in each country in both inflation and devaluation, depending on the government the country has at each moment.

There are governments that are more focused on the interest rate, the third factor that we should consider. And they pay attention to the interest rate, and they leave the currency to flow free. There are other countries paying more attention to devaluation so the interest rate turns high. So it's a very complex situation, and it depends on the current philosophy of each government.

In Argentina, just to give you an example, we've had inflation and devaluation of the local currency for the last seven years, and that devaluation has been forced by the government in order to neutralize the effect of the inflation. The inflation in Argentina in particular is driven by the printing of bills [cash] in order to pay expenses.

So there are a lot of [Argentinian] *pesos* around to convert into dollars, based on the research of the Central Bank, the USD. So our peso is more worthless than before because of the printing. That's an issue, and nobody could figure out how to stop that because stopping inflation means to cut public expense. Nobody would like to take that risk because cutting public expenses means an increase in unemployment.

For a Socialist government, that's something impossible to do. Argentina is a very particular place in the world, I may say, different from other Latin American countries.

Colombia nowadays is facing a devaluation of their currency because of the oil, the value of the barrels in the market. It underwent a devaluation, at least 27 percent is the last year, but they don't have inflation. So for common people, the ordinary people working in Bógota and not dealing with USD, the devaluation doesn't mean anything, if they don't buy imported things. But it's tough.

Brazil is also facing a situation similar to Argentina because they have raised the public expense. They have to print extra bills as well, and to allow their *reals* [Brazilian

---

7. Articles.latimes.com/1987-03-31/news/mn-1496_1_stolen-car.

dollars] to devaluate, because they're having inflation. They are not on the same scale as Argentina, but they are facing that kind of situation.

So I'm going to give you an example. We prepared a budget for Argentina, using an exchange rate of 14.6 pesos per dollar for this whole year. The currency, the accurate currency for Q1 was 8.8 pesos per dollar, which means that our peso was worth more than budget. We sold the same in pesos—our revenue is the same—but because of the exchange rate, we have more variance in the budget, and I have to explain that in each analysis.

In Colombia, it's the contrary, the opposite. We ran a budget using an exchange rate of 2,000 Colombia pesos for the whole year, and now the Colombia peso is 3,082. It's a large devaluation. So that is something: reporting needs to done in USD, but running the businesses in local currency implies an explanation of that, of the currency.

INFLATION FORCES US TO ASK FOR SALARY INCREASES— OR THE EMPLOYEES WILL LEAVE

Regarding inflation, we have to go in front of the company asking for a wage increase for all the employees that are not protected by the union, because 90 percent of our employees are protected by the union. So the wage increase for them or COLA [cost of living adjustment] is mandatory. For the rest of the employees, we need to adjust the salary just because of the market, you know, because, if you don't raise their salary, they will go elsewhere.

So when we have to go in front of the senior management asking for a wage increase for those employees not protected by law, and they say, well, "How much would you like to increase?"

I say, "[We'd like] about 30 percent of their current salary."

They say, "How much?" [Laughs.]

I say, "Yeah, 30 percent. That was the salary increase that was agreed in the union we're paying. So we need to do the same with them. Otherwise, they start looking for a different job in the market who is willing to pay more than us."

And then we have to go in front of the clients, asking for a price increase to offset our inflation on the expense side. So that's something we have to bill every year, at least in Argentina, where those variations are really material and out of the average in the world. There might be three or four countries in the world with such a level of inflation like Argentina: Venezuela, Russia, Greece—with my fingers on one hand, I can count the countries with such level of inflation in the world. So we are a special case. [Laughs.]

WORST MOMENTS ON THE JOB

In terms of worst moments, the four countries that I mentioned, that I manage, are not in good shape. They were not performing pretty decently well in the last two or three years.

That takes me to what I mentioned regarding cultural matters and the way of doing business. In 2012, the managing director of Latin America left the company for his own reasons, and someone from the States came down to Córdoba and took over that role in the company.

That person was based in Portland. He didn't move to Latin America. He managed the company from his house in Portland, and basically, long story short, he screwed that up.

We lost relationships with clients, because you cannot deal with clients in the American way in Latin America. We get along in Latin America by personal relationships. You have to know someone who works there if you want to bring some new business into the company. It's not a public offer, by writing, etc. And you close business in a dinner, basically. This person only had experience in the U.S. So that was not a clever idea for the company. We started to lose businesses and money in 2012, and 2013 was a mess.

WE LOST $13 MILLION, AND I HAD TO TELL THEM WHY

As a messenger back to the company, I ended up with so many bullet holes in me We lost $13,000,000 in the year 2013, which was a record for us. We had never lost that kind of money. So, at that time, Xerox turned a profitable Latin American company into a money-losing company, losing *big* money.

And then I had, as the finance manager there, not only to take care of the finance report, but also to take care of the cash of the countries. I had to face corporate several times, asking for money, explaining to corporate guys in Norwalk [Connecticut] why we were losing money, and why we need money, and why they should give money to Latin America to keep the business working.

You've got a guy in front of you, and you're saying, "We lost $13,000,000, and I need more for next year;" you try that! That's what I had to say, on several occasions.

It had zero percent to do with local politics here. One hundred percent of the losses we had and we still have in the country, in the region, not only Argentina, but also in Chile, were due to bad decisions made by that managing director.

The president of the company phoned me. He called me asking for an explanation, because he couldn't understand what was going on here, and I had to say the truth. We're making bad decisions down here. I said, "We are thinking of business in the wrong way, and my recommendation is to make a change immediately." So they did that because of me. That was my advice.

Now we have a managing director that is from Latin America and lives in Latin America, and we are turning the thing around. We are starting to promote again. So those were my tougher days in the company, explaining to the corporation why we were so bad and recommending top senior management to separate [terminate] the managing director from the region.

LOTS OF HAPPY MOMENTS, LIKE WHEN MY PEOPLE LEARN TO LEAD

I've had several happiest moments in this job. I love working with people to develop long-term plans, comparing them with actual results, detecting deviations, and providing corrections.

All of that is driven by human behavior, so interaction and understanding people, in essence, are key to performing this work. I also love it when I can see my people being recognized as good workers, and when I feel that I was able to teach them something, and they can put that to work. When I can go out on vacation and leave someone in my team in the frontline, and when I come back, my boss or whoever is telling me that my team is excellent: That makes me feel very happy, because I like developing the skills of my people so that I can grow or I can move away.

TRAVELING NEAR AND FAR WITH MY FAMILY

When I go away, I always travel with family. I usually take two weeks during summer because I have four weeks a year vacation. In summer, and we usually go to a beach with the family. Last summer, we went to the north of Brazil for the second time. The year before, we spent some time in the Dominican Republic. And we are saving to go to the south of Mexico. There are beautiful beaches there.

In winter, I like to drive around the country, going to places that I've never been before. We have a beautiful country. There are mountains with snow. There are beaches. There is warm weather, cold weather. It's a large country. So I like to take the car with the family and drive miles and miles, going new places.

BEING AN ARGENTINIAN, A LATIN AMERICAN, AND A GLOBAL CITIZEN

When we greet someone in the street, you know, we say, "Hey, how are you doing today?"

"It's so good to be Argentinian," they say. [Laughs.] That's a saying that means we are good, considering that [because] we are Argentinian. So people joke about that.

From a world perspective, being Argentinean, we always have to make a differentiation between Argentinians living in Buenos Aires, the capital city, and Argentinians living in the rest of the country. People living in Buenos Aires, just like people living in Rio de Janeiro, Brazil, think that they are the cleverest people in the world, that they are successful, and they have solutions for everything. They are arrogant,[8] you know?

That's what people from other countries and other cities think of people living in Buenos Aires. So, when you go to a different country, even for vacation, people ask, "Where are you from?" and you say, "I'm from Argentina—but not from Buenos Aires." [Laughs.]

You make that clear. They say, "Ah, that's okay. That's okay." So it's not easy to be an Argentinian because, in the past, we were proud of being an Argentinian because people think, "Oh, Argentina, Maradona, Maradona," or they said, "Argentina, *Evita.*" Or now they say, "Argentina, Messi," who plays on the Barcelona soccer team.

But now people say, "You know, Argentina, oh, Cristina Kirchner, your president sucks." She's a friend of Hugo Chávez from Venezuela. They think your government doesn't like the Mercosur, which is the economic union in the southern countries of the regions. They fight the U.S., they're a friend of Iran…You know, we are seen like bad guys in the world because of the government we have.

So it's not easy at this moment being an Argentinean in a global world. As for the borders, we don't care about that, you know? We are all the same. We can live with that.

Being in Latin America, I don't see that there's any particular matter on that. It's

---

8. Read why, from a native's perspective: news.terra.com/argentine-arrogance-myth-or-reality,5108fcde942f7310Vgn-CLD200000bbcceb0aRCRD.html.

part of a growing region that has got governments that are more aligned to this protecting not only the people but also the companies, and justice. It's getting better that way here and in Brazil, Chile, Peru, and Colombia. They improve their institutions a lot, and they're getting respected by other continents. So I think that being in Latin America nowadays, it's okay. There is nothing to be embarrassed about because of that.

In terms of being a global citizen, for business, we live in a virtual world, and all the connections are on the [Inter]Net. You don't need to travel to meet people and be places.

But, you know, I'm kind of old-fashioned regarding my personal life. To be considered to be a global citizen, I would like to be in the place, you know, physically in that place.

For now, from a working standpoint, from a job standpoint, yeah, I might be a global citizen. From my desk, I can work for any company in the world. But, for my personal life, I'm interested in visiting places and seeing the landscapes with my own eyes. As I said, I'm old-fashioned in that way.

MY OWN COMPANY: I DON'T KNOW HOW MUCH LONGER I CAN GET ALONG WITH BOSSES

I've thought of starting my own company. I'm almost forty years old. I don't know how long I could get along with some kinds of bosses. I think to be respectful with my boss, you know, that person at least cannot be stupid. [Laughs.]

It's getting more and more difficult for me to get along with that kind of people. I have to say things, what I think. That is something that is a characteristic for people from Argentina: We are not—I don't know the word, but—maybe *shy*.

We say what we think, whether you like it or not. We're pretty direct and straightforward. We strive to express our feelings or our thinking. We shout when we talk. That's my way. And sometimes I have to back up and say sorry. But that's the risk you run when you are open. So I don't get along with people that are not at the level they should be, to be my manager. I was more tolerant in the past, but I'm not sure that I can tolerate that in the future or when I turn fifty, you know?

The second aspect is that I spend twelve hours a day working for someone else, making money. So I am pooling all my efforts on my chance for someone else taking the cash. If I could spend that time at my own project, I could make that in my company. My contribution to the company could to *me*, go into my pocket, but first I have to find the business that I could actually run or to create.

In addition, considering the type of work I perform, being tied to rules is a must. We have policies, internal controls, and procedures to follow. Here, there's not much room for creativity in my job. I think that my new dream of running my own business has something to do with that.

So I'm taking some entrepreneur courses, just to learn. As I am in finance, I am not a friend of risk. And when you run your own business, you should get familiar with risk, because no one will succeed in the first try. That's a rule. And so I, I have to lose the fear to fall and start again.

That is my main fight to make that decision, because I have a family. I have kids in school. I have to save for their wellness, and I'm not sure I'm prepared to run the risk of failure. That's my only issue here.

1at relies on you—that doesn't make things easy. But I've discussed
1 my wife, plans and ideas, and what about working more hours a
1ess meetings, saving some money, just in case. We have gone back
:. Meanwhile, here I am, still at Xerox . . .

MY PHILOSOPHY OF MONEY

I am a finance guy by choice. It is my own choice. That means I think that, like it or not, money moves the world. If you want to get a life, you need money for that. That's reality.

I remember, when I was first born, my parents lived in a room in my grandmother's house. They didn't have a house; they didn't have a car. My father was fired just when they got married, and I was born one year later. So my father was just starting a new job.

But they didn't care. Work was for the basics. You spend eight hours a day working to get enough money to survive, but life is after those eight hours. I think that now life is different, and we have to spend at least ten hours a day working, both the husband and wife, working to get enough money to the school, the car, the new house, the vacation. Everything is paid by money. That's reality.

Otherwise, I wouldn't work so many hours. I could get a part-time job; my wife could work a part-time job, and we could spend half of the day with kids, drinking coffee, and just being with them.

I'd love spending time with family and visiting new places with them. I always say that I don't have enough time to help other people with basic needs. I'd be more dedicated to them for sure. I'd spend more time playing sports every day.

But in a global world, the ideal life is shortsighted and online. So when a new car is launched in the U.S., we can see that down here, and we want that car, you know? That car might be too expensive down here, but we want the car. If we see a snapshot of an island in Asia, we want to be there. That's money. That's money.

So: money rules. That's reality, and it's very sad. I have to recognize that. It's very sad. Sometimes we are spending so much time to earn money that we don't take care of the core of our life that is our own personal life and our families. It doesn't make sense: We make a lot of planning to take our families on vacations, but [snaps his fingers] like that, you no longer have a family. So why are we wasting so much time working? Money confuses us. That's my deep thought on that.

I have always had an internal conflict, which is how much should I dedicate to the job in any company? How much should I dedicate to other things? How important should work be in my life? Thus far, the job is winning, because I spend most of the day working. That's something that I would like to rethink and see how I can figure out. That's an open thought…There's no conclusion there.

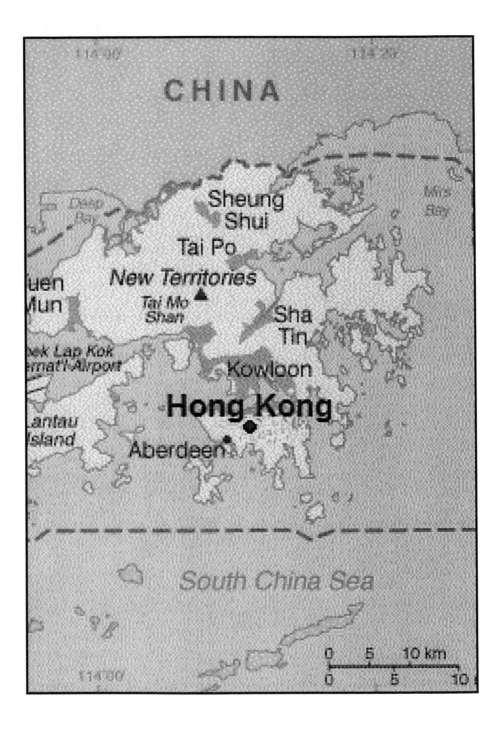

NIK

EQUITY INVESTMENT MANAGER

HONG KONG, CHINA

Editor's note: Nik Rowold is a German citizen working for an American company in Hong Kong. Prior to now, he's lived in Bonn, Moscow, Washington, D.C., Philadelphia, and London. He speaks German, Russian, and English (with an American accent picked up during his Maryland years) and is trying to learn Chinese and Korean. His U.S.-born wife also "grew up all over the world," and their two children, born to bicultural American-German parents, have Chinese citizenship from birth.

This is Hong Kong (population 7.2 million),[1] an endless sea of a montage of humans—not just international but, as Nik talks about later, diversely inter-Asian. Flower stands and food stalls pop up at the feet of mighty skyscrapers in Central, the city's financial district and center of Nik's posh world.

---

1. Hong Kong Island is a bit bigger than New York City in landmass, but less densely populated at 7.2 million versus 8.5. For comparison, London is 8.6 million, and Tokyo and Moscow each has around 13 million—but Mainland China, across Kowloon Bay from where Nik lives, boasts three of the world's most densely populated cities: Shanghai at 24 million, Beijing at 22 million, and Tianjin at 15 million.

Nik hasn't done much of life following any standard formula. Having moved as a nine-year-old from Germany to the "Wild East" and witnessed the fall of the Soviet Union, he later moved from Moscow to the capital of the U.S. (Washington, D.C.) for high school, then back to Germany for social service and a quick company startup stint, before returning to Maryland for college. Then he was off to London Business School for his master's in finance, and after that, the world was his oyster.

Nik says he got more out of college because he'd already worked a couple of years as an entrepreneur, with a young startup team that later sold the company for over a billion dollars. He didn't stick around long enough to pocket any of the proceeds. Besides, for a numbers guy whose job is to invest and generate massive piles of wealth, Nik appears to be pretty detached from money. He's an equity manager who says, "Don't focus primarily on earnings."

His job may seem glamorous, but he says, "I think most kids stick to clichés when they make career choices." Nik wants to debunk false notions of what it takes to work in finance and whether wealth can bring any happiness at all.

His number one hero is Manjula, his college buddy who forewent Wall Street to spend decades fundraising for kids' scholarships in his home country of Sri Lanka. Nik has supported Educate Lanka (educatelanka.org) by running an Ultramarathon[2] (50-100 kilometers or 31-160 miles) in Nepal, raising $14,000 for student scholarships.

He's striving to develop aspects of himself beyond his 80-100 workweek at Providence Equity. "At the end of the day," quips Nik, "I hope I'm more than just a guy in a suit."

GENERATING NEW BUSINESS FOR AN INVESTMENT FIRM IN THE WORLD'S FINANCIAL CAPITAL

My name is Niklas Rowold; I'm thirty-three years old. I'm in business development for a private-equity firm, Providence Equity.[3] It was launched in 1989 and is run by a gentleman named Jonathan Nelson. We manage forty-five billion in assets. It's a fairly small firm, about three hundred people, and it's set up in seven offices, in the U.S., in Europe, and then there's my team in Asia.

The idea behind private equity firms is, you develop a certain level of expertise in a sector or a region, and then you look for companies you want to invest in. We're the largest media investor in the world.

We invest in communications media and some education. We own a lot of large education businesses. For example, in communications, in Hong Kong, there's a dominant cable station called TVB [Television Bureau of Advertising, Inc.]. So we own a quarter of TVB along with other investors. In the U.S., we started Hulu. We started that together with a couple of strategic partnerships with NBC and Fox Networks.

---

2. Join Nik for a short bit of his run in Nepal, via video: youtu.be/OX7_VeFu25U.

3. Update: Nik changed jobs in early 2016 and now works in a similar capacity for a larger firm, CVC Capital Partners, a division of Citicorp that's invested $71 billion into 60 companies since its inception in 1981.

The idea is finding premium content and building businesses around premium content or the delivery of that content, essentially. There's a lot of value in that. So we said, Let's create a company that essentially markets that content, delivers it to fans, and then monetizes it.

We started the Yankees Entertainment Sports (YES) Network. Before the Yankees Sports Center, that concept didn't exist. Now you have a lot of TV stations or channels that are for divisions in college sports in the U.S., or for other regional sports teams, such as Bulls TV for the Chicago Bulls.

In education, we own Blackboard. We own a lot of vocational training schools. Ascend Learning teaches nurses. We've bought businesses like Vector Learning, which did compliance training. Study Group is a business that helps foreign students place into schools in the U.S., U.K., and Australia. So, for about ten years, we've invested a lot in the education fund, for-profit education.

All we do is we look for companies that do things very well in their sector, and then my job (because it takes capital to buy these businesses) is to convince investors that they are the best at that, so that they give us the capital. We invest on their behalf. We charge fees for those investments, and then hopefully make money on the investments, return the capital plus the profit back to the investors.

I'm the head of the business development function in all of Asia. I'm the one who raises capital from large institutional investors to allow us to invest in these companies. My clients are corporations, endowments, sovereign wealth funds, and some very large families. So basically institutional pooled capital across Asia.

GROWING UP IN GERMANY AND THE SOVIET UNION

I'm German. I grew up in West Germany, in Bonn. I didn't grow up with wealth, but I grew up comfortable. There was never anything that I didn't have that I really wanted. I had a really good childhood, great parents, comfortable, no wealth, but comfortable. And when you're little, wealth doesn't mean anything.

My father's name is Manfred Rowold. He was the first university graduate in his family. He was a political journalist for a big German daily newspaper. He became one of the main foreign correspondents when the Berlin Wall fell, and it looked like there was going to be a strike, and the Soviet Union was going to bring Communism to an end. Armies of journalists were sent from all over the world to Moscow to cover that. He covered that for *Die Welt*. He retired in his early fifties.

And my mother was a teacher who stopped teaching kindergarten when my brother (who's four years older) was born. So she's been a full-time mom ever since, and she still is. I admire my mother for always supporting various parts of the family. We have a small family with various issues, and she's very active, flying around, just being a mother in the true family sense. Certainly I've looked up to my father at times, and it's typically family that you look up to, but I wouldn't say there's just one person that's been like that my whole life.

One of the best things that happened to me, in my development, was that we moved to the Soviet Union in the late eighties and stayed there through 1995. We moved from Germany to Russia. Career-wise for my father, it was great. We were there for six years.

We were a normal family in West Germany doing absolutely fine, and then, in the late eighties, our life changed fairly dramatically when he was sent to Moscow; for me, the world just opened up. I was introduced to foreign things, things that were not German, and I really, really liked it. I embraced the Soviet Union because it was very imperfect. There was nothing there. I was nine.

I learned to improvise. There were no toys. There were no playgrounds. It was dirty. It was cold. My parents were very liberal in letting me play and just experience it. From a developmental perspective, that was fantastic because you're not sitting back. You're not being fed stimulation. You actually have to go out and find it.

So in Moscow, foreigners lived in these ghettos basically, compounds all bunched together. You lived with people from all over the world. I remember my best friends being from Algiers and other parts of North Africa, just everywhere. So my English is decent just because I started speaking it when I was nine, with all of these kids. I also learned Russian then. I can read it now.

In the Soviet Union, we were under surveillance constantly. All of the apartments were bugged; all of the embassies were bugged. This was the epicenter of the Cold War. The country was at the brink of collapse because poverty was everywhere. The system had clearly failed. You did have relatively high crime rates. We went from a small town in West Germany to a gigantic city. And my parents were fantastic because they wanted us just to embrace it. They didn't protect us all that much. They didn't put a cage around us.

WITNESSING THE COLLAPSE OF THE SOVIET UNION IT WAS THE WILD EAST

Then when the Soviet Union collapsed in the early nineties, everything changed. It was a free-for-all—a lot of social change, and social change brings unrest. There were protests. There was fighting. The tanks were patrolling around the building they called the White House. I was shot at near the Duma. I was there with my father, and they shot at us from the building where we were standing. My dad had several of his colleagues killed in an assassination in some part of Moscow.

It was the Wild East. It was definitely volatile, the end of the Cold War. It changed the lives of every person on the planet. It doubled the size of the global workforce. It was the single most important geopolitical event of all of our lifetimes.

Nothing is close, in my opinion. China wouldn't be China, and Russia wouldn't be Russia. We wouldn't be sitting here today if we still had the Cold War going on. Think about the implications of the crash of the Berlin Wall and then a couple of years later, the end of the Soviet Union, Boris Yeltsin stepping in for Mikhail Gorbachev, and everything that followed. It opened up the world. The entire Eastern Bloc would be closed today, but it's not. That's where all the growth is coming from. What would Europe do if China didn't exist right now, if China wouldn't trade with them? So the implications are massive, right? It affects everything.

MOVING FROM MOSCOW TO MARYLAND: THEY COULDN'T BE MORE OPPOSITE

Then in 1995 we moved to D.C., which was the opposite. We went from downtown Moscow to Potomac, Maryland, which was quiet and safe. You didn't lock your doors. It was just perfect. I didn't like it better, but it was just completely different. We lived in a small house in Potomac, but it was in a really nice neighborhood. So that was my first taste of wealth, seeing big houses and bigger cars, when I was about fifteen; but we were never wealthy. We lived close to the school. There was a German school there.

I picked up an American accent when we moved to D.C. Prior to that, I had an accent that was probably a mix of a lot of things, and then it became American over time.

I then graduated from high school. I did a lot of different things. I went back to Germany. I did social service in a hospital for a year. I helped start a company, Hybris, in the late nineties when I was just out of high school. I was one of the first employees, basically. The company hit a wall but actually survived, and some of the guys who started it stuck with it and sold it to SAP, a tech company, for a billion plus a couple of years ago. Great story. A great, great story and really good guys, too.   .

RACING THROUGH UNIVERSITY TO EARN TWO DEGREES IN THREE YEARS

Then I went to University of Maryland for three years. I was not on scholarship. My parents supported me, and I also worked doing translations and other little things for Hybris. When I left to go to college, they were kind enough to give me work off and on, so I could have some income while I was there. And my wife Stephanie was a teacher. She taught kindergarten. She was in the final year of her education and started her work meanwhile. I think she made $1,600 a month. She supported me for two years.

I got into the school of economics first, but the business school had the better reputation. So then I decided, "Let me just do both," and then I just ended up doing both. They're actually very different fields.

If you want a career in finance, you can study whatever you want, in my opinion. You don't need to study finance or economics. That's not what banks actually are looking for.

IF YOU WANT TO WORK WITH MONEY, STUDY ANYTHING *BUT* ECONOMICS AND FINANCE

I believe, to be successful, you should study what you love, and just make sure that you're really smart.

I remember interviewing at Goldman [Sachs, GS]. I was really lucky getting into Goldman, by the way, totally lucky to get the interview. I remember at GS sitting in my training class. There were about 140 of us just in investment management, and about 70 percent of them were *not* finance or economics majors. No business majors at all—English, psychology, whatever you want.

If you're that young coming out of school, the thing that employers typically care about is, "Are you intellectually curious? Do you have self-awareness, and do you have awareness?" Those are two different things. Self-awareness is knowing what your weaknesses are, being okay with them, and knowing how to address them. Awareness is, "Are you aware of your surroundings?"

Nobody expects you to actually know anything about what you studied. You don't learn that much [in school]. It sounds really harsh, but you can sit in four finance classes and learn the basics. For finance in particular, it's not rocket science. You can pick it up. But are you smart? Are you driven? Are you intellectually curious? Are you quick on your feet?

When we interview the 4.0 finance majors, we're like, "I'm not so sure." I'd rather have somebody who's 3.8, 3.6. Look at who does well at banks? Athletes do. People who have done interesting, challenging things in their life. Look at how many athletes actually run banks, football players. The guy who runs Goldman right now, the Number Two guy, is a hockey player.

If you're in training positions in banking, it's about winning. It's about fighting. It's about perseverance. Those are the intangibles that really, really matter. If you're easily offended, or you're thin-skinned and people can get to you, that industry is not for you. You can be a wizard on a spreadsheet, you can be the best accounting student, and whatever upward mobility you wanted without all the intangibles, you're never going to get it.

STRAIGHT OUT OF COLLEGE, I WORKED FOR GOLDMAN SACHS

After university, I went straight to Goldman in Philadelphia. Stephanie and I were living together. Our relationship was interesting in that she grew up the way I did: We lived all over the world. She had an opportunity to live in Hong Kong for six months and then move to India to teach, where she had lived for eight years growing up. So she did that; that meant that the whole time that I was in Philadelphia working for Goldman (which was two years and my last year at university) we were separated.

And then after two years at Goldman in Philly, I moved to London with Goldman. I moved there in 2007. We got married in 2008.

I then quit Goldman in 2009 to start a business with a client that was focused on family offices. It was a family-office advisory business. This was at the height of the [Great Recession and] distrust in banks. He was a very wealthy man, and he wanted families to come together to basically transact together without having to rely on the Goldman Sachs, the J. P. Morgans of the world. So, if you wanted to buy a business and you need aggregate capital, we could be the link to connect you to other private pools of capital and then start to transact together.

MY CHANCE TO MOVE TO CHINA AND ADVANCE WITH GOLDMAN

So I did that for a year and a half, and then he and I had disagreements on where to take the business. And then it was again a coincidence: My former boss called out of the blue. I hadn't talked to him in years. He opened the conversation with, "Hey, Nik, this is Larry. Do you want to move to Hong Kong?"

They knew I knew the business background. It was just a matter of me getting adjusted to Asia.

I had just agreed with my business partner that we were going to part ways. So that's how I ended up in Hong Kong. In-between, in 2010, we had our son, Benjamin. Then I moved here in January 2011.

Benjamin was only three weeks old, brand-new. By then I had been at Goldman for two years. So I worked at Goldman for a total of about seven. The thing that struck me was, one reaction of banks in the crisis was to consolidate decisions, where they're made and by whom they're made. And if you're in a remote office like Hong Kong, that's very difficult.

So a big reason why I decided to leave was that Goldman prides itself on being very entrepreneurial, and they are. Of all the banks, I still think they're head-and-shoulders above everybody else for many reasons. But it made it difficult to really be very responsive and to run it in an autonomous way, the way I would have liked to.

LEAVING THE BIG GUN TO RUN A SMALL INVESTMENT FIRM

And then my current opportunity presented itself. Providence found me through a headhunter, and I decided to leave, and that was a good move.

Autonomy is crucial for me. There are people that work better in larger organizations where they have a process, and they execute that, and they're world-class at executing that. It's a set of tasks and a bit more controlled environment. You know where you are. You know where you fit.

I'd rather have more responsibility and live with the volatility that comes with it, than have less and have very limited influence over ultimately my destiny. If you work for a company with 40,000 people, that's the case.

With me, what always appealed to me was imperfection and uncertainty. I wanted to drive the business, make decisions and then live with those: enter a situation that is imperfect or incomplete, and then improve it. If you're an entrepreneur, you have all of those things to the extreme. What attracted me to what I do now is that it was a great institution with a very unique profile, but a limited footprint, in a fast-growing market.

The appeal was to take this institution and make the investor base aware of the brand and capability set. That's a unique setup. You have strong brand, a strong franchise, a great leadership facing a huge market that's untapped, and you have to connect the two. And so if you're in the business-development profession, that's interesting.

Hong Kong Providence has been here about seven years now, but it's very small. People will know TPG, Carlyle, K.K.R., Blackstone: the giants of the private equity world. Providence has been around just as long or longer, and has as much capital in some cases, but it's just a very low-profile brand.

FROM SMALL STARTUP TO BIG COMPANY, AND BACK TO VERY SMALL

Private equity, believe it or not, is different. It's a lot more intimate, a lot more private. Day-to-day, my headquarters is thirteen hours removed. I can design my day the way I like it and then measure my results. That's great. That's a huge appeal, leaving a big bank and going to a smaller firm. The stress is more, and the work is more, but the way I can divide it up is a lot more up to me.

Banks are competitive places, and they should be. Post-crisis, they're increasingly regulated. Everybody's looking at each other. So everything you do, you look left and right, and that's just the function of it being a bigger institution. There's a lot of pressure on performance.

And so private equity is very competitive, but it's also just a smaller version of a bank. The office that I'm in here has seven people, very small. So it's a very collegial, family-type atmosphere, where we just work together and try and get results, but there's no elbows. You don't have to take somebody out to get ahead. You just do well, and you're hoping to be rewarded for that, and you do it again, and you try to have fun in the process.

SHAPING STRATEGY AND GETTING A RETURN ON OUR INVESTMENTS (ROI)

A decent ROI [return on investment] is probably 2X or a 2-½X, just because they can be mature businesses. That's not particularly high. So a lot of guys would tell you 3X, 4X, but that's not really realistic anymore. I think the market's too efficient. But if you can double somebody's money, or generate 150 percent on it over four or five or six years—annualizing a 20, 25 percent return—people tend to be pretty happy. In Asia, the return threshold is a little higher because you have higher levels of inflation, but that's sort of the idea.

This is all equity in private businesses. They're not traded on the Stock Exchange. We typically buy, control, and then run these businesses. So we appoint new management, or we back existing management. Sometimes you like the assets of a business but you think the way they're deployed is wrong. We set strategy from a value-creation standpoint, and either our companies continue doing what they're doing, or we change the direction.

The firm runs its portfolio globally out of one pool. The last fund we raised was five billion dollars. The other before that was about twelve billion dollars. That was at the height of, sort of pre-bubble investment activity.

I INVEST IN MY OWN COMPANY, TOO

We have investment professionals globally that can run that capital. I participate through personal investment into that fund. Depending on your seniority in private equity firms, the way you get compensated is that you participate in the performance-based fees of that firm. So if you actually end up making money for investors, then you can, as an employee, take a portion of those profits.

You want to be aligned. It's not so much an expectation as it is an opportunity. I think most people who do what I do believe in the asset class of private equity, because private markets provide an efficient fee that liquid markets typically don't, or not as much, because there are more eyes looking at deals, and it's traded and information is omnipresent. In private markets, that's not the case.

One of the drawing points of being in this industry is that you actually eat your own cooking. You invest heavily in what you represent. It also gives you credibility in front of your investors, if they know that you're investing, even though the amounts are tiny, a couple of hundred thousand dollars, compared to the hundreds of millions of dollars that we get from investors. Your personal contribution is tiny, but it still matters.

MARRIED TO A KINDERGARTEN TEACHER WITH TWO CHILDREN

My wife's thirty-four. My son, Benjamin, he's four. My daughter's name is Lillian, and she turned two in October. My wife has taught kindergarten, but right now she works at home. At some point, she will resume teaching. There's a German/Swiss school here where our son goes; my wife may teach there.

Here's another thing about finance: You'd be surprised how many bankers have teachers as their spouses. It's a higher percentage than you would think. There's something about having people with completely different values, that orientation, that somehow find themselves together. I'm not sure that can be statistically verified, but the number of people that I know where one of the two is in a finance job, totally Type A, and the other is in a really different job where it's about social impact, teaching, etc., I've always noticed.

My wife and I adopted our daughter Lillian. That's not socially terribly accepted here. It's frowned upon. There is a big belief here in having bloodlines, strong family ties, and strong family histories. So even people I know, Hong Kong Chinese people who've adopted, don't tell anybody. They would never talk about it. They keep it completely quiet. There are certain social stigmas associated with things like adoption.

It's not the fact that we're Caucasian and we've adopted a Chinese daughter; it's just adoption in general. Those are things that you wouldn't feel coming here [as a tourist], but they exist. In terms of racism, I don't really see it as much, but I may not be the right person to ask. I'm a Caucasian living on Hong Kong Island in Central [District].

WHEN I'M NOT WORKING, I'M RUNNING, DIVING, AND PLAYING WITH MY KIDS

Outside of work, I'm primarily a dad. I spend most of my time with my family, and then I do a little bit of sports. I was always an athlete. Way back when, I played hockey and basketball. Then for many years, I didn't.

I started running again about a year ago. I've lost about twenty-five pounds in the last year through working too much, running, exercise, changing diet, everything.

I also started diving and taking diving lessons. In Asia, you can dive everywhere, but I'm just getting started. The Philippines, everywhere. Everything's so close. The great thing about Asia is that you're in Thailand in two-and-a-half hours; you're in Burma in three. You're in the Philippines in two. I'm going to Australia this week: I enter the plane at 7:00 p.m. and I wake up at 6:00 a.m. It's perfect, easy. Maldives is six hours away. Wherever you want to go, it's very quick.

The kids go to bed fairly early. On weekends, we go to the beach a lot. On Hong Kong Island, there're lots of beaches and islands around. The kids have activities, or we go to markets or Hong Kong Park. What else do we do? Playgrounds. Sometimes no playgrounds, if the air isn't that great [pollution]. And lots of birthday parties. I feel like some kids' birthdays are twice a year, there are so many birthday parties! Every weekend, you just go.

IT'S EASY TO MAKE FRIENDS HERE

In Hong Kong, it's very easy to find friends. Most people who live here have a similar profile to us in that they've moved here. So they're welcoming to others who've moved here.

Let me contrast that to Germany. If I moved back to Germany, the people who would be my neighbors have been there probably their whole lives or most of their lives. If they're in their mid-thirties or late-thirties, they have no interest in meeting somebody else. They have their group. Hong Kong is the opposite. Everybody's welcoming.

"You just moved here—great. Let's go here, let's do this. Our kids should play."

So my wife, within weeks of moving here, had the same friends she has now. Especially if you have children, it's very quick. The ecosystem is typically around your children. Thousands of restaurants. We go out to dinner a lot.

The quality of life in Hong Kong is quite good, because you have domestic help. That actually matters a lot. You have a live-in helper that takes care of your household and looks after your children. They actually have their own living quarters, which in some cases are in horrible shape.

We just have one nanny, a helper. She looks after the house and the kids, cleans, does little things. Quality of life-wise, it's huge, and she's great with the children.

I MAKE DECENT MONEY, BUT I DON'T WANT EXPENSIVE THINGS

I cannot complain about the standard of living that I can afford for myself and for my family, and I earned all of it with the support of a lot of people as the years went by. But clearly I'm in a position where I'm doing well to afford the things in life that I would like to afford.

I drive a Kia. I think driving a fast car, in Hong Kong in particular, is stupid, because you can't drive it anywhere. I don't own an expensive watch; I don't have a big car. I don't have anything that's really expensive. If I were to tell you what my suit cost, you'd laugh at me.

My suit costs $200. The shirt's fifty. I don't have any jewelry, nothing. That's not the value set. I have two kids. It's like, are they healthy? Can you afford vacations? Can you pay rent in Hong Kong, which is unbelievable? If it's not the highest in the world, it's the second highest in the world. It puts New York to shame, if you want a comparison. Nobody spends less than $12,000-13,000 a month on anything sort of decent. We have a decent three-bedroom apartment, and we spend a little less than $13,000 a month.

But the taxes are low. I'm not a U.S. citizen, so I pay local tax. Most other things are expensive, rent in particular, but taxes are going to be 15 percent flat, and they take that only once a year. They don't take that out of your paycheck. So versus in New York, that's a key career consideration. Do you want to pay 55 percent or do you want to pay 15?

I think I get a fair wage. I earn a fair wage locally and globally because I can afford a standard of living that I'm comfortable with. I can afford the things in life that I want to afford, and those are not excessive. I don't have any excess in my life. My value set and my wife's value set is just different. It's a little bit off-putting.

THE EXCESS WEALTH AND ENTITLEMENT IN THIS CITY IS ASTONISHING

Hong Kong is defined by excess in every way—big cars; you walk along Queen's Road and it's all expensive jewelry and bags. It's just about having wealth and showing it, even if you don't have it. People show wealth immediately the second they acquire it; the second they earn it, they show it off. So we're not like that. We won't be like that.

People go shopping here with Prada bags, but they have H&M mascara inside. Then something that's somewhat unique, when you think about a country like China, which has grown at double-digit rates for the last couple of years, the speed with which wealth is being created here is astonishing.[4] The entitlement that people feel about being wealthy is even more astonishing.

Not only are people wealthy, they feel entitled to be wealthy. This is a statement that I have to be careful about how I phrase it, but not all of that wealth is on the back of working hard. A lot of it is on the back of other factors. [Laughs.]

I compare it to the Soviet Union. You have a lot of wealth created in a very short period of time, and you can just be at the right place at the right time. You can have the right level of connectivity, government contracts that are afforded, this and that. Look at everything that's happening in the anti-corruption campaign in Beijing[5] right now. That's a power-consolidation play. If everybody has something to hide, then you can go after whomever you want. So it's that kind of dynamic.

You have an incredible amount of wealth created in a short period of time, the entitlement that comes with it, and money's just burning in people's hands. They want to show it off.

WHAT'S MY NUMBER FOR SUFFICIENT MONEY IN THE BANK? I DON'T HAVE ONE

I don't have a number that would make me feel like, *this* is enough money. I don't associate a number with wealth. Wealth to me represents the ability to make decisions without constraints. You get to the point where the money you've earned gives you the flexibility to decide based on what you *want* as opposed to based on what you *have* to do. So everyone's got a different number.

I don't have a number in my mind; I don't. I live in Hong Kong, so it's a bigger number. If you actually want to make decisions purely based on what you want, it has to be close to probably ten million dollars before you can say, "The pressure's off, I can do what I'd like to do;" but I don't live my life that way, and I'm glad I don't. It's just something that I know exists.

But one of the reasons why I quit banking is because a lot of people live their life that way, and the problem is, that target moves. Wealth becomes relative very quickly,

4. Bloomberg reports that one in five people in Hong Kong lives in poverty and the gap between the rich and poor continues to widen all the time: bloomberg.com/news/articles/2013-09-29/hong-kong-poverty-line-shows-wealth-gap-with-one-in-five-poor.

5. Ibtimes.com/chinas-anti-corruption-campaign-top-beijing-shanghai-officials-under-investigation-2179252.

actually very, very quickly. So if you don't have a lot of money, there's an absolute level. You want to afford certain things. The second you can afford them, the appeal of that goes away.

The day I could afford a Porsche or a Ferrari, there's no incentive to buy it anymore. You could buy a Porsche, but it's just kind of like, when things are out of reach, you want to get there, but the second you've reached them, they kind of lose appeal, and then when you're in an environment like banking can be, and it wasn't all bad, but everybody around you, their wealth increases, too, and so it becomes a race.

AS A WHITE MAN, I'M NOT THE TOP DOG AROUND HERE

As a white male in China, I am not top dog. That's the way it used to be. Now the Chinese are top dog. From a consumer perspective, it's not even close. Go to the luxury stores on Queen's Road. They have Mandarin speakers, and they have different types of Mandarin dialects. The Chinese consumer drives Hong Kong's wealth. They drive the property market. They drive the retail market, everything.

So probably in the nineties and early 2000s, it was the foreigner who was on a big expat package and was making a few million dollars. Now, it's the Mainland Chinese. They come in tour buses. They are in the new territories, and they bus in, and they buy Queen's Road dry.

It's absolutely like that. You buy an apartment in Hong Kong for a certain amount, and then you get a Hong Kong ID, and then you just leave the apartment empty. You don't even rent it out. I've told you what you can earn in rent, but you don't need to, so you don't.

It's the Chinese that are on top. I'm one of many. I do well, but from the consumer perspective, it's clearly driven by the Chinese.

HONG KONG AND MAINLAND CHINA ARE LIKE TWO DIFFERENT COUNTRIES

There's a separation between Hong Kong and Mainland China, and it's growing. Hong Kong, by and large, they do not see themselves as Mainland China. It's everything: It's cultural, it's visa policy. One's a free country. The other one isn't. People forget that China is communist, full-blown communist.

There was an article recently in the *South China Morning Post*, and this is not unique information of any kind, that at universities in China, they're banning books that profess Western values.

People are fooling themselves to think that this isn't like the Soviet Union twenty-five, thirty years ago. It is. It's a very capitalistic set of communism, but it's not a free country. There's no freedom of religion, no freedom of speech. There's none of those things. In Hong Kong, there're all of them. In Mainland China, none. And there's no Internet. You can't Google whatever you'd like. Facebook is blocked. Bloomberg is blocked if they write their own article; so is CNN. The press is controlled. It's an atheist country.

So, at the very foundation of things, Hong Kong is one of the most liberal countries/cities I can think of, at least overtly. There's a lot of discrimination under the hood.

But overtly you can practice whatever religion you want, you can be of any race, you can criticize the government, even the Chinese government. There are regular, massive protests against the Chinese government and everything else here.

That's the starting point, and then the divide really is that you have a whole generation of Hong Kong Chinese that grew up feeling, "We're Hong Kong; we're not China."

Everybody who's twenty now grew up being Hong Kong and not China. So even though power was passed back to the Chinese, there are gigantic differences in every single way. If you go to Mainland China, it feels different. People are different. They behave differently, think differently, and speak differently.

So you read about, "Will China ever take Hong Kong's thunder as a business leader?" There's no way, in my opinion, that that will happen in the next twenty or thirty years. I think it's very unrealistic to believe that.

Hong Kong is like a test case for Mainland China, much like Macau is. But Hong Kong, I don't think they're going to leave Hong Kong alone. They're going to gradually become more visible here.

There is a level of anxiety because if Mainland China wants to just change things in Hong Kong overnight, they can. Hong Kong is governed by Beijing completely. There's autonomy because they granted it, not because Hong Kong can take it. China is so powerful that nobody would actually mess with Beijing, if they did anything to offend Hong Kong's liberties. So all of that is leading to tension.

CULTURE, RACE, AND TEAMWORK IN A GLOBAL COMPANY WITH VAST REGIONAL DIFFERENCES

When I was at Goldman, we had 160 people or so on the floor. I was the only non-Asian on the entire floor. Similarly now, there's one senior advisor in our office. Culturally, it doesn't really matter. We get along great, really great. It's a great group of people. In a small company, that's essential. Culture is paramount. It's the number one thing.

Our Beijing office is all Mainland Chinese. We have an Indian office where they're all Indian. In the Singapore office, we have a Taiwanese lady and two Singaporeans. I'm the odd guy out. I'm the German in Asia.

But it's not been an issue, and I would never expect it to be an issue, partly because it's Hong Kong, and partly because we have great people. What's interesting in my job is that people say, "Don't you have to be Chinese? Don't you have to be Japanese to do the job?"

People underestimate regional differences within Asia. If I'm Japanese, and I go to China, that doesn't help me. If I'm Chinese and go to Japan, it doesn't help me either. So the argument I made to Providence, convincingly it seems, as I work there now, I said: "Look around and look at who runs business development functions in Asia. It's typically people with a global or a western profile." Half are Chinese and half are Asian, and that tends to work really well.

So that's not been an inhibiting factor so far, certainly in our culture, or with our investor base. But, as I mentioned, once the second and third tier of institutions come in, I will need to hire people to go there. I will not be as effective.

IN FINANCE, IT'S A SMALL WORLD AFTER ALL

Hong Kong is a tiny finance community, very small. The population is over seven million, but everybody sits on top of each other. Within a one-mile radius from where we sit right now, you have every major bank in the world, every one of them, all of them, in probably less than one mile.

What I do is fairly specialized. As a result of that, we all know each other. There are maybe twenty of us in all of Hong Kong that do what we do, probably less, actually. So the job description is fairly unique. The skill sets are fairly unique. When opportunities enter the market, if the firm is hiring, we know about it instantly.

We all talk to each other, and for one reason or another, we either like it or we don't like it. So it becomes something that we entertain. This is sort of on a personal basis. "Hey, these guys are hiring. What do you think?" and then we all talk about it. It's ad hoc, informal. We're all friends.

When it comes to what differentiates each of our firms and the IP, the intellectual property, there's obviously no collaboration, but when it comes to things like somebody's looking for somebody to fill a certain role, the way companies hire people in Hong Kong is, in our business, it's all recommendations. So I get calls from headhunters, and I might recommend somebody, and somebody else recommends the same person, and that's how the pipeline of people get the jobs that they have.

WORKING FROM CHINA TO THE U.S., MY DAY IS A BARBELL, WITH 6 A.M. AND MIDNIGHT CALLS

My company's based on the East Coast. I have a twelve- or thirteen-hour time difference, depending on what time zone. I have to make sure that I stay connected with them. I wake up early. The first thing that I do in the morning is I call New York [City] or I call Providence [Rhode Island].

I call at 6:00 a.m. to 7:00 a.m., which is evening in the U.S. And then late at night, my calls start at 9:00 p.m. and go through to midnight. That's most nights. I get calls at midnight; people don't think twice about it. So part about being in Asia and working for a U.S. company, an East-Coast company, is you have to deal with that. My day is a barbell. It's very early morning and very late at night.

My job day-to-day is being on the phone with investors, prospective investors, colleagues in the region, intermediaries, consultants, what have you, planning trips. I traveled last year I think 152 days or so. Asia is a face-to-face region. You want to do business, you have to go see them. It's cultural. People will say, "If you want business from me, you have to make the effort to come see me."

I SPEND A LOT OF TIME ON AIRPLANES

This year, I've been in seven places so far, including Singapore, Brunei, Korea, and Taiwan. I'm going to Australia next week. I'm on the road constantly. My job is speaking to these investors, spending time on the road, seeing them. I spend a lot of time on planes and just fly all across Asia to meet with them. We talk in-person about what we talked about over the phone, and we build relationships. We build trust.

I fly business class. On long flights, I sleep. On short flights, I work. I go to Sydney on a Sunday night. It's a ten-hour flight. I'll work the first couple of hours, and then I'll sleep the next. I don't take any medication. A lot of people take sleeping pills; I don't do that. I just try and find a rhythm and fall asleep on my own.

The thing is, the way I travel and the way most people who do what I do travel: You do day trips to countries. A typical trip is to do Monday Beijing, Tuesday Tokyo, Wednesday Seoul, dot, dot, dot. So you actually have no time to get tired. You're definitely not jet lagged—you don't really have time to get tired because you're moving constantly, and it's not the flights that are dragging. The flights, you're sitting and comfortable, you have something to drink. It's the connecting. It's immigration. That's the real drain.

My day is waking up, spending a lot of time on the phone, preparing these trips, and doing the follow-ups to these trips. Ultimately the idea is to try and close business, having an investment proposition that was presented to an institutional investor that they then take through a due-diligence process. That can take a year to a year and a half, they hopefully make a decision to sort of vote with their capital and trust in my firm to then manage those assets, invest those assets…and I do that constantly.

WINNERS AND LOSERS IN OUR INVESTMENT PORTFOLIO

In terms of investment winners, it always takes time for these to show. From a business perspective, I'll give you two recent deals. This is just in terms of winning and raising capital, not performance.

So we worked with a large Chinese investor on the mandates that would allow them to lend money to U.S. mid-market corporates. Interest rates are at zero everywhere. There's no cash yield to be had, and there's an inefficiency in the U.S. in the middle market. Think of companies that have operating profits of ten to fifty million, because they used to have regional banks lend money to them or even big banks lend money to them. They no longer do because post-crisis, these desks have been fired, and regulation has made it very expensive to lend money to small, unrated companies.

We were able to work with this Chinese investor to come up with a structure where they entrust us to make loans, and these U.S. corporations pay interest, which then obviously gets back to the investor. That deal took a year and a half to close. Due diligence was a year, and then the legal negotiation was another seven months.

We do consider Small to Medium Enterprises [SMEs]. Post-crisis, if I were Bank A and I would make thirty-million-dollar loans to companies that didn't have a credit rating, what happened in the Dodd-Frank Act and the Volcker Rule and things of that nature, was invest in something that owns a capital charge.

So if you're a bank, you can do that, but regulators would deem that particular loan, because it is illiquid, because it is not rated to be risky. In order for you to make a thirty-million-dollar loan, you have to keep a much larger number in cash or cash-like investments on your balance sheet. Banks have focused on larger transactions and bigger deals where there's a credit rating associated with it and less perceived risk, and the capital charges are a lot lower.

Funds have gone to larger businesses and moved away from these smaller businesses, which is the majority of U.S. companies. What we've done and many other firms have done this, too, is we've said, "Anytime that banks leave a market, that's a good thing. That means there are opportunities. There's a vacuum."

That's a huge pipeline, and that will stay there, because the regulations won't change. The SEC [Securities and Exchange Commission] is not going to change their mind on how banks are measuring liquidity. So we think that's a near-permanent mismatch between demand of capital for SMEs and supply of capital from banks. I'll give you a stat. Loans to middle-market companies today from banks are at 12 percent [interest]. It used to be 70, ten years ago. It's a business that's dominated by nonbanks.

We're focusing on that market because relative to all the other opportunities to generate big yields, we think this is a great time.

And it's been very successful. Going back to the Chinese investor, they believed we could do a good job. They also gave a similar mandate to a couple of managers like us. That was a success.

A deal where it wasn't a success was where we had worked on a transaction, and we actually had accumulated demand for the transaction. We were bidding on the asset (a company), and then we just lost the bid. Someone else won the deal. So you work six months on raising capital. You have the capital. Everything's done, and then you bid, and then you lose. Then it kind of all goes away.

SOMETIMES YOU HAVE TO JUST WALK AWAY

Sometimes, the deal's too big for us. So what we do, is we go to the investor and you say, "You can give us capital just for this specific transaction," but you still could end up losing the deal.

That happened last week. You win some and you lose some. You lose 95 percent of the deals that you focus on—and you should, by the way. If you win most of them, something's wrong. If you win most of them, you're either paying too much, or you're not seeing any risks. If anybody tells you we make half the deals we look at, then that's not a good thing. So pricing discipline is key, and being very stringent about how you underwrite your deal is key.

There are certain prices that will make you just stop. You're not going to pay more. And there are certain conditions that you need to have present in order for you to do a deal. If those go away, you just don't do the deal. But the consequence of that is that somebody else may be more aggressive. Somebody else may disagree with you on risks and be more liberal on how they allocate capital, and then you lose.

Part of the reason why I'm so active, my team is so active, it's a little bit of a numbers game. You have to be out there. You have to show yourself. You have to make sure that you connect into all of these capital players, because there's a significant component that's just being in the right place at the right time.

BUSINESS DEVELOPMENT IS SALES OVER A VERY LONG CYCLE—LIKE 10 YEARS

So, again, business development is sales over a very, very long sales cycle. That's how I would describe it. Ultimately you're selling yourself and that somebody would believe that you have integrity, that you know what you're doing, that you're knowledgeable and professional, and that you follow up.

This is unique to private equity. If they decide to invest in you, they do that for ten years. They can't get out. So they're making a long-term commitment. You have to be an incredible representative, etc., personally. And then you have to be able to convey what your firm does in a way that's honest and compelling and applicable. People need to understand how it benefits them and how it relates to them.

That's different from short-cycle sales, where it's a simple product, or a specific need, like selling a product in a store. The person is in that store because they want to buy something to begin with.

In my line of business, they have the world to choose from. They have endless amounts of capital typically, and what we do is highly complex. So they will engage in multi-month question-and-answer sessions with us to get to the bottom of a certain question.

SKILLS YOU NEED FOR LONG-TERM CONVERSATIONS WITH MULTILINGUAL SPEAKERS

The skill set is being patient, persistent, smart, able to articulate complex concepts in a simple way without losing the substance of what you're explaining. That is especially hard in a region where everybody you talk to, English is their second language. That's a big challenge that comes with Asia. When I'm in meetings in some countries, I talk very slowly. I use simpler words and repeat concepts over and over and over again. It's just because it's a second language to them.

You also need to be very flexible. You need to be able to hear "no" a lot. You have to keep coming back. If somebody says no, they don't say no to *you*. It's not that they don't want to deal with you, but it's not the right place, not the right time, not the right strategy. The common ground between what a firm does and what an investor needs is narrow.

Where you need to get to is a relationship where they want to meet with you because you add value to them. You share market intel. You just talk about what's going on. They feel like it's worthwhile, building a relationship with you. If you can't do that, you're not going to be successful. So that's what it starts with, and then patience is the second big factor.

FINANCIAL-MARKET PROCESSES IN ASIA ARE TWENTY YEARS BEHIND THE U.S.

A little unique to Asia, again it's unique to my business, but in the United States, you have endowments, pension funds, very sophisticated institutions that have established processes. If they look at the opportunity, they know how. They know which questions to ask. They have a decision-making cycle. So, if they tell you they liked something, then there is a process on the back end, and they take it through their process. At the end of the process, there's a decision.

The Asian market is probably twenty years behind the U.S. market in terms of sophistication, institutional structures, the seniority of the team, the language skills of the team, etc. A challenge that comes with the region is that the processes aren't set. It is not clear, if there's an expression of interest, what the outcomes are going to be. They can take way too long.

You can think that you're in for nine months, and then you're out, instantaneously. There's a lot more turnover at institutions because they're typically government institutions where the career path is limited. All of that is changing very gradually as the market matures and the market becomes institutionalized, but for the time being, that's a struggle.

The other challenge that I have right now is that the institutional investor base is quite small. The ones that matter, that have capital to deploy, they're deploying, they're smart, and they all speak English. They all went to school. Many went to school in the U.K., the U.S., etc.

At some point, the fact that I don't speak Chinese or Korean or Japanese is going to become an issue. So, as these markets open up, as these markets become deeper, what I need to make sure is that I hire people, build the business, produce results, hire people that will allow me to hire regional specialists that are Japanese, that are Korean, that are Chinese. So, I'm working on that.

The goal is always to make yourself obsolete if you run a business, right? That's what you want. So I'm working on that; it's a long-term thing.

WE LOST MY WIFE'S BEST FRIEND, AND IT STILL HAUNTS US

Probably the worst experience of my life was much worse for my wife, which was when lived in D.C. This was 2004. My wife's best friend was living in our place because she was in a marriage dispute with her husband. Her name was Maggie. She was a PhD student at the University of Maryland.

She was Chinese, Mainland Chinese, married to an American, and she committed suicide. She jumped off the roof of our building. We lived in a high-rise. She committed suicide. She lost a restraining order on her. And then the shame that that brought with it vis-à-vis her parents was too much. So she went to the roof of our building. She wrote a very thoughtful, calm, rational thank-you letter addressed to my wife and me.

She just took off her jacket, took off her shoes, and left the scarf that my wife bought her as a gift, folded everything neatly, and jumped.

My wife was home when she did that. She came home from work. So Maggie's on the roof, and she jumps down. I'm at university. They find Maggie still breathing very faintly but then she dies shortly after. I get a panicked call from my wife, and I rush home. They accused my wife for a second because they thought there was some sort of dispute, which there wasn't. So they dropped that literally within hours.

And then my wife had planned a trip to India a few days later and actually went. So I was left to handle basically the entire funeral proceedings, cremation, her parents coming over, Chinese, didn't speak a word of English. I gave the speech that my wife wrote for her at the ceremony. We planted a tree in front of the department of sociology at the University of Maryland, which is still there, and her name plaque and everything.

That was a wake-up call. You go through college in your early twenties, thinking that things are good. She was only twenty-four at the time.

That was tough. That was really tough. We still have a big picture of her in our living room now.

I'M NOT A RELIGIOUS PERSON, BUT I HAVE A FEAR OF DEATH AND STRONG BELIEF SYSTEM

I'm not a religious person, I never have been. I wasn't raised that way. I'm not anti-religious, but just not religious. I think my parents decided early on that they were going to let me choose whenever I could make up my own mind what I would, which religion I would choose, and whether I wanted to choose it.

This is very personal: I've had a fear of death for a long time. It's been a phobia I've had for like twenty years. It probably started with the passing of my grandmother when I was nine. So, ever since then, it's a part of my life. The topic of my death and where I go afterward has been very, very relevant to me, very present.

Nothing triggers the fear: It's random. It's not always with me, but it kind of comes. It just kind of happens, and then it goes away. So you learn how to manage it. I've read books like *Mortality* by Christopher Hitchens, a famous atheist and he's also an anti-aid, right? He's both. I like him a lot because I think he's intellectually stimulating.

I'm not religious, and I don't really have a strong belief system. I don't know where I'll go when I die. I have had things like déjà vu that make me think twice. I think I live my life with a sense of urgency, and probably because of my fear of death, I live it with a heightened sense of urgency. I'm very conscious of there being a start and a finish. Steve Jobs, I think gave a speech at Stanford and said he likes the fact that there's an end because that means you work hard.

When I started developing this phobia, my brother, who's always had a very natural relationship with death, said it would be awful if I *never* died. He said it would be horrible. He said then all of this would be pointless, and there would be no motivation to do anything. I would just lounge around. I was at the opposite end. I was like, "I don't want any of this. I don't know where I'll go."

WHAT I WANT TO DO NEXT IS TO GIVE BACK

I look up to people like my friend Manjula, who runs a nonprofit called Educate Lanka, because one of the hardest things to do in life is actually to live on conviction. Manjula could have every job on Wall Street that he wanted, and make a lot of money, and have a lot of things that he now cannot afford.

It's hard to live your life doing the things that you have conviction behind because typically, noises emerge that lead you on to a different path—needs, wants, relative perception of yourself, peers, whatever, right? So it's a combination of things.

If I had infinite money…How do you know that I'm not already a billionaire? [Laughs.] I'm kidding. No, I'm not.

I do have the view that, with wealth, comes responsibility. If I were in a position where I would be very wealthy, I would try and find smart ways to get rid of ills and improve things, whether it's medical issues, educational, what have you, injustices. That would be the objective.

MY PERSONAL DREAM: TRAVEL THE WORLD AND LEAVE MY IMPACT

I think in terms of some of the more personal things, I would travel a lot. I have this dream that I don't want to leave this planet without having seen it all. That's a big thing of mine. I want to see *all* of it. Do the extremes: go to the North Pole, the South Pole. It feels strange that you leave and you haven't seen the place.

Anybody who says they wouldn't spend some of their money on themselves if they had it, they would. I would live in a nice place, and I would have certain luxuries. It would come down to seeing the world and living my purpose.

A good friend of mine who used to be my boss runs a very big part of Goldman in Asia, and he can attest that, "Charity at the end of the day, you do for yourself." You do it for others, but ultimately you do it for yourself. So I would try and find things that I'm passionate about and just do that.

WHAT I CURRENTLY GIVE TO CHARITY: MONEY AND TIME

In terms of what I devote towards charity right now, is probably around 5 percent of my income. I just started doing this. I've not been in a position very long at all to be able to do it. This is recent. I don't come from wealth, and I'm not there yet. So I'm just beginning to do it.

The reason I went to Manjula was because I knew that if there's one person who would pour his heart and soul into it, it would be him, and I knew him and I liked him. What he's doing, I think is actually really smart. I think how he's approaching education for kids is really smart.

RUNNING MARATHONS FOR STUDENT SCHOLARSHIPS

So my wife and I donated a little bit to Educate Lanka, and then we raised $14,000 from the Ultramarathon on top of that, and I want to do this every year. Maybe not run the marathon, but definitely give money and raise money, both. That was good. But also when you work a lot, and you have a family, sometimes the decisions you make in life are about you for a while, and then they become about others.

If you work eighty hours a week, a hundred hours a week, and then the remaining hours, you spend with family. Running the Ultramarathon was a little bit to recapture myself. And running it and doing well at it, and building a fitness level and all of that, then just making it about Educate Lanka, was easy. It ended up working well.

Our other cause is Mother's Choice, the orphanage that our daughter is from. I'm on two committees, on the finance investment committee, and I'm a financial supporter but not a big one. So that's really mostly time, probably eight to ten hours a month, something like that. I try to help and then little bits and pieces here and there.

I DON'T NEED TO GO LAUNCH ANOTHER CHARITY

I don't need to create my own thing. I think that there are a lot of egos in nonprofit, and that's always bothered me a tremendous amount. Everybody needs to start their own as opposed to just finding who does it really well and just enabling them to do it.

For a while, I thought about having a foundation in my children's name, a very small one to do little things like paint a park, renovate a retirement home, little tangible projects. I was like, "Well, I can do that, but that exists [already]. Let me find the people that do that and let me enable them to do it."

What I'd like to do is take a portion of my annual income and just dedicate it to those causes. I almost see it like a tax, if you will. It just goes out in the air.

WHERE I GET MY VALUES AROUND MONEY

I have to credit my parents for raising me with a certain set of values. That's what it comes down to. We didn't grow up with wealth, and we never distanced ourselves from poverty. In Moscow, you saw terrible, terrible things. My wife, living in Egypt and India, saw people with cut-off limbs banging on the window of the car and begging for money. It's just reality.

I was raised with an understanding that there's people who live really well, people who do okay, and people who don't do well. You can have a choice if you want to distance yourself and cut yourself off from what's probably half of the world's population or more—the ones who do not do well.

I'm very fortunate. Look at where we're sitting now, in an exclusive dining club in Hong Kong. I'm doing fine. Whatever that 1 percent is, I'm in it, and I'm only thirty-three. You have to recognize that that is part achievement, but also part luck.

So reconciling the two, to me, is very normal. I was always worried that I would lose [that attitude]. I just kind of pity people that don't see it that way, who think it's all entitlement, and who think the world's built on them, and everything they've achieved is just because of them.

CAPITALISM VERSUS SOCIALISM

I'm a liberal. [President] Barack Obama said, "You never achieve success on your own. It's everybody around you."

I see it that way. I think I deserve where I am today, but I'm also lucky. And then the natural thing is, as soon as I can afford to, try and make somebody's life better, then you do that. It's the most logical thing in the world for me.

To tie that back to capitalism, how we can fix it: We can fix it in a way that Manjula does it. I don't believe in handouts in the sense that you plug a hole, but the pressure that's going to reopen that hole is constant. So the second you remove the plug, it's there.

What Manjula does is, he says, "These kids are smart. They should go to school, but they can't. Cover the costs at home, let them go to school, and then they become productive members of society, and the [virtuous] cycle has started."

I believe in that. I think capitalism can play a vital function in making sure that the cycle that creates poverty is broken. Over time—this is a gradual process—income levels will rise, wealth will rise, accessibility of water, everything else will rise...

Capitalism allows people to basically create their own destiny and then reap the rewards. You just enable free markets and then go out and if you can achieve, you achieve.

To me, where capitalism could help to alleviate poverty is finding ways to channel that type of spirit or enable children or enable people in different social classes to believe in it and then actually act on that opportunity.

I would describe myself as a social capitalist. Germany has that system. I do believe in free healthcare. I think it's nuts that it doesn't exist in places like the U.S., where a broken arm can bankrupt you. I believe in some form of free education. I believe in the government finding means to enable people to actually act on or further their potential to break a certain cycle of poverty. I do believe in that.

What I don't really believe in is this trickle-down notion. I think that's bogus, to be frank. It's the Robin Hood concept. It just doesn't work. The number of poor versus the number of rich, the dynamic is completely proportionless. Capitalism needs to have a component to it that recognizes that the system enables wealth and wealth creation, but then once that wealth has been created, a portion of that should go into leveling the playing field.

I don't think living in a capitalist society and having capitalism recognize the need for some level of equal access are irreconcilable. I don't see why it has to be one extreme or the other.

MY LEGACY: MY CHILDREN

I always believe in doing the first thing that comes to mind, like if I ask you, "What's your favorite movie?" the first movie you think of, that actually should be it. So the first thing I thought of, when you asked me about impact, was particularly the life of my children. I think the only way, if people want to be immortal, is if you can instill certain traits in the people that are close to you. Building that up in my children, I think that has to be my legacy.

And with philanthropy, you try and expand that legacy by helping people like Manjula impact hundreds of children, and then, by extension, thousands of people over coming generations. The work that he's doing, I think he's brought a couple of hundred people through his program. Think about a hundred years down the line, what that will have meant. It's tremendous, right?

So just multiply that by a hundred. Children, children's children...If some of these kids do well, literally he's impacted thousands of people in that entire community. That's real impact. That's where there's going to be a Manjula statue at some point. Who knows? But that's impact.

BEING A TYPE A HAS ITS DOWNSIDE, IF YOU FORGET THE HAPPINESS COMPONENT

I'll tell you one thing that people struggle with that have my profile. This is going to sound pretty cheesy: But, for people who are in their early twenties or maybe thinking about changing careers from A to B or what have you, the metric that nobody talks about—the *dimension* that people rarely talk about, is actually happiness. It's not talked about in high school really, or in college, because it's hard to define, and it's so subjective.

Guys and gals like me, you breeze through college. I had one B my entire collegiate career, and that was after Maggie killed herself, [an exam] that next day. It should have been an A. It screwed up my GPA.

You have like overachievers who do well in school and in their career. And then they put their head down and rush, and succeed. At some point most people like that put their head up and look around, and what they have is a little bit of money. They may have property.

Hopefully they have a healthy family, but oftentimes there's still a void, and it's extreme because this happiness component is neglected very, very early on. You start living for other people's expectations or your own expectations that others teach or push on you. It's ultimately your responsibility, but the dimension that's so hard to quantify or to tap into is what actually will make them happy.

What does that look like? Where do you want to live? How do you want to live? What do you think the marginal return on the next value earned is going to be to you?

Studies have shown that at [a salary of] $75,000 or more, your margin level of happiness doesn't really increase.[6] So at some point in people's lives happiness becomes the main focal point, but it typically happens too late, and then people either can't make those choices or those choices are painful.

You want out. You're miserable. You're in a rat race. You have four properties and you need to pay mortgages, and you can't quit. You've invested in this personality that you think you wanted to be, and now you can't quit for the next five, ten years. There're thousands of them in New York, London, Hong Kong, Singapore, everywhere, where the pressure to perform, to earn money, is massive.

I'VE HAD A GOOD LIFE, SO FAR

So for me, the Ultramarathon was part happiness. Philanthropy was part happiness. Let me do things that feed myself. I think if that is done earlier in a more honest and supported fashion, I think that would save people a lot of time.

I have definitely had a good life. Not "charmed" in the sense that things were given to me, but a good life. I've been lucky. I hope I'm not just the guy in the suit who goes to work. How sad would that be? That happens to people.

The job is what you do, but it's not who you are, right? So it enables you to be who you are. That should be the idea, in my opinion.

---

6. See this article in Time: content.time.com/time/magazine/article/0,9171,2019628,00.html, or read the study by Princeton University to which Nik refers: princeton.edu/~deaton/downloads/deaton_kahneman_high_income_improves_evaluation_August2010.pdf.

MUSIC & ARTS

· ·

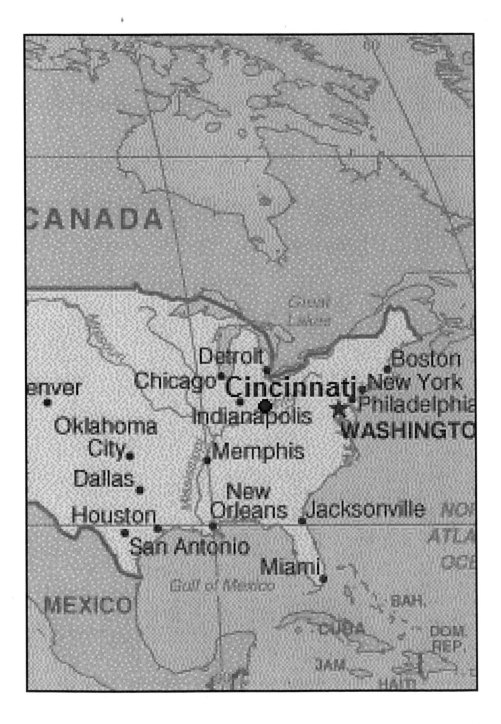

KEVIN

ARCHITECT

CINCINNATI, OHIO, U.S.

Editor's note: If you work in architecture, Cincinnati might inspire you, with its prominent bridges (including a suspension bridge that became a model for the Brooklyn Bridge) leading from Kentucky across the Ohio River, to a grand skyline framing its Riverbend Music Center amphitheater and cluster of slick glass skyscrapers interposed with German gothic-revival and French art-deco monoliths. This is home to Kevin Kluender, whose firm designed a mixed-use residential center, The Landing,[1] to support families of children with life-threatening bone-marrow and oncological illnesses while renting homes to neighboring families in a park-like facility with ponds and trails.

The Landing was conceived by The Dragonfly Foundation,[2] a noble project that emerged from tragedy: the near-death encounter with Hodgkin Lymphoma

---

1. Thelanding.org.

2. Dragonfly.org; for the story of how Dragonfly Foundation got started, see dragonfly.org/our-story.

Stage 3[3] by Matt, the then-ten-year-old son of cofounder Christine Neitzke.[4] Christine is my sister Sylvia's friend; their sons went to school together in the Cincinnati suburb of Mason.

Christine and her cofounder Ria Davidson have served over 600 pediatric patients and 2,500 of their family members, bringing their mission of "comfort and joy" through hygiene kits, toys, electronics, hospital visits, family events, and peer playtimes. Christine's son Matt survived and now is thriving as a senior in high school. Recognizing a need for a center for out-of-towners and low-income families (one that's longer-term and larger than, say, a Ronald McDonald House), Christine set to work with Kevin and his team at Drawing Dept[5] to create The Landing.

Kevin has worked as an architect since college (through a co-op program). He relishes all the mundane realities of his job, as filing paperwork and calculating taxes. He doesn't like surprises, and he'd rather keep his own ego out of the design process when figuring out what a building wants to be. He drives an old gray-green Mercury sedan that he calls his "rolling office." He prefers high-maintenance clients, as long as they back their demands with aesthetic passion.

Kevin readily admits that the children who will live in The Landing have, at their tender age, have already faced "a lot more adult ideas than I have had to face." To prepare the design, Kevin and his team spent many hours talking with the founders of The Dragonfly Foundation and were literally "on the floor" playing with little kids in treatment for and recovery from cancer. He wanted to give the building "a sense of wonder and light"

After fifteen years in the business, Kevin still enjoys the variety of projects. "One of the reasons I wanted to be an architect is that no two days are ever going to be the same," he points out.

I'VE BEEN AN ARCHITECT SINCE COLLEGE

My name is Kevin Kluender. I am 38. I am an architect. I started architecture on my first day at the University of Cincinnati and studied it all the way through college. I graduated in 2001 with a bachelor's of architecture, which is not a graduate degree. This degree hardly exists anymore. It's gotten phased out because architects can charge more if they went to grad school. But to get your registration, you just have to have a bachelor's of architecture. So that's what I have, and I've been an architect for fifteen years.

Our firm is in a part of town called Oakley, which is in the northwest suburbs of the city. Oakley is like a first-ring suburb out from downtown Cincinnati. You're really looking at an industrial area there. When there were some really bad floods[6] in the

---

3. This stage indicates cancer in the lymph nodes on both sides of the diaphragm and possibly another organ: cancer. net/cancer-types/lymphoma-hodgkin/stages.

4. Stay tuned for Christine's story: Her chapter will appear in the sequel to this book: My Job 2.

5. Drawingdept.com.

6. Oakley, named for famous markswoman Annie Oakley, is currently a young professional district of Cincinnati. The flood to which Kevin is referring, the Ohio River flood of 1937, left one million people homeless and 385 dead. It caused $500 million in damages (= $8.7 billion today).

downtown areas of the city that wiped out the industrial basin, all the big factories and stuff came up to Oakley. So there's ample commercial opportunity there.

At this time last year, there were six of us in my firm, Drawing Dept. Today there are eleven people, seven men and four women. We're growing like crazy.

THE MONEY IS PRETTY GOOD FOR WHAT I DO

I earn $80,000 a year. That's probably a little bit on the low side for most other people in my profession at my age, but a lot of that has to do with just the nature of the architecture industry. You can make a lot of money, and you can work at a firm that does nothing but design Kroger's grocery stores. Here in the Midwest, every Kroger grocery store comes out of the same Cincinnati firm.[7]

You'd be surprised—you can't just use the same plan for every new store. You've got to adapt, expand, whatever. It's pretty mundane stuff, right? You can make a lot of money doing that, or other stuff, like healthcare design. It's like these never-ending corridors and that kind of stuff.

So, I accept a pay cut to do something that I find value in.

I think that, if I pushed it, I could probably be a partner, but I enjoy the flexibility of not being a partner.

That means there's more to life than work, and it means that there's more to work than maybe what my job entails right now. The people that I work with now, I've worked with for fifteen years. Maybe I see things a little bit differently? And so a partnership is sort of a long-term horizon thing, and I don't know if my horizon is necessarily that long [with this firm]. There's maybe a little bit of a generational difference between me and our lead partners, a different sort of mentality. I don't know. This might not be my forever job…I think I'm happy with it for now. It might be my forever job.

GROWING UP THE ONLY CHILD OF HARDWORKING PARENTS

I grew up in the south suburbs of Detroit. I'm an only child; just me and my parents. They worked hard. My mom was a middle-school math teacher. My dad was in sales; he sold industrial piping and other things like that.

We were pretty middle class, I guess, or lower-middle class. We had the worst boat of anyone I knew. I think we got it from another math teacher who was retiring or something. And it was yellow. No one has a yellow boat!

Now my parents are both retired. They spend seven weeks a year in Florida. So they're there right now.

As a child, I always liked putting stuff together and taking it apart. Just kind of figuring out how things worked, was fun. My grandparents would have Tinkertoys[8] at their house. But I didn't really know any architects, growing up.

---

7. The firm, CR (Cole + Russell Architects), has designed over 500 Kroger grocery stores: cr-architects.com/expertise/all/kroger/?r=56.

8. Invented in 1910, Tinkertoys (similar to Lincoln Logs and Erector Sets) are wooden wheels with holes all around and sticks that connect them to build abstract shapes: toyhalloffame.org/toys/tinkertoy.

In middle school, I would draw a lot. I would take a lot of art classes and just draw houses or buildings or whatever. It was easy.

So I can't remember, but probably my grandma or someone just said, "Have you ever thought about being an architect?" and it was like, "Okay." So I picked it up and thought that was good. It's been really interesting. I like it a lot.

MY FIRST JOB WAS IN 4ᵀᴴ GRADE AT THE FARMER'S MARKET

I had my first job when I was in fourth grade. I worked at a farmers' market that was by my house growing up. This guy I worked for, he would go down to Detroit to the big farmers' market down there, and then he would just buy all the stuff and bring it to our town. My friend and I walked in and said, "Do you need any help doing any work?" and he said, "Yeah."

I don't really know why we did it. We were bored. He needed someone to, you know, deadhead the pansies and the impatiens, shuck corn, and do stuff like that. I got paid under the table, $2 an hour.

If I go through my whole growing-up list of jobs, I worked as a caddy for a couple of summers and as a dishwasher for a summer or two. I've been a temp, too, and I had dozens of different jobs through that agency.

WORKING IN AN AUTOMOBILE FACTORY IN DETROIT

During high school and the first summer after freshman year of college, I pulled cars off the line at a Mazda plant in a south suburb of Detroit. The cars get to the end of the line, and you get in the car, and the car has a tag on it indicating where it's supposed to go, and then you drive the car from there to some other parking lot. So you're the first person ever to get into some of these cars.

For some reason, that summer after freshman year, I felt like I needed a lot of money for school. That was because everyone else was home. All my friends were trying to do the same thing. [Laughs.] I think it was just for pocket money. College was like out-of-state rates—*so* expensive. No money that I was making was going to make a dent in that. My parents had to help there.

At the Mazda plant, that shift started at 6:00 p.m. and work went until 3:00 a.m. or something like that. That was a really sketchy shift.

That pulling the cars off the line job was bad. By the time you get through that, it's 2:00 in the morning, and you take your car out and you sit in this van and drive back. And as a nineteen-year-old kid, you're sitting in this van and a lot of the people who are also in the van are pretty rough. They're going to stake their claim and show everyone else how tough they are by getting into you a little bit.

So, man, I got roughed up, not like physically roughed up but just like some of the women were just filthy, [they used] filthy language. It was really an eye-opener. It's hard to talk about the people in the van as being bad people or evil people. They were working hard, and they were just different. But I couldn't imagine. Those guys all had kids. That was their *job*. That was their life. I just felt like, "I do not want to work in a factory anymore."

And then during the school year, I would work at an art gallery on campus. I'd be just sitting there for a while, getting paid five bucks an hour or something. Then, later, I started the co-op program in architecture.

I HAD ANOTHER WEIRD FACTORY JOB WHERE I INHALED A LOT OF GLUE

I also had a weird job as a temp and had to put together these two-piece shoe inserts that they would sell on TV late at night. So I worked in this weird factory, gluing these foam things together.

There's a fume hood, a sneeze guard that's supposed to take everything up, but like a lot of people who work there were like shorter, like the women. Some people were, like, hunched under it. So that was really awful. By the end of the day you had just inhaled so much glue. So I did that for three or four days. Yeah, that was rough.

MOVING FROM SMALL-TOWN MICHIGAN TO URBAN CINCINNATI

For college, I decided to go to the University of Cincinnati. The community I grew up in is pretty small, like 10,000-12,000 people there. My parents grew up there. So it was a little claustrophobic at the time. I wanted to get away. And some of the schools in Michigan I got into, you didn't start architecture school until the third year, and I just didn't want to wait around till then.

Cincinnati has a really good architecture program, and for a long time, it has been one of the top ten or top fifteen architecture schools in the country. It's a six-year program. You're on campus for four, and then you're out working for two years in the co-op program. So you go out, and the university helps set you up with jobs and things like that; and then there's a 100 percent job-placement rate.

As someone whose parents were really concerned with what job I had, it was really good to come out of college with three or four professional contacts and be able to have a job. I don't know why they were so worried. It's just what you do: you get a job. That was kind of an important thing, having a job. I guess it was just important to be stable.

I am a proud member of the "never getting better than a B in almost anything" club. I can get a B in everything. There's not anything I'm really great at, yet there's also not anything that I'm really terrible at. I can just get a B. If I really work hard and apply myself, I can get like an A-, but it just doesn't appeal to me as much as taking it easy and getting a B.

THE CLASSES AND CO-OP TRACK I TOOK IN COLLEGE

Design studio was really fun. It was like a social thing. Architecture and history classes were good. I struggled a little bit with the heavy calculus of some of the structural classes. Some of the more abstract classes would be a little rough for me. So I enjoyed practical things, I think, as a whole.

So when you go co-op, you generally end up being the youngest person in the whole office. You just figure it out, and then you're also changing offices the whole time. So I worked for two quarters at a firm in Virginia and did everything from answering phones and organizing carpet samples to, you know, measuring existing buildings and then doing some design charrette[9] work, some actual design work.

You'd grab whoever was around the office and available, and you'd just say, "Here's the project: We're supposed to be doing a competition to do like a mausoleum. What are some of your thoughts about that?"

You design it with a team of people. You get to do a full range of things. Then, as you get a little bit older, you might do a little bit more toward model-making or renderings or things like that, but you're generally at the lower end of the pile. It's good.

I worked for two different quarters at a firm in Virginia, and then I went and worked in Seattle for a quarter, and then I worked in Cincinnati for two quarters.

MY SCARY QUARTER OF TRAVEL ABROAD, ALONE

Then I took a travel quarter, where I just did Europe for two months. I was twenty-three, twenty-four. I went from Rome to Berlin by myself, just me and my backpack. I took a really long, slow trip.

It was pretty damn scary. It was good. Everything good happened. Nothing bad happened, but you get off of an airplane, and they speak Italian. Then you go somewhere, and you don't know how to get there. I'm trying to think of what year this would have been. It would have been 2001. So the Internet is barely a thing. You don't have a cellphone. I'm still like unfolding pieces of paper to figure out how to get from the airport to my hotel. You can't tell somebody—it's just a whole different thing now.

You just are kind of navigating, and you sink or swim. You find some people whom you like, maybe students from the schools there, and then they go on their way, and you have to find a new group, or you don't.

Then, all of a sudden, you accidentally get off the train after you've been studying Italian for a month, and everyone speaks French, and you're like, "I didn't study any French." So it's a little scary. I only did Italy, Switzerland, an accidental day in France, and then Germany. So, not very much. I wish I would have done more.

MY DESIGN STYLE WAS NOT REALLY AFFECTED BY EUROPE

I don't know whether these travels influenced my design style. I think when you're like twenty-three or whatever, you don't really have much of a design style. You're just kind of winging it. I have no idea whether I would be working any differently if I hadn't taken that trip. Because then when you're thirty-eight, looking back to what you were doing when you were twenty-three, you realize you didn't know shit. You didn't have a design style.

So what the hell is my design style now? I have to think about that one . . .

I guess there's this idea that architects have about visual style, that you could tell a

---

9. A charrette is an intensive planning session that often takes place near the building site, in which designers and citizens collaborate on their vision for a project: tndtownpaper.com/what_is_charrette.htm#http://www.tndtownpaper.com/what_is_charrette.htm.

building that was by Architect A because it looks a certain way, and Architect B would have taken a building that had the same exact sort of program and site, and it would have looked like a building by Architect B.

But that's not really what I feel is my "way." My style would be that I don't have a style; that there's a way that a building operates and functions and looks that is immediately appropriate for every situation and piece of building, if that makes any sense. There's a part of myself that I bring to a project, but that's not *the thing*. There are other pieces of the project that also go into that. So sometimes those things are more important than how something looks.

FIGURING OUT WHAT THE BUILDING WANTS TO BE

For example, I do a ton of renovation work. So, figuring out what a building that I would do, looks like, is kind of a different thing. Sometimes it's just a matter of scraping away things to reveal the truth about something rather than saying like, "This is me, and this is my blood and guts. It's a *Kevin* project."

To say that there's "a style" is a little bit tricky. To say that there might be a common ethic or a common sensibility of how something is arrived at, is probably more accurate. I don't know exactly how to say this. It's definitely way too nuanced. I should probably just say that I like buildings that are rectangles…but I don't always like buildings that are rectangles.

Probably some of it is just figuring out what the building wants to be, instead of imposing myself on it.

In my whole life, I've done a lot of single-family residential work, both brand-new and renovations. I'm designing three or four art studios on my plate these days, and those are mostly renovations of warehouses or factories in which we insert gallery and artist spaces; certain sorts of event spaces, and yet there are also operational spaces, like bathrooms and things like that.

These buildings are here in town. There's one that was a factory that made tool-and-die type stuff. Some people bought it, took it over, and wanted to start a glass-making school there, like an art studio complex. That was the first one of those that we did, in 2008.

We've added a few more here and there, but they're all different. They all look different and all sort of act different. They all have a different mission, based on extremely different people who are involved with the projects, and the history of the building, and the history of the site.

That's why it gets a bit tricky to say, "That building is my style," or "This one isn't my style"; because some of those buildings are so loaded. I mean, I feel like it's a positive thing to say that "That's my style" doesn't override other things that are going on there.

MY TYPICAL DAY AT THE OFFICE

I live less than a mile from the office. It's walk-able, but I use my car for work all the time. During the week, I might be in the office like 80 percent of the time. The other 20 percent, I'm out at different job sites and things like that.

I drive a Mercury sedan. It's kind of green-grey. It's more and more green. It's pretty much a driving office. I just drive around and my hard hat, my mail, and junk accumulate in my car.

HOW WE PRODUCE BUILDING PLANS

In the office, we do a lot of drawing. We do draw by hand a lot. We draw on computers and then produce paper. I didn't start drawing on computer until after I got out of school. Most of my basic sketching comes from drawing and then goes into computer drafting. So in my client meetings, it's just really easy to sketch [on paper] really quickly.

Our office uses AutoCAD [a software program for designing in two or three dimensions], which is just a really nuts and bolts. It's used in 90 percent or more of offices. It evolves. It grows up a little bit. We update. And then some people use other bigger programs.

It's not hard to keep up with technology for drafting and stuff. But then, the older I get, the less I do. I just do a lot less drafting now, so the technology matters less and less. We sometimes create models, but we would assign them to our co-op level students. We use them not in a regular way, but just sort of like on an as-needed basis. We don't have someone permanently on staff that is in that role at this point.

NO TWO DAYS ARE THE SAME

One of the reasons I wanted to be an architect is that no two days are going to be the same. You're working on different stuff all the time. No six months are the same. So, for example, right now I'm in a real difficult six months where everything that was just on paper six months ago is now happening on a construction site. And sometimes that's good.

Right now, I should be drafting some projects that will be in construction soon. There's so much stuff coming back from the field. In a normal situation, you'd have one in construction while you're drawing another one, and they'd kind of chase each other. But when the recession [the Great Recession of 2007-2009][10] happened, everyone kind of hit the reset button. You started everything all at once. So everything was in the design phase for a long time, and then a lot of that stuff either died or got taken over.

Unfortunately, right now, my schedule is such that everything's in the same place. So during a normal day, I might get five emails about five different projects and five different emergencies happening at once. I have to respond to those in like two days, and then I might get nothing for two days and then have to draft on somebody else's project or do something else. So it's pretty hectic right now. It's not my favorite thing.

THE WORST IS WHEN A CLIENT BUTCHERS YOUR PLANS

The worst thing that's happened is you work really hard and present a client with a plan, and you think it's brilliant, and then they call back two weeks later and say stuff like, "Well, we've done a little work on your plan." It's like a total butcher job. They've ripped out the heart of it. That happens. That's about as injurious as it can get.

---

10. Stateofworkingamerica.org/great-recession.

It's rarely about money as much as it is that we already have a ton of work to do. It's more painful to have to redraw something to make into something that I hate.

You kind of let all the air out of the balloon, just like all the enthusiasm goes out. You end up stuck with something that you just know is going to be a monster. It's going to be terrible. You don't want to put your name on it.

This will sound really bad, but those are the ones [clients] that are really high maintenance, and you can't get away from them for two years. It's a construction thing. You're going to hear about this now for the next two years. This voice is going to be on your phone like, "This isn't how I wanted it" kind of stuff. It's rough.

I think one of the good lessons of the past year has been like, *You just really need to sell it.* If one of the things we've done in the drawing is in question, we just need to be aggressive with it and believe in our vision, whether it's a creative vision or not. We need to believe in it because once you open that door that anybody can be doing anything, then anybody will do anything, and you're going to end up with a pile [of shit] at the end, and you're going to hate it.

There's such a thing as too much collaboration.

That's probably the worst part of my job. It's not filing papers…Filing's great. Papers, tax returns—it's just like you need Document A, Document B, Document C, and that's it. You're done.

It's not that I like being organized, so much. It's that I like having a finite path. I like knowing, "This is what you need to do to get stuff accomplished."

With architecture, that's often not the case. It's often hard to say when to start, and when to stop. It's hard to know if someone values you as much as you value your own work. That's probably a necessary part of the job. It's not the high-maintenance people themselves. It's just you do care and, sometimes, you know, we work with clients who don't care, and that's worse.

They say, "Couldn't you make it cheaper?" and then, "Could you be cheaper, too?"

High-maintenance clients are great. I mean, they're involved, and you know, they may or may not want the same things as you aesthetically, but they generally have the best interest of what they're doing in their mind.

There's definitely a difference between high maintenance and meddlesome. I prefer high maintenance. I'd hope they would say like, "Well, I'm an accountant, and I don't know about 25,000 years of architectural history like you do, and so I'll respect your expertise in this and be involved that way," versus saying like, "Well, I can do this, too. I have graph paper. Can't we just fit a closet in right here and then"—you know, and while they're doing that, the toilet just keeps getting smaller.

It's like, "No, you're just doing it wrong, and we've done this before." There's a difference between collaborating and being told what to draw, especially when it's absolutely horrid. Then you just are stuck. But this is a for-profit business.

THE MOST HIDEOUS BUILDING I'VE WORKED ON

Gosh. I'm trying to think of the absolute worst project I've ever worked on. I did a storefront renovation for a building in our neighborhood. Our client wanted to take out this beautiful wood-and-iron storefront, really ornate, nice stuff, and wanted to put it back with basically hideous, modern sort of stuff. It was a big job, a complex job, thousands of square feet of glass. We had to get permission from the City. There was a lot of work to do, which made everything worse. And it broke my heart.

The materials [we removed] were so old. You start taking them apart, and they just fall apart. It would have been great to do anything else with them, but, again, you're on that spectrum of the care index where the contractor doesn't care about re-keeping or salvaging it. He just wants to get somebody in there to trash it as fast as possible.

Stuff like that is painful. I [still] drive by that building every day. It's got these black tinted windows, and it looks like it got its eyes poked out. It's just this lifeless thing, and it exists, and we got paid.

My conscience is on that. No one can look at it and see my name. So that's fine. But *I* know.

MY FIRM HAS WON A DOZEN AWARDS

I've not really won any awards as Kevin Kluender, architect. I've won probably about a dozen awards[11] for projects that I've worked on through the Drawing Dept. They're all local Cincinnati awards. Cincinnati is the second-biggest city in the nineteenth-biggest state in the country. So it's not that great of a deal. It's not a huge thing, as far as awards go, but it's nice to get recognized.

I am particularly proud of an award I won last November. That was a project that I basically worked on from start to finish. No one else was allowed to touch it. So that one, I feel like it says "Drawing Dept" on it, but if you scrape underneath the surface, it would have my name on it.

I'm really happy with that project. There was this woman who took over her family's wood-flooring factory and warehouse. She wanted to put an art gallery in it and do a stone-carving studio and things like that.

So, inside this big warehouse, we put this tiny gallery box, and it's just beautiful. It's really great. When people deal with family stuff, it's always an awkward thing. Maybe some sort of therapy happened there, but it turned out great. So that was a really good one, and it's been a fun ongoing project.

I did another project, a house for this older lady. She was really great. She had an unbuildable site with a creek running through the middle of it. She came to us and said, "I want a log cabin." My boss designed it. He built this log cabin that spanned over the creek. It has a sloping grass roof. So he handed it over to me.

I was all of twenty-two, straight out of college; it was the first thing I did. I had to figure out how to build this thing, and I did. So I worked with the contractor. This woman, who was eighty-five when the construction started, she drove by every day and took a picture with her disposable camera—every single day.

And it took a really long time to build. She never really lived in it, but she died in it. It was finished and she had just moved in, and there was this beautiful bedroom that was open to a birch forest. Since there was a hillside above the creek, her bedroom was in the

---

11. Drawingdept.com/newsite/architecture_drawingdept_awards.php.

air. So there were all these yellow leaves falling around her.

We've been in close contact with the family. They were like, "That house kept her going." She would come back from vacation, and she was just like, "I've got to see the house."

The house was definitely one of those rare architectural masterpiece houses, but that's the last thing I cared about. It was just really nice to be able to give her that for her life. That was a good thing.

I'M DESIGNING A CARE CENTER FOR CHILDREN WITH CANCER

I'm also one of two major collaborators on The Landing, a place that serves to assist the Dragonfly Foundation. Their mission is making the lives of people who have families in various cancer crises easier.

There's a whole bunch of different ways that they do that there: Part of it is creating a free play space for kids with immune system compromises to inhabit in a sort of childlike way. It's also a space for volunteer and donor opportunities. So a huge number of volunteers will come in and go out, providing assistance for out-of-building opportunities, whether it's delivering toys, or their blue-bag care packages [full of toiletries and comfort items for hospital stays], or things like that.

Then other areas will be for the administration and offices and marketing for the foundation. That section also serves as sort of a fundraising venue, so that when they have different activities, they can have one centralized space to do that. At this point, my firm has designed just the main building, not the residential piece of the project.

WORKING WITH DRAGONFLY FOUNDATION

When they were accepting bids for the job, Dragonfly put together a really well-respected team of contractors and builders and client representatives. They sent out essentially a brief or a request for proposals [RFP] to five or six architectural firms and asked, "Here's this project we're thinking about doing. What do you guys think, and how much would it cost? What are your visions? Can you reply to this by this time?"

So we put together a response to that, and they selected us. Or they narrowed it down to three, and then we did an interview process, and then they selected us. I can't remember, but I want to say we might have had ten weeks and $50,000, something like that, to complete the drawings.

That's an all-inclusive rate. That includes other engineers and professionals being involved to a smaller degree, rendering packages and things like that.

So, after we got the job, we spent a lot of time with them in their current offices. They would walk us through, basically the tour that visitors get to take, and then we talked. We had long interviews with them about what else they want to be doing with the space, kind of breaking that down.

Then we spent a good chunk of time here interviewing the employees; I don't want to say "observing," because it sounds creepy—but time with the family and some kids who were here, just playing and being a part of that.

The founder, Christine, had been gathering information and ideation for many years about this project. So we're sitting down and doing intense interviews with her and pulling all of that information together, putting that into a central document that we call a *program*, and then presenting that program to the team. Then basically we're using that program to start a fairly fundamental set of diagrams, how things are organized and functioning. All of that gets arranged and then we figure out how each space wants to look, what the character of that is.

GETTING PULLED THIS WAY AND THAT BY THE BOARD OF DIRECTORS

What's been tough about this project is, it's hard working for a board. When you work for a board, you don't have a single point source of information. You have like *ten*. And so Board Member A pulls you aside and says, "Listen, I really think that this needs to do this, this, and this; don't listen to Board Member B."

Then Board Member B pulls you aside and tells you the exact opposite; so you're constantly having to evaluate everybody's information about what they're hoping for and then also having to be really firm with them.

The reason they bring us on is because we have expertise, and we know what we're doing. So you have to be really firm and aggressive with your vision. That's not something that comes really easily for me, to be aggressively defensive, especially with a board of people who are—I don't want to say "make it, break it" people, but they're *big* people.

OUR DESIGN IS MEANT TO CAPTURE PLAYFULNESS, AND LIGHT

I think that we've managed to capture an image that's somewhat familiar: the dragonfly itself. It provides a good contrast to the sort of clinical places that these kids are accustomed to. That was really important for us. I think we've been successful at coming up with a building shape and size that's starkly in contrast to what we'd understand as a very common hospital.

So we said, "We don't want this to be just about building a house. We want this to feel more comfortable, like a residence, with some people that live in apartments and others in ranch houses, and there are some people in cancer treatment."—But we still wanted it to have a domestic character to it as opposed to like a hospital building, endless floor plates, and flat roofs, and things like that.

For example, the front elevation is a pair of gables. You're seeing two gable ends, and there's an uncanny recognition between a gable and a human figure or human face. Presenting two gabled faces as a front of a building gives the building façade a sort of recognizable face.

Other things we really worked on to contrast that sort of clinical thing, like these never-ending corridors with the room on one side and the window: We tried to make sure that a lot of the spaces were getting two light sources in, whether via two perpendicular walls or from each side of the one wall. That makes the space a little more rich.

It might be too subtle, but there's also a patterning in the materials that takes a nod from the dragonfly wing pattern, It's one of those things where we don't want it to explode into like, you know, "That building's a dragonfly." We want it to have a sense of wonder to it, but we don't want it to get pushed into a really literal thing.

We've talked a lot about this with Christine. These kids have dealt with cancer. They've had to face a lot more adult ideas than I have had to face as an adult. So, we've made a concerted effort not to treat them like children and not to make a place where like circles are red and triangles are blue, and that type of kindergarten talk. But we also wanted to visualize the building as having a layer there that might be a little more imaginative.

GETTING CREATIVE WITHIN A FRAMEWORK

You know, being creative is a tricky thing. It's not strictly a creative endeavor. It's not like painting, where I could just paint whatever I want: It's a structure, with function.

"Clever" is a good word. It's having a response that solves two or three problems at once. That's really rewarding to me, like having a sort of aesthetic detail that is involved in heating and cooling and lighting and structure and things like that.

I don't dream this stuff. I've never solved a problem in my sleep. I think of things sometimes when I'm jogging. I guess I mostly think of things in the shower. It's that distracted type of insight, I guess. When I'm doing something else, an idea pops into my head.

LIFE BEYOND WORK: MY GIRLFRIEND, FAMILY, AND HOME

When I'm not working, I run a couple of times a week. My girlfriend, Christi, and I live in a house in Cincinnati, and we do our best to try and make that work. Marriage is not really relevant right now. I'm happy with the partnership. I don't know if I want to have kids.

We're pretty much homebodies. We just stay home, veg on the couch and watch TV, cook or go for a walk, or something like that. It's pretty simple. We also both like to hike.

It's always a little dicey like having family out of town. So you're balancing trying to stay in town and go out of town, just being around family and stuff. I don't know. There's nothing super exciting in my life.

This is the year of me working forty hours a week. Last year was, to me, a lot more difficult. So my resolution this year was to like say, "I'm not doing this."

The flip side of the coin of only working forty hours a week was picking up some volunteer activities. So I do—it sounds cooler than it is—I volunteer for a reading-for-the-blind program, an organization that tries to get every written periodical into a voicemail system for blind people to be able to access and understand. So I am part of that.

It's been weird. One of the discoveries is my voice sounds amazingly different outside of my head. So it's strange. You have to listen to these messages. Who is that? That's *me*. [Laughs.]

They're a really great group. You don't have to try out. They have hundreds of volunteers, and they have pretty much everything covered. I ended up getting stuck with reading *Men's Health* magazine. So I am the *Men's Health* reader. And it's good; I enjoy it.

I guess it's like the biggest program in the country [here in Cincinnati]. There are people around the country and around the world that call into this thing.

Other than that, I'd like to do some traveling. After school, most of my friends moved away. So we usually will try to travel somewhere to see some of them. One of my good friends moved to Florida. So we'll try to go see them, or we'll see old friends up in Michigan. Some of my other friends live out in the Northeast, in Vermont and Boston. So we'll try to get to see them as well.

I'M SECRETLY OBSESSED WITH THE APPALACHIAN TRAIL

I also will say I've been secretly obsessed with the Appalachian Trail for the past three months. So that would be a thing I would like to do. That would take like five months. And, you know, I probably would kick it back to Europe and just get to the rest of the stuff I didn't get to, and maybe even go back to the stuff that I did get to see, and look at it with older eyes.

IF I HAD ALL THE MONEY IN THE WORLD, I WOULD STILL DO ARCHITECTURE

If I had all the money in the world, I think I would probably figure out something else to do in architecture. I'm still enamored enough with it that I would be interested. I don't know what I would do: Build mansions in France, eco-housing in Alaska…We do some green building now.

As for my dream house, you know, I'd be totally lying if I said that I never doodled a cabin in the woods for myself, or something like that. That's just something that you do.

I'm sure if I would have been mindful of it, I probably should have been keeping these [sketches] for the past fifteen years, because it would have been a really interesting evolutionary study.

Mostly, my dream house is like a rectangle. It has some bigger windows. I don't know. Fifteen years ago, I probably would not be at all interested in any sort of *statement*; the architecture would be like a rectangle with maybe a window that's larger than you're accustomed to and really well-oriented to let a nice view in, and some decent sunshine. Fifteen years ago, I would have told you it would be this famous-making thing. Today, my vision is totally different.

MY WORK PHILOSOPHY CAME FROM MY GRANDPA

My first understanding about work, or the first piece of work advice I ever got, was from my grandpa. He was a doctor. He was just a general physician. He had an office in Detroit; and when it was in the 1940s, Detroit was like the Paris[12] of everywhere.

My grandpa worked until 2006. He was ninety-some odd years old. He would drive

---

12. Detroit in the late 19th and early 20th centuries was nicknamed "the Paris of the West" because of its verdant parks, stunning architecture, and eight-spoke-wheel city design: writinghistoricalnovels.com/2013/05/25/early-20th-century-detroit-the-paris-of-the-west-by-de-johnson.

the half-hour drive from our suburb to his office to give out flu shots and cortisone shots and stuff, and he would accept all kinds of things as payment. The neighborhood went through some transitions from being white working-class to black working-class to being just straight Mexican. You could go over to his house, and he would have a jar of tamales that he took for payment, or cakes or cookies, or whatever.

He was probably the first person ever to tell me that if you like what you do, you won't ever have to work a day of your life. That's, I think, a good thing. I like architecture. If I go on vacation, I go look at some dorky buildings and drag people along with me to do it. That's probably really trite, like too much of an inspirational-poster kind of thing.

But in terms of a worldview, I have no idea. I wish I had one. I don't know.

Very early on, would have thought that my work was a sort of problem-solving, but I think now I consider more of what I do is to sort of bring or give *meaning*. I said this to a student the other day—we get involved with coop-student critiques every once in a while, and it just came out. How did that come out and make sense?

Architecture is like this: You're translating someone's values into built form. Whatever that means, that's what that is. If that person's values are cheap storefront windows, then that's what your job is. If that person's values are helping a kid that's sick feel a little bit better today, that's what your job is. So it feels like that's what my work is.

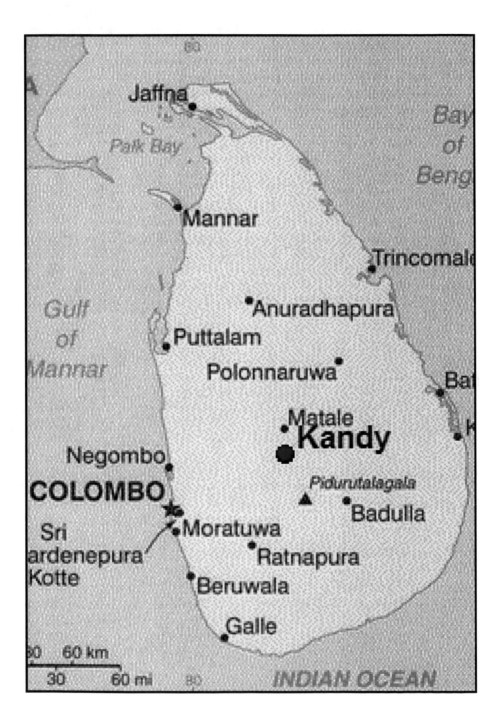

PURNIMA

INTERIOR DESIGNER

KANDY, SRI LANKA

Editor's Note: Sri Lanka, whose name means something like "honorable, glittering gem," was called "Ceylon" (as in, tea) by its British occupiers until 1948. It's shaped like a gem, dangling just south of India, with steamy lowland beaches and nippy inland mountains in a country the size of West Virginia.. Known for tea and cinnamon, coconuts and rubber, its pristine coastline and ancient sacred sites, it's a nation that's still recovering from natural disaster (the 2004 Indian Ocean tsunami) and civil war (1983-2009).

Purnima arrives in a stylish Western dress made of denim. Her long nails are perfectly polished and her big brown eyes dart around the room, taking in every detail. More than anyone else in the building, Purnima has been trained to imagine what the room *could* be: She's an interior designer who's worked on grand homes, offices, a pub, and even the stately Old Parliament Building.

She speaks a little English; but soon after we exchange pleasantries, she shifts to the comfort of a full-range vocabulary with her mother tongue, Sinhalese.

With me are the nonprofit Educate Lanka's[1] country director, Dhanu, who will translate for me from Sinhala into English. The organization's founder, Manjula,[2] also joins us toward the end of the conversation.

However, the biggest detriment to Purnima's candor seems to be the person closest to her, both at the table and in life...Purnima's mother. She smiles for the pictures I ask to take with my cellphone, but her smiling countenance belies a tough character who is here for one reason only: to protect her beautiful daughter from the "shady characters" around Kandy and, if necessary, from us.

Purnima's mom never really relaxes. She watches everyone like a hawk, and she is ready to swoop in if she perceives any threat whatsoever to her darling girl.

Purnima tells me that even while living away in the capital city of Colombo, earning her master's in design and working as an apprentice, she must call her mother on her mobile phone to ask permission to cross the street or sit down for tea. There is nothing facetious, no exaggeration here. At age twenty-six, she sends home half her salary (which surpasses her father's; her mother makes no income as a stay-at-home parent) yet has to ask permission to buy a new dress.

This is what love looks like, to them. Mama and daughter share stories of how Purnima nearly died from a mysterious illness at age four, how she's the only daughter and so they all rally to spoil her, and how dangerous it is for a girl of her beauty to be out and about...Mama shakes her finger at Dhanu and frowns at me. No one's going to take advantage or even ask an inappropriate question: We'd have to get through her, and she looks perfectly capable of taking us down.

As I listen intently and watch both women's body language, my emotions as a Western woman who values my complete and utter freedom, shift from bewilderment at Purnima's situation (several of my American nieces are her age and they live across the U.S., Europe, and Asia, building careers and enjoying friends and boyfriends), to frustration at what looks to me like a cage built around her.

Translator Dhanu tells me later that Purnima is unusually old-fashioned in the way her parents protect her and the way she must report "to my home," as she puts it. That means she must get permission for every action from her father, through a chain of command of Mom to Dad. Dhanu says this is not so common among the youth of Sri Lanka today. Mom knows she is dating a guy but Dad cannot know, because it's not acceptable to be in a relationship while a girl is still in school.

Eventually, my brain cracks open just enough to discern that Purnima is... happy. She still suffers from debilitating food allergies, and she takes great comfort in her mother, brothers, and father fussing over her health. They're profoundly grateful she survived her near-death experience, and they don't take for granted any moment of her life.

---

1. Educate Lanka is a partner of the SFF (skees.org) and my connection to Purnima, a scholarship alumna of their program. See: educatelanka.org.
2. Manjula Dissanayake, the Sri Lankan-American who launched Educate Lanka, tells his story here: youtu.be/ FUN0uISPE3A.

Given the derogatory attitudes toward women in many parts of the world, their near-worship of their little girl for her intelligence and beauty, ends up striking me as pretty sweet.

Bottom line is, the protection and worry don't seem to bother Purnima. Rather, as she builds her career, breaking into a male-dominated field and winning awards for her ingenuity, as she ventures far beyond where even her educated father ever studied or worked, Purnima seems to take comfort in the way they sort of virtually stalk her everywhere she goes, even if only via a mobile phone.

Given how highly accomplished Purnima has been in school and work, winning scholarships and awards, the fact that she said plans to chuck all her education and career the moment she marries (which could be next year) seems sort of tragic. Conversely, when Dhanu walks away for a moment, Purnima informs me that she intends to be a successful career woman.

I WORK FOR A WORLD-FAMOUS FURNITURE AND INTERIOR DESIGN FIRM

My name is Purnima Wanigasekara. I'm twenty-six years old. I'm an alumna of Educate Lanka, and I currently work at Don's Interior, a branch of H. Don Carolis and Sons Private Limited.[3] It's a private company, an island-famous and world-famous furniture and interior design company. I have worked here for one year (more than that if you count the in-plant training we're required to do in advance) as an interior designer. This is my first job.

Don Carolis is a huge company. They have a manufacturing plant and a furniture plant, and there are 150 carpenters working in that plant. And the sales team, there are fifteen. There are twenty executives, and, in the design team, where I'm working right now, there are three training designees and two senior designers in charge.

Our clients are both men and women. But for domestic projects, mostly it's just women coming in, because they're the ones who do the choosing for a house in general. So they're the ones who come for design.

I LIVE AWAY FROM HOME, NEAR SRI LANKA'S CAPITAL CITY

I live in a boarding place in Moratuwa, fifteen kilometers away from Colombo towards the south. The boarding place is all girls. It's more like a dorm kind of a boarding place. I have lived in this place since I went to university. There is a matron there. There are thirteen girls on our floor and many floors in the building. I share the room with a friend, but I'm not really friends with the other girls. They are much younger. They are still university students, and I'm now working. So it's not as friendly.

I work in Colombo Monday through Saturday. I take the bus when I can visit my family. I do not drive. My brothers drive, but as they don't own vehicles, we all just take the bus. I visit home every other weekend.

---

3. For more information, see facebook.com/donsInterior or doncarolis.com.

I GREW UP IN A VILLAGE IN THE CENTER OF THE ISLAND

I was born in Kandy, in a village called Teldeniya. I would like to explain about my family. My father is a government employee. My mother is a housewife.

I have two younger brothers. Both of them are now students. My older brother is studying at the Vocational Training Authority at Jirella. My younger brother is studying at Open University Polgolla.

My brothers all spoil me terribly. Yes. [Laughs.] As the only girl, I am spoiled. In Sri Lankan culture, it's kind of hard for a woman to do things alone. I always have to rely on my brothers or my mother or father. My mother always follows me wherever I go.

Even when I was at the university, whenever I'd come home, she'd be working in the home, fussing over me. Then again, now, whenever I come to Kandy, my mother is going to [ride the bus to Colombo to] pick me up, and my father is going to drop me off. That's just how it is.

Compared to other cultures or like Western cultures, it's not quite the same here. For a girl, it's not the same. There are so many restrictions imposed by society or for the culture alone. You can't really do stuff. So it's always my mother or my brothers looking after me.

I will give you three examples. One is nightlife. For example, if I were in Colombo and I wanted to go to a party at night, I'd have to check it with my father through my mother, because I'd have to have permission. Two, when the Educate Lanka staff asked that there's going to be an interview [today, for this chapter] with a foreigner, I had to get permission from my father. The way it works is, I have to ask my mother to ask my father, to get it approved. And three, if I want to wear something, I have to check it with my mother, like buying a new dress or something, if it's okay or not.

My brothers also check on me. Like when I came to the this meeting, my brother was like, "Where are you now? Did you come to hotel? Did you meet Dhanu?" and likewise.

My elder brother and my younger brother also still go back to our parents and talk to our mother and check it out, get their permission—not permission, just really running things by them before going. My older brother is twenty-nine years old. Now he is looking for a partner, a girlfriend, and he's also asking our mother about that.

WHY I WOULDN'T JUST LIVE THE WAY I WANT TO

There are a couple of reasons why I wouldn't just live the way I wanted to. I would always ask my parents for permission, because my parents always call me. It has always been like that. It's not just every night: It's like morning, day, evening, night, afternoon, checking if I had breakfast, checking if I had lunch or tea; and if I said I hadn't had tea, then they'd be like "Why didn't you have tea?"

Even if I could go to a party, for example, without them knowing—say I tell them I'll just be visiting a friend the next town over—well, *I* know it's not true, and I will probably show that. It's the trust. If that's not there, then there's no point.

This is the reason why I wouldn't lie: trust. Even if I'm not specific, I may be not lying but leaving something out. I may be saying something like, "I'm in such-and-such town, just passing by Kandy Road," but if my father would be like, "Are you sure? Are you in

Kandy now?" I might be like, "Oh I didn't open the windows so I can't see exactly where I am right now," but it just wouldn't sound right. It's not the way I want to be.

MY NEAR-DEATH EXPERIENCE AS A LITTLE GIRL CHANGED ME

I almost died at one point, at a younger age, and I'm still quite sick. It's a stomach issue. I get sick quite easily.

When I was four years old, I had a stomach infection. No one knew what it was, but I couldn't eat anything. I would throw up everything that I would eat, and I had intensive diarrhea and severe dehydration. [Cries.]

They were treating me in the village hospital, the Teldeniya Hospital, and the doctors, they just thought it was just a diarrhea issue, and there was nothing serious about it. They weren't really like treating it in the proper way. A germ had gotten into my stomach. It wasn't a parasite to our knowledge, but some sort of germ.

But for doctors to do anything about it, they would have had either to give some medication through the mouth or right away through the blood, but I was unconscious. My eyes weren't open. I was barely living. One by one, my limbs were like actually falling apart, and they couldn't do anything for me.

Then, things got really worse. They had to take me to Kandy General Hospital. That's where the doctors really checked me and said, "This is not just diarrhea. There's something serious here, and we have to do something about it."

It was quite late, and I was unconscious at the time that I came to Kandy Hospital. So my father went out and knocked in the doctors' [living] quarters and woke them up, pleading, "We need to do something about this." He got a couple of doctors to come and see me. The doctors actually gave up on me, saying, "We can't do anything about this."

But my father went and talked to another doctor and said that he would like them to try something, anything. So they had another team check in on me. They found like one vein that was visible, and gave me intravenous medication, and then I was saved.

Until the last moment, they weren't sure if I would live. When the doctors actually found that one live vein that they could inject antibiotics, even more than my parents, I think the doctors were so happy! They were shouting and yelling. It was very chaotic in there. My parents didn't understand what the doctors were saying because they were speaking English, but they said that I was very lucky.

So you see, this is the reason why my parents are also quite worried about me and what causes them to fret all the time.

Even to this day, I have a really sensitive stomach. If I don't drink purified water, I get sick. So we have to be very careful with the fountain water.

I never even had plain tea—normal tea—until I went to university to study. That's when I actually had tea and knew the taste of what tea is. Previously, there were really hard times at home when everybody was drinking tea [and I couldn't have any]; but because they wanted to take care of me, so they had to seek a stash of milk powder for me.

Milk is expensive compared to tea! But my mother would say to the other family members, "She's a sick person, so let us give the milk to the daughter." She would come and tell me, "You just hide this. No one knows about it. You just have it. Hide it for yourself and have it."

I have to emphasize this point, because it shows how much I was being spoiled. [Laughs.]

Today, when I was coming out of the house, my father was crying. My father has been crying since this morning because I'm leaving, going to Colombo right after this meeting, going back to work after two days of holiday. My father told my mother, "You are lucky because you have the chance to actually go in the bus [with her]." He doesn't have that opportunity.

I EARNED MY DEGREE IN ARCHITECTURE, WITH A HANDS-ON INTERNSHIP

I attended the Department of Architecture at the University of Moratuwa. I have been affiliated with Educate Lanka for four years. I joined Educate Lanka in the second year of university. When I was in my third year at university I did my in-course training for six months at the same place where I am working right now. It's like a mandatory internship. It's called "in-plant training" so we could get to understand about marketing and production, the final production.

THEY DIDN'T BELIEVE I COULD DO MY FINAL PROJECT, BECAUSE I'M A GIRL

For my final-year project, I wanted to do a project with throw-away parts, like discarded car parts. When I was about to submit this idea to my department, it was not welcomed because people said, "It's about cars, and what do you know about cars? You haven't actually been in a car. You don't know what the spare parts are, and you haven't even probably ridden in a car as a guy would do, and why would you want to do this?"

I was designing a lobby area for an upscale [auto] service station. So I wanted to do the lobby using spare parts, using them creatively. So because of that, I actually went to the Bosch Service Station.

Bernard Gomez[4] is an architect, like a really famous one in Sri Lanka. He had done the building for this service station. So I met him and consulted with him. Then I went to the service station and checked how things worked: I saw where the drivers sleep and where the cars go, and I looked at spare parts. I was going in and getting under the cars and actually trying to understand all that. Because they said that cars are a man's thing and not a woman's thing.

I wanted to bring out the *womanness* of a car and bring that out into the lobby. It was a six-month project. I had to spend a lot of my own money for the final production. I had to purchase some stuff to show this. I did finish the project.

This was for the Bosch Company. The people who judged my project were foreign examiners. There was one Australian, one Indian, and one German. These three panelists who came for the final-year project were mocking me and saying, "More than your product, we actually like your eyes and your beautiful smile."

---

4. Bernardgomezarchitects.com.

But they were really like happy to see this product. They said it was like a white person's. The term we use is "soap dust," which means "white" or "whiter." That's a compliment to us but it would actually be quite derogatory for a white person.

THEN THE FIRM HIRED ME, AND EVEN MORE WOMEN, TOO

After I graduated, I was hired at the company where I did my in-course training. The chairman of the company actually liked the way I worked. Initially, the company didn't like to hire women, because there's a lot of machinery to be working with in the furniture manufacturing industry. There's a lot of hard work and solid work and maybe traveling. So they didn't like it [for women].

But there was an interview where two males and two females reviewed me, and based on my internship, they actually changed their perception of what women could do in this field, because of the way I worked. They thought that females could be adding something to this field because they would be double-checking safety and paying attention to detail.

When I first joined the company, of that five-member designing team, there were no women there, but now there are several women among the new trainees. So now three out of five in my staff are women. In the plant, where the manufacturing is done, sanding and painting and carving, there are women working there, because their work is neat. Also, the sales team is now predominantly women, because they know how to use their mouths to get the sales.

I MAKE MORE MONEY THAN MY PARENTS, AND I SEND HOME HALF

My basic salary is 30,000 rupees [$208/month], but I'm still in training. From the 30,000, I send home 15,000. I earn more money than my father, and I chip in. My mother and father do not ask for any more, because they think I'm a beautiful girl who should be wearing beautiful clothes and be beautiful. I also pay the boarding house 5,000 rupees [about $35/month], and there are also class fees, tuition fees, and training. I manage to pay all my expenses from my own salary. And, I still take classes in English.

Unlike with common jobs, there's no particular protocol for saying that right after training, *this* is the amount that you're going to get. These are huge private companies. So based on our interest, our performances, and our commitment in terms of time, like how long I'm going to stay with this organization or whatever else, the salary could be open to discussion.

I DON'T FEEL DISCRIMINATION IN THE WORKPLACE

I have a friendly relationship with the male coworkers because it's more like family than [corporate] peers. It's like I'm the youngest among them, so they treat me always like *nangi, nangi*: That means "little sister." You say that in this country, in Sri Lankan culture, when the person is close to you. That's the relationship we have.

I am also pleasant and very friendly with everybody else. I would share anything that I would get with the whole office. So, we have a very friendly relationship.

I don't feel discrimination in the workplace. Let me use the example of Educate Lanka. Every student who's at a certain age group gets the same amount of financial support without any differences between the gender, ethnicity, age, knowledge, or qualifications. The Sri Lankan culture is also like that.

It has more to do with, if you speak good English or don't speak good English. If somebody fails, it's the nature of the Sri Lankan people to actually carry that person along and go together, rather than just leaving this person behind. So that could be why there's no difference that I see in terms of treatment.

It could be this thing about Sri Lankan culture, why the coworkers are not treating me ill, or any differently, based on my gender—because Sri Lankans don't want to discriminate or be discriminated against in any way.

A DAY IN THE LIFE OF AN INTERIOR DESIGNER

Usually I wake up at 6:00 a.m. I take a half-hour train ride to work. I get to the office at about 8:00 a.m., and I work from 8:00 a.m. to 6:00 p.m.

Meals are actually a problem because of my sickness. I can't eat a lot of outside food. But since I am used to eating from the university canteen [cafeteria], I get my breakfast from there.

When I go to work, that's in Colombo, I don't have a proper lunch. I have some biscuits or some snacks, and then when I go back to Moratuwa, I eat at the university canteen, where I'm more comfortable. I do that for health reasons and also because it's much pricier to eat in Colombo. I have to send some money home, and it's quite hard for me to afford some meals in Colombo.

As an interior designer, I make design concepts and new furniture. I work with lighting, flooring, color combinations, wall colors, tile colors, and all things according to customers' requirements. I work on both new homes and renovation projects like offices, hospitals, and hotels.

I prefer to work on domestic interiors, but there were a couple of other projects that I really liked, too. I did some work at the Presidential Secretariat's office (that's in the Old Parliament Building) and some of the houses of ministers.

I also worked on a restaurant in Rajagiriya that I really liked. It's a pub, but it has a reception area where you could host functions. And there's also the baby area for the kids, too, like a playpen. The client wanted the nature effect. So I thought I should bring in a lot of timber colors. I changed the colors, and I showed all of the concepts that I had in mind in 3DS MAX [a computer program that makes models and animations] to show how the lighting would work in the reception hall, and how it would work in the pub area, and to see if that would reflect what they needed.

THE DESIGN PROCESS ENTAILS BOTH SKETCHING AND ONLINE RENDERING

I do all of the designing in AutoCAD [a software program for designing in two or three dimensions]. When I have to do rendering, I use 3DMAX, because the customer pays quite a bit of money so for the final product, they [our firm] want to show the customers what they are really going to get. And if they want to do any adjustments, say that the armrest is not good, or the colors in the pub area are not good, then they could change it and redo it right there in the program.

I'm self-taught in this software. In the university, there was a program that teaches about this software, but it was in the last year of courses [too late]. When I was in my third year at my internship course at this company, I saw the people who were working there using the software. So I came home and asked to borrow a friend's laptop and installed the software and actually tried to learn what I saw in the office. I did the training at the same place where I actually work right now.

My favorite project was the lobby area of the Ida Denna[5] TV show, which is our at our national television headquarters. It was a minimalist theme, what they wanted, in black and red, and they had already designed the reception counter. So I had to design everything based on that reception counter. But it was easy because it was minimalist. It was straight lines and cubes, and I tried to match it with the other areas where they used white carpets.

It was difficult in that I had to stick to what I had to do more than inspiration or what I would *like* to do. I had to look into the logo and the colors already there, and also there were big columns inside the building architecture. And also the lines, they were like straight lines in the buildings. So if I went with curved furniture or curved interior, that would not suit well because it would be messy for the eyes, and the contrast would not be suitable for viewing. So I had to look into all of this when I worked on this project.

WHERE I GET MY INSPIRATION FROM: THE PAST

Going back to the inspiration: It's easy for a designer to come to a place and show their creativity, to show their knowledge or what not by just suggesting randomly looking at the space there.

But if you were to do a really good job, you have to look into the history of the building. If I were using this place [the hotel] as an example, I'd have to see who has been living here, why the previous people had ordered this kind of furniture and not something else. I'd begin at the history and the context and also work the sketch up to the 3-D level with different perspectives and looking at it. That's how I would arrive at my final plan.

BIG MISTAKES I'VE MADE ALONG THE WAY

I have made mistakes. Given the nature of the work, even a small word, one word, can make a huge difference. For example, I gave an order for the manufacturers of the company for a particular plan, saying that they needed a wardrobe, whatever, but I forgot to put in the one [crucial] word, "fix onsite" [assemble onsite], so that it wouldn't arrive assembled. They wouldn't have been able to use the finished product. Apparently this was for the fifth floor, and you can't carry the huge thing up there. So it was like a

---

5. *Ida Denna* is a popular Sri Lankan teledrama produced by the government: rupavahini.lk/sinhala-teledrama/ida-denna.html.

huge mistake, that one. There've been small mistakes, too.

I have done that two times. The other time was for an apartment complex, I think. The lift in the apartment complex was small, and I didn't order it to be assembled onsite.

When I do mistakes like that, the product gets returned to the company, and the company must refund the client because it's our fault, the company's fault. In that case, there's an inquiry. What I would do when that happens is just go to the chairman directly. I would go in and specifically say, "This is my mistake. This is the reason that I did that mistake. I didn't notice it," and I would elaborate my side of the story.

The chairman would always say in Sinhalese, "Just don't come to me after making a mistake and tell me about the problem with a tearful eye, because I can't scold you." [Laughs.]

MY FUTURE: HOUSEWIFE OR SUCCESSFUL DESIGNER?

Actually, I would like to become a successful designer in my field. I want to help my family, and I want to help my younger brother to complete his degree. I graduated with honors as an upper-second in my class, but I only lost being the first in class by two points. I really want a master's degree.

Saving money has always been a habit. So even when I was getting the Educate Lanka scholarship I was managing it in a way that I could stretch it as much as possible. I asked my father's help to get my bachelor's degree without any financial support from outside sources. I can't do that for my master's or wherever I go from here. So I save 5000 rupees [about $35] every month. But then again, there are other things that I have to look into, like my brother's education. There is spending as well, but I am definitely saving, and I'm committed to doing that.

I haven't yet traveled outside of Sri Lanka. I would like to go to Canada because that's where my teacher studied and did his master's. And even he has said, "If you go to Canada, I can help you out." So that's why I would like to go to Canada.

I would like to study overseas, but I need to go for my English first, and complete my master's or PhD in my university.

MY SECRET SWEETHEART COULD BE THE PATH I CHOOSE

My boyfriend is from Peradeniya, the University of Peradeniya. That is in Kandy. I had no romantic relationships when I was still in school—absolutely none. Even when I met this person, in the final year of university life, the funny thing is, I didn't actually tell it to my "house"—by house, I mean, my *father*. My mother knows, but she hasn't told my father. I want to be a little bit stronger in my life so I can actually take it [the news of the relationship] to my father.

I don't know why I like him. I don't have answers for these kinds of questions. But then again, we're just in the talking terms of the relationship. Maybe I just don't know yet.

He's just a good person. My mom says there are a lot of bad people in Sri Lanka and that, "We just can't let a pretty girl like this get into the wrong hands."

My mom knows him. They have met each other more than once or twice. Whenever

I see him, I always go with my mom. He talks very nicely with my mother.—But then again, I can't commit to something beyond that at this point.

I will get married someday. According to the ways of Sri Lanka, we have to do it. I need to get married by the time I'm around twenty-seven years old [next year]; but then again, there's so much for me to complete. This was the reason why I didn't want to commit to a boyfriend when I was in schooling or even when I was in the university.

I still have a lot to learn. I want to finish learning. I want to build as much as I can by learning and doing everything before I get married. After I'm married, I don't want to learn or study. I don't want to actually work or build my career. I want to be like my mother, looking after the children, and bringing someone else up, rather than focusing on my own career.

I CONSIDER MYSELF A REALLY LUCKY PERSON

I consider myself a really lucky person from the beginning, from when I was four years old, that accident or that mishap that I escaped and survived.

Going on from that, I was not born into a rich family, but I have rich parents. My parents are rich in *qualities*. They're wonderful parents, loving parents who take care of each other. So that was a blessing.

Starting from there, and then going to a village school and being able to get past my O level exams and actually go to a different school after O levels; then to finish up the A levels the first time, and get selected to the University of Moratuwa, and to get into this good program and have the support of the university, the people doing the program, the administration, and finding Educate Lanka Foundation, and being able to get their support and guidance, and then get a job right after university . . .

That is all quite rare, and I was so lucky I got the job right after university as a trainee.

And even today I was quite scared about the [book] interview, but then again, it turned out that Dhanu was there to translate, and I wasn't sure that he was going to be there, but then I got to meet you, and all of that. So I feel that I am really, really lucky.

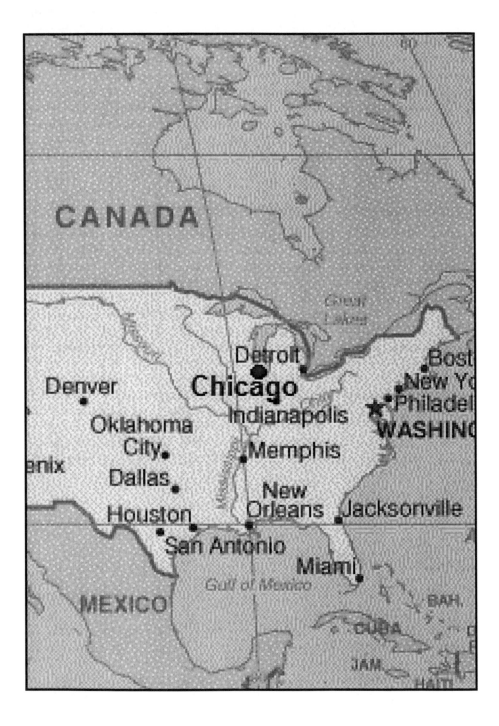

DARIUS

HIP-HOP ARTIST

CHICAGO, ILLINOIS, U.S.

Editor's note: Growing up in what's been dubbed "the murder capital of the U.S."—Chicago's South Side—Darius deftly sidestepped both gangs and jail; he dabbled in and then discarded drugs. While other young-adult Americans see the bleak legacy left to them of a crumbling economy, accelerated global warming, persistent racism and inequality, political parody and governmental paralysis, Darius Clark remains stubbornly optimistic about his life, his country, and his world. He credits his amazing mother and grandma—yet lots of other young guys in his restorative-justice program[1] come from loving families, too, but don't end up with his positive attitude.

I met Darius the first time I visited PBMR or "The Center," our nonprofit

---

1. Restorative justice is a system of criminal justice that focuses on the rehabilitation of offenders through reconciliation with victims and their community. Darius has not been convicted or served time, but he spent much of his youth at "The Center" (PBMR) in his neighborhood that offers restorative justice programs as well as educational, job-skills, counseling, and family support. See: pbmr.org.

organization's partner[2] whose tiny staff of heroes strive to keep youth off the streets and out of jail simply by offering them choices: alternative schooling, academic tutoring, peer and adult counseling, family support, sports and conditioning, art and music, and theatre. Perhaps The Center's most vital service, according to members I've interviewed, is the bountiful free meals they share anytime a kid and/or his family shows up—along with kinship of peers and adults who sincerely care over time, and a place to be safe, away from the lure of gangs and the range of stray bullets.

Getting to know The Center's members, I've been struck by their open hearts. Not what I expected. Perhaps the peace circles[3] held at The Center every week, during which members share their experiences of violence, prejudice, trauma, and dreams, have made the difference. While the city right outside their doors wages wars over drugs and girls and turfs, inside The Center, a kid can be exactly and all of who he is. And with Darius, that's a lot.

There's something almost mystical about Darius. He is at once profoundly humble, a tall, rail-thin dude who blushes easily and would never hold himself superior to any other human being; yet he's also supremely confident in his ability to manifest his dreams.

He will top the hip-hop[4] charts, not just in Chicago, but in the nation; and it will be soon. He will become a "trillionaire" and buy a Lamborghini and an oceanfront home in Hollywood. However, his plans for wealth and fame far surpass any material luxury you might imagine. Darius got out of "gangland"[5] while remaining 100 percent loyal to his friends and family; he smiles his way through the aisles of his day-job at Target to pay his grandma's rent; he mentors younger musicians; and he composes music in the predawn hush of 4a.m. He's resilient, brilliant, and somehow, strikingly innocent.

YOU'LL ALWAYS HAVE SOME HATERS: THEY'RE ALSO YOUR MOTIVATORS

My name Darius Clark. You can use my name. It don't matter to me. This is real, what I'm speaking.

I'm twenty-four. I was born on July 7, 1992.

It's been a blessing to do hip hop and R&B [rhythm and blues]. I'm also working at Target right now. I'm a team leader and a team trainer now.

[Shakes his head and laughs a little.] Yeah, I'm amazing. Yeah, I'm definitely going to make it—everybody say that. Talking about my music, I don't say nothing. I just tell

---

2. SFF (skees.org) has provided general operating support as well as funding of youth leadership, tutoring, and job-skills training programs at PBMR.

3. Peace circles, a core component of restorative justice, originate from a Native American tradition of passing a "talking stick" and taking turns expressing experiences from trauma to healing; for example, from victim to perpetrator, youth to family, or opposing gang members.

4. Check out Darius's music on MTV: mtv.com/artists/darius-clark.

5. Nickname for Chicago. Learn more about Chicago gangs at: chicagogangs.org.

them, "Thank you all. Thank you all. If you don't like it, somebody else is going to like it. I don't care what you all say. I'm just doing this, what I love doing," and that's what I've learned is the key.

People will hate you; but without haters, there ain't going to be motivators. That's why I'm motivated from my haters. [Laughs.]

I feel completely different than the last time you saw me. I'm much more mature now. I've grown more wiser now. I know stuff. It's been a long time. I just thank God that I'm still here, doing what I love to do. It has been a blessing for me.

RIGHT NOW, I'M LIVING WITH MY GRANDMA

Right now, I live with my grandma on the South Side of Chicago. Her name is Riola Cross, and she's like sixty-five years old. My mom's got her own place, too, but she lives far away. I'm just in my grandma's house because she lives closer to my work. She lives close to the rail line, and she can just drop me off for work, and when I come back, she comes to get me. I got my job at Target, like a year ago. I'm just thankful I got that. That's still going well.

My grandma don't work. No, she just helps me as a kind of mama. She's always moving around and staying active. What she loves to do, she loves to go to the casino. She loves, she *loves* that.

I think she be on that Social Security stuff, but we pay some of her bills. So she gets money, you know, from the state, and then she paying her bills out, too, and then we helping out, too.

MY FAMILY: MY MUSIC

I'm also a hip-hop, R&B musician. To me, my music is my real job.

I'm married to my music. I'm single with no kids. And it's like, if you do try to get into a relationship, it's really hard because they don't understand. Like, you tell them what you've got to do, but they still want to spend time with you, but you can't because you've got to fulfill your dream.

And that's why I end up being single all the time. I know that sucks, but this is more important. This is what I always wanted to do ever since I was a little kid. So this has always been my dream. I've wanted to be a musician ever since I was twelve.

GROWING UP IN CHICAGO WITHOUT A DADDY

I grew up in the house where I live now—my grandma's house. My oldest brother, Deyonce, my sister, Yasmin, and my little cousins, all grew up in the same household.

And my best friend, John Jones, he grew up right next-door. He comes to The Center too, so look for him here. Me and him been through the thick and the thin, been through it all, fights, everything, uh huh. I grew up with my brothers, sisters, cousins, nieces, man, aunties, and grandmas—like a whole big family grew up together.

My parents are still married, but they're separated.

I have a brother and sister on my mama's side. And on my daddy's side, there's a bunch of us. Yeah. My youngest brother, I think he's nineteen now. And then my oldest brother, he's like twenty-nine.

When I was a child, my father was in the Navy. He was in the military for a long time, I think. Basically, what I know is that him and my mom was married. And at the time I was a kid, I think he was in the Gulf War or something, whatever war they had then; and he couldn't see me. So he was gone for like a few years, I think.

And then when he came back, I saw my father when I was around like five. I don't know for sure. My mom said I saw him then. But, you know, they got back with each other. I think it wasn't working out, and they separated, but they still talk off and on. I don't really know much about him. He's just doing his thing.

MY MOM IS A SOUL-SURVIVOR, AN ANGEL

My mom's name is Brenda Clark, and she's forty-four. Oh, man, she's powerful, strong, independent; a soul survivor, an angel.

I love her so much. She did everything for me and my brothers. She did *everything*. There were no handouts being granted to her. I think my mom went to college, but I don't really remember, like she don't talk about her college life, but I know she did go to school.

It's hard trying to be a single parent, but she did it, you know. She did it. She works at FedEx. She's a team leader. She's been there for ten years now, her and her sister, my auntie. They both got hired at the same time. So they're both like team leaders now. My mom's got her own office and everything. She's a big shot, as they call it. [Laughs.]

Yeah, so, she moved out of the neighborhood. The next position, she's going to move up north. So, if I don't have my own place by then, I'll just be at her place with her until I get my stuff together and fulfill my dream. Then I can do everything else.

When I do become somebody, I'll make sure she'll be all right. I'll make sure of that, for a fact. My mom has been struggling. That's the hardest thing. She's just been struggling, trying to take care of my brothers and sisters and all of us.

That's why I want to do music, so I can take care of her and my brothers and sisters, and make sure they be all right. I want to make sure nobody have to struggle or nothing like this again. That's always been my dream, to help out, because she's been there through thick and thin.

If I make bad songs, she's always going to play my songs and support me, no matter what. She's always there to support me 100 percent. Like I say, she's just an angel. I'm just happy that I have her.

All my other friends, they don't got no mothers or dads, or they don't got both, and they look up to me like, "Darius, how is it to have a mother?" and I'm like, "It's just a blessing. Your mother, she's a blessing, too, even though she's passed. She's still watching over you. She wants you to do better and keep out of the streets."

MY FAMILY WAS DIFFERENT FROM OTHER FAMILIES

Basically my family, compared to other families, it was kind of different, you know? My mom had a job, and my grandma was cooking for people in the neighborhood, giving out food to people who need it, basically being like a grandma to everybody in the neighborhood. She was giving out food for free.

Everybody respected her. She was helping them out, like some of the gangbangers[6] in the neighborhood, they'd be hungry. So she'd make food for them, or I'd go out there and give them food.

So we'd have a cookout, feeding kids and the youth. They'd basically have a big block party. They'd have jumping jacks for the little kids and races...You'd win and get your money. That's how they helped out the kids. If everybody was going to school, they'd give them stuff for school, like school supplies, erasers, books, everything you need.

THE CENTER IS LIKE FATHER KELLY'S BIG-BRAND COMPANY

That's when Father [Dave] Kelly started coming along, and that's when people started going to The Center. The Center has become the heart of this area. You get everything you need. You want to come up there and study; you need some advice; you need somebody to talk to. It's like a big brand. It's like his own company. [Laughs.]

To me, I have a lot of role models. Father Kelly and Father Denny are my role models. They've been with me since I was ten, eleven years old. My friends started telling me, "You'd better go to The Center. They're giving out food." So I went there. I started getting into these programs, and then I was painting murals, all around the city. It's just been a blessing to me.

Father Kelly and Father Denny really are angels. They always help out people. If somebody has been incarcerated or something, they let them come here and do their service hours here. Father Kelly gets them jobs, like in the summertime, they'll be working in the garden or painting murals, or they'll be doing arts like painting, you know, putting some money in your pocket. Just being around The Center is good: cooking, cleaning up, just helping them out with jobs, because so many people, young people have been felons. They got locked up.

If somebody gets locked up for some nonsense stuff, Father Kelly and Father Denny, they help you out. They get you out. So that's why I said they're angels, and I'm just so blessed that they're in our neighborhood.

Father Kelly and Father Denny, they could be in a rich neighborhood, if they wanted to, but they just choose to be in our neighborhood because they know that it's real, and they know that we're struggling. They know that we need jobs. Some of them have been incarcerated. So, none of them can get jobs. If somebody needs stuff for school, we've got computers and stuff here, and you can learn. You can just soak it in like a sponge. This is like another home. This is a safe place, a real safe zone.

Before everything got hectic [in my neighborhood], the safest place was at Sherman Park, but it's like a 50-50 chance there now. It's scary to go up there now.

Other gangs come to The Center, too, but the one thing about The Center is that we all respect each other and respect Father Kelly. Nothing is going to happen. Outside is a different story, but in The Center, everybody is family. That's how it is.

---

6. My young friends at The Center have taught me that on the South Side, you have to be a gang member. You're only a gangbanger if you commit crimes and fight.

THE GUYS I GREW UP WITH—I'VE LOST A LOT OF THEM

I grew up with the people at The Center: Lamont, Jonathan. Man, we all grew up in the same neighborhood. We was all little kids together.

When I was a little kid, I was all the time outside playing on the block with my friends. We were having the time of our life, block parties. We had food fights. I think that was the most funnest time in my life, being a little kid. You don't got to pay no bills. You were just running around free. We used to go to the same grammar school. It was crazy how we started.

We all started off doing different things. Some people always wanted to be in the NBA. Everybody wanted to be the best basketball player, and we'd go against each other, like playing for a dollar. Whoever would win would get the money, but the good thing about it, we still share with each other. That was when all my friends were alive.

I've lost a lot of friends I know over violence, mistaken identity, crazy stuff. Gang stuff. They were not gangbangers, but it was like they was in the neighborhood, in the area, and people thought they was gang members. They'd come to The Center, too. So there I was, seeing them, and then someone would say, "They just killed him."

I would say, "That's crazy. I just saw him like a day ago."

And then, another person passed a month later. He was a mentor of the whole neighborhood, helping out with basketball tournaments, and he died, too. He got shot, too, and died, over some crazy stuff. I think it was mistaken identity.

Everybody was hurt. I was like, "Man, it's crazy." You think about like what my grandma say, "You never know when your time is up." All you can do is just do good and do what you're supposed to do. That's how it is.

MY FRIENDS AND FAMILY ARE IN OPPOSING GANGS

I have never been in a gang. But I've got a lot of family and friends in gangs, and some of our families are in the opposite gangs and are fighting the other gangs. It's crazy, like this is *real*.

This is real tough. I've got one side of my family like is GDs [Gangster Disciples] and the other side of my family is like Stones [Black P. Stone Nation], and they interact with each other. That's basically how it is. Like all my cousins and siblings are on the opposite sides of gangs.

We've had a big family event, like a reunion or something like that, and they all respect each other because it's a family thing. They're like, "Okay, we're family."—they *know*, the gangs intuit each other, but still they just respect one another.

The crazy thing about it, even though I'm not in a gang, they probably think like, "Oh, he with them" and then the other side, "Oh, he with us."

I've never been in jail. That's a blessing.

I HAVE A PROTECTIVE SHIELD AROUND ME—I DON'T KNOW WHY

And then my friend told me, "Every time something happens, you're never around. Have you noticed that?"

I'm like, "Wow." I didn't even know.

This friend, her name's Morgan. She's a Christian and also a psychic reader. I used to work with her, but she got transferred to another Target.

She was saying that I'm going to be a musician. She said I'm going to have kids, everything. She said that I'm a motivational speaker. People look up to me. People love me, and people just want to be around me because I make them feel good, and so I've got to give back. I was like, "Man. That's crazy." She told me the reason why is that I'm blessed. She said that God favored me.

I said, "Why me, out of everybody in my family and out of everybody just good?"

She said, "There ain't no reason. God just picked you, handpicked you. He favored you because he know that, before you were born, it was something that was in you."

I was like, "But what is it?"

She's like, "I don't know, but you know."

I was like, "I don't know it, either."

She said, "Have you ever realized that every time your family's being jumped, somebody gets hurt or in a fight, you're never around. Does that start making sense?"

It's true. Anytime something bad happened, like somebody was getting killed or somebody was getting shot, around the block or somewhere on the block, I'm never around. Or I just got in the house or I just made it two seconds later or something, dodged it, or watched over me.

I started thinking, maybe she's right. And I started believing it, and now I believe that's what it is. She said God got a shield over me and he's protecting me. And that makes sense.

She said, "He wants you. He knows you're going to do it, be successful. That's why he's protecting you."

I was like, "Man, this makes absolute sense." I was so happy.

GANGBANGERS TAUGHT ME WHAT'S WRONG AND RIGHT

Because I really didn't have a father, I had to teach my own self how to become a male. I watched the people on the streets. Dangerous people.

The gangbangers taught me what's wrong from right. They would tell me like, "No, you don't want to follow in our footsteps. You see how we is? We've got to survive. You see us out here selling drugs," like they don't want me to be doing that. They told me to stay in school, to keep following my dream. They told me I got the talent. They always tell me to keep doing what I love to do and just keep being respectful.

What I learned about how to become a man, it's basically like looking at their footsteps. They say, "Go to school. Better yourself and move out of the neighborhood," or they say, "Follow your dream. Come out of the neighborhood and make it better," you know, something like that.

They're saying, whatever I want to do, just don't forget where you come from.

IF YOU GET OUT, THEN YOU HAVE TO GIVE BACK

I came from nothing, and that's been my dream to help out my community, just like The Center.

I want to give back to the community, just like Derrick Rose. He was in the Englewood area, the NBA player, Derrick Rose. He made big fame. He helped out the neighborhood. He put the money back in, helping out the schools, taking care of people. I want to be like that, a role model, so the [young] people in The Center would look up to me.

Things started changing when I started getting older, like they say a "reality check." So when I started getting like sixteen, seventeen, that's when I started looking at things differently: "Okay, things are starting to get real. I've got to find something to do. I've got to get a job."

I just thank God I didn't have no children and thank God I still don't. I thank him for that.

I started realizing, okay, I know wrong from right. I know if I do this, I'm going to jail. If I do this a certain way, I've got to watch out and make sure I'm nowhere outside. I come to The Center, work, work, work, go back home. And then if I do go out in the car with my friends, we just go to the mall, get some clothes, have fun, and go out and just enjoy ourselves or go to the beach or somewhere.

MY SCHOOLING IS NOT DONE YET

I went to Richards Career Academy for high school. When I was in high school, I worked here at The Center. Father Kelly let us work so we could pay off our school fees. Our school fee was like almost $1,000. So we worked for Father Kelly, and I had like $500 saved up, and my mom paid the rest, for everything, my graduation, my lunches, my school fees. She said she had been saving.

In high school, the classes I was good at were journalism, writing, and reading. I love to write, and that's why I think I'm good at it.

I was not good at math. But my math teacher, I'll never forget this—I struggled so hard. The classwork was easy; it's just that I'm a bad tester. When test time came, I'd always fail. I failed it over and over again, and I told my teacher, "But I'm doing all the class work." I think I was going to get held back, but she told me, "Darius, stay after school. I'll teach you one-on-one," and she taught me what to do, and I passed! I passed my math test with a C+.

But I wanted to make it better. I wanted to get a B or an A. She told me to just stay and help out, cleaning in the classroom, and then she bumped my grade up to a B because I was one or two points away from getting a B.

That was what I really wanted. I don't like Cs. A "C" means you're just "seeing" your way through. That's what it is. I wanted to be "B." I wanted to be "better." And an "A," you "achieve" greatness, you know, something like that. [Smiles.]

MY GREAT-GRANDMA PASSED AWAY A WEEK BEFORE MY GRADUATION

One of the hardest times I've been through is when my great-grandma passed away a week before I graduated out of high school. That was devastating. I was going to make her happy, and then she passed away.

And then my mama say, "She knows. She knows you did good. Don't worry about it. She's watching over you. She knows you graduated." Actually, out of all of my brothers and sisters, I was the first kid to graduate out of high school, like that was my dream, to be the first one to graduate out of high school. And then my sister followed in my footsteps. And then my brother got his GED.

After I graduated from high school, Father Kelly helped me go to college. I went to a community college, Kennedy-King College. So I did a semester, to see how I liked it or not. I didn't want to go to university at first. I liked community college. I basically went for graphic design, and I'm always going to go back. Father Kelly told me, "If you want to go back there, just let me know, and we can put you back in there."

FROM GRAPHIC DESIGN CLASSES TO MY FIRST REAL JOB, AT TARGET

After I did college, I was on the website looking for jobs, and then my godbrother, he told me, "You know, Target, they're hiring." So I just signed up for it, and then they called me like a day later, and I went for my interview, and they told me, "You're hired." I was like, "Dang! This easy?"

He was like, "There's something about you" that got me hired. They said I was different. They said I was "the three Fs." The "three Fs" means fun, fast, and friendly. They said they liked me.

And people in the store, they were walking up to me, and I would like it. I could make everybody feel loved. I like making people feel good. They're feeling down, and I make them feel good, lifting them up. That's always been me. I think that's one of my gifts.

The Target is on Peterson. It's by the cemetery, right on the side of it. I started there last summer, like in June, I think. I was a cart attendant, moving the carts around the store and stuff. Then I learned guest service. I know cashier; I know sales flow. I can do everything in the store, and I'm still learning every day.

Based on my next position, I'll be like a manager. That's what they're saying, "We see you doing that." I made a name for myself, and I'm a team trainer. I train the new people that come in, doing the carts. Or if they need cashier stuff, I'll train them in cashier, too.

I LIKE WORKING AT TARGET: EVERYBODY RESPECTS EACH OTHER

I like working at Target. It's a lot of young people. Uh huh. [Laughs.] Some are students, some fresh out of college. They're like the big bosses, but they're still young.

There's one older man. He's been there since like twenty years, and in his picture

[I.D.], he's got black hair. Now his whole head is grey; it's crazy. I think he's probably like sixty. But he's an overnight team member. Everybody shows him respect because he knows everything.

Everybody gets along and respects and loves each other. Everybody motivates everybody. If somebody is feeling down or they need a day to switch—there's a lot of people in there that go to school and college, and they'll be switching days with each other. So we're helping each other out with hours. If I need somebody to help me out, they'd come help me out because I'd do the same thing for them.

I used to have issues with some of the supervisors. But now, you know, I'm used to it. They was trying to make you do everything, boss you around, but after you start making a name for yourself, and people start giving you recognition and giving you shout-outs, they start respecting you more, "Okay, you're a good worker."

They start showing you the most respect, and then you feel good. So that's how it works, how to make a name for myself and show people that I really know how to work, that I'm a good team member and help out guests. That's our first priority, helping out our guests first. And that's what I do. They be like, "Man, we like him." [Laughs.]

MY SCHEDULE, SALARY, AND BENEFITS

I do the daytimes. The overnight people come in around twelve, and they end at around six or seven. Then the morning people come in around eight, and the rest of the day is like that. The store closes at night, but then the overnight people come in and do everything, get the store ready to open again. They're restocking everything and cleaning. After that, the day shift and the customers come in.

Basically I work 9 to 5 four, five days a week. But I work overtime all the time. When I started, my salary was $8.75. Then it went up to $10.00. It's across all the state of Illinois. It's a lot of employees, working there. I don't really know for sure how many, but there's people getting hired every day. It's a big place.

I just got the benefit packet a week or two ago. I've gathered over a thousand hours now. I'm like, "Dang, already!" It's like healthcare and all that, but I've got healthcare already through my mom at FedEx. I also get a 5 or 10 percent discount at the store. You get a little thing called cartwheels. You get an extra discount, and you start getting more and more. Everything starts dropping prices.

I've bought a PS4 and the games that came with it. I bought some jewelry for a friend. I bought candy. And junk food. My weakness is Hot Cheetos. I like them, man. I love hot chips, for some reason. I eat a lot, but I'm still so skinny. My metabolism is like really high. And I'm always on the move.

It's a natural high for me: I'm always hyped up, energized. I'm always like this. If I can get a few hours' sleep, I'm still energized. I don't know how. It's just like that. I used to get tired, but now I don't no more. I don't take nothing [no drugs].

NO TV OR TV NEWS FOR ME

I used to watch the news, but I don't no more, because every time I watch the news, there's always somebody down, somebody getting killed, a shooting, people getting raped. Like they say, "If it bleeds, it leads," and that's what it do. I don't watch the news at all, like I know what's going on. I'm a self-taught person. I know, every time the news comes on, people getting crazy.

Now I'm just a YouTuber and Internet, Google person, and what else, and a gamer and a musician. When I used to watch TV, it was like brainwashing: I'm watching every single day, not doing what I need to be doing. I was trapped. My mind was stuck. When I broke out of that habit, like three years ago, then I started doing what I'm doing now.

TAKING CARE OF MY FAMILY

I'm working right now to help out people in my family, to help out my grandma. I'm not doing the college thing: College is going to be in the future. I see myself always going back to college, like, you know, educating myself, bettering myself. But I probably won't go back for like three or four years.

If I was in college, my family would be struggling and needing some help, and then I'm not around. So nothing would be happening, the lights would get cut off, the bills get cut off. I have to help out my mom because she needed the money to get her place. So I give her a few hundred dollars.

But I'm also saving my money. So far, I got a nice little amount in the bank. My plan for it is to get my own place. I want to live up north, like North Avenue, somewhere closer to my job.

I always like being an independent person. I don't want anybody to give me handouts. I want to earn it. I like to work for it, and then I'm like, "Man, this is what I've accomplished," and then success feels really good. That's how I've always been since I was little. [Income from] my music's helping me out, too.

I STARTED WRITING SONGS AT AGE TWELVE

I started writing songs when I was twelve. I got a binder, and it's got all types of songs. I didn't even know I wrote so many songs. It was just ridiculous. I've put a lot of time and hours into this work. That's why I think it's all paying off now.

I wrote my first real song when I was fifteen. I'm not going to lie to you: When I was younger, I was so weak, I didn't know what to say. I was just saying random stuff, talking about shooting people and all types of crazy stuff.

Then I started getting older and I started reading. I started listening to other artists to better my skills. I was reading the dictionary. Eminem said he read the dictionary. That's why he's so talented. Everything he say is *crazy*. People don't know what he's saying because he's too lyrical. And then I started learning, and my skills are getting better and better.

When I was first starting out, I spent all day on music. Now I just write something real quick, and that's it. Now I could probably get a song done in a day. It used to take me like three, four days or five days to get a song done. Now, if I know it's going to be like a gold track, it's going to take a minute, but [otherwise] I can just get a song done as quick as possible, and it's a hit, and get out of the way, and next. Next song? Next song? Next song? Just like that.

It's channeled. It's like a wave is going through me. It took me a long time to learn that. It's a gift. Most people get writer's block. Like my other friends, other musicians like, "Man, I've got writer's block," I'm like, "Yeah, because you be thinking of something." I don't think. I just let the pen flow.

And then, when I go back over it, I proofread it. That's when I think. I've got to proofread it like three, four, five times to make sure everything is all right, make sure it's down pat, and then I put it out there to the world. They like it; or they don't like it. I still appreciate it because they're listening to us.

I can write at my home, just in my bed. I'll be up at like three, four in the morning, writing songs. When you're a musician, you never sleep, and that's true because I don't sleep no more. If I'm up, I'm writing a song. I just love music.

MUSIC IS MY WIFE, AND MY STORIES ARE OUR BABIES

Creativity is something you've got to find within yourself. That's why I think it took me a long time, and I finally found out what I was good at, and what I'm good at is making songs and making stories, and that's why I call them my stories and my babies.

Like Prince said, "These are my babies right here." You write down whatever you *want* to feel. That's why I say music is like my wife, because no matter how I'm feeling, no matter if I'm crying or sad, she's always going to be there. She's going to listen to me. When I write it down, she's going to agree with anything. Even though if it's bad, she's going to agree with it. She ain't going to argue. She ain't going to fight. She's going to support me 100 percent. That's why I say music is my wife, and we make a *lot* of babies. [Laughs.]

Every time when I write a song, I can see it like a vision. I see how the song gives life, and then I write it down. I think that's another gift. I can *see* it, and then I write it down. People like it because they know I'm talking about their situation. I can use somebody's situation that's been in the neighborhood and put it in the song, but I'm not just talking about them. I'm talking about the whole world.

I also use it [visioning] in other parts of my life. That moment I got that job at Target, the crazy thing about it, I was actually like seeing myself getting hired and what I'm now doing, and then when I went there, I got hired, and then I was doing it. I'm like, "Dang, this is coming true!" I'll be seeing myself every night, like a visionary, seeing myself doing better, and going up the ladder, and doing what I love to do. It's an amazing feeling. I'm going to say that comes from God, man. He blessed me.

GHOSTWRITING FOR PEOPLE WHO JUST CAN'T GET THEIR SONGS OUT

I also ghostwrite for other artists. They want to talk about shooting people. They want me to make a song for them because, you know, "I just can't talk about this."

I say, "Okay. What type of style do you want? What type of song do you want me to write? Like a party song or just a song about the struggle or something like that?"

Then I just write it down and give it them. Like I don't want to give it to them because these are my babies, and I'm writing, but still, they pay me. So I do it.

Every song is like a different type of story. I can make a song for the teens. They like smoking, so I'll make song for them about smoking. Or, I can make a song about how they grew up in their neighborhood, or about being a star, "I see myself in the starlight." I can make a song about how good I rap; crazy things. I'm universal now. I can make a song about anything.

It really depends on what type of beat it is, but you know, with an R&B beat, I can make a song for a girl. The way I do it is this: If you make a song for a woman, you basically write the song thinking that you made it for that one girl, but all the girls in the world think it's about them. That's how you do it.

The best part about music for me is that you can write down anything that's on your mind. I think this the right path for me to go. I see myself doing this for the rest of my life.

I'M WRITING FOR YOUNG PEOPLE, OLD CATS, EVERYBODY

I'm writing for everybody, like every single body, even people who have become older cats. I just get in with the young crowd, and really talk about the music, and then write for the older crowd and get the older fans, too. They'd be like, "Oh, this kid, he's got something on his shoulders."

I'm doing it level by level, little by little. The older I get, the more mature my music get.

I've made a lot of songs, hundreds of songs, but I didn't even release them yet. All my songs are a different style. Like my songs are happy, angry, or emotional. I've got lovemaking songs, club songs, weed songs, crazy songs. All types. It took a minute to learn the craft, and now I've learned it, and it's just real easy.

I'VE STARTED MAKING A NAME FOR MYSELF

During the time when I was at community college, I started making a name for myself in music. I started doing shows. People started noticing me. Now my fan base is crazy. I've got like over 40,000 followers on my Instagram. On my Twitter, I've got 26,000 followers, and on my Facebook, I've got over 2,000.

I've got thousands of fans now, and I'm getting paid for shows. My other cousin, he just got signed with a label, and I'm glad for him. He got *signed*. I guess I'm up next now. Hopefully, I'm supposed to get signed this summer. I want to get signed with Def Jam or G.O.O.D Music [Getting Out Our Dreams; Kanye West's label]. G.O.O.D is a record label like Def Jam; there are a lot of Chicago artists on it.

Def Jam is an international label—the label I see myself with. You know, like Warner Brothers or something like that, but I prefer Def Jam because Kanye West, he's with that record label. He's got his own record label in there.

So it's good music, and I fit, and I want to fit with him because he's produced Common, a great artist, and Big Sean, and other great artists. So I see myself with them.

Now I think I'm buzzing. *Buzzing* means that I'm trending. People are looking up to me, searching my name through Google and everything. And then my music's on Amazon now, and everything. It's been crazy.

You've got to create yourself. It took me a long time to get where I am at today. You don't just work it overnight. You've got to have the steps. At first, if you asked me, "Where's your music at?" I would say, "I don't got any." But now they ask me where my music's at, "Boom. Go here. You can download it here. Pay money. You've got to spend it here."

Now my music is on Amazon, Atoll, Spotify. I think it's on Pandora, too. I'm not sure. It's on a PlayStation thing, on Xbox, this song I made called, "My Bars Be Killin'."[7] It's basically talking about how good I rap, and people say I sound like Big Sean.And then there's another song I just released called, "Dat Loud," and that song is for the young crowd. It's a party song, you know, for people in the club who like to drink or smoke, dancing, or just having fun.

I'M NOT FAMOUS, BUT I'M SUPER CLOSE

People think I'm famous, but in my head, I'm not, yet. I'm super close. I've got my fan base, my music videos get 100,000 views and all type of crazy.

"Man, Darius, you're up next." That's what they say, and I really think so.

Now they're saying that fame is like a curse, and it's a death. You don't want to quit doing this because you've got people looking up to you. If you try to quit, they think you let them down. So basically like, "Oh, you let me down, we believed in you. You was *this close* to getting signed with a label." I don't want to quit because like I'm super close now. I've never been super close in my life.

It's too late now, so I might as well keep going.

MAKING IT TAKES PATIENCE, AND I'M GLAD IT'S HAPPENING SLOW

Patience is the key, and it's just a matter of time for everything to happen. And I'm glad that it's happening slow. When you do make it, you appreciate it more. I'm happy that it didn't happen when I was just starting out, all at once. That would have been a different story. I would have been doing some crazy stuff. I would have been in jail. I'm happy with the slow pace. When I do achieve it, I'll appreciate it more, and I'm way smarter and know way more about the business now.

Like the celebrities, they get famous too fast and start doing drugs and all types of things.—I probably would have been one of those crazy people. I'm glad it happened at a slow rate because as I get older, I'm wiser. I know the right choices. If it would have happened too fast, I would have been famous not for too long; like, "Oh, he got famous. He's just crazy, psycho." People start putting rumors on your name.

I WRITE AND SING, AND I MAKE MY OWN BEATS

I produce my own music. I write my own lyrics, and I actually produce my own beats. Other musicians have helped me, but I'm going to make my own beats now. I don't play any instruments. I used to know how to play the piano, but I think I lost it. I started playing when I was young, like ten. I didn't have a piano in my house. I just played it at school and on the computer.

---

7. See this song: youtu.be/Rzpo1hHAEeY, and Darius's others here: youtube.com/user/DariusClarkevevo.

So basically everything is all me, and I put it out there. I go to a studio, and in The Center, they've got a studio, too. I've got my own music stuff, my own copyright stuff. I'm my own artist, and I get all my money. So I put it out there on the Web and then get paid. People play my music and spin it, like my music videos. It just feels so good when you hear yourself playing, you know, outside or playing on the radio, and people are like, "I heard your stuff on the radio, your songs. Man, you, you got it!"

They keep showing me love, and I'm getting paid. So that's how it is. DJs follow me—*famous* DJs follow me. It energizes me. It's what I want to do.

I get royalties for my music. The amount of money varies every month. I also get money from YouTube, based on how many times a song got played every month. One month, I made like, $1,500. I was like, wow! I didn't even know that song was so popular.

I also make money from writing songs for other people. My rate varies. Basically, it's $500. But if I know you, or, if you show loyalty to my music, I'll only charge you $100 or $200. I'm still getting something. But if you're somebody I grew up with, I'm like, "I know you," then I won't charge you nothing because I know you're on the same strive as me. You're trying to come up, too. I still get credit: Just say the song was written by me.

That's what Ne-yo do. Like Ne-yo, he makes songs for people. Even though he's a singer, he makes songs for people, like he did a few Beyoncé songs, and you look at the credits, it says, "Produced by Ne-yo."

MY MOST EXCITING GIG SO FAR

The most exciting gig I've done so far, it was at this club that got shut down, but at the gig, I was opening for a celebrity, August Alsina. He's a R&B singer, famous worldwide. The place was packed with hundreds of people. And I performed my song, and my friends came onstage. They be helping me, hyping up the crowd. It was crackin'. That was the most crazy show.

I don't get stage fright. I got kind of nervous a long time ago, when I did my first performance at a place called Street Level. I used to record my songs there, and that was my first time. After that, I don't get nervous no more. I just do my thing. This is what I love to do.

THE DOWNSIDE OF MAKING MUSIC: YOU CAN'T HAVE A RELATIONSHIP

The only thing I don't enjoy about it is like you really can't have no relationship. You can't. You try so hard, you don't get no sleep. If you're somebody that's popular, you can't go nowhere because people run up to you, want to shake your hand, and take their picture with you, want to just be by your side, like, "Hey, I know him."

They want to give you hugs, and groupie-girls come out of the blue. They want to be with you, lie, and say they've got your baby, all type of crazy stuff.

I love it, but sometimes it really gets annoying. That's why I said like it's a curse and it's a blessing. The curse is that you can't really do things that a normal person can do no more. People are going to look at you different.

I DON'T GO TO CHURCH, BUT I PRAY EVERY NIGHT

My faith is super strong. I don't go to church, I'm not going to lie. [But] I'm a spiritual person. What I do is every single night before I go to sleep, I pray.

I pray just like a check-in and check-out, like I tell God how my day was and I always thank him, and I always bless people that are less fortunate than me, and people that are starving and hungry. I ask God to keep on blessing me, keep pushing my music harder, and just keep my family safe. My guardian angel protects me through the day and night and makes sure everything is all right. And I just say "Amen," and, you know, these blessings just keep coming like crazy.

I GOT SAVED FROM MY DEMON—DRUGS

I think I really got saved last year. I think I got *saved*. I was going down the wrong path. I was using marijuana, liquor, pills. It was crazy. It was a tug of war going on between me and the devil. It was pulling me. I was on drugs, but I still knew what was going on.

I was just having fun with my friends. They were used to doing drugs; I wasn't. I'd get to a certain point, and I was visualizing and going crazy and stuff. But they stayed doing that. I said I was never going to do it, and then I lied and broke the oath I made with God.

Then I asked a Sister, "Can you get saved without going to church?"

"Yeah, people get saved without going to church."

It happened at my grandma's place. I was outside. I was by myself. I said, "Please, God. I'm sorry. I won't do this again. Please save me, save me."

I felt something got pulled out of me. I know something got pulled. I know for a fact that there was a demonic spirit, a demon or something that got pulled out of me. I used to have crazy dreams. It was like something just got pulled out of me. I felt it leap out, like pulled, and I fell to my knees.

My mom, she was at work. My brother saw it, and he was like, "Man, what's wrong with you?" Everybody thought it was something wrong that happened. Everybody thought I was going crazy. They called an ambulance.

They took me to my grandma's house. I calmed down, came back home, and then my cousin said, "Boy, you crazy; boy, you trying to kill yourself?"

I'm like, "No, man."

I finally told my grandma what happened, but I never told the rest of my family this story, like they don't know about this. So they will hear it now.

I know I got saved that day. They say that when you get the Holy Ghost, you feel that love-spirit. It was like whole-body chills, and I still get that [feeling] every single day, every time something good happens. I'm not going to lie: I still drink. I like drinking, but I don't smoke at all. I don't do pills or nothing like that. I feel like angels are patting me on the back, like to tell me, "Congratulations." It's just been so good.

I don't got no fears. I don't fear nobody but the man upstairs, and God keep blessing me and keep me out of harm's way and keep my music going. That's the only person I need on my back. I don't care about nobody else. As long as I got God, I'm good. [Laughs.]

MY FUTURE: I'LL BE LIVING THE DREAM IN L.A.

I want to move to L.A. That's where I want to live. When I get famous, when I get signed, I'll move to L.A. and just live my dream out there. I want to do shows every night and get paid and just keep making music. And then after I make music, I want to make movies, too. I want to build my own empire up and start investing in myself. I want to start my own label, "Summit," and open up my own company. I'm going to do it the smart way.

I think if I ever do get married, it's going to be somebody else that's in music industry, and I think I know who. [Laughs.] Yeah, it's this singer. Her name is Janai. She's a famous R&B singer worldwide. She's around my age, probably like twenty-three or twenty-four. I think she's from LA. And she's *hot*. Super hot. So I'm coming for you, girl! And I also imagine having kids and a dog.

My house is going to be a fortune. I don't want too fancy of a house. I just want a little mini-mansion, you know. I'll have me a pool and a basketball court in the backyard and have my own studio in the basement, and that's it.

I would drive a fancy, foreign car like a Lamborghini. That's one of my dream cars. And a Range Rover—that's my favorite truck. What else? My favorite street car is a Nissan Skyline. I love that car. Let's see, what else? I'd get me a jet plane and a boat or something.

When I was a kid, before I dreamed of being a musician, I wanted to be a wrestler. But I was too skinny. I didn't actually do any wrestling in school. I did basketball and volleyball and football and everything else, but we never had wrestling at school.

I'VE WON AWARDS, BUT MY ULTIMATE IS A GRAMMY

I've won so many awards. I don't remember. I've received awards from DJs in big clubs and radio stations, too. So far the awards I got was music certificates, little trophies, and stuff like that for doing good with my songs.

But my ultimate goal is for me to win at least one Grammy. A Grammy is like an NBA championship ring. So I just want to win one, and then I'm cool. If I won more than one, it would be a blessing, but I just want to win one to show people that I really love doing this.

MY MUSICAL IDOLS AND MY OWN STYLE

I want to make music with other artists. Kanye West is one of my musical role models. His music is on a whole other level. People don't like him; they don't understand. They always say he's cocky, arrogant. He's not. It's just you all don't understand him. He's got his own style, his own weight, like he's in a different league of his own.

And Jay Z, he's a motivated speaker himself. He's got his own company. I think he owns a basketball team or something like that. He's a role model, too.

And my two artists right now that's killing the game: Drake, I've always been a fan of Drake. I love his music. He knows exactly what to do. He can change his style, the way he sing or rap. And I'm going to have to say Chris Brown. People don't like Chris Brown because of that incident [with Rhianna], but you can't still hold a grudge. You know, he's a better person now. So I'm going to have to say Chris Brown, Drake, Kanye West, and Jay-Z. They're my four people right there.

But I've got my own style. I listen to other artists, and I suck it up like a sponge, you know, get their knowledge, what they're saying. I learn from them. I learn from old-school artists, new-school artists, and then I just do my own thing. People like my stuff because everything is all me. I don't try to sound like the other artists. I'm trying to do my own thing, but still be up there and match what they're trying.

I listen to all kinds of music. I listen to pop, a little bit of rock, and different styles, too: R&B, jazz, instrumental and Island music, overseas music. I've been listening to a lot of music from England. Their music is way different. I'm soaking this stuff up, trying to use it and put it in my music. It's like, "Whoa! Are you from England?"

Taking knowledge from the other artists and putting it to your music: That's what it is.

I'M GOING TO L.A., AND THEN I'M GOING GLOBAL

You don't use their beat. You make your own beats, but you make it sound a little bit like how they beat it, but you put them to your own music, and they're like, "Hey, this dude, we see that he has a little bit of our style," and then you start getting their fans out there, and you start becoming an international star, like Beyoncé. That's my dream, to be an international star. All my music being played over here, in China, Africa, Europe, Japan, everywhere. I want to be global.

So basically, yeah, I want to travel to L.A. I want to go out there so bad. You can come to them, and they can be like, "Dang," and sign you right there on the spot. But Chicago, we don't got no labels or nothing like that. We just got a beautiful city and big buildings. That's all we got.

I want to travel all over. The first place I'll go is Brazil. I love Brazil. I always want to be out there. It's fun out there. And Spain. I've got three family members in Spain. So I'm going out there to Spain.

Africa, Tokyo, Russia, where else? Basically all around the globe, all around the world. That's what my dream is, just to travel all around, and let my music go through the whole world. I just want to do what I love doing and act with other artists and make films and just become an international superstar.

WHAT I WOULD DO IF I HAD A TRILLION DOLLARS

If I was a billionaire or a trillionaire, the first thing I'd do, I made a promise and I made a deal to God. I told Him that all of these blessings I'm getting right now, I'm going to give back. So basically what I'm going to do is give back to charities, give back to people that need it, people that are starving, and homeless people that need somewhere to sleep and eat.

I'm going to open up a little company for the homeless people to come in and bathe. I be seeing them homeless people that ask me, when I be going on the train, can I have a dollar or something? Sometimes I give it to them. Sometimes I don't. But you know, the people that are really, really starving or something, they don't ask for money. They just want to get something to eat.

I want that power so I can do that. Right now, I can't. When I become bigger, like

Jay-Z-big or Kanye-West-big, I'm going to come back and give back, you know, help out the community.

I'm [also] going to put my money into The Center, to make it even bigger than what it is, have more people drawn back into it. I'm going to make sure that everything's good and get the neighborhood safer, so people can walk through here without being in danger.

I would have more security or more police, and people not harassing the young black males or the young black women. I would make sure the police really is protecting and serving and doing their job. The way it is right now, they're always accusing you of doing something or they just see like a group of young boys, and they bother them. I've seen this with my own eyes, people [police officers] harassing girls and throwing them on the ground. It's like you can't do *nothing*. If you "see" something, they're going to come and bother you and beat you, too.

It's going to take some time. If I do become this successful person, as I hope and believe I am, it's going to probably take like a year to do all that. Like I really see myself doing it.

This is where I grew up. I'm never going to forget where I came from. We'll do little events like once or twice a year, like Father Kelly be passing out turkeys in the neighborhood. They pass out food to the homeless people every Wednesday. They feed the community. One time, Father Kelly took me to this place all the way up north [of the city], and I had to speak in front of a big crowd. I was nervous. I was like, "What has Father Kelly got me into, man?"

I told them about the area I was born in, and they was like, "Man, we like you," and then Father Kelly said, "I told you. This guy's the real deal." That was a cool day. I'll never forget that day.

IT'S NOT ABOUT YOUR RACE; IT'S ABOUT THE FAMILY YOU WERE BORN INTO

If I was born into another race, I think I'd have it easier. Just because I'm coming from Chicago and a young black male that's doing music and everybody else in the city doing music, that's hard because I'm competing with everybody else in the neighborhood. But if I was like, another race, like Indian, or a woman...

It basically depends on the type of family you have. Say my family was like all business people and college heads. I'd want to do what they'd want to do. I'd want to be a college head, go to school, be a businessperson like them; or if my family owned like a Fortune 500 company or something, I'd be next on the throne. I'd probably be arrogant, be cocky, looking down. Them guys just look down.

That's why I'm glad that I'm where I am right now, because it makes you appreciate more. Then when I do become rich, I'll look at things way different because I worked hard. I'm not going to look down on people. I'm going to help them out. I know how it is.

That's why God put me here, to do this, and to do music. And then when I do get on, he knows I'm going to appreciate him more and know what I've got to do. I've got to help people less fortunate than me because, you know, I made it. Now I'm going to help out people and motivate them so they can try to be better.

EVERYBODY HAS A DESTINY, AND A CHOICE

Everybody has a destiny. I really believe in destiny. The way I see it, it's like a road. You can go this way, or you can go this way. It's whatever you want to choose. You can go the good path or the bad path.

And the path I'm on is to success. I see myself as—I don't like saying a "superstar," but like being this popular icon, you know, being a role model to people, being a musician. I know it's going to happen because this is what I love doing. It's like, whatever you love to do, why not go for whatever you love to do?

MY MESSAGE TO THE WORLD IS LOVE

I want to let the world know that I'm just me. Everything you're reading here is 100 percent me. It comes from my heart.

I just thank everybody that's been with me through thick and thin and keep helping me out day by day. God bless them. Father Kelly and everybody at The Center, because this is like another home. Without this, I think we all would have been going through some crazy times, but I'm so grateful that we've got a Center in this rough neighborhood. It's just a blessing that we can come here and show our feelings, and let people know how we really feel, and let the people know that this is what we be living, day by day. It's always been a dream to do my thing.

Thank you all. I love you all. [Laughs.]

APPENDIX

INTERVIEW METHODOLOGY

The interviews for this book emerged from a standardized set of twenty-five questions that narrators reviewed in advance and addressed in the interviews. I used similar questions to give context to a wide range of geographic and sociocultural settings; for example, How much do you earn? Is that a fair wage for what you do?

However, the narrators' uniqueness also shines through in the off-track tangents, traumatic and ecstatic experiences, and definitive personality traits that diverge from the list. So I also asked questions particular to their own situation; for example, How did the Nicaraguan Revolution impact the way Mayra acquired her coffee farm? Or, what if Chicago hip-hop artist Darius had been born into another race and place?

The end results surprised and fascinated me: Each chapter took shape in its own way, emphasizing the values and vision of each narrator, shaped by economics, ethnicity, and—above all, as Darius concludes—the family you're from.

—Suzanne Skees

MY JOB INTERVIEW QUESTIONS

1. Do I have your permission to use your story and images in the *My Job* book and any related online and print materials?

2. What is your name and age?

3. Please describe your job.

4. How long have you had this job?

5. What work did you do prior to this?

6. Tell me about your family: whom you live with and who else is in your family—names, ages, occupations, relationship with you, how often you see them, and what you've learned/inherited from them.

7. How did you end up in this particular job?

8. What's the most challenging aspect of your work?

9. What's the most misunderstood aspect of your job?

10. What do you most enjoy?

11. Tell me about your coworkers and how you do/do not get along with them.

12. Tell me about the other people who work in this industry. How do you compare with them?

13. When you were younger, what was your dream job? Do you still wish for that job?

14. If money were no object, what would you be doing with your days?

15. Have you ever been injured or abused on the job?

16. Have you ever won an award or received acclaim for your efforts?

17. Are you able to express your creativity through your job? Describe how that is for you.

18. What do you earn? Is that a fair wage for what you do? Is it enough to live on?

19. How does where you live affect your wages, livelihood, and day-to-day life on the job? Do you think it's different for people in your job in other parts of the world?

20. Tell me about your worst day.

21. Tell me about your best day.

22. What do you want readers to know about what it's like to work in your industry?

23. How do your gender, race, and age impact your experience of this job?

24. What are your goals for the future?

25. What else do you want people to know about your situation?

ABOUT THE EDITOR

A journalist specializing in social-justice storytelling, Suzanne Skees travels from schools to slums, prisons to farms, serving as a storyteller for nonprofit workers, social entrepreneurs, and their courageous clients, who toil every day to end poverty. She somehow lucked into the best job on Earth: spending three years listening to people across the U.S. and around the world, talking about their work, life, struggles, and dreams - which became the book, *MY JOB: Real People at Work Around the World*. She also works in international development as director of the Skees Family Foundation, which supports innovative self-help programs in the U.S. and developing countries in education and job creation. Skees studied English literature (Boston College) and world religions (Harvard Divinity School) but has learned more from the school of personal mistakes and quiet listening. She lives in the San Francisco Bay Area, surrounded by a loving network of family and friends both near and far, and enveloped in the peace that comes from just savoring life's infinite blessings.

PREVIEW OF *MY JOB* BOOK 2

Stay tuned for Book 2 of the series, *MY JOB: Real People at Work Around the World*, to come in 2017. Book 2 will feature Mary, a banana farmer from Uganda; Greg, a Mideast peace diplomat from New York; and Mike, a gambling-addiction counselor from England; as well as many other colorful characters who happen to be real, talking about much more than just their jobs.

Get updates at myjobstories.org.

Join us on Facebook at Facebook.com/myjobstories and Twitter at @myjobstories.

You also can support jobs by donating directly to our nonprofit partners at myjobstories. org/create-a-job.

INDEX

children. *See also* education for children
adopted, 209, 220
envisioning the future for, 73, 75, 103–4, 123–25
as heads of households, 99, 101
as legacy, 222
pressures imposed on, 21–22
punishing, 113–14
supporting the family, 13, 99, 101, 102, 128, 249, 250, 257
videogames and, 146
with cancer, 237–39
Chile, 185
China (mainland) vs. Hong Kong, China, 212–13
Christina. *See* Ganim, Christina
Cincinnati, OH, 227
circumcision, 114
Clark, Brenda, 258
Clark, Darius
on becoming a man, 261
on The Center, 259–260
on creativity, 266
described, 255, 256
on destiny, 274
drug use, 270
education, 262–63, 265
envisioning the future, 262, 265, 266, 272–73
family, 257–260, 262–63, 265
friendships, 260
God's shield protecting, 260–61, 270
on grades, 262
on haters as motivators, 257
income, 264, 269
on relationships, 257, 269
religion, 270
at Target, 256, 257, 263–64
on tv news, 264–65
values, 261, 262
Clark, Darius, hip-hop artist
awards, 271
the best and worst moments, 268–69
envisioning the future, 267–68, 271–73, 274
fame, 267–68
fan base, 267
income, 269
production, 268–69
role models, 271–72
songs, ghostwriting, 266–67, 269
songs, writing, 265–66
climate
adapting business to the, 28
Barpeta, India, 27–28
drought and the Maasai, 110–11
drowning, deaths from, 65–66, 70
rickshaw pullers and, 100
climate change, 111, 163
Clinton, Hillary, 67, 73–74
Clinton Global Initiative University (CGIU), 168
Clo Intimo, 51
Coelho, Paul, 23
Cold War, 204
college
costs of, 186
need for, 21–22, 23, 206
Colombia, 51, 185, 192, 193, 194
coming out, 169
commitment, 47
Common, 267

communications media, private equity investment in, 202–3
communication with multilingual speakers, 191, 217
competition, 37, 50
Computer Management Consult Company (CMC), 90
Confederation of Indian Industry (CII), 30
confidence, 157
Córdoba, Argentina, 184
corporate sponsors, 7
corruption, 87, 211
cows, the Maasai and, 110–12, 117–18
creativity
in architecture, 239
Darius on, 266
me in, 16
mental dysfunction and, 11–12
Cross, Riola, 257
crowdfunding
education, 162, 166–67, 174
filmmakers, 47
financial transparency in, 166
musicians, 7
culture
adapting business to the, 28
in global corporate management, 213
Hawaiian, 19–20
of shame and suicide, 218–19
shaping art through, 18–19
cultures. *See also* globalization
bridging, 109, 188–89, 210
conflict resolution across, 59
customer expectations, 50

Dana Holding Corporation, 186, 187
Darius. *See* Clark, Darius
Dasgupta, Arindam
background, 25, 30
Driiti nonprofit, 29, 30, 34
Dasgupta, Arindam and Debaleena. *See also* Tamul Plates
courtship, 25–26
envisioning the future/dreams, 39–40
families, 29–30
income, 38
life beyond work, 35–36
marriage, 30–36, 39
professional relationship, 33–36
dating, 25–26, 31–33
"Dat Loud" (Darius), 268
Davidson, Ria, 228
death rituals, Maasai, 110
debt due to injury, 100–101
dedication, 12
Def Jam, 267
Denny, Fr., 259
DePaul University, 44, 46
destiny, 12–13, 103, 157, 221, 274
determination, 23, 141
Dhanu, 244–45, 246, 253
dharma, fulfilling one's, 5, 13–14, 20
difference, creating, 36–37
Dinh Thi Song Nga. *See* Nga
dinnerware, disposable. *See* Tamul Plates
disability, persons with, 150–51, 157
discrimination
gender-based, 249–250

CPSIA information can be obtained
at www.ICGtesting.com
Printed in the USA
LVOW10s2221281016
510691LV00003B/4/P